Commission of the
European Communities
in Cooperation with
Verein Deutscher Ingenieure

Proceedings of the International Seminar held in Düsseldorf
13–15 February, 1984

volume 3
Applications
and Technologies

Edited by
A. S. Strub and H. Ehringer
Commission of the European Communities

**VDI** VERLAG

Verlag des Vereins Deutscher Ingenieure · Düsseldorf

CIP-Kurztitelaufnahme der Deutschen Bibliothek

Energy conservation in industry: proceedings of the
internat. seminar held in Düsseldorf, 13–15 February, 1984;
[results of the Europ. Communities Energy R & D Programme
(1979–1983)] / Comm. of the Europ. Communities.
[Ed. by A. S. Strub and H. Ehringer.
Conference chairman A. Strub. Rapporteurs M. Groll...].
– Düsseldorf: VDI-Verlag,
   ISBN 3-18-419095-1

NE: Strub, Albert S. [Hrsg.];
Europäische Gemeinschaften / Kommission

Vol. 3. Applications and technologies. – 1984. –

Organization of the Conference by
Commission of the European Communities
Directorate-General for Science, Research and Development, Brussels

Publication arrangements by
Commission of the European Communities
Directorate-General for Information Market and Innovation, Luxembourg

EUR 9236
Copyright © 1984, ECSC, EEC, EAEC, Brussels and Luxembourg, 1984
ISBN 3-18-419095-1

Published by VDI-Verlag GmbH for the Commission of the European Communities
Postfach 11 39, D-4000 Düsseldorf 1

D
6 21. 4
E N E

Printed in the Federal Republic of Germany

PREFACE

The main objective of the Communities' Energy Policy consists in securing a sufficient energy supply to meet the present and future demand of its Member States, and in reducing the Communities' dependence on imported energy. In spite of the temporary fall in oil prices energy saving measures will continue to remain imperative, as resources will continue to diminish rapidly. This ist the reason why – since 1975 – the Community has been stimulating universities, industries and national laboratories of the EG Member States to perform under cost-sharing contracts R and D work aiming at energy saving.

Within the framework of the Communities' Second Energy R and D Programme (1979 – 1983) more than 85 contracts concerning new energy saving technologies in the industrial sector have been concluded. The work carried out under most of these contracts has ended and many results have become available.

The International Seminar ENERGY CONSERVATION IN INDUSTRY organized by the Commission of the European Communities in cooperation with the Verein Deutscher Ingenieure (VDI) highlighted the results of these research projects and conveyed them to representatives of national authorities, public, industrial and financial organisations.

The Seminar was opened by Dr. A. PROBST, Staatssekretär of the Bundesministerium of Research and Technology (BMFT) in the Federal Republic of Germany, and by Dr. D.H. DAVIES, Deputy Director General of DG XII at the Commission of the European Communities.

In a plenary session on the first day, recognized energy experts illustrated the need for energy conservation research and commented on the potentials of various technologies in this field.

During the next two days results of research work carried out by contractors were presented in four plenary sessions and poster sessions on energy saving technologies, engines and flywheels, electrical energy storage devices and industrial applications of energy saving technologies. During each session an overview of the work was given by a rapporteur and some contractors. At the end of the conference, overall conclusions and recommendations were developed by the Conference Chairman Dr. A. STRUB, Director at the Commission of the European Communities and by the Session Chairmen.

Dr. Hermann EHRINGER
Head of the Energy Conservation
Research Division

Conference Chairman	Dr.-Ing. A. Strub
Scientific Chairman	Dr. H. Ehringer
Opening Speakers	Dr. A. Probst
	Dr. D. H. Davies
Keynote Speakers	Dr. W. M. Currie
	Prof. Dr.-Ing. A. Kuhlmann
	Dr. R. Dumon
	Dr. J. J. T. M. Geerards
	Prof. Dr. G. Briganti
Chairman	Prof. Dr.-Ing. R. Quack
	Prof. Dr. I. E. Smith
	Dr. F. Ehrhart
	Prof. Dr. P. Hagenmuller
	Dr. J. Limido
	Dr. A. Rossi
Rapporteurs	Dr.-Ing. M. Groll
	Dr. J. Carrasse
	Ir. J. A. Knobbout
	D. A. Reay, M. Sc.
	Dr. J. Durandet
	Prof. Dr.-Ing. U. Essers
	Prof. Dr. P. Wauters
	Dr. E. Voss
	Dr. R. L. Vic
	F. Audibert, M. Sc.
	Prof. Dr. J. M. Schissler
	Dr. P. S. Rogers
Secretariat of the Commission	Dr.-Ing. P. A. Pilavachi
	G. Hoyaux
	Ir. P. Zegers
Local organisation by VDI	E. Piski
Publication arrangements of the Commission	D. Nicolay

Opening Session : (from left to right) Dr. H. Ehringer, Dr. D.H. Davies, Dr. A. Strub, Dr. A. Probst, Dr. H. Vetter

CONTENTS

Volume 1: Combustion and Heat Recovery

Session I. Part A: Energy Saving Technologies
Chairman: Prof. Dr.-Ing. R. Quack

Heat Exchangers

Session I. Part B: Energy Saving Technologies

Chairman: Prof. Dr. I. E. Smith

Fluidized Bed Combustion

Combustion

XI

Volume 2: Engines and Batteries

Session II: Engines and Flywheels
Chairman: Dr. F. Ehrhart

Concluding remarks by Dr. F. Ehrhart

Session III: Electrical Energy Storage

Chairman: Prof. Dr. P. Hagenmuller

Advanced Batteries

XV

XVII

Concluding remarks

The stand of the Commission

Poster session

Poster session

SESSION IV
APPLICATION OF ENERGY SAVING TECHNOLOGIES – PART A
Chairman: Dr. J. Limido

Rapporteurs:
F. Audibert, M. Sc. (Chemical Industry and Catalysis and Coal and Peat)
Prof. Dr. J. M. Schissler (Metallurgy)

CHEMICAL INDUSTRY AND CATALYSIS
COAL AND PEAT

Presentation by Rapporteur
F. Audibert, M. Sc.

Institut Français du Pétrole
F-69390 Vernaison

Modification of cracking furnaces of existing plants to increase yields of
valuable products and to reduce oil consumption by Riveda (ex Montedipe),
Italy :

The aim of this research is to design a new radiant coil to improve
olefins yields and to reduce the dilution steam consumption at constant
conversion.

It is reminded that the optimum of olefins yields is achieved, at constant
conversion, when the cracking gases are operated at a residence time and
hydrocarbons partial pressure as low as possible.

In the proposed technique the monotubular coil of existing furnaces is
replaced by a split coil with a new alloy. This improvement allows to
reduce both the contact time and the hydrocarbons partial pressure. New
alloys, operating at a higher tubewall temperature make it possible to
increase heat fluxes and reduce the coil length.

At the inlet, where the coking rate and gases specific volume are still
low, splitted coils of small diameters can be used allowing a higher
surface to volume ratio. At the outlet, small tubes can be collected in a
single coil of larger section.

As a consequence, the new split coil is characterized by lower contact
time and pressure drop and is therefore more selective in desired olefinic
products.

Selective removal of H_2S from gaseous mixtures containing CO_2
by Snamprogetti, Italy :

The selective removal of H_2S in the presence of CO_2 has always been of
great interest when treating acid gas or natural gas.

In this research, various amine-solvent combinations have been tested and
from vapour-liquid equilibrium determinations at various pressures and
temperatures, a selection has been made.

Subsequently, the selected absorbing media have been studied in a pilot
plant consisting essentially of absorption and regeneration columns.

On the basis of experimental research results, the following conclusions
can be drawn off :

3

- Dimethylethanolamine - N Methylpirrolidone is the most interesting amine organic solvent combination allowing a solvent stream three times smaller than a classical one as NMP-Water.

- Small water concentrations in the 6 to 10 % w range do not affect the selectivity of the absorption system.

Energy conservation in the chlor-alkali industry
by The City University, UK

To reduce the energy consumption, it is proposed to replace the classical mild steel cathodes with electroplated or teflon bonded Ni CO_2 S_4 electrodes. Both systems lowered appreciably the hydrogen evolution overvoltage.

In addition, these Ni-CO-S electrodes maintained their activity after the electrodes had been left at open circuit voltage in the same electrolyte for a number of hours but with time the cobalt component dissolved out in the NaOH solution.

An improved catalyst made with Fluorinated Ethylene Propylene bonded electrode gives hydrogen evolution overvoltage similar to the Ni-CO-S and maintains the electrode performance after leaving it at open circuit.

A typical figure is hydrogen evolution at $1A/cm^2$ in 17 % NaCl and 15 % NaOH at 70°C at an overvoltage less than -175 mV vs RHE (-137 mV vs DHE) for over 500 hours.

Thermal depolymerisation of waste tyres by heavy oils -
Conversion into fuels by Institut Français du Pétrole, France :

Laboratory work has been achieved at the Compiègne University of Technology. In view of the promising results obtained, the INSTITUT FRANCAIS DU PETROLE was assigned the development stage.

The process consists in treating whole tyres with heavy hydrocarbons which transfer the heat required to reach around 380°C and to dissolve the oligomers resulting from devulcanization and depolymerization reactions.

The tyre is converted into moderate amount of gas and gasoline and mainly into heavy oil loaded with finely dispersed carbon black.

The viscosity and the pour point of the heavy oil produced are markedly decreased in the process compared with the feed oil.

The advantages of the process are summarized as follows :

- the tyre is treated as a whole
- practically any kind of hydrocarbon can be used
- the fuel oil produced can be processed in conventional equipment.

The energy savings correspond to about 60 % wt of the whole tyres and are then of 0.52 TOE per ton of tyres feedstock.

A critical evaluation of anaerobic fermentation of waste products
(A Management Study) by International Research and Development Co. Ltd.
United Kingdom :

The objective of this evaluation is to examine the contribution that
anaerobic fermentation of waste can make to the Community's energy
requirements. A large number of enquiries made in the Community countries
has led the author to the following main findings :

1. Despite the extensive worldwide activities in anaerobic digestion,
   the basic mecanisms controlling it are still not completely understood.

2. There is little improvement noted in the last few years in gas yields.

3. There are problems such as : straw containing wastes; waste collection
   and handling; storage and use of biogas; sludges disposal.

4. The performance is low - Economic data are available from the operation
   of full scale digesters but anaerobic digestion is more likely to be an
   economic means of dealing with environmental pollution than as a source
   of energy.

5. The maximum possible contribution from the anaerobic fermentation of
   wastes is not more than 3 % of the Community's primary energy demand.

6. However, if account is taken of all the practical restrictions/problems
   which arise in its wider use, the actual contribution from an overall
   Community point of view can only be marginal, although suitable applications will no doubt provide local benefits.

7. On a final cautionary note, the author warns that there is little
   justification for claiming that especially grown energy crops could be
   a viable proposition in a European context.

Alcohols formation by cobalt catalyzed reduction or carbon monoxide
by Université de Liège, Belgium :

The main purpose of this research programme is to find and develop an
efficient, cheap coordination complex catalyst to hydrogenate carbon
monoxide into oxygenated compounds, emphasis being laid on ethanol.

The catalysts first explored were Co species as n-cyclooctenyl cycloocta-
diene cobalt. This catalyst appeared to be active at 200°C and high
pressure but the efficiency was rather poor due to the low conversion rate
with a too high proportion of hydrocarbons and olefins. The impregnation
of this complex on various supports like bentonite and morganite is
mentioned.

Attempt was made to associate cobalt-rhodium and cobalt-ruthenium to
decrease the amount of precious metal. The cobalt-ruthenium system was the
most efficient to produce oxygenates together with hydrocarbons under high
pressure (200 bars).

Finally, the rhodium based catalyst was the most efficient and selective
catalyst for ethanol production.

Selective Synthesis of Diesel Hydrocarbons from Synthesis Gas
by Katholieke Universiteit Leuven, Belgium :

Katholieke Universiteit Leuven (Belgium) in association with Compagnie
Française de Raffinage (France) using new catalysts are developing a new
Fisher Tropsch Technology which will allow a substantial increase in the
selectivity of narrow hydrocarbon cuts and, in consequence, a considerable
improvement
of the conventional process economy.

Upgrading deasphalter by hydroconversion with finely divided catalysts
by Cerchar and Institut Français du Pétrole, France :

In the coming years, the refining industry will have to upgrade increasing
quantities of atmospheric and vacuum distillation residues of crude oil.

The proposed scheme consists of two steps : Applying a deasphalting
process developed at IFP, these residues are separated into a deasphalted
oil valorized by conventional processes and an asphalt extract.

Then, due to the very high contaminants content of the extract, a
catalytic hydroconversion is applied to the dilute asphalt using an
entrained catalyst in suspension. This technique allows the impurities
that are formed during asphalt conversion to be transported out of the
reactor.

This development stage has been achieved on a continuous coal hydrolique-
faction pilot plant at CERCHAR.

The results show a high conversion of the asphalt greater than 65 % and
the content reduction of asphaltenes, metals and sulphur is in the range
of 60 to 90 %.

Kinetics of ferrous sulphate liquid phase oxydation by Thio-Bacillus
Ferroxidans under continuous and batch growth conditions
by ENEA, Italy :

The aim of the work is to investigate the capability of Thio-Bacillus
genus bacteria to oxidize sulphur in the inorganic compounds of coal. It
is reminded that inorganic sulphur is present as iron sulphide. The
biological desulphurization can be direct when the insoluble iron sulphide
is oxidized in soluble sulphate and indirect when the oxidizing agent is
the ferric sulphate. The ferrous sulphate obtained is reoxidized to ferric
by the bacteria. Many bacteria strains of thio-bacillus Ferroxidans have
been tested and harvested in sulphur springs and in acid drainage of a
coal mine. The best growth medium selected was the "Silverman 9K".

Batch experiments ware carried out to study growth rate and ferrous
sulphate oxidation kinetics at different T, pH, initial ferrous and ferric
sulphate concentrations and carbon dioxide supply values.

Furthermore, a kinetic equation for ferrous to ferric sulphate oxidation
was calculated from continuous operations.

Peat harvesting machinery for operation on smaller bogs
by National Board for Science and Technology, United Kingdom :

The objective of this application project is to produce an inexpensive peat cutting attachment usable with a medium powered agricultural tractor.

The present method for peat harvesting involves large bog clearance and drainage and the use of big and expensive machines.

The proposed harvesting method is also applicable to a few acres of bogland.

The equipment consists of an auger powered by a tractor and a sodspeader which casts the cut peat to one side of the machine.

Following some expected improvements, it is believed that these machines could produce an additional 3.5 millions tonnes of peat, at 25 % moisture, to the Irish Market. It is said that this production would be equivalent to 1 MTOE.

MODIFICATION OF CRACKING FURNACE OF EXISTING PLANTS TO INCREASE YIELDS OF VALUABLE PRODUCTS AND TO REDUCE FUEL CONSUMPTION

Dr. E. Gugliotta and Ing. M. Spoto

Riveda S.r.l. – Casella Postale 11 – Priolo (SR), Italia

Summary

For a long period of time, and up to 1973, Virgin Naphta availability in Europe was higher than demand and its price lower than other petroleum pro - ducts.
Therefore almost all steam cracking plants were based on Virgin Naphtha as primary feedstock.
Many of the existing cracking monotubolar furnaces, which are the heart of an Ethylene plant, designed within the above framework, do no longer comply with the new market constraints: reduced V. Naphtha availability, higher feedstock and energy costs.
The aim of this research was to design a new radiant coil which could improve olefins yields and reduce feedstock and energy per unit of product and give a maximum flexibility on feedstocks.

INTRODUCTION

The cracking furnace is the heart of an ethylene plant: in fact about 80% of the energy required by the plant is supplied, as fuel, in the furnaces; in addition, the selectivity of the cracking reactions to desired products (ethylene, propylene, butadiene...) is strictly related to the radiant coil geometry and, with a proper design, condensation reactions are minimized.
In a modern cracking plant material and energy flows are large so that the need to reduce feedstock and energy consumption is pressing.
A new design of radiant coils (split-flow coils) and the use of new alloys, have permitted, in the last years, significant improvements as far as yields and energy consumption are concerned.
Nevertheless, a large number of the existing cracking furnaces are still e-quipped with monotubolar coils and do not fit the new production require - ments: high conversion and high selectivity.
In the past, with the goal of obtaining the maximum ethylene output, plant operators used to increase more and more the coil outlet cracking tempera-ture up to the maximum allowable value. A further increase in cracking severity causes a selectivity loss and a rise in the cocking rate because of the long residence time and the high pressure drop typical of the conven - tional monotubolar coils;

as a consequence, valuable products such as propylene and butadiene continue
to decrease, ethylene degradation starts, aromatics rise.
The deposit at the tubewall of heavy aromatic compounds and their further de
hydrogenation mean frequent shutdown for decocking.
Substantial improvements can be achieved only through the reduction of the
contact time and the pressure drop which both depend on the coil geometry.
The aim of this research program is the design of a new radiant coil: this
goal has been reached using our own experience on steam cracking operations
as well as a reliable computer model able to simulate the steam cracking
coil reactor.

1. DESCRIPTION

To understand how we have retrofitted the existing furnace let's describe
its previous geometry and layout:

1.1. - Old monotubolar furnace

The old cracking header was a typical Lummus SRT-1 single coil design,
with the following characteristics (see fig. I, II)

- convection section

14 tubes, finned and bares type, internal diameter: 67 or 91 mm; lenght
:3380 mm

- radiant section

10 tubes, internal diameter: 108 mm; lenght: 7000,8040 and 8710 mm.The
furnace is equipped with 24 wall burners and has a nominal feedstock capacity of 2,500 Kg/h. Feed enters into the top of the convection section where
it is mixed with dilution steam at a fixed ratio. The mix, fully vaporized
and heated up to about 600°C by the flue gas, enters the radiation section
where cracking reactions occur. The cracking effluent are then quenched with
oil in a quench pot before been fed to the primary fractionator.

1.2. Furnace modifications
General considerations

As it is well known, the optimum of olefins yields is achieved at a
fixed conversion degree with the lowest residence time and the lowest hydrocarbon partial pressure (HCPP).
Under these conditions, selectivity of cracking reactions to the desired pro
ducts is at the maximum value and condensation reactions are discouraged. At
a fixed feed rate and severity degree, both residence time and HCPP depend
on the absolute pressure level at radiant coil outlet, steam dilution rate,
coil geometry and lay-out.

Coil design

According to the above mentioned concepts, a study has been carried out
to replace the monotubolar coil of the existing semiscale furnace with ano -
ther one of improved performances. By using a split coil geometry and a new
alloy it is possible to reduce both the contact time and the pressure drop.

New alloys, operating at a higher tubewall temperature, allow to increase the heat fluxes and, as a consequence ,to reduce the coil lenght.

A team of ours experts has worked out several coil arrangements looking for the optimum S/V (surface/volume) ratios along the reactor. At the inlet where the cocking rate and gases specific volume are still low, splitted coils of small diameters can be used: pressure drop and residence time are low and heat fluxes are high.

At the outlet, where gas specific volume is higher and the cocking rate in creases, small tubes must be collected in a single coil of larger sectio - nal area: the pressure drop and the tubewall temperature are still in the desired range.

The next step was to simulate the performance of the proposed coils with SPYRO program by Pyrotec Company. SYPRO is a reliable theoretical model to predict furnace performances.

Analysis of simulation has shown that the reactor with the best performance is a multiple diameter coil with the following tubes lay-out and size (see fig. III, IV)

- 4 small tubes in the first and second pass (ID 64 mm)
- 1 larger diameter tube in the third and fourth pass (ID 130 mm)

The total length is 31 meters, the radiant volume 0.4 cubic meters and to- tal surface is 24 sq. meters.

The selected coil, with respect to the old monotubolar coil of the experi- mental furnace, is characterized by lower contact time, lower pressure drop and high selectivity.

The construction material of the tubes is the new alloy Manaurite XA produ- ced by "Fonderies et Acières du Manoir". Manaurite XA is an iron, nickel chromium alloy with special additional elements (Al, Nb) and is characteri- zed by improved resistence to the carburation and creep. In addition, the new alloy, because of the passivanting action of the aluminium, should in- crease the on stream time of the furnace.

2. EXPERIMENTAL WORK

In order to make a proper comparison between the performances of the old and the newcoils, it is mandatory to operate the furnace with the same "feedstock" before and after its modification. To do that, a tank of suf- ficient capacity has been filled with a naphtha with the following proper- ties:

- composition (% wt): Normal paraffins (37,5), Isoparaffins (29,9), Nafte- nics (22,3) Aromatics (10,3)

- ASTM %V: IBP (78°C), 10% (93°C), 30% (102°C), 50% (111°C), 70% (127°C), 90% (148°C), FBP (180°C)

- Specific gravity: 0.729

Before to start with the furnace modification a test has been executed on the conventional coil.

The ranges of operating variables have been:
Coil outlet temperature   = 800 ÷ 840°C
Steam dilution ratio   = 0.4 ÷ 0.7   (Kg steam)
                                            (Kg naphtha)

Naphtha flowrate   = 2250   (Kg/h)

The yields of main products are shown in fig. VI, VII.
The temperature profile of the cracking gas flowing into the coil is shown
in fig. V.
After the furnace modification a test has been executed to evaluate the
performances of the new split coil.
The virgin naphtha fed to the new reactor was the same fed to the old reac
tor.
The ranges of the operating variable have been:
Coil outlet temperature   = 800 ÷ 860°C
Steam dilution ratio   = 0.3 ÷ 0.7   (Kg steam)
                                            (Kg naphtha)

Feedstock rate   = 2250   Kg/h

The products yields are shown in fig. VI, VII.
The temperature profile of the cracking gas flowing into the new split coil
was continuously monitored by six recorders located along the coil (see
fig. V).
Analysis of the two temperature profile (fig. V) shows the new coil operating at higher temperature level (temperature level = $\int Tdl$.
In addition, we have to note that the calculate contact time of the new
coil is 0.4 sec. against 0.8 sec. of the conventional coil; pressure drop is
also halved (from 1 Kg/cm^2 to 0.5 Kg/cm^2).

From the above said considerations it follows that the new coil is more
selective than the conventional coil because it is operating at:

HIGHER TEMPERATURE   LEVEL
LOWER PRESSURE   LEVEL
LOWER CONTACT   TIME

and from the analysis of the gas effluent from the furnace before and after modification (see fig.VI, VII)it follows that the new coil is more se
lective in valuable products than the conventional coil:

HIGHER ETHYLENE
HIGHER BUTADIENE
LOWER METHANE
LOWER AROMATICS AND FUEL OIL

3. ECONOMIC ASSESSMENT
   The economic assessment of this project has been achieved on the basis
of the following products values (US $/ton): Ethylene: 526, Propylene:369,
Butadiene: 676, Raffinate-1: 330, Benzene: 424, Toluene: 335, Xilenes:380,

Light end/Raffinate/Heavy aromatics: 294, Fuel Oil: 166 US $/ton.
Hydrogen, Methane, Ethane, Propane and Residue have been accounted on the basis of their heat values.
Figure VIII shows the economics of the radiant zone retrofitting vs coil outlet temperature.
The maximum economic value obtained from the new split coil and from the conventional coil are respectively 391 and 379 US Dollars/ton of Virgin Naphtha.
The payback period to retrofit an existing furnace of nominal capacity of 10 ton/h is therefore:

$$10 \times 8300 \times (391-379) = 1.000.000. \text{ US \$}$$

$$PBP = \frac{500.000}{1.000.000.} = 0.5 \text{ year}$$

if 8300 are the on stream hours per year of the furnace and 500.000 US $ the investment.

EXPERIMENTAL FURNACE
OLD MONOTUBULAR COIL

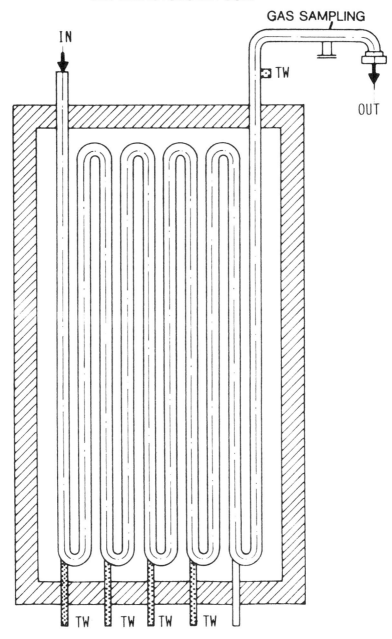

FIG. I

EXPERIMENTAL FURNACE
SIMPLIFIED DRAWING AN PROCESS ARRANGEMENT

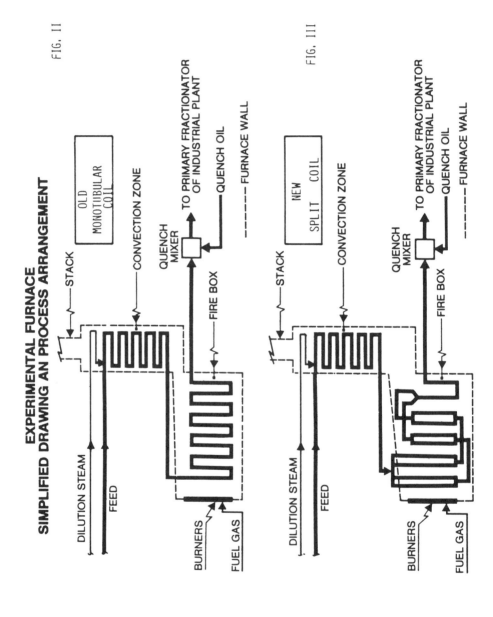

FIG. II

FIG. III

EXPERIMENTAL FURNACE
NEW RADIANT SPLIT COIL

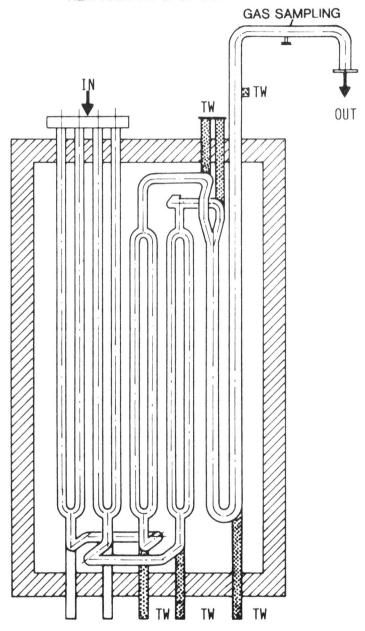

FIG. IV

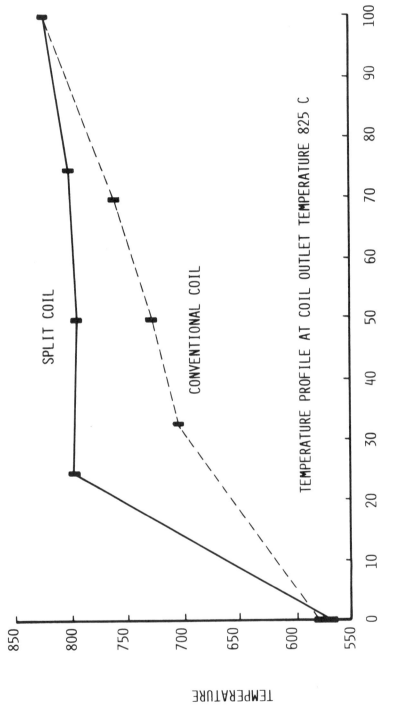

FURNACE : B 1043

SPLIT COIL

CONVENTIONAL COIL

TEMPERATURE PROFILE AT COIL OUTLET TEMPERATURE 825 C

% COIL LENGTH

TEMPERATURE

FIG. V

16

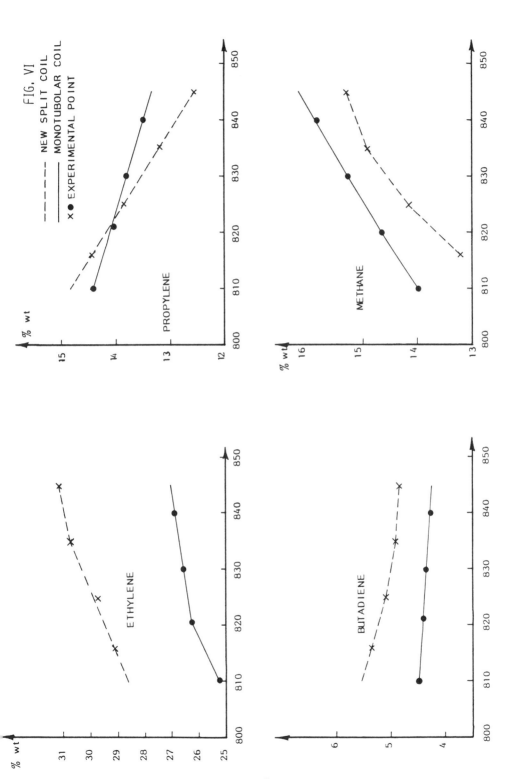

FIG. VI

----- NEW SPLIT COIL
——— MONOTUBOLAR COIL
x ● EXPERIMENTAL POINT

PROPYLENE

METHANE

ETHYLENE

BUTADIENE

17

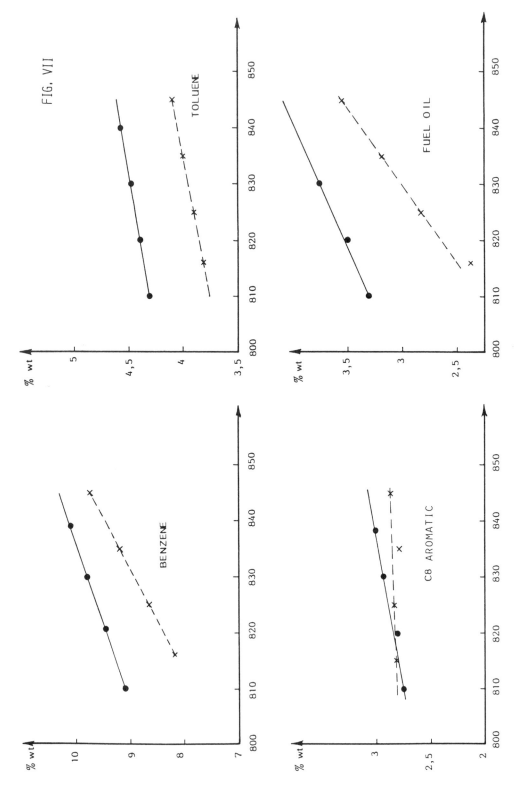

FIG. VII

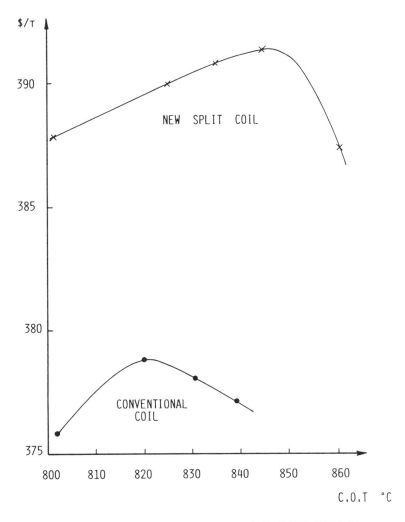

ECONOMIC VELUE OF GAS FLOWING FROM THE CRACKING FURNACE

FIG. VIII

SELECTIVE REMOVAL OF H₂S FROM GASEOUS MIXTURES CONTAINING CO₂

C. Rescalli and L. Gazzi
Assoreni – Snamprogetti S.p.A.
Via Alcide de Gasperi 16, I-20097 San Donato Milanese

Summary

The selective removal of H_2S from gaseous mixtures containing CO_2 is a problem which has been examined for a long time and which is not yet efficiently solved. The object of our research concerns a highly selective process
based on the reactivity difference between H_2S and CO_2 towards tertiary amines in suitable anhydrous solvents, with energetic advantages since CO_2 is
left in the main gas stream. Possible applications are very numerous in the
field of natural gas and in the preparation of synthesis gas.
An experimental laboratory work has been carried out concerning said selecti
ve separation of H_2S. Various amine-solvent combinations have been tested
and, from vapor-liquid equilibrium determinations at various pressures and
temperatures a selection among different absorbing media has been made.
Subsequently the most interesting amine-solvent combinations have been studied in a pilot plant in order to collect further informations on their behaviour and on
the real possibility of using them in an industrial plant. Particularly, at
standard conditions, tests have been carried out to determine and compare
the minimum acid gas feed/ solvent stream ratio that allows the recovery
from the top of the column a gaseous stream with $\leq$ 1 ppm H_2S while H_2S is
discharged from the bottom of the absorber with the minimum amount possible
of CO_2.

1. Introduction

The selective removal of the H_2S from gaseous mixtures containing CO_2
is currently carried out by means of:
- physical absorption processes (Selexol, Rectisol....)
- oxidative processes (Gianmarco, Streetford,)
- liquid gas washing processes based on the most favourable kinetics of absorption of the H_2S with respect to CO_2 in water-Methyldiethanolamine
  (MDEA) solutions.
The industrial application of these processes has met with considerable difficulties for both ecological problems and for the considerable cost
increase due to selectivity losses when a complete removal of the H_2S is re
quired. It is well known that primary and secondary amines react with CO_2
according to different mechanisms:
- by hydration followed by bicarbonate formation,

- by carbamate formation.

Tertiary amines react by bicarbonate formation only. On the contrary there is no difference between primary, secondary and tertiary amines in their behaviour with respect to H_2S which reacts by salt formation only.

With the aim of developing a simplified and competitive process, we have examined the possibility of using a chemical selective absorption of H_2S by tertiary amines in suitable organic solvent, on the assumption of two hypothesis:

- a solution of a tertiary amine in a reasonably anhydrous organic solvent hardly reacts with CO_2, because of the low H_2O concentration (CO_2 should first react with water to H_2CO_3 and only then ionize and react with the tertiary amine)
- the same solution will allow the salt formation of H_2S with amine since H_2S contains protons and its ionisation can take place also in organic solvents.

In practice a part of CO_2 will always be absorbed with the H_2S because both of the physical absorption phenomena and the reaction with the small quantities of water: the water is present in the initial solvent, can enter with the gas phase, and therefore its concentration can increase in the amina-solvent solution according to the operating conditions.

2. Description of the research program

We can identify two stages in this research program: a preliminary laboratory evaluation has been carried out in order to verify the hypothesis mentioned above and then to specify, among several tertiary amines and organic solvents, the most interesting materials on which the further experimentation should concentrate: we also examined the effect on the selectivity of the small quantities of water eventually present in the various amine-solvent mixtures and absorption-reaction H_2S and CO_2 kinetics to get to equilibrium conditions. The second stage has been carried out in a pilot plant, working under conditions suitable for an effective gas stream treating, in order to collect further informations on the behaviour of the selected solvents, identify the most effective ones and identify possible difficulties that could arise during their use in industrial plants.

3. Experimental development set up

The experimental apparatus used in the first stage to determine the quantities of CO_2 or H_2S present at equilibrium and described in fig.1, consists essentially of:

- a cell for the gas-solution contact (10)
- two autoclaves for feeding the gas - H_2S or CO_2 - (5) (5a).

This experimental apparatus allows the determination of amount of gas present in solution without chemical analysis. Each gas is measured separately. The equilibrium cell consists of a stainless steel autoclave, of the capacity of 337,7 cm^3 in a isothermal water bath at 25 °C $\pm$ 0,1. Stirring is assured by a high couple magnet.

21

For the exact measure of the quantity of gas absorbed by the solvent, the manometer scale of the feed autoclave has been calibrated at 0,5 kg/cm² intervals, by weighing the effluent gas.

Referring to Fig.1, the experimental procedure can be summarized as follow: 150 cm³ of solvent are charged in the absorption cell (10); the cell is immersed in the thermostatic bath (9) and connected through valves (7) and (7a) with the autoclaves containing the gas to be absorbed.

After connection vacuum is made, through valve (8),in the cell and in the connecting line in order to vent inert gases (time 2' at 1 Tor ca.).

Heating of bath (9) at the operating temperature is then started and once this temperature is reached, the cell is ready for absorbing the gas.

Through valves (7) and (7a),gas to be absorbed is contacted with the solution of cell (10) where is kèpt stirred and, through the manometers (3) (3a) of the gas feed, the flow of the gas from the autoclaves to the solution is monitored. Equilibrium is attained when the system pressure is constant for 10'. When measurements at different temperatures are required, valves (7) and (7a) are closed, the temperature of bath (9) is set at the desidered value, and when this value is reached, the same procedure is repeated.

The system pressures are recorded at the beginning and at the equilibrium points. From these values through the calibration curve, the gas absorbed in the contact cell is determined (in order to know exactly this quantity, the gas phase in the ceiling of the cell must be substracted).

Following the above procedure, the absorbed gas at the equilibrium conditions is calculated by utilizing the formula:

$$\frac{gr\ gas\ in\ solution}{100\ gr\ solution} = \frac{A-(\frac{P.V}{KT}.Pm)}{W} \cdot 100$$

Where:

A= weight of the gas lost by the autoclave (5) or (5a) (gr)

P= cell pressure (ata)

V= ceiling volume (lt)

K= universal gas constant $(0,082 \frac{ata\ lt}{°K\ m})$

T= temperature (°K)

Pm=gas molecular weight (gr)

W= weight of the solution charged in the absorption cell (10) (gr).

Each amine-solvent mixture has been tested with pure H_2S and pure CO_2 separately: vapor-liquid equilibrium has been evaluated at various temperature (40,60 and 80 °C) and pressure (1-15 ata). Absorbing solutions have been obtained from the following compounds:

AMINES		ORGANIC SOLVENTS	
Methyldiethanolamine	(MDEA)	Sulpholane	(SOL)
Dimethylethanolamine	(DMEA)	N-Methylimidazole	(NMI)
Diethylethanolamine	(DEEA)	N-Methylpyrrolidone	(NMP)
Methylmorpholine	(NMM)	Tetramethylurea	(TMU)
Amino-Dimethylethyl 2-Ethoxy	(EtEA)	N-Methylformamide	(NMF)
Dimethylaminepropane 2-ol	(DMPA)	Dimethylsulfone	(DMS)
Iminotripropane 2-ol	(TPA)		
Dimethylaminomethylacetate	(DMAM)		

22

The experimental apparatus used to determine absorption-reaction kinetics to get to equilibrium condition for both acid gases consists essentially of a glass cell (with a smooth and well defined gas-liquid contact surface) and of two flow-meters to misure the fed and discarged gas; absorbed gas flow, in the time and surface unit, is calculated by utilizing the formula:

$$V_{i,t} = (F_{i,t} - D_{i,t}) \Big/ S = Nl/sec \cdot cm^2$$

where: $F_{i,t}$ =fed gas flow (Nl/sec) at time (t) in the equilibrium reaching

$D_{i,t}$ = discarged gas flow (") " " " " " " "

S = gas-liquid contact surface of cell (cm^2)

H_2S and CO_2 have been tested separately with a SOL/DMEA/AQ (63/34/3 p.) absorbing solution, at T= 40 °C and P= atm.

The pilot plant used in the second stage of work can be divided into three sections:
1) feedstock preparation
2) separation columns: a first H_2S absorption column and a second stripping column to regenerate continously the solvent utilized (in the Fig.n°2 is reported a simplified flow sheet of the cycle of this section)
3) effluent gas wasting equipment

The acid gas feedstock is prepared mixing high purity N_2 and CO_2 with a gaseous mixture of H_2S in nitrogen (5 mol.%); each component is taken from suitable storage bottles at high pressure: their flow-rates, and conse quently the flow rate, composition and pressure of acid gas feedstock, are controlled by PVC and FIC pneumatic instruments.

Both columns are made up of several steel pieces with a number of pla tes varying from 10 to 25. The plates are the bubble - plate type (two per plate and inside diameter = 50 mm); the pieces are separated by intermedia te plates equiped for:
- temperature measurement and sample collection of the liquid phase
- introduction of the feed stream or sample collection of the vapor phase

Referring to fig. n°2, the experimental procedure can be summarized as follow. The acid gas feed stream ($N_2/CO_2/H_2S$ = 79,5-80/20/0,5-1 vol) and the selective solvent stream, after heating in E1 and E2, are introduced at about T=40 °C and P=30 ate into the selective absorption column C1(44 p.p.), at the bottom and at the top of the column respectively. The H_2S-free ga seous stream is continously obtained from the top (PIC 1): the bottom li quid stream, containing the H_2S is discarged (PIC 2) and expanded (at 2÷3 ata) into the vessel V2.

The V2 liquid phase is sent by means of metering pump P1 and through the valve V1, after heating in E3 at about 95 °C, into the regeneration co lumn C2 ($P_T \simeq$ 0,6 ate, 44 p.p.) at one of the intermediate plate, together the gaseous phase (PIC 3). A distilling head on the top of C2 continuously provides both for reflux of the liquid stream and discarge (PIC 4) of the gaseous stream containing all the H_2S fed into C1.

The H_2S-free product getting out of the reboiler E4 is sent into the vessel V1 and afterwords will be again sent and utilized as selective solvent, by metering pump P2, into absorber C1.

A process gas cromatography continuously analyzes the feed and the gaseous streams leaving the top of the columns; other analytical determinations are carried out on the liquid streams to allow a more accurate knowledge of the separation. To avoid H_2S wasting above TLV in the working area, gaseous products discarged from any point of the cycle are sent to an incinerator or, if this is out of use, to a specific air dilution equipment. Tests have been carried out by H_2S low concentration feed stream ($\leq$ 1% vol) because:

- the separation meets with considerable difficulties and large operating costs whenever a complete removal di H_2S ($\leq$ 1 ppm) is required working streams characterized essentially both from high CO_2 concentrations and a few thousands of H_2S ppm.
- results obtained at low concentrations can be extrapolated to high concentrations without difficulties
- natural gas and synthesis gas usually contain a few hundreds of H_2S ppm but usually can be utilized only with H_2S contents $\leq$ 1 ppm.

At first experimentation has been carried out by the most interesting amine-solvent of laboratory research (DMEA), then has been used MDEA to verify the separation with a mixture characterized by a low vapor pressure and consequently low losses. Beside N-MP, tests have been carried out by SOL because the same is less expensive than N-MI and therefore preferable for an industrial use.

Particularly in pilot plant tests have been carried out in order to determine and compare, at standard conditions, and for the different absorbing media proposed:

- the minimun solvent stream/acid gas feed ratio to recover from the top of the absorber a gaseous stream containing $\leq$ 1 ppm of H_2S;
- CO_2 absorbed with H_2S and discarged from the bottom of the absorber
- further informations on behaviour and on the real possibility of the same media in an industrial plant.

4. Main results and discussion

On the basis of experimental results of the first research stage and their evaluation in terms of selectivity α' and H_2S transport power β' defined as:

$$\alpha'_{H_2S-CO_2} = gr\ H_2S\ sol/gr\ CO_2\ sol. \qquad \beta'_{H_2S} = gr\ H_2S/100\ gr\ sol.$$

the most interesting amine-solvent combinations are DMEA-NMP and DMEA-MMI; among the amines, beside DMEA, the DMPA is the most promising. In the following table the α' and β' values (calculated at 40 °C and 4 ata) of main tested mixtures are given:

	α'	β'
SOL	4.3	4.9
NMI	8.2	10.5
NMP	7.0	13.0
NMP-DMEA-water (64/34/2 w)	8.8	16.6
NMI-DMEA-water (")	8.8	15.4
SOL-DMEA-water (")	6.1	14.8
SOL-DMPA-water (")	6.4	11.1
SOL-MDEA-water (")	4.6	9.7

Tests carried out with SOL-DMEA-water (63/34/3 w) showed that CO_2 initial absorption reaction kinetics is about seven times smaller than that of H_2S ($V_{CO_2} \simeq 3.0 \ 10^{-6}$ e $V_{H_2S} \approx 2.1 \ 10^{-5}$ Kmoli/sec. m^2) and that their ratio changes unfavourably in the course of the equilibrium attainement.

The interesting behaviour of DMEA-NMP-water has been checked also in a pilot plant run, whose main results are given in the following table:

	X_{H_2S} (% vol.)			α''	β''	Temp. (°C) str.
	Feed	Head abs	Head str.			
NMP-water (87/13 w.)	1.0	$\leq$ 0.0001	21.4	6.2	0.11	142
NMP-DMEA-water (59/34/7 w.)	1.0	$\leq$ 0.0001	21.8	6.9	0.37	149
NMP-DMEA-water (59/34/7 w.)	0.5	$\leq$ 0.0001	14.4	7.0	0.19	149
NMP-MDEA-water (50/40/10 w.)	0.5	$\leq$ 0.0001	11.6	5.2	0.10	148
SOL-DMEA-water (59/35/6 w.)	0.5	0.0004	10.6	5.0	0.14	140
SOL-MDEA-water (56/34/10 w.)	0.5	0.0006	7.3	3.3	0.07	142

where the selectivity (α'') and the transport power (β'') have been calcula ted respectively by:

$$\alpha''_{CO_2-H_2S} = \left(\frac{Y_{C1 \ feed}}{Y_{C2 \ head}}\right)_{CO_2} \left(\frac{Y_{C2 \ head}}{Y_{C1 \ feed}}\right)_{H_2S} \qquad \beta''_{H_2S} = \frac{H_2S_{C1 \ feed}}{C1 \ abs. \ solution} \cong moli/Kg$$

Particularly from these results we observe:
- working at the same conditions (P,T and $X_{H_2S,Feed}$), the DMEA-NMP-water mixture allows to recovery from the absorber head a gaseous stream contai ning $\leq$ 0.0001% v. of H_2S using a solvent stream tree times smaller than that of typical industrial physical absorption solvent as NMP-water (to- tal separation selectivity is substantially the same for both systems);
- small water concentrations (6-10% w.) do not produce a marked effect on

the selectivity of the absorbing system and allow an easy complete solvent regeneration (stripper exercise is carried out avoiding both high
temperature or low pressure levels);
- do not appear possible to increase the total separation selectivity, by
absorption - reaction kinetics control;
- the sulpholane is not advantageously proposable as organic solvent for ab
sorbing media.

5. Conclusion

The research program carried out has demonstrated the possibility of
selectively removing H_2S from a gaseous stream containing also CO_2, by using
solutions of tertiary amines in organic solvents at low water concentrations.
The most interesting results have been obtained by the use of mixture of
Dimethylethanolamine and Methyldiethanolamine in N-Methylpyrrolidone containing a few % w. of water. In order to perfect the process it is felt
that work should be carried out on a larger plant to determine with accura
cy the energetic requirements and therefore to specify the energy savings
connected with this new process and to optimize the cycle.

SELECTIVE REMOVAL OF H₂S FROM GASEOUS MIXTURES CONTAINING CO₂

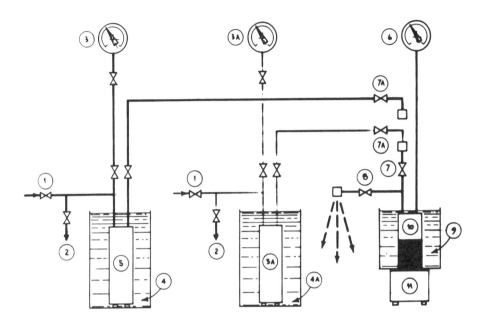

FIG. 1. SCHEMATIC DRAWING OF APPARATUS FOR VAPOR LIQUID EQUILIBRIUM DETERMINATIONS.

①		INLET VALVE
②		OUTLET VALVE
③ ③A ⑥		MANOMETERS
④ ④A ⑨		THERMOSTATIC BATHS
⑤ ⑤A		FEED AUTOCLAVES
⑦ ⑦A		VALVES FOR COLLECTING FEED AUTOCLAVES ⑤ ⑤A TO ABSORPTION CELL
⑧		VALVE TO VACUUM, FOR FEEDING SOLUTION AND OUTLET GAS FROM ABSORPTION CELL
⑩		ABSORPTION CELL WITH MAGNETIC STIRRER
⑪		MAGNETIC DRIVER APPARATUS

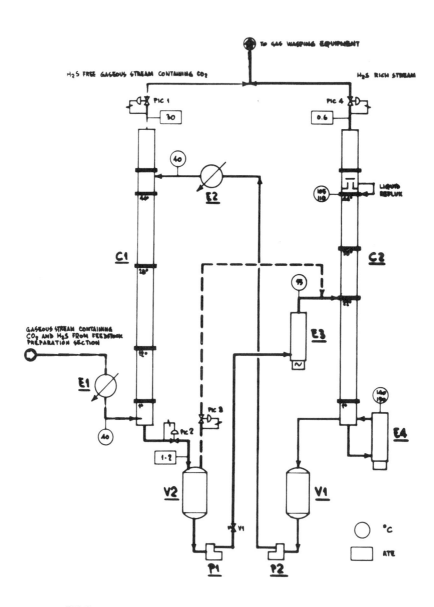

FIG. 2. SIMPLIFIED FLOW-SHEET OF SEPARATION COLUMN SECTION.

ENERGY CONSERVATION IN THE CHLOR-ALKALI INDUSTRY

A. C. C. Tseung and A. R. Goodson

Chemical Energy Research Unit, Deparment of Chemistry
The City University, Northampton Sq,.
London EC1V 0HB, U.K.

ABSTRACT

One of the main obstacles in the use of active hydrogen evolution cathodes to replace the inefficient mild steel cathodes is the corrosion of the cathode catalysts at open circuit. This paper gives an account of some studies on the mechanism of corrosion of active cathode catalysts and suggests possible methods for solving this problem.

1.   Introduction

The chlor-alkali industry consumes about 1.5% of the electricity produced by developed countries. Therefore, there is a need to improve the efficiency of the chlor-alkali cells. One approach is to use active hydrogen cathodes, such as Raney nickel instead of mild steel cathodes but this has not been successful since the life of the active Raney nickel catalysts is relatively short. Recent attempts to use transition metal sulphides (1-2) or Ni-Mo catalysts (3) have resulted in significant improvement in performance but it is still not certain whether such catalysts can function in a real chlor-alkali environment where the cells are subjected to scheduled and unscheduled shut-downs. The objective of the present study is to elucidate the mechanism of corrosion of active hydrogen evolution catalysts at open circuit as a function of temperature and time.

2.   Experimental Procedure

2.1.   Materials

2.1.1. Nickel sulphide catalyst

Nickel nitrate hexahydrate (10.1g) was dissolved in 100 cm^3 of distilled, deionised water. This solution was stirred vigorously and 85 cm^3 of 10% sodium sulphide solution was added. The precipitate was then filtered, washed with distilled water and dried in nitrogen at 200°C for 5 hours.

2.1.2. Nickel cobalt sulphide catalyst

Potassium polysulphide (50g) was dissolved in 150 cm^3 of distilled water and this solution was filtered. Nickel nitrate hexahydrate (15g) and cobalt nitrate hexahydrate (30g) was dissolved in 50 cm^3 of distilled water. The polysulphide solution was added to the nitrate solution with constant stirring and the nickel cobalt sulphide precipitate was dried under nitrogen at 125°C overnight.

2.1.3. FEP bonded electrodes

The sulphide catalysts were ground into a fine powder with mortar and pestle. The catalyst was then mixed with FEP dispersion (I.C.I.) in ratio of 75:25. The resultant slurry was pasted onto previously degreased 100 mesh nickel screens. The electrodes were then dried for 5 mins at 80°C, followed by sintering at 300°C for 1 hr.

2.1.4. Nickel-molybdenum alloy electrodes

A blue homogeneous solution was prepared by adding ammonium molybdate (1.17g), nickel nitrate hexahydrate (3.66g) and ammonia solution (4 cm^3) to 10 cm^3 of water. The 100 mesh nickel screens were then dipped into the solution and then heated over a bunsen flame. The process was repeated several times until the desired catalyst loading was achieved. The electrodes were then subjected to hydrogen reduction treatment at 500°C for 1 hour and left to cool to room temperature (3).

2.2.   Characterisation of materials

2.2.1. X ray powder diffraction analysis

Cu target was used for the study of NiS and Ni-Mo catalysts; Mo target was used for the NiCo$_2$S$_4$ catalyst. Apart from examining the as prepared catalysts, the electrode coatings were also investigated before and after electrochemical tests. The specimens were obtained by scraping the coatings from the electrodes.

2.2.2. Sulphur analysis

The sulphur content of the sulphide catalysts was determined by a Carlo-Erba Elemental Analyser Model 1006, using a sulphur channel with a poropak QS column.

2.3.   Electrochemical test procedure

2.3.1. Test cell

Half cell measurements were carried out in a U-shaped Pyrex glass cell, using a 20 cm^2 nickel sheet as the counter electrode. The tests were carried out in 20% NaOH at 70°C.

2.3.2. Reference electrode

The reversible hydrogen electrode (RHE) was used as the reference electrode. The potential was checked periodically against a separate Hg/HgO reference electrode.

2.3.3. Measurement of ohmic drop

The ohmic drop was determined by the interruptor technique.

2.3.4. Test procedure

The tests were done in 20% NaOH since this is close to the operating environment in a membrane cell. The open circuiting experiments were controlled with a time switch. Each current interruption cycle was for 4 hrs but the thermostat of the water bath was not turned off. This simulates the situation in a real chlor-alkali plant, since it will take quite a long time before the temperature of the cell reaches ambient value on shut-down due to the large thermal mass of the cells.

3.   Results and Discussions.

3.1.   Effect of periodic open circuiting

Fig. 1 shows the change in voltage of the three types of electrodes (FEP bonded NiS, FEP bonded $NiCo_2S_4$ and Ni-Mo alloy) on repeated open circuiting (4 hrs at open circuit, 70°C and open circuiting at room temperature during weekends). In the case of NiS, there was hardly any change in the overvoltage at 300 mA/cm^2 after the electrode has been subjected to 6 cycles of open circuiting at 70°C, though there was a slight increase in the open circuit voltage (134 mV to 164 mV). Thereafter, both the overvoltage and open circuit voltage increased and by the end of the fourteenth open circuiting cycle, the overvoltage increased to -437 mV and the open circuit voltage rose from 164 mV to 1285 mV. This result is comparable to those obtained on a 100 mesh nickel screen electrode tested under similar conditions. In the case of $NiCo_2S_4$, the decay pattern was similar, except that the drastic increase in overvoltage and increase in open circuit voltage occurs earlier, i.e. after the third cycle. For the Ni-Mo alloy electrode, there was also a gradual deterioration as the number of open circuit cycles increased and by the end of the fourteenth cycle there was significant increase in the overvoltage (-59 mV to -275 mV) and the open circuit voltage (142 mV to 582 mV). These results showed that repeated open circuiting will lead to changes in the nature of the electrode surface. Fig. 2 shows the changes in Tafel slopes of the electrodes before and after the open circuiting experiments confirming that the catalytic activity of all the electrodes has deteriorated.

3.2.   Cyclic voltammetric investigations

3.2.1. Cyclic voltammograms between -500 mV and 1500 mV

Fig. 3 shows that when a NiS electrode which ran for 20 hrs at 1 A/cm^2, was subjected to potential cycling up to 1500 mV (oxygen evolution), the subsequent hydrogen evolution performance was drastically affected, dropping from -100 mV to -350 mV (300 mA/cm^2). In addition, it is worth noting that there was a very massive oxidation peak at about 350 mV. On the second cycle, this oxidation peak virtually disappeared. The hydrogen evolution did not recover when the electrode was recathodised at 1 A/cm^2. Fig. 4 shows the cyclic voltammogram of a $NiCo_2S_4$ electrode. In this case the oxidation peak at about 300 mV was very much smaller and there was hardly any change in the hydrogen evolution performance after the first two cycles. Fig. 5 shows the cyclic voltammogram for a Ni-Mo alloy electrode, again showing that there was drastic decrease in hydrogen evolution performance after the first two cycles. It is worth noting the first anodic oxidation peak was substantially less in the second cycle and there were no second and third oxidation peaks in the second cycle. Since the results in Fig. 1 shows that the performance

31

of the NiS electrode was stable up to six open circuiting cycles and the
open circuit voltage only went up from 134 mV to 164 mV, it was decided to
investigate the potential range at which the NiS hydrogen evolution activity
is unimpaired despite open circuiting.

3.2.2. Stability voltage range for NiS electrodes

Fig. 6a shows the cyclic voltammogram for a NiS electrode which has
been cathodised at 1 A/cm² for 20 hrs and then subjected to potential
cycling up to 230 mV. During the first two cycles, there was a slight
improvement in the hydrogen evolution performance. However, the hydrogen
evolution performance deteriorated significantly on further potential
cycling (25 cycles, Fig. 6b). On further cathodising treatment at 1 A/cm²
for 20 hrs, the hydrogen evolution recovered to the original value (Fig.
6c). Fig. 6d shows that when the electrode potential was raised to 500 mV,
there was another large oxidation peak and the hydrogen evolution
performance deteriorated. Further cathodisation treatment at 1 A/cm² failed
to recover the original performance.

3.3. Physical and chemical characterisation of the electrodes before and after OCV experiment

3.3.1. Chemical analysis of the sulphur content of the sulphide electrodes

Table 1 shows that at the end of open circuiting, most of the sulphur
has been removed from the sulphide electrodes. Furthermore, qualitative
analysis confirmed the existance of sulphate ions in solution

Table 1

electrode	weight % sulphur	
	before	after
NiS	27.89	1.17
NiCo₂S₄	42.07	0.59

Table 2 shows the sulphur content of the NiS electrodes after they have
been cathodised at a constant current for 40 hrs.

Table 2

current density mA/cm²	overvoltage mV vs RHE	weight % sulphur
standard	0	31.2
100	65	14.7
300	95	9.91
1000	157	4.82

3.3.2. Chemical analysis of the spent NaOH solution

Atomic absorption analysis indicated that only 0.25 mg of Ni was
dissolved in the spent electrolyte from the NiS test. (total Ni in NiS
electrode, 15.19 mg.). In the case of NiCo₂S₄ electrodes, the amount of Ni
in the spent solution was 0.25mg, and that of Co 0.5 mg. though there was
evidence of solid sludge at the bottom of the U tube, which was found to be
mainly Co(OH)₃. The total amount of Ni and Co in the electrocatalyst was
4.54 mg Ni and 9.09 mg of Co. There was only 0.12 mg Ni and 0.85 mg of Mo in
the spent Ni-Mo test solution (the amount of Ni in the Ni-Mo coating was
12.83 mg and Mo was 11.07 mg).

3.3.3. X ray powder diffraction

Table 3 shows the changes in the crystal structure of the various electrocatalyst coatings before and after the open circuit tests.

Table 3

catalyst	crystalline products identified (4)	
	before	after
NiS	$Ni_{2.824}S_2$	$Ni, Ni(OH)_2$
$NiCo_2S_4$	amorphous	n/a
Ni-Mo	$NiMo, NiO, MoO_2$	$NiMo, NiO, MoO_2$

The results indicated that the surface structure of NiS has changed ($Ni(OH)_2$). In the case of Ni-Mo there was no evidence of new compounds forming but the results did not preclude changes in the amount of NiO present.

3.4. Conclusions

Since all the active catalysts evaluated in this study are composed of at least two materials of different electrode potentials, short circuited corrosion current will definitely be set up at the cathode on open circuit, regardless of whatever protective atmosphere is used. Variation in the electrocatalyst composition will only increase the time by which the active Ni component remains free of non-conducting films but this will not provide a long term solution acceptable to the chlor-alkali industry. Therefore, it is necessary to consider the use of cathodic protection methods if active hydrogen cathodes are adopted in the chlor-alkali industry.

4. References

1. A.C.C.Tseung, P.Rasiyah, M.C.M.Man, K.L.K.Yeung, "Optimisation of Gas Evolving Teflon Bonded Electrodes." Final Report (1st Nov. 1977-31st Dec. 1979), EEC contract No. 311-77-11 EH UK.

2. A.C.C.Tseung, M.C.M.Man, British Patent, 1 556 452, 1979.

3. D.E.Brown, M.N.Mahmood, European Patent Publication No. 0 009 406.

4. "Powder Diffraction File." JCPDS. Pensylvania (1978).

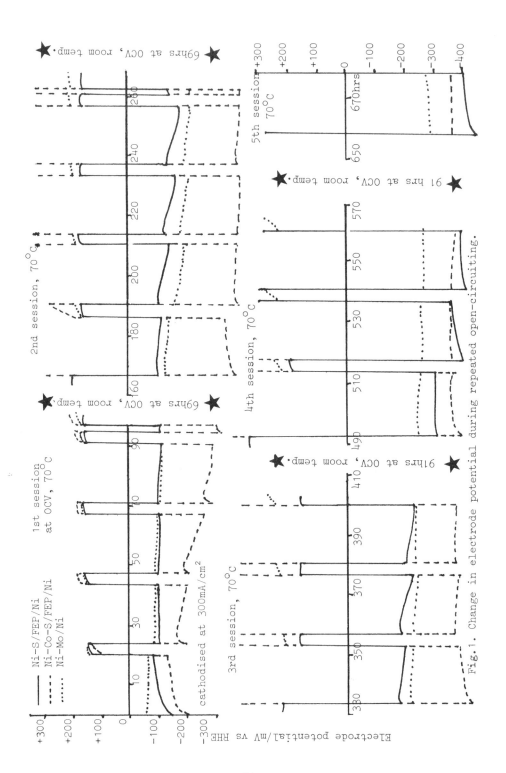

Fig.1. Change in electrode potential during repeated open-circuiting.

34

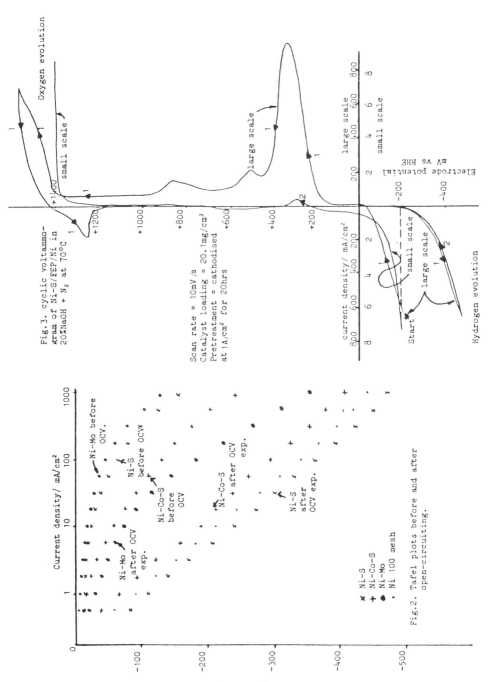

Fig.3. cyclic voltammo-
gram of Ni-S/FEP/Ni in
20%NaOH + N₂ at 70°C

Scan rate = 10mV/s
Catalyst loading = 20.1mg/cm²
Pretreatment = cathodised
at 1A/cm² for 20hrs

Fig.2. Tafel plots before and after
open-circuiting.

✗ Ni-S
+ Ni-Co-S
● Ni-Mo
. Ni 100 mesh

Current density/ mA/cm²

iR corrected electrode potential/ mV vs RHE

Oxygen evolution

small scale

large scale

large scale
small scale

Electrode potential   mV vs RHE

current density/ mA/cm²

Start

small scale
large scale

Hydrogen evolution

Ni-Mo before
OCV.

Ni-S
before OCV

Ni-Co-S
before
OCV

Ni-Mo
after OCV
exp.

Ni-Co-S
+ after OCV
exp.

Ni-S
after
OCV exp.

35

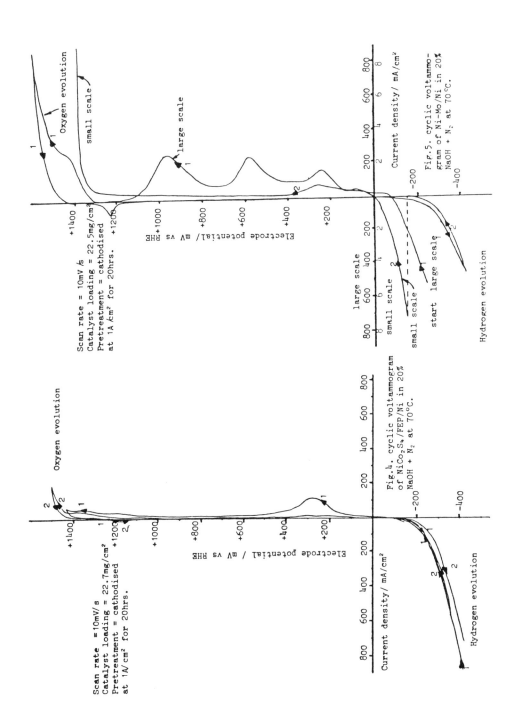

Scan rate = 10mV /s
Catalyst loading = 22.5mg/cm²
Pretreatment = cathodised
at 1A /cm² for 20hrs.

Fig.5. cyclic voltammo-
gram of Ni-Mo/Ni in 20%
NaOH + N₂ at 70°C.

Scan rate =10mV/s
Catalyst loading = 22.7mg/cm²
Pretreatment = cathodised
at 1A/cm² for 20hrs.

Fig.4. cyclic voltammogram
of NiCo₂S₄/FEP/Ni in 20%
NaOH + N₂ at 70°C.

36

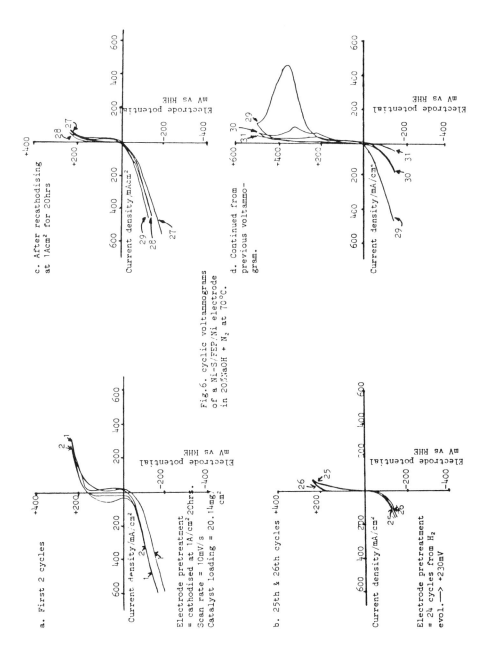

a. First 2 cycles

Electrode pretreatment
= cathodised at 1A/cm² 20hrs.
Scan rate = 10mV/s
Catalyst loading = 20.14mg/cm²

b. 25th & 26th cycles

Electrode pretreatment
= 24 cycles from H₂
evol.—> +230mV

c. After recathodising
at 1Acm² for 20hrs

d. Continued from
previous voltammo-
gram.

Fig.6. cyclic voltammograms
of a Ni-S/FEP/Ni electrode
in 20%NaOH + N₂ at 70°C.

37

THERMAL DEPOLYMERISATION OF WASTE TIRES BY HEAVY OILS CONVERSION INTO FUELS

F. Audibert and J. P. Beaufils

Institut Français du Pétrole
B. P. 311, F-92506 Rueil-Malmaison Cedex

Summary

Since 1974 a chemical engineering team at the University of
Compiègne has been developing thermal degradation of rubber on a
laboratory scale. On view of the promising results obtained,
the Institut Français du Pétrole was assigned the development stage.
The process consists of treating whole tires with heavy hydrocarbons
which transfer the heat required to reach 380 °C and to dissolve the
oligomers resulting from devulcanization and depolymerization
reactions. To gain better understanding of the fied of rubber and
tires, I.F.P. became associated with the MICHELIN MANUFACTURES.

The tire is converted into moderate amount of gas and gasoline and
mainly into heavy oil loaded with finely dispersed carbon black.

Beside used tires application rubber wastes can be treated such as
composite metallic and rubber parts from the transport vehicle
industry. This latter case is of great interest for recovering the
metallic portion.

The energy saving corresponds to about 60 % wt of the whole tires and
is then of 0.52 TOE per ton of tires feedstock.

Results have been obtained on a large size pilot plant making the
process directly applicable to the industrial scale.

For a 8 000 T/y whole tires plant the estimated pay out is of 3 years
before taxes and the rate of return of 16 % after taxes.

1. INTRODUCTION

For a long time researchers have been involved in trying to valorize
waste rubber. Their attention has particularly focused on reclaimed material mixed with fresh rubber. For more than ten years efforts have been
made in this field for both environmental an energy saving purposes.
Thus, since 1974 a chemical engineering team at the University of
Compiègne (Professor M. Gelus and his assistant J.M. Bouvier) has been
investigating the thermal degradation of rubber on a laboratory scale.
Because of the promising results obtained, the Institut Français du
Pétrole was assigned the development stage.

2. DEVELOPMENT PHASE

The process aimed at consists in treating whole tires of all types with heavy hydrocarbons which transfer the heat required to reach around 380 °C and dissolve the oligomers resulting from devulcanization and depolymerization reactions.

To gain better understanding of the field of rubber and tires, I.F.P. became associated with the Michelin Manufactures. This company has provided financial aid, and support has also been obtained from european and french public institutions (European Economic Community and Agence Nationale pour la Récupération des Déchets).

The development work was done during two distinct periods. The first one was completed in 1979, using a medium size pilot plant representative of the contact phenomenon. The second one started early in 1982 in a large pilot plant suitable for problems of scaling up.

Both plants were operated in batch vessels designed for 8 hours of complete operations.

The medium size pilot plant included a batch vessel with a capacity of a few cars tires and has demonstrated the feasibility of treating whole tires.

2.1 Large pilot plant description - Process description

The large pilot plant built at the end of 1981 is described in the inclosed figure and comprises the following main parts :
- the whole tires (100 to 300 kg) are put in a basket (R_1) ;
- the contacting oil representing a total volume of around 600 l per batch is recirculated in the main loop with the pump P_1 at a flow rate of 30 to 60 m^3/h depending on the viscosity of the bulk liquid (on an industrial plant the relative oil recirculation would be markedly decreased) ;
- the circulating liquid is heated in the electric heater E_1 up to 380 °C within 3 h ;
- the liquid is sprinkled in the vessel making contact with tires by trickling and involving much less liquid than with complete immersion ;
- as the different reactions proceed involving thermal cracking of rubber and to some extent of the oil the light compounds produced condense in the air exchanger E_3 while the gas goes through the condensing part and is volume metered before exiting ;
- when the depolymerisation reactions are over, the bulk liquid phase including the compounds resulting from the tire degradation is cooled in the air exchanger E_2 down to around 100 °C ;
- at this stage of advancement of the operation the liquid in the main loop, which is quite comparable to viscous fuel oils is diluted with the light hydrocarbons coming from the bottom of E_5 which favorably decrease the viscosity and the pour point of the fuel. The role of E_5 is to remove the necessary amount of light gasoline to set the flash point of the fuel oil at the specification (> 70 °C). Eventually E_5 can supply an additional amount of gasoline to fit the energy requirement of the plant which could be normally provided by a mixed-burner (gas and gasoline).

2.2 Material balance

For each operation the rubber stock is placed in contact with an amount of fresh oil representing about three times the quantity of rubber by weight. When the temperature increases and reaches the range required,

the amount of gas and light compounds formed is dependent on both temperature and residence time. This is the reason why heating is stopped when the
rubber has depolymerized. Obviously any fresh oil distilling before the
required reactor temperature will supply additional condensates.

We describe hereunder a material balance with somme data included
within a given range because of the differences existing in the type of
tires and oils that can be treated. In our experiments we used the oils
described later on in this paper.

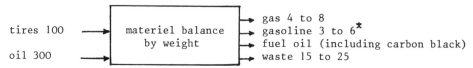

* 1 to 3 are to removed to get the flash point specification of the fuel
oil.

As a first approach the oil can be considered to act as a solvent and
heat transferring agent.

In an industrial plant the effluents from the reactor would be separated in a column. The amount of gasoline removed from the top can be
ajusted so as to supply (with the gas) the energy requirements of the
plant. The top effluents (gas and gasoline) are then separated in a drum.

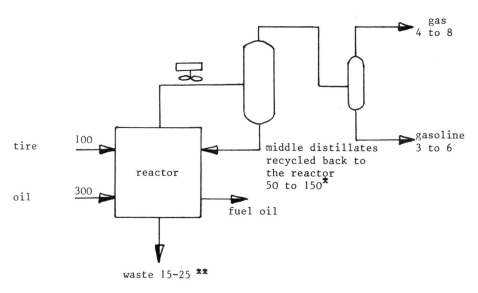

* amount sensitive to temperature level and residence time and of course
to the distillation curve of the contacting oil.
** A few percent of undissolved but depolymerised rubber does stay mixed
with the metallic waste depending on the nature of the reactants (aromaticity of the oil and tires composition).

2.3 Contacting oil analyses

As said above in the text, various oils can be used as long as they
are available at low price and have a moderate amount of volatile compounds
below 380 °C.

Beside waste oils which can be used, two kinds of oil have been systematically explored and are described below :

	Aromatic extracts from lube manufacturing		Heavy fuel oil of the market
	150 ssu	400 ssu	
Specific gravity at 20 °C	0.997	0.998	0.984
Viscosity at 50 °C (cSt)	104	300	362
Viscosity at 100 °C (cSt)	8.47	22.85	33
Pour point °C	+ 12	+ 27	0
Flash point °C	-	-	> 70
Conradson carbon wt %	0.22	2.2	13.7
Asphaltenes (wt %)	-	-	5.3
Sulfur (wt %)	4.7	4.9	3.7
5 % distill. (°C)	402	477	240

Table I

2.4 Products analyses

Gas	Average analysis % vol.	Gas	Average analysis
CO	1.2	C_3H_8	8.8
H_2	3	C_4'	18
CH_4	16.5	nC_4	7.8
CO_2	2	C_5'	6.6
C_2H_4	1.3	nC_5	11.5
C_2H_6	8	C_6'	2.5
H_2O	1.3	C_6	1.7
H_2S	5	undetermined	0.5
C_3H_6	4.3		

Heat value calculated (net)		10 400 kcal/kg
Average molecular weight		45.3 g

Table II

Gasoline :

Typical analyses are given for gasoline having a 200 °C end point. Data are included within a range because of some composition variation due to altogether rubber depolymerisation and cracking of the oil.
ASTM

Initial point	73 °C	
5 %	105	
10 %	111	
30 %	125	
50 %	137	
70 %	149	
90 %	165	
95 %	173	
E.P.	194	

Specific gravity at 20 °C	0.770 to 0.800
Nitrogen ppm	500 to 1 000
Sulfur wt %	0.6 to 0.8
Bromine number gBr/100 g	50 to 80
Maleic anhydride value mg/g	10 to 20

The bromine number and maleic anhydride value provide information on the olefin and diolefin contents which are about :

olefins	33 to 53 %
diolefins	2.5 to 5.5 % (include also some aromatic rings with olefinic branched chain)

Fuel oil :

The so-called product corresponds to when the contacting oil has dissolved the rubber and contains no more gasoline and gas.

The thickening effect of the depolymerised gum dissolved is largely compensated for by the diluent effect of the middle distillate recycled back to the fuel oil after each operation.

It should be borne in mind that these middle distillates come essentially from rubber depolymerisation into oligomers and to a less extent from some cracking of the oil.

It is very interesting to compare the analyses of the fuel oil obtained to those of the corresponding contacting oil (table I).

	150 ssu + rubber	400 ssu + rubber	heavy fuel oil from the market + rubber
Specific gravity at 20 °C	1.025	1.019	1.007
Viscosity at 50 °C (cSt)	90	266	223
Viscosity at 100 °C (cSt)	–	–	–
Pour point °C	– 9	+ 3	– 3
Flash point °C	152	114	146
Conradson carbon %	7.14	9.3	18
Asphaltenes wt %	–	–	5.3
Sulfur wt %	3.95	3.88	3.14
Zinc wt %	0.38	0.32	0.48

Table III

As it can be seen above the finely dispersed carbon black increases the Conradson carbon of the corresponding feeds by about 5 absolute percents.

3. PROBLEMS SOLVED IN DEVELOPMENT

Reactor :
    The pilot reactor is made of carbon steel and operated at atmospheric pressure. Because flammable and foul-smelling products are raised to high temperature, it must be tight.
    The door of the pilot reactor is a reinforced thick steel plate, and some elasticity of the seal was required. For this reason several kinds of seals were tested, and viton was selected. Some cooling was required to prevent destruction of the seal. On an industrial unit the tightness would be ensured by bright-parts making possible more efficient cooling of the seal.
Mixing of the reactants :
    In the pilot reactor the liquid was sprinkled on the tires placed in a fixed position in the basket. Another way of contacting could consist either in sprinkling the liquid through a rotating sprinkler or making the basket rotate slowly in order to improve the mixing of the reactants. Some mecanical mixing is required in the rubber dissolving.
Main pump characteristics :
    When depolymerisation occurs gas evolves in the bulk liquid circulated with the main pump. The presence of the gas might drop or stop the sucking action of the pump. This problem has been fully solved by focusing attention on the pump characteristics and its proper location in the loop.
Heater :
    No special attention except the observation of a sufficient liquid velocity. After several months of batch operations we found clean pipes.

4. ADVANTAGES OF THE PROCESS

    - The whole tire treatment is shown to be feasible so that shredding is no longer necessary (cars, trucks, earthwork vehicles) ;
    - the trickling contact between oil and tires involves moderate hold-up of the liquid and shortens the time required for heating and cooling the bulk liquid ;
    - practically any kind of hydrocarbonscan be used as long as the oil doesn't distill too much before 360 °C or so ;
    - the rubber is converted into fuel oil and forms a homogeneous liquid with the contacting oil and then is processed in conventional equipment. No decantation of the carbon black was ever observed in all the liquid fuel oils obtained ;
    - the resultant fuel was burned with success in a 6 300 MJ/h boiler. The carbon black did not affect the quality of the smoke ;
    - on the other hand various rubber wastes can be treated such as composite metallic and rubber parts from the transport vehicle industry. This latter case is of great interest for recovering the metallic portion ;
    - the operating conditions enable viscous fuel oils to be valorized by decreasing their viscosity and pour point as the result of lighter compounds formation and the additional cracking of the hydrocarbons.

5. MAIN FEATURES OF AN INDUSTRIAL PLANT

    The large size pilot plant drecribed above gives a most representative view of what an industrial unit will be.

For economic reasons a batchwise process requires paying special attention to the stream time with regard to the equipment cost. For this reason it may be more advantageous to associate a couple of reactors timed so that only one heater could be used twice a shift.

Each oil batch feedstock is preheated by the fuel oil produced in the alternate previous loop which is to cool before storage.

One column and a vessel make the light effluents separation.

On the other hand the gas and gasoline produced can be used on the site to feed the heater.

Concerning storage it would be most advantageous to have several tanks for the various possible contacting oil.

6. ENERGY SAVING

On the passengers cars tires basis the recoverable fraction can be so calculated :

metallic wastes with some undissolved tire constituents : 22 % of the tires
tire fraction equivalent to process utilities consumption : 14,5 %
undisolved waste (depending on the aromaticity of the oil
feed) :   3,5 %
recoverable fraction :   60 % wt

Basis	8 000 T/year of waste tires
Recoverable fraction	4 800 T/year (8 700 kcal/kg)
TOE recovered	4 176 T/year
TOE recovered per ton of tires	0.52
Investment B.L. per TOE recovered	11 000 KF/4 176 T/y = 2 600 F/Ty

7. ECONOMIC EVALUATION

The erected investment cost approximates KFF 11 000 B.L. on the following basis :
- tires capacity   8 000 T/y
- stream factor   8 000 h/y
- batch duration   4 h
- batches/shift   2

The above cost includes gas storage and booster. It has not been considered the cost of feedstocks storage and tires handling which can be largely dependent on existing facilities of the site.

The operating cost as calculated from table IV data includes a capital total charges of FF 145/T of produced oil assuming a payback time of 3 years before taxes and giving a rate of return on investment capital after taxes of 16 %.

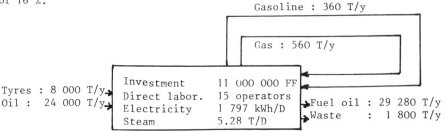

Gasoline : 360 T/y

Gas : 560 T/y

Tyres : 8 000 T/y.
Oil :   24 000 T/y.

Investment	11 000 000 FF
Direct labor.	15 operators
Electricity	1 797 kWh/D
Steam	5.28 T/D

Fuel oil : 29 280 T/y
Waste   : 1 800 T/y

Remark :
- gas and gasoline fit the heater energy requirement
- waste produced have not been rated.

| | Operating cost | |
	KFF/y	FF/T of Produced oil
Fixed costs		
Capital to depreciation	3 700	126
Working capital	560	19
Maintenance + Insurances	660	23
Direct labor	1 800	61
Running costs		
Electricity .2 FF/kWh	120	4
Steam 144 FF/T	250	9
TOTAL	7 090	242

Table IV

The minimum sale price of produced oil giving the above payback time and rate of return corresponds to the total operating cost plus the feed oil and waste tires prices per ton of produced oil applying the above yields.

If the sale price of the produced oil is given, the maximum purchase price of feedstocks can be calculated assuming same payback time and rate of return.

For instance, it can be shown that if both the contacting oil and the produced oil are priced at the number 6 FO of FF 1 600/T the waste tires cost cannot be higher than FF 170/T.

VALORISATION OF WASTE TYRES
CONVERSION INTO FUELS

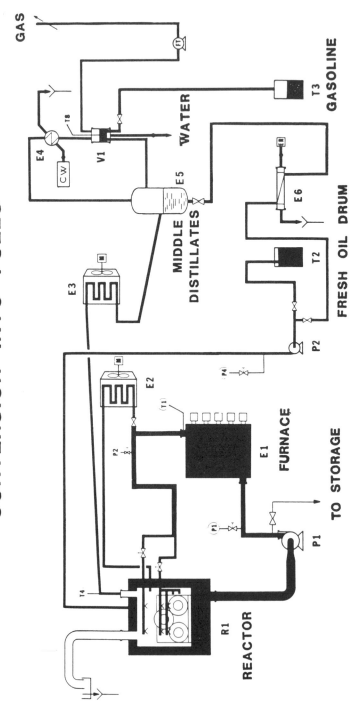

UNITE DE DEMONSTRATION IFP

A CRITICAL EVALUATION OF ANAEROBIC FERMENTATION OF WASTE PRODUCTS (A MANAGEMENT STUDY)

M. F. Anderton and D. F. Gibbs

International Research & Development Co. Ltd.,
Fossway, Newcastle upon Tyne, NE6 2YD, U.K.

Summary

The main aim of this study has been to evaluate whether anaerobic fermentation of waste products can produce a significant saving in the Community's primary energy needs. In carrying out the study the authors have reviewed the current state-of-the-art of the technology and the specific interests and current research being pursued in individual Community countries. Particular interest has been taken in those factors which may affect the implementation of anaerobic fermentation techniques in the Community.

The technology review showed that anaerobic fermentation developments in terms of the efficiency of biogas production, have not significantly advanced over the past few years. Current research is aimed at improving this performance either from a better understanding of the processes involved or by improvements in plant design. From estimates of available wastes, it is concluded that the maximum possible energy contribution that anaerobic digestion could make is no more than 3% of the Community's primary energy demand. However, when all the practical factors such as transport requirements, preprocessing, storage, etc. are taken into account, the net benefits will be marginal. Overall the real value of anaerobic digestion lies with its environmental applications.

1 INTRODUCTION

The fermentation of waste products to produce methane has been known from historic times through the production of 'marsh gas' but only in recent years have the potential benefits of 'biogas' come to be realised. Anaerobic fermentation is particularly applicable to agro-industrial wastes because their highly biodegradable character makes biological treatment an attractive process in terms of efficiency and economy. The worldwide energy crisis encouraged wide ranging activities in anaerobic digestion, not only in connection with waste treatment projects linking energy conservation with pollution control, but also more generally on energy production from biomass in the broadest sense, including energy crops, forestry and algal systems.

In submitting their proposal to the Community for appraisal of anaerobic digestion, the authors felt that a great deal of time, money and effort was being invested in too many projects, some of which appeared to have no positive aim and many of which either over-lapped in content or were duplications of one another - a view which was strengthened during the course of the project.

The primary intention of the study was to place the anaerobic fermentation of waste products for energy conservation (and to a lesser extent other biomass products) into perspective with current European energy and agricultural policies.

It was evident that the first major task was to carry out a comprehensive state-of-the-art review to provide a foundation for the project. Parallel discussions were held with experts in several of the individual member states as this was felt to be the most effective way of collecting the most relevant information on anaerobic digestion research and development, commercial practices and other factors affecting its exploitation in the Community countries.

In considering subsequent stages of the project it was necessary to bear in mind that anaerobic digestion originated as a pollution control method which provided a balanced stabilised effluent for disposal whereas the conservation or production of energy by anaerobic digestion techniques is a comparatively recent development. Furthermore, whilst there may be significant benefits to be obtained by using anaerobic digestion as a pollution treatment system, there are many barriers to its use for energy saving and energy production particularly on a Community scale, where substantial national and multi-national finance would be involved.

Consequently, one of the main objectives of the project has been to identify these barriers and assess their importance in the light of the Community's current and expected future energy demand and waste arisings. The benefits to the Community in exploiting anaerobic digestion are clearly dependent both on its significance as a potential contributor to energy demand and on the limitations imposed by the availability of agricultural wastes and crops. Other factors affecting exploitation such as environmental considerations, agricultural policy, climatic uncertainties, etc. have also been examined.

The conclusions of the study summarise the salient results of the authors' investigations which are presented in full together with recommendations in the final report (1) from which the present severely abridged version has been condensed. Most of the detailed findings have thus had to be omitted from this summary report, although the conclusions and recommendations appear in a largely unchanged form.

2   STATE-OF-THE-ART REVIEW
2.1 Sources of information
The state-of-the-art study accounted for a considerable proportion of the total effort committed to the project and involved an in-depth literature review, attendance at relevant conferences, considerable correspondence and other contacts with individuals and organisations and, most important of all, direct personal contact with a large number of experts in the field.

This latter activity was important not only in providing an input to the review but also in obtaining a view of the current situation on anaerobic fermentation in the member countries and opinions on future prospects and barriers to exploitation.

In the final report on the project the information obtained by the above means has been summarised in a state-of-the-art review covering biomass and biomass potential; basic microbiology/biochemistry; digester types; sewage/sewage sludges; agricultural wastes; food residues; municipal refuse/landfill; and other sources of methane production. Limitation of space in this present summary report allows no more than a brief reference to one or two salient points in each of the above areas of interest.
2.2 Biomass and biomass potential
World net photosynthesis produces annually approximately ten times the world's annual energy needs but extraction of this energy in a convenient form is a major hurdle. However, setting this aside, for temperate indstrial regions like Europe having a high energy and food demand, biomass could never be expected even in the most favourable of circumstances to produce any more than a small fraction of the Community energy needs. On a more restricted front however, the conversion of biomass waste by anaerobic

fermentation processes is relevant to European conditions although its potential contribution to total energy needs is still small.

2.3 Basic science and technology

Despite extensive work carried out on the basic microbiology and biochemistry of anaerobic digestion there are still many uncertainties regarding the precise behaviour of the bacteria involved in the process and of the biochemical pathways concerned. Achieving a complete understanding of their behaviour is difficult owing to their inherent nature; as strict anaerobes they are difficult to isolate and study, their metabolism is not fully understood and they have a restricted tolerance of substrates. Significant improvements in digester technology are perhaps unlikely to be achieved until a more detailed understanding of their behavioural characteristics is known.

2.4 Digester types

The potential applications of anaerobic digesters are wide ranging; to reduce pollution loading; to conserve energy and/or produce energy; to reduce objectionable odours; or to stabilise sludges for disposal. Each of these applications (or combinations) has an impact on digester design. Current digester designs range from simple, historically ancient digesters which are still used in great numbers in China (with over seven million in use), India and developing countries, through the classic digester of sewage treatment to modern digesters based on improvements derived from R & D into more efficient waste treatment/energy conservation systems. Generally speaking the design of pollution treatment digesters is simpler than that for energy generation systems but all depend on adequate information regarding the substrate, dilution rate, thermal performance (i.e. heat loss rate), retention time and temperature.

Some of the newer systems which are briefly reviewed in the final report include anaerobic filters, anaerobic contact digesters and the upflow sludge blanket (UASB) process. More recent developments on fluidised bed and similar techniques are also covered.

2.5 Sewage and sewage treatment systems

The importance of sewage treatment and disposal in a European context is self evident and it is therefore hardly surprising that much of the early work on anaerobic digestion was undertaken with this application in mind, particularly in the UK and Germany. Because of the nature of raw sewage (mainly its low solids content) anaerobic processes are largely used for treating sewage sludges rather than for primary treatment. Despite this restriction they are an important feature of many modern treatment plants and provide substantial quantities of biogas. Typically, it is estimated that London's ten largest sewage works (serving seven and a half million people) could produce 250,000 M^3/day of gas from an input of about 660 tonnes/day of sludge to offset a substantial proportion of the power requirements for primary treatment. Current uncertainties regarding such applications for anaerobic digestion concern not so much technical capability/performance as economics, particularly with regard to the minimum viable plant size.

More speculatively, as far as technical developments are concerned, some workers have suggested that plant based on the UASB digester may eliminate the need for the aerobic stage of sewage treatment. If so, this would be of considerable economic importance.

2.6 Agricultural wastes

Animal wastes and crop residues are a highly important potential source of energy at local level with one estimate indicating that some 950 million tonnes of Community agricultural waste was generated in 1979. It is significant that most development work in the field of anaerobic digestion

49

has been concerned with agricultural wastes, the major part of which has been carried out in the US. Much of the information in the report, particularly with regard to animal wastes, is based on US experience and this suggests that the required scale of plant to deal with animal wastes on an economic basis is considerably larger than any in Europe. From a European point of view, pig and poultry wastes are a more important aspect of animal waste treatment and most of the larger pilot/demonstration plants in Europe have been designed to handle pig wastes; very little work on poultry waste has been identified.

Until recently little information was available on the anaerobic digestion of crop wastes but, with increasing awareness of the need for energy conservation and better utilisation of available materials, this situation is changing. Agricultural crop wastes in Europe are dominated by straw (85M tonnes produced in 1976) but the 'surplus' availability is difficult to estimate. Unfortunately straw is unsuited to anaerobic digestion techniques in an untreated state and much of the current work in this area (including a number of CEC contracts) is concerned with improving methods of pre-treatment.

2.7 Food and food processing residues

Food processing wastes tend to be characterised by large water flows with high biological oxygen demand containing dilute sugars and starches. They are therefore particularly suited to anaerobic digestion techniques primarily as a means of reducing pollution problems although recovery of valuable materials can be a bonus in certain cases.

Commercial plants exist and are in use in many industries; notably in the sugar industry whilst others include the fermentation industry itself (breweries, distilleries, cheesemaking), fruit and vegetable processing and slaughterhouses.

2.8 Municipal refuse and landfill

Again much of the work in this area has been carried out in the US and is thus, strictly speaking, outside the scope of the study but the main features of US developments have been covered in the final report for the sake of completeness. Plants using anaerobic digesters have been developed or studied by the Institute of Gas Technology and Dynatech but the most advanced is the Pompano Beach, Florida plant based on the Refcom process which has two 31,300 M^3 digesters.

In Europe, domestic and urban refuse is mostly incinerated as landfill sites become scarce, with some being pyrolysed or used to make refuse derived fuel (RDF). Landfill sites can be regarded as 'natural' anaerobic digesters as the natural breakdown of organic wastes (once the small amount of oxygen is used up) produces methane. Uncontrolled, this can lead to dangerous situations through the gas seepage and this has led to development of methods for the collection of gas and to the development of sites based on the profitable collection of biogas.

2.9 Other sources of methane

Although outside the scope of the study, as they are energy crops rather than wastes, the possibilities of methane production from algae (chlorella, kelp, seaweeds, etc.), from other plants such as water hyacinths, and from peat have been briefly reviewed.

3   ANAEROBIC FERMENTATION IN COMMUNITY COUNTRIES
3.1 Sources of information

As mentioned in Section 1 above, the most valuable source of information on activities in the Community countries has been through direct personal contact with active investigators either by visits to recognised centres of excellence or at conferences and backed by correspondence with other centres where visits were not possible.

One major difficulty experienced in this part of the investigation was the recurrent problem of confidentiality when discussing the performance/economics of commercial equipment or processes and in most cases this has prevented a detailed economic assessment being made of many of the processes.

3.2 Belgium

Three major institutions were visited in Belgium; namely the University of Ghent; the University of Louvain-la-Neuve; and the University of Namur. In each establishment, discussions were held with the senior researchers in the appropriate fields.

In summary, because of forward looking Government policies, Belgium is in the position of having an advanced research programme in biomass and anaerobic digestion. They also have significant internal and industrial/commercial funding for much of the development and demonstration work. It is felt that the results of many of the research programmes, if verified by additional financial and technical data, will not provide encouragement for long-term investment in anaerobic digestion within the Community. However, the individual research programmes currently in hand should provide good hard data which will be particularly useful locally and which could be exploited successfully in the developing and poorer countries.

3.3 Denmark

Work in Denmark on three demonstration projects for large farm units has shown both the potential and problems of using anaerobic fermentation technology for animal waste treatment. Their economic evaluations show that many assumptions have to be made, the validity of which cannot be easily determined but it is apparent that construction costs and operating costs are generally too high and gas utilisation is underestimated whilst environmental advantages are beneficial but cannot be easily calculated.

One of the assumed benefits of anaerobic fermentation which is being studied by many groups is that the digested slurry is a better manure than raw slurry but a two-year study in Denmark on this subject has concluded that this is not the case.

3.4 Eire

A fairly intensive programme in research and development and applied technologies is being carried out in Ireland at two main centres - University College, Galway and at several of the Agricultural Research Institute stations such as that at Johnstown Castle. Funding for most of this work comes from the Irish National Board for Science and Technology and from the CEC's Solar Energy Programme.

Much of the work undertaken in Ireland concerns the development of a two-stage digestion system which can be easily managed in situ on any farm and can, in theory, be used to treat either animal or crop residues. The basic unit is an efficient hydrolysis reactor followed by an anaerobic filter for short retention time methanation. The projected benefits from the operation of a two-stage system for high solids substrate digestion include reduced capital costs and greater methane yields.

3.5 France

Two institutions were visited in France, the Institut National de Recherche Agonomique (INRA) and the Institut National Polytechnique de Lorraine, whilst detailed information was received from the Commisariate a l'Energie Solaire (COMES), the authority responsible for the national programme on renewable energy sources.

Although it has been felt in France that it is behind its neighbouring countries in methanisation techniques, it is catching up rapidly and has a thriving national programme of research and development and application, largely funded by three ministries. Results to-date indicate that agro-industrial wastes are suitable for anaerobic fermentation waste treatment and also wastes from the larger farms, ideally with more than five hundred pigs or one hundred cows.

Generally, it is believed that present technologies are too expensive and that heat production is the best use of biogas, but this in itself requires a minimum number of animals(e.g. thirty cows). However, before installing an anaerobic treatment system account must be taken of equipment already existing (such as that for manure handling), its operation must not take up too much time, the end use of the biogas must be understood and costed and the agronomic use of the residue must be considered: points which are not particularly well understood by many of the plant manufacturers.

The French are also aware of the major problem which exists throughout the Community, that there is, to-date, no flexible, commercially viable continuous fermentation system for what the French call 'fumier' - that is cattle waste, inclusive of its straw, bedding, etc.

3.6 Germany

Three organisations were visited in Germany: AHT in Essen; FAL in Braunschweig; and KTBL in Darmstadt. In addition, the 2nd International Conference on Anaerobic Digestion in Travemunde was attended. The German programme on anaerobic digestion and biogas appears to be very progressive. although some university projects are financed under the terms of CEC contracts (e.g. Wagener's work on Mariculture at Jülich) most research and development appears to be as a result of intensive Government backing. The economic assessments to-date indicate that biogas systems will not be an economic means of energy production for a number of years yet. The degree of Government involvement in the German programme, suggests that additional funding for research and development may not be required, particularly as it is known that a number of industrial organisations are also active in this and related topics.

3.7 Italy

Despite a number of requests for information on the status of anaerobic fermentation in Italy, no response was obtained and the information in the final report is based solely on published data and a few personal communications.

Italy produces quite a high proportion of agricultural residue within the Community but the average farm unit size is very small. This militates against any serious investment in anaerobic fermentation technology and is no doubt the reason why Pirelli and the CRN (the Italian National Research Council) are funding research on low cost systems for small dairy farms.

It is believed that there are a number of digesters working on large pig farms in Northern Italy with a common biogas collection line, but detailed performance data are not available.

Published information also indicates that several groups in Italy are working on two-stage digestion systems and on the basic problem of breakdown of ligno-cellulosic wastes.

3.8 Netherlands

Visits were made to the Agricultural University in Wageningen and to TNO, Zeist from which the general impression was gained that the trend in the Netherlands seems to be away from agricultural wastes towards more unusual substrates for anaerobic digestion treatment, particularly those encountered in dealing with a wide range of waste waters.

Views were also expressed that the rapid commercialisation of UASB type digester systems to large plant scale is possibly premature in the light of the limited amount of intermediate testing completed. This opinion was backed by various comments that were made at Travemunde at the 2nd International Conference on Anaerobic Digestion.

Considerable emphasis was placed on commercial opportunities in third world countries for the export from Europe of simple, low cost hardware and expertise, but industries in Holland and elsewhere in the Community appear reluctant to do so because the returns on investment are too long term.

3.9 United Kingdom

Visits in the United Kingdom included five in England to Leicester Polytechnic, the Agricultural Development Advisory Service, Water Research Centre and Warren Springs both in Stevenage and ETSU (The Energy Technology Support Unit); three visits were made to Wales to the Polytechnic of Wales, University College, Cardiff and the Cardiff University Industrial Centre; and one visit to Scotland to the Rowett Research Institute in Aberdeen. In addition, the Brighton Conference on Energy from Biomass was attended in November 1980.

It was clear from the discussions that there are many active research programmes on anaerobic fermentation in the United Kingdom but despite this, there is no comprehensive national policy on anaerobic digestion nor is there likely to be any strong Government commitment to anaerobic digestion as a means of energy conservation or as an alternative source of energy. There was however some indication that the need for demonstration systems is being recognised, but this may be affected by a recent Government decision to reduce funding for most alternative energy research programmes.

4   WASTES ARISING IN THE COMMUNITY WITH RELEVANCE TO ANAEROBIC FERMENTATION

Clearly, evaluation of the potential contribution that anaerobic digestion of suitable wastes might make to Community energy requirements requires a comparison between energy demand on the one hand and the availability of suitable wastes on the other. Both subjects were considered in the study but space considerations limit comment in this report to a summary of the sources of suitable waste. As far as energy requirements are concerned, suffice to say that a figure of 930 million tons of oil equivalent (MTOE) was taken as a measure of the total Community primary energy requirements in 1980.

With regard to the availability of suitable waste within the Community (and its potential as a source of energy) the authors, in reviewing the relevant literature, were unable to reconcile the wide variability in published estimates owing to the many uncertainties involved in converting raw agricultural statistics into estimates of usable energy. Typical uncertainties include such factors as the mean daily output from different animals, the usable/fermentable fraction of total waste produced, its dry content and proportion of organics, the average efficiency of conversion and the net/gross energy ratio, etc. In view of these uncertainties the authors used the CEC's 1981 Agricultural Report, together with some recent French and UK data to make a simple, approximate estimate of the maximum possible energy potential of fermentable wastes so that it might be put in perspective with Community energy requirements.

Three categories of waste were considered; animal wastes, crop wastes and agro-industrial wastes. Deliberately excluded were sheep and goats (as their wastes are essentially non-collectable), forestry wastes and straw (as suitable fermentation techniques are not available).

Using these estimates together with UK figures for methane yields gave an upper gross limit for the potential energy in Community waste of approximately 50 MTOE (i.e. about $5\frac{1}{4}$% of the primary energy requirements).

It must be stressed however that this is very much a theoretical upper limit and if allowance is made for several relevant factors (the effectiveness of waste collection, seasonality, inefficiencies in biogas production and use, etc.) this figure would be significantly reduced to well below 3%. Consequently the authors believe that the net gain in energy from anaerobic digestion of waste is likely to be marginal.

5 CONCLUSIONS
5.1 The basic technology of, and equipment for anaerobic fermentation

5.1.1 There has been little progress over the past three-five years in achieving greater yields of biogas by means of an increased understanding of the basic processes involved in anaerobic fermentation, and little improvement is evident in the generally quoted average yield of $0.3M^3$ of gas produced for every kilogramme of volatile solids digested.

5.1.2 Nor is there any significant evidence of improvements in gas yield by the alternative approach of advancements in the technology of equipment, although pilot scale studies in Denmark and Eire on two-stage digester systems for the treatment of straw show some promise.

5.1.3 There is a lack of convincing evidence on the economic justification for specific anaerobic digestion installations and the authors doubt whether it is possible to generalise about the economics as each application must be judged according to its merits.

5.1.4 With the exception of major sewage treatment digesters which, although well established, are considered to be a special case, there are few full scale digesters, other than agro-industrial types, operating in the Community to allow any significant technical or economic assessments to be made in the context of this study.

5.1.5 To-date, little attention has been paid to waste handling equipment required to feed a digester or to the downstream requirements after digestion - in particular to the use of discharged sludges/slurries and the storage and use of the biogas.

5.1.6 Cattle wastes form the largest usable proportion of current waste arisings but the inevitable presence of straw in the waste is a major problem as there is at present no low cost, flexible, off-the-shelf system available to deal with straw-containing waste.

5.2 Anaerobic fermentation in the context of national policies

5.2.1 With the apparent exception of the United Kingdom, Eire and Italy significant funds are allocated to anaerobic fermentation studies in the other member states as part of their substantial national energy programmes.

5.2.2 The majority of the member states have conducted their own surveys and forecasts of wastes arising within their own borders; the results being remarkably variable and at variance with those calculated at a Community level. This highlights the dangers associated with the interpretation of the large volume of statistics available within the Community and individual countries and the assumptions that have to be made in carrying out what can become complex calculations.

5.2.3 The scientific/technological status of the individual national programmes varies considerably with Belgium being one of the most advanced in terms of research and development. Commercially, whilst many organisations have at some time been involved with anaerobic fermentation plant, many have either subsequently withdrawn or are concerned with a single experimental/trial plant. Consequently, only a few companies in the Community can be regarded as being actively engaged in the anaerobic fermentation plant business on a significant commercial scale.

5.3 Anaerobic fermentation within the Community

5.3.1 Work carried out during the study has indicated that the maximum upper limit of the contribution to the Community's energy requirements from the anaerobic fermentation of waste is no more than 3% of the total primary energy demand. It is unlikely therefore that anaerobic fermentation of waste will be a significant factor in reducing the Community's dependence on overseas sources of energy supply.

5.3.2 However, because of the geographical distribution/concentration of wastes, it is quite reasonable to expect that useful savings can be made at a local level within agricultural communities, provided the most suitable applications are selected by a realistic evaluation procedure.

5.3.3 Similarly there may well be worthwhile applications for anaerobic fermentation in the treatment of certain agro-industrial waste waters which would be of financial benefit to the company concerned and of environmental benefit to the Community as a whole.

5.3.4 The financial structure of the European farming community is so dependent on the Common Agricultural Policy that the availability of, or return on capital may be insufficient to justify the installation of anaerobic digesters and related equipment and if the Community wishes to promote the use of such equipment then the possibility of offering financial incentives will have to be examined.

5.3.5 The research and development activities associated with anaerobic fermentation are spread widely through the Community and the sources of funding are also spread widely both on a national and Community level. This is a situation that inevitably leads to duplication in research - as evidenced by much of the information currently presented at conferences, meetings and in the relevant literature published throughout the Community.

5.3.6 Although not strictly within the scope of the project, the authors consider it appropriate to sound a cautionary note on the enthusiasm in some quarters for the prospects for energy production on a substantial scale through the anaerobic fermentation of specially grown crops. For a variety of reasons but especially in connection with the central issue of land availability and competition with food production and forest products, the authors firmly believe that energy production by this means is not a viable proposition on any significant scale in a European context.

5.4   Factors affecting the exploitation of anaerobic fermentation

5.4.1 The effective implementation of anaerobic fermentation for agricultural waste ideally requires the installation of relatively expensive equipment, good waste handling systems, etc. on large farm units. In reality a large proportion of the Community farm holdings are small labour intensive units essentially incapable of justifying or providing the necessary capital investment. Even for the larger farm units, the present economic trends in interest rates, energy costs, feed costs, etc. are such as to inhibit capital investment in equipment of a non-essential nature; and applications which would otherwise be ideal for anaerobic digesters may therefore remain unexploited until the present financial restraints are lightened.

5.4.2 As yet, there are few specific legal restraints on the design and operation of digesters but most of the Community countries are active to a varying extent in the preparation or implementation of codes of practice or other safeguards. It seems quite possible that when these codes are finally issued the designers, manufacturers, installers and operators of anaerobic fermentation systems will have to comply with safeguards which will add considerably to the capital and running costs of such units. This could further inhibit their exploitation except in the most favourable economic circumstances.

5.4.3 Any decision to install anaerobic fermentation equipment to deal with agricultural waste will be (or should be) based on an economic evaluation taking into account all relevant factors including the value and regularity of the energy generated set against the investment required. Clearly, the effect of climatic variations is important in this respect and in the extreme, should the main crop fail or be substantially reduced, the installation will fail to pay for itself.

6   RECOMMENDATIONS

6.1 It is recommended that CEC funding for anaerobic fermentation technology be reviewed by the Commission as the authors believe that significant reductions are possible in the light of the level of funding already available in the member countries from national and other sources and in view of the relatively small contribution that the process can make to energy savings in the Community.

6.2 Such funding as remains should be directed towards research in specific areas that will advance the technology of anaerobic fermentation particularly in those areas which may be beneficial to other technologies in the longer term. Should this lead to significant improvements then there is no reason why funding levels could not be increased again to assist in exploiting the improvements.

6.3 If the research is to be cost effective, it should be closely co-ordinated within a planned programme of objectives and projects so that unnecessary duplication is avoided. It is suggested that work in each of the three main areas of interest, namely: basic microbiology and biochemistry; design and ergonomics; and economic evaluation be centralised in a limited number of centres of excellence.

6.4 Whatever decisions may be taken regarding the scope of the chosen programmes of work or their co-ordination, it seems likely from the nature of the work that it will continue to be carried out in institutions mainly of an academic character. It is therefore recommended that appropriate industrial advisors and possibly potential users be given the opportunity of commenting on the objectives of the proposed programmes and on the progress of the work to ensure that the ultimate aim of commercial viability is kept in mind.

6.5 It is recommended that the CEC should examine the commercial prospects for supplying the technology to developing nations - the so-called third world countries as there seems to be a large market in these countries for simple, low-cost anaerobic fermentation systems backed up by effective technical assistance. Apart from the Eastern bloc countries, few commercial concerns are pursuing these opportunities, either because of lack of knowledge of the demand or doubts about the commercial returns. If the Commission can provide encouragement, perhaps through market intelligence to quantify the demand and/or by financial incentives to counter commercial difficulties then it is believed the long term prospects for business are considerable.

REFERENCES

1   ANDERTON, M.F. and GIBBS, D.F.   IRD 82/20 Critical evaluation of anaerobic fermentation of waste products (a management study) - Final report, Contract No. EE-B-4-180-UKH.

NOVEL METHODS FOR ALCOHOLS PRODUCTION (FUELS AND HYDROCARBONS SUBSTITUTES) FROM SYNTHESIS GAS

J. Drapier, A. F. Noels, A. J. Hubert and Ph. Teyssié

Laboratory of Macromolecular Chemistry and Organic Catalysis,
University of Liège, Sart Tilman, B-4000 Liège

Summary
    The direct production of oxygenated products, parti-
cularly alcohols such as ethanol, by CO hydrogenation is of
major industrial interest. Owing to the high cost of the best
known (rhodium) catalysts, the present work reports on the
relevance of cobalt catalysis in this field. Reduced cobalt
species (Co(I)COD) appeared to be active for CO hydrogenation
under a wide range of pressures (from 1 up to 500 bars).
Olefins rich hydrocarbon mixtures (CH_4 being the main component
however) were obtained under low pressure (1 bar) using a circulating system (recycling of syngas and trapping of products).
Oppositely, small amounts of alcohols were detected when the
reduction was effected in autoclaves under high pressure (150
bars). The reaction appeared to be very sensitive to different
factors such as the temperature, the use of a support (such as
bentonite-Tixoton and Triton-Kaowool (alumina silicate)), the
pressure. The selectivity in alcohols (relatively to other
oxygenates) was generally good but remained however very low
relatively to alkanes production (5-16%). Moreover, the catalyst was readily deactivated (except under the low pressure
conditions with recycling of the gases and trapping of products).
Therefore, the present results indicate that the alcohols production seems to be limited to very few catalytic cycles.
An investigation of bimetallic systems (Co-Rh) was also approached, the objective being the use of decreased amounts of the
selective (but expensive) rhodium catalysts while preserving
catalytic activity. The cobalt additive led however to increased alkanes production.

1.1.   Introduction
    The preparation of organic chemicals directly from
synthesis gas ($CO-H_2$) is essentially related to the recent
energy crisis linked to petroleum shortage. Therefore, the
preparation of synthetic fuels from coal (via synthesis gas)
has already received a great deal of attention.
    However, the old processes can only be applied to
the preparation of hydrocarbons mixtures (essentially paraffins), oppositely the problem of the selective direct synthesis
of valuable industrial chemicals (eg, oxygenates such as
alcohols, aldehydes, carboxylic acids ... or olefins such as
ethylene, propene, ...) has not yet been satisfactorily solved
(except for methanol synthesis) despite recent spectacular pro-
gresses (for example : the direct ethylene glycol synthesis by
the UCC process). The direct production of alcohols from syngas
is in fact an important aspect of these problems, the preparation of ethanol being particularly desirable as this alcohol
can be considered as an interesting precursor of several key

raw materials of the chemical industry (ethylene, acetaldehyde ...).
    The design of the catalyst is determining :up to now the
best results for ethanol production have been obtained with
rhodium based systems (1,2),the support (for example,lanthanide
oxides)(3) being an important factor.The common drawback of
these systems is the cost of the essential component (rhodium)
together with prohibitive pressure requirements (ethylene glycol
synthesis) and problems related to the selectivity and stability of the
catalyst.The search for stable selective catalysts avoiding the
costly rhodium component has therefore received much attention:
particularly interesting results have been obtained by the IFP
group(4) who reported on the efficient and selective synthesis
of alcohols mixtures(C_1-C_6) directly from syngas on mixed oxides
catalysts(Co,Zn,Cu,Cr,Al). In opposition to the rhodium catalyst,
this system is not selective for ethanol production, mixtures
of alcohols being the rule.
    The aim of the present work was therefore to realize an
exploratory investigation of alcohols formation (emphasis being
laid on ethanol) on catalysts based on cheap metals :
    Cobalt complexes have been first considered owing
to the activity of this metal for CO hydrogenation but also
for the homologation of methanol to ethanol (1,2,5).
    Experiments with rhodium catalysts have also been run
for comparison (Rh-Co systems).
2.   Realization of the work
2.1.   Apparatus and techniques
2.1.1.Analytical procedures
    The gas phases were analysed by GLC (columns:Spherocarb
(9feet,1/8inch) for CO,CO_2,CH_4; Al_2O_3 capillary PLOT column
(30meters, isothermal 60°C): hydrocarbons. FFAP and chromosorb
W:alcohols). Identification of the gases was based both on chromatographic
methods (retention times) and mass spectrometry.
2.1.2.Equipment and operating conditions
    Low pressure (1-1,4bar) experiments were run in a glass
reactor at 200 to 250°C with continuous trapping of the reaction products (7).
    High pressure experiments were carried out in stainless
steel autoclaves (PROLABO).The dried catalyst (contained in a
glass jacket under nitrogen) was introduced into the autoclave
CO and H_2 pressure being then applied. The reactor was then shaken at the
required temperature during 40 hours. The gases were collected in a reservoir after cooling and analysed by GLC whereas the liquid fractions were
condensed in a cool trap (liquid N_2). (V autoclave = 100ml).
2.1.3. Catalysts
    n3-cyclooctenyl1-π-1,5-cyclooctadiene (Co(I) was purchased
from Emser Werks A.G. or prepared according to a reported procedure (6).
    Supports :Bentonite-Tixoton is a commercial clay (presen-
ting base character) available from Süd Chemie A.G.,(München).
Triton K_aowool (alumina silicate fibres) is available from Morganite Ceramic Fibres Ltd.,Tebay Road,Bromborough,WIRRAL, Mer-
seyside L62 3PH UK.
    Preparation of supported catalysts : impregnation of the
dried supports was effected by slow evaporation of a catalyst solution in pentane, followed by drying overnight in vacuo (<1mm)
at 25°C.

2.2. Results and discussion
2.2.1. Reduced cobalt (Co(I)) based catalysts.
Activation of CO hydrogenation catalysts is classical-
ly effected by hydrogenation of supported metal salts or oxides.

However, Petit, Mortreux and Vanhove (7) reported on
interesting selectivities in olefin productions with a Co(II)-
AlR$_3$ catalyst in solution : the formation of low oxidation states
as the active cobalt species (eg Co(I)) was therefore strongly
suspected to take place under the reported procedure for the
catalyst preparation (Co(I) complexes are in fact formed under
similar conditions).

Moreover, we envisaged that the relatively high selectivities in olefins could result from dehydration of alcohols
precursors or that the catalytic sites responsible for olefins
production (for example : hydroxycarbenes or metal-formyl
species) could be directed towards alcohols production (by ac-
ting on the reaction conditions such the temperature, the pressure, the CO/H$_2$ ratio and particularly, by using different kinds
of supports or additives, ...).

Therefore preliminary attempts were run with cobalt(II)
salts reduced with NaBH$_4$ in the presence of a diolefin as ligand
(L) (L=butadiene,1,5-cyclooctadiene (COD)). In fact, in a second stage, the use of pure preformed cobalt reduced species
(Co(I)) was investigated under different conditions.

2.2.1.1. Preliminary attempts (CoCl$_2$ reduced by NaBH$_4$, L=butadiene, COD).
These experiments were run in autoclaves under pressu-
re (120 bars) of CO-H$_2$ (1:2) in the absence of solvents (the
solvent used for the catalyst preparation was evaporated in
vac uo prior to the CO-hydrogenation experiment : see chapter
2.1.3).

These experiments led to the formation of a mixture of
n-alkanes (C$_1$-C$_6$) and traces of olefins together with a mixture of oxygenates (mainly alcohols (C$_1$-C6) and aldehydes(C$_1$-C5)).
However, the selectivity in alcohols relatively to other oxygenates appeared to depend strongly on the conditions (see table
I) such as the solvents used for the reduction of the cobalt(II)
salt, the presence of an added solvent, the nature of the ligand
L (BD,COD,Cp),(the nature of the metal is of course of determining importance : NiCl$_2$-NaBH$_4$ affording only traces of methanol
(and alkanes) under the same conditions).

2.2.1.2. Investigation of preformed Co(I) complexes as catalysts.
The preliminary attempts were an indication for the
participation of low oxidation states of cobalt (particularly
as Co(I) entities) as the active catalytic centre, the ligand L
stabilizing the cobalt (I) species. In fact, the used conditions
(as well as those reported by Petit, Mortreux and Vanhove (7))
are compatible with the formation of n^3-cyclooctenyl-π-1,5-cy-
clooctadiene cobalt(I)(Co(COD)) : cobalt (I) complexes were
therefore investigated as catalysts.

It appeared that both the activity and selectivity of these catalysts were very depending on the ligands : CpCo(CO)$_2$ was inactive for oxygenates production (the main products corresponding to the hydroformylation of the ligand) whereas alcohols were formed, sometime with a good selectivity relatively to other oxygenates with Co(COD), but the yield relatively to hydrocarbons remained always very low.

2.2.2.   Investigation of Co(COD) as catalyst
The sensitivity of the catalytic performance to small modifications of various factors appeared readily when different crops of catalysts were prepared in the laboratory. However, alcohols were always present with good selectivities in the aqueous phase, aldehydes being always minor products as compared to the former.

The catalytic efficiency and the selectivities appeared to depend markly on the reaction conditions such as the pressure, the type of reactor (autoclaves : no trapping of products, no recycling of the gas. Circulator : continuous trapping of products, recycling of the gas), the temperature and the use of supports.

a) The pressure : the conversion rate decreased readily with the pressure for the experiments run in autoclaves. However, alkanes and alkenes were formed under low pressure (1.4 bar) when using a circulating device (see below).

b) The reactors : the catalyst appeared to be readily deactivated (the conversion decreased by a factor of ten in some cases after the first run) when the reaction was performed in an autoclave. The reaction products (particularly water, the alcohols) could therefore contribute to catalyst deactivation : in fact, the catalytic activity remained practically unchanged during several successive utilisations (up to 18 uses of 6 hours each) when using a low pressure circulator (1.4 bar) (see the scheme page 9).
However, the selectivity in hydrocarbons changed appreciably during the first 6 utilisations (molecular weight distribution, olefins to alkanes ratio, α to β olefins ratio, cis to trans ratio)(see fig. 1).
The isomerising properties (particularly as far as the positional isomerism of the double bond was concerned) appeared to increase notably with aging of the catalyst. Oppositely, the branched to linear hydrocarbons ratio was not much affected. These effects were strongly accelerated when increasing the local concentration in cobalt on the support (see fig. 1, dotted lines). The detailed description of the phenomenon related to the hydrocarbons has been described in a recent publication of our group (8).
However, oxygenates were practically absent under these conditions, particularly in the aqueous phase.

c) The temperature appeared to be an important factor : the distribution of products in the gas phase (hydrocarbons, CO$_2$) and in the liquid phase was notably temperature dependent. An investigation with Co(COD) on Triton Kaowool (Morganite) as support showed that the yield of alcohols was

60

particularly affected : the total amount of alcohols present in the aqueous phase decreased by a factor of 10 in the liquid phase between 235 and 265°C (the yield remained however very poor even at the lower temperature (see table II)). The analysis of the gas phase showed that the methanation and particularly the water gas shift (CO_2 formation) reactions were strongly enhanced by increasing the temperature. Moreover, an organic liquid phase was also present and consisted in a mixture of higher hydrocarbons (C_4-C_9), the distribution of these alkanes being little affected within this range of temperature ($C_6>C_7>C_8 \sim C_5>C_9>C_4$).

d) <u>The supports</u> : different supports were investigated in order to try to stabilize the catalytic centre responsible for alcohols production. In fact, it is now well established that supports and additives are an important factor as far as the control of the selectivities(1,2,3,9) is concerned (alcohols production with rhodium catalyst was reported to be particularly promoted on basic supports such as ZnO, La_2O_3, $Mg_2Si_3O_3$, TiO_2 ...
Additives such as KI and Na are also beneficial in some CO hydrogenation processes whereas CH_3I is commonly used in the now classical rhodium and cobalt catalyzed homologation of methanol to acetic acid (and to ethanol)(4).
The results obtained with different supports can only be described as general trends of the catalytic performances of Co(COD) as the results were poorly reproducible and depended particularly of the catalysts preparation and aging of the Co(COD) solutions. Moreover, the dispersion mode of the complex was obviously a key factor. Dispersion on an " inert" support such as glass wool or glass beads showed that hydrocarbons distribution was markly affected by increased dispersion of the catalyst (higher molecular weight alkanes are formed) but the selectivity in oxygenates was low (4-15%, ethanol:1-7% relatively to hydrocarbons together with other oxygenates).
The use of Triton Kaowool (an alumina silicate from Morganite) and of bentonite Tixoton (a basic clay) led to some improvement of the efficiency and selectivity of the catalyst : alcohols are formed with appreciable selectivities relatively to other oxygenated products.
However, in some cases selectivity in alcohols (C_1-C_6) relatively to the hydrocarbons appeared to be located within the same range of a typical ethanol producing catalysts (Hoechst) used under low pressure (1 bar) conditions.
Zinc oxide supported Co(COD) catalysts were tentatively explored in relation with the potential activity of the cobalt complex as a methanol homologation catalyst when used in combination with the zinc based system. Moreover, a patented methanol catalyst (10) (Zn-Cu-Al-(W)-O) was prepared and tested in autoclave under our conditions (150 bars,250°C) : high yield of methanol was obtained (4g of practically pure methanol). The catalyst efficiency appeared to be very sensitive however to minor changes in the preparation procedure (notably to the presence of the tungsten additive).

The use of the above methanol catalyst as a support for the Co(COD) complex led to a sharp decrease of selectivity in alcohols : alkanes were formed and the total amount of alcohols decreased (0.15g instead of 4 g), some homologation being observed however ($CH_3OH > C_2H_5OH > C_3H_7OH$).

Practically identical distributions were obtained with ZnO as a support for Co(COD), the selectivity for the homologation products being however improved with a SiO_2-ZnO support C_2-OH > C_3-OH > $CH_3OH > C_4$-OH > C_5-OH >> C_6-OH) as well as with $Zn|Co(CO)_4|_2$ on bentonite-Tixoton (analysis of the aqueous liquid phase (1.35g) : C_1-OH:0,23; C_2-OH:0,36, C_3-OH:0,38; C_4-OH:0,28; C_5-OH:0.06%. Po-Pf=150-105 bars.T=250°C. t=40h. Alkanes : 3% of the remaining gas phase).

A bimetallic system (Fe-Co(COD)/bentonite) led to high catalytic activity but the selectivity was poor in alcohols relatively to alkanes production. However, Fe-Co(COD) led to the formation of an aqueous phase containing essentially alcohols (beside water) whereas Fe/bentonite yielded an aqueous phase containing at least 22 products.
However, this type of catalysts were characterized by the formation of a relatively important organic phase (not miscible with water) consisting in a very complex mixture of compounds (more than 30 constituents of the mixture being detected).

2.3. Rhodium-base catalysts : Ichikawa has reported on the selective alcohols synthesis (with preferential formation of ethanol) under low pressure (∿1bar) when using a circulating device and trapping of the reaction products. The catalyst was a rhodium carbonyl cluster supported on a lanthanide oxide. The patent literature reported also on the use of $RhCl_3$ based catalysts (SiO_2-MgO supported) (9) : good selectivities in ethanol were observed when using a circulating device under high pressure (100 bars).
In autoclaves (without trapping of the products), alkanes appeared as the main reaction products, the alcohols being formed in traces amounts.
However, Hoechst catalyst appeared to afford alcohols ($C_2 >> C_1 \approx C_3$) even under low pressure (1 bar) when using a circulator allowing trapping of products. It appeared therefore that the trapping of reaction products is essential to get complete evaluation of a catalyst.
An exploratory study of a bimetallic system based on $RhCl_3$ associated to $CoCl_2$ on a Hoechst type support led only to enhanced alkanes production, alcohols formation being not improved (the selectivity for C_2-OH being however maintained).

3. Conclusions
Cobalt catalysts are active for promoting carbon monoxide hydrogenation, oxygenates being formed together with alkanes and olefins. Co(COD), a preformed reduced cobalt (I) species, led directly (without hydrogen treatment as it is the case for classical catalysts) to the formation of the hydrocondensation product of CO. It appeared however to be extremely sensitive to the reaction conditions (aging, dispersion mode

on supports, origin,...) the results were therefore poorly reproducible and general tendencies can only be given.

When used in autoclaves, the catalyst displayed a moderate efficiency during the first run, then its activity decrease markly. Hydrocarbons were the main reaction products but alcohols (C_1-C_4) accounted for the oxygenates fractions with a good selectivity, ethanol being the major constituent of this fraction in some cases.
Both the efficiency and the selectivity were improved by using high pressure (100-500 bars). The temperature appeared to be a key factor : the alcohol fraction decreased sharply within the (235-275°C) range whereas the methanation and particularly the water gas shift reactions increased dramatically.
The support of the Co(COD) complex was very important : the best results for oxygenates production were obtained with bentonite Tixoton (a basic clay) and with Triton Kaowool (an alumina silicate), the selectivity in alcohols relatively to the oxygenates was good but this fraction represents only a minor fraction of the reaction product relatively to the hydrocarbons. The use of zinc oxide based supports afforded methanol as the main constituent (as expected from the zinc oxide own catalytic effect) together with some homologation products (ethanol, propanol).
The low yield in oxygenates may result from the instability of the Co(I) species (as shown by the fast deactivation of the catalyst in autoclave and the decreased alcohols production when the temperature was increased) in fact, the initial Co(I) complex was progressively destroyed and the metal is finally formed under our reaction conditions. The alcohols production appeared therefore as a reaction close to stoichiometry relatively to the catalyst and as a minor pathway relatively to hydrocarbon production. The failor to reach good efficiency may essentially result from the impossibility to stabilize the Co(I) species (for example, by a support effect).
Further studies should in our opinion, be centered on polymetallic catalysts (similar to IFP catalysts : Zn,Cu,Co,...).
The use of a circulator allowing the recycling of the synthesis gas with continuous trapping of the product showed that the catalyst (Co(COD) on bentonite-Tixoton) was active even at low pressure (1-4 bar) and, in opposition to the experiments in autoclaves, the activity was preserved after extensive utilisations (more than 18 utilisations of 6 hours each).
However, alcohols are not formed under these conditions but the olefins represented an important part of the hydrocarbons fractions. The use of a circulator under high pressure (100 bars) would be therefore of interest in the context of this works.
If the present study shows that cobalt catalysis is not yet a practical method for alcohols production, the reported results bring significant information on the role of different parameters in this reaction : the oxidation state (Co(I)) of the metal plays obviously an important role.

Rhodium catalysis is characterized by the best efficiency and selectivity in ethanol production reported up to now in the patent literature.

The prohibitive cost of the catalyst together with the fact
that the undesirable hydrocarbons production could not be sufficiently avoided, prevented its industrial application up to
now : it would be of interest therefore to decrease the required amount of the costly rhodium metal by association with
another one : our investigation of a supported Rh-Co system
led only to the promotion of hydrocarbons formation, alcohols
production being not improved. Further investigations in this
direction would however be of particular interest when considering the association of rhodium with other metals than
cobalt(such an approach of the problem has been considered when
using a rhodium-manganese catalyst [11])).

Abreviations

COD : 1,5-cyclooctadiene
Co(COD):n^3-cyclooctenyl,π-1,5-cyclooctadiene cobalt (I)
C_p = cyclopendadienyl
L = ligand
$C_n^=$ = olefin, n = carbon number, $c_{4p}^=$ = 2-butene

References

1) C$_1$-Based Chemicals from Hydrogen and Carbon Monoxide,
    M.T.Gillies (1982). Noyes Data Corporation, New Jersey USA.
2) Catalysis in C$_1$ chemistry. W.Keim (1983), D.Reidel
    Publishing Compagny.
3) M. Ichikawa, K. Shikahura, K.Sekigawa and T.Tanaka (Sagami
    Chemical Research Center) European Patent 22358 (1981).
4) A. Sugier and E. Freund, U.S.Patent 4,122,110 (1978).
    Ph.Courty, D.Durand, E.Freund and A.Sugier, International
    Symposium on Catalytic Reactions of One Carbon Molecules
    Bruges (1982). J.Molec.Catal.17,339 (1982).
5) W.E. Walker, U.S.Patent, 4,277,634 (1981). H.M.Feder, U.S.
    Patent 4,301,312 (1981).J.Gauthier-Lafarye, R.Perron and
    Y. Colleuille, J.Mol.Cat.17,339 (1982).
6) Inorganic Synthesis,17, 112 (1977).
7) M. Blanchard, D.Vanhove, F.Petit and A. Mortreux, J.Chem.
    Soc.Chem.Comm.,908 (1980). D.Vanhove, M.Blanchard, F.Petit
    and A.Mortreux, Nouv.J.Chim.,5,205 (1981).
8) 2nd Belgo Hungarian Conference on Catalysis. De Haan-
    Belgium (1983). Acta Chim. Acad.Sc.Hung.-to be published
    in 1984.
9) H. Hachenberg, F.Wunder, E.J. Leupold and H.J.Schmidt
    (Hoechst Aktien Geselschaft). European Patent 21330 (1981).
10) P.G.Bondar, O.N.Goroshko, L.E.Suskaya, V.V.Lavrova, V.E.
    Leleka and E.G.Ilko, U.S.Patent, 4,107,089 (1978).
11) P.E.Elingen and M.M.Bhasin, U.S.Patent, 4,014,913 (1977).

TABLE I : Hydrogenation of CO on reduced cobalt catalyst (CoCl$_2$+NaBH$_4$+L) : exploratory experiments (typical results).

catalyst :	
CoCl$_2$.NaBH$_4$. BD(CH$_3$OH) (a)	gas phase:C$_1$>>C$_2$∿C$_3$>C$_4$>C$_3$=>C$_5$>C$_4$=>C$_5$=>C$_6$>C$_2$= liquid phase : alcohols:C$_1$-C$_4$ aldehydes : traces
CoCl$_2$.NaBH$_4$.COD (CH$_3$CN) (b)	gas phase : C$_1$>>C$_3$>C$_2$∿C$_4$>C$_5$>C$_6$ liquid phase : n-C$_3$OH, n-C$_4$OH, 2-methyl-1-propanol
CoCl$_2$.NaBH$_4$.Cp (CH$_3$CN) (c)	gas phase : no hydrocarbons liquid phase : traces of CH$_3$OH
CoCl$_2$.NaBH$_4$. COD.dioxane (d)	gas phase : C$_1$>C$_2$∿C$_3$>C$_4$>C$_5$>C$_6$ (traces of olefins) liquid phase :C$_1$OH>n-C$_3$OH>C$_2$OH (e) aldehydes : C$_3$>C$_4$>C$_2$

(a)CoCl$_2$:0.005mole,NaBH$_4$:0.010mole,L=butadiene(BD)Solvent(used for the preparation of the catalyst):CH$_3$OH(20ml).(b)L=COD: 0.010mole.Solvent:acetonitrile.(c)L=cyclopentadiene.(d) CO-H$_2$ reaction run in dioxane as solvent;sequence:n-propionald. >n-butylald.>methanol>n-propanol>acetaldehyde>ethanol.

TABLE II : Influence of the temperature on the distribution of products.

gas phase (%W)				aqueous liquid phase			(%W)
	235°C	250°C	265°C		235°C	250°C	265°C
CO	75.42	30.3	0.67	H$_2$O	70.3	92.85	99.68
CO$_2$	6.46	24.06	40.25	CH$_3$OH	9.87	1.99	0.059
CH$_4$	12.13	31.58	48.09	C$_2$-OH	7.30	1.67	0.034
C$_2$	0.43	2.35	2.66	C$_3$-OH	5.93	1.72	0.053
C$_3$	2.03	4.36	3.95	C$_4$-OH	1.94	0.63	0.02
C$_4$	2.1	3.98	3.19	C$_5$-OH	0.36	-	0.0025
C$_5$	0.96	1.34	1.19				

Conditions:Pf:150atm.(autoclave:154ml).C$_6$H$_2$/1/2.T=245°C.t=40h.
Catalyst : Co(COD)(0.001mole on alumina silicate (Triton-Kaowool)(2g)
Total weight(g) of the liquids phases, relative volumes ratios (__) of organic to aqueous phases : 0.43(0.12),0.40(0.1), 0.92(0.1).

TABLE III : Hydrogenation of CO with Co(COD)(0.001mole) on bentonite-Tixoton (1g).
Liquid phase(W%) : H$_2$O:94.64; CH$_3$OH:1.29; C$_2$OH:2.02;
C$_3$-OH:1.25;C$_4$-OH:0.41; C$_5$-OH:0.17;
C$_6$-OH:0.62%. Weight:0.51g).
Gas phase : CO:90.93; CO$_2$:1.09; CH$_4$:4.04; C$_2$:1.01;C$_3$:1.40;
C$_4$:0.83; C$_5$:0.68%.
Conditions : Po-Pf=150-105 bars. T(°C)=245°. t=40h.

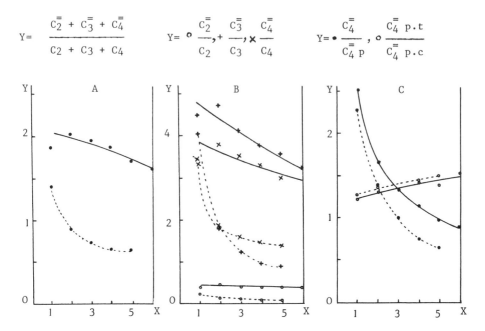

$$Y = \frac{C_2^= + C_3^= + C_4^=}{C_2 + C_3 + C_4}$$

$$Y = {}^\circ \frac{C_2^=}{C_2}, + \frac{C_3^=}{C_3}, \times \frac{C_4^=}{C_4}$$

$$Y = \bullet \frac{C_4^=}{C_4^= \, p}, \quad \circ \frac{C_4^= \, p.t}{C_4^= \, p.c}$$

Fig. 1 : Evolution of the Co(COD) catalyst during successive utilizations (X=number of runs, 6 hours each).
A and B : evolution of olefins to alkanes ratios with the number of runs
C : evolution of positional and geometric isomers distribution with n.
Co(COD) : 0.001 mole.(—) on 5g bentonite.(---) on 0.5g bentonite then 4.5g bentonite added (higher local concentration of cobalt than for (—)).

Scheme of the circulating systems (1 bar and 100 bars)

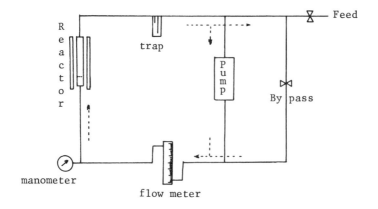

SELECTIVE SYNTHESIS OF DIESEL HYDROCARBONS FROM SYNTHESIS GAS

P. A. Jacobs, K. Willemen, L. Leplat and J. B. Uytterhoeven

Katholieke Universiteit Leuven
Laboratorium voor Oppervlaktescheikunde
Kard. Mercierlaan, 92, B-3030 Leuven (Herverlee)

SUMMARY

The conversion of a CO/H_2 mixture to hydrocarbons is reported for increasing time-on-stream, using a Fischer-Tropsch catalyst which contains alumina as support and cobalt metal deposited on the support as active phase. The unit used is a bench scale high pressure continuous flow reactor, which allows on-line analysis of the products up to carbon number 25. For all times-on-stream (up to 70 hours) and at 200 °C reaction temperature the activity of the catalyst remains unchanged at about 20 % conversion in CO, its carbon material balance reaches 100 % and the growth factor is always around 0.75, at least for the hydrocarbons in the C_2-C_{12} range. The selectivity for the other hydrocarbons (C_1 and those in the diesel range) drastically varies with time-on-stream : C_1 increases and C_{12}-C_{20} decreases. In this way, at least during the first 30 hours of operation, diesel yields are obtained, which are higher than those reported for the SASOL plants.

INTRODUCTION

The synthesis of liquid fuels and more particularly the synthesis of hydrocarbons in the gasoil and/or gasoline range from coal with synthesis gas (CO + H_2) as intermediate has proven its technical feasibility in the SASOL plants in South-Africa (1). These processes are generally denoted as Fischer-Tropsch synthesis. The presently operated process is highly unselective and requires expensive post-synthesis treatments of the hydrocarbons. Results from the SASOL plants (1) indicate that there exists an interrelation between the various product cuts. Therefore, the maximum selectivity for gasoline and diesel is limited. In practice maximum yields of 42 and 18 % by weight car be obtained, respectively. The detailed distribution of the product carbon numbers can be described reasonably well by a chain growth polymerization mechanism, a polymerization distribution law (PDL) or by the so-called Schulz-Flory kinetic formalism :

$$W_n = n\alpha^{n-1} (1-\alpha)^2$$

67

W_n represents the weight fraction of carbon number n and α the growth factor of the hydrocarbon chain on the catalyst surface. The selectivity according to these models only varies with the growth factor α. In recent literature (for a survey see ref. 2), strong deviations from these models have been reported and thus enhanced selectivities for certain carbon numbers in a Fischer-Tropsch synthesis can be obtained.

It has been the primary goal of the present research to verify whether the enhanced selectivity of products in the gasoil range, reported for cobalt metal on alumina (3), can be obtained in a reproducible way or whether they are just the result of experimental artefacts.

In a previous paper (4), the results obtained in a batch-type Fischer-Tropsch reactor have been reported. In such a reactor the cumulative amount of products synthesized after 2 days was analyzed. For low Co loadings on alumina, enhanced selectivities in the diesel range were found. Therefore these Co catalysts do not seem to obey the PDL-formalism.

In the mean time <u>a new bench-scale reactor</u> was constructed, allowing :

- to perform sampling of products on-line to the reactor, up to product carbon numbers of 25;
- to determine accurate carbon mass balances : i.e. to compare the amount of carbon present in the synthesis-gas to the carbon analyzed at the reactor exit;
- to determine actual product distributions at different reaction times. In the previously used batch reactor, only cumulative amounts of products could be determined.

The time-on-stream dependence of the Fischer-Tropsch products is followed for catalysts which in the batch-reactor showed deviations from a statistical product distribution.

EXPERIMENTAL DETAILS

Reactor

The unit is a continuous flow high pressure reactor, the exit of which is connected to the sampling valve of a high resolution capillary gas chromatograph. It can be loaded with 2 g of catalyst and is able to operate at a total pressure of 6000 kPa. The compartment linking the reactor exit to the sampling valve is kept at such a temperature (usually 295 °C) that hydrocarbons up to C_{22} remain entirely in the vapor phase. The unit is dual : when reaction occurs in one reactor, another catalyst can be pretreated and activated in the second reactor. A flow sheet of the reactor as well as of the analytical equipment is given in Figure 1.

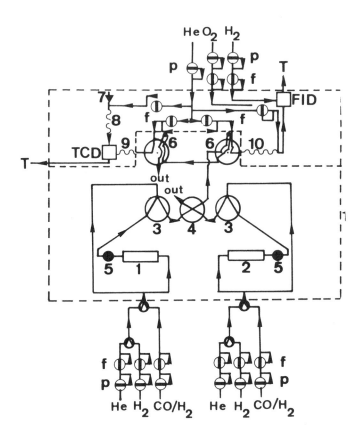

FIG. 1 : Flow sheet of the high pressure continuous flow bench-scale reactor and analytical set-up;

f, flow-regulator; p, pressure-regulator; 1, reactor 1; 2, reactor 2; 3, 3-port valve; 4, 4-port valve; 5, needle valve; 6, 6-port sampling valve, with sample loop; 7, manual injection port; 8, capillary column, fused silica (OV 101, 50 m); 9, packed column (carbosive B, 3 m); 10, capillary column, fused silica (OV 101, 50 m); 11, gaschromatografic part; 12, thermostatted part; FID, flame-ionization detector; TCD, thermal conductivity detector; T, terminal.

Analysis

Samples of the reactor exit are taken by means of two 6-port sampling valves. The first valve injects samples on a sorption column, kept isothermally at 80 °C (3m Carbosieve B with 3.2 mm internal diameter), which in its turn is connected to a thermal conductivity detector. Separation and detection of H_2, Ar, CO, CO_2 and light hydrocarbons is possible. The second sampling valve is connected to a capillary column (50 m OV 101 on fused silica with internal diameter of 0.3 mm) and a FID detector. Most of the hydrocarbons synthesized in the carbon number range C_1-C_{21}, can be separated and quantified this way. A typical chromatogram as well as the temperature profiles of the columns are given in Figure 2. The analytical set-up also allows to analyze product condensates off-line via a manual injection on a second capillary column connected to the TCD detector.

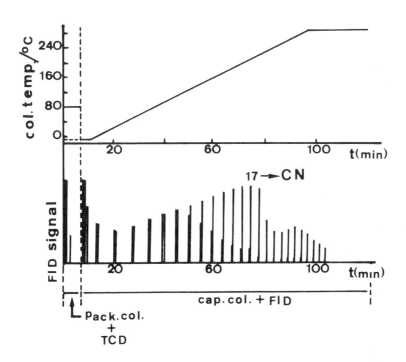

FIG. 2 : Typical chromatogram with temperature profiles of the columns.

Procedures

The air-dry catalyst powder is pressed, crushed and sieved. 0.6 ml of the 0.5-1 mm particles are diluted with an equal volume of inert quartz chips of similar dimensions and loaded in the reactor. After removal of the last traces of air from the system, the catalyst is reduced with hydrogen at 400 °C. The catalyst is then cooled to reaction temperature, then synthesis gas ($CO:H_2$ volume ratio of 2:3) is allowed to the system and pressurized till 1600 kPa. The reaction is then followed for at least 60 hours. Samples are periodically withdrawn from the reactor exit, usually one every 4 hours.

Data handling

The data were obtained from a gaschromatograph Hewlett-Packard 5880A. The calculations were done on a HP-1000 computer.

a. <u>CO-conversion (% K)</u>

$$\% \ K = (1 - \frac{(CO/Ar)exp}{(CO/Ar)st}) \times 100$$

where $\frac{CO}{AR}$ = area ratio's of CO and Ar in experimental (exp) or standard (st) conditions

b. <u>Carbon-balance (% C)</u> [*]

$$\% \ C = \frac{C_{output}}{C_{input}} \times 100$$

[*] Assumed is that the sensitivity factor (FID) for all hydrocarbons is equal to 1.

$$\% \, C = \dfrac{\dfrac{\Sigma C_{Ni}}{16xQ} + \dfrac{(CO_2)}{44+48}}{\dfrac{(AR)_{exp} \times \dfrac{CO}{Ar}_{st} \times \dfrac{\% \, K}{100}}{42}} \times 100$$

where : ΣC_{Ni} = area sum of all the hydrocarbons

Q = conversion factor FID $\rightarrow$ TCD

$(Ar)_{exp}$ = Ar-area in experimental conditions

(CO_2) = CO_2-area

c. <u>Chain growth factor α</u>

$$W_n = n \, \alpha^{n-1} \, (1-\alpha)^2 \qquad \text{(SF kinetic formalism)}$$

or

$$\log(\text{mol} \, \%) \cong n\log\alpha - (\log\alpha - 2\log(1-\alpha))$$

By plotting $\log(\text{mol} \, \%)$ versus the carbon-number n the chain growth probability factor α can be determined for each run by measuring the slope of the line.

73

RESULTS AND DISCUSSION

As mentioned in the introduction, literature data as well as own results using a batch-type reactor indicate that on some alumina supports loaded with cobalt metal, Fischer-Tropsch products are synthesized, the carbon number distribution of which does not obey the so-called PDL- or Schulz-Flory (S.F.) formalism. It was attempted to confirm this behavior at different times on-stream using the new bench-scale flow unit.

The reaction conditions in which the catalyst was tested are summarized in Table 1.

TABLE 1 : F.T. synthesis conditions using a CO on alumina catalyst

	Bench-Scale tests	Batch-tests**
$CO:H_2$ of syngas	2:3	2:3
$GHSV_{CO}/h^{-1}$ *	700	–
Total pressure/kPa	1600	800
Reaction temperature/°C	200	190

* Gaseous hourly space velocity in carbon monoxide
** Ref. 4

The carbon number distribution of the products synthesized at different times-on-stream, is given in Figures 3 and 4 in weight % and as the logarithm of the molar distribution, respectively. The growth factor α in the carbon number range 1 to 12, hardly changes with the time-on-stream (Fig. 4) $(0.74 < \alpha < 0.82)$. The methane selectivity (C_1) is significantly higher than the one expected from the polymerization distribution law. This is an indication that certain sites exist on the catalyst surface which do not possess any growth capability, i.e. sites

74

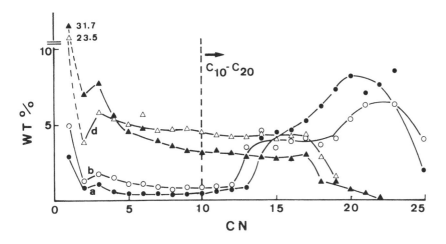

FIG. 3 : Fischer-Tropsch product distribution from Cobalt-on-alumina at
200 °C and different times-on-stream :
a, 22h; b, 29h; c, 53h and d, 72h.

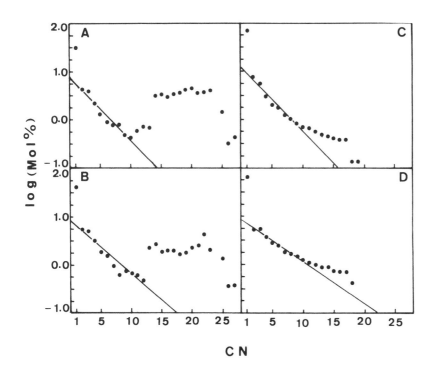

FIG. 4 : Schulz-Flory plot of the FT product distributions on
Co-on-alumina at 200 °C and for different times-on-stream :
A, 22; B, 29; C, 53 and D, 72 h.

which exclusively perform C-O bond scission and have hydrogenation capacity. It is known that the concentration of such sites can be manipulated by changing the average metal particle size distribution. The latter in its turn can be influenced by decreasing the average pore diameter of the alumina support.

Changes in the product selectivity in the C_{12}-C_{25} carbon number fraction with time-on-stream are remarkable. Initially, i.e. up to 30 hours on stream, significant deviations from the PDL-model are found (Fig. 4). For longer times-on-stream, this deviation gradually declines and the product selectivity comes closer to the PDL-model. It is remarkable that even after 71 hours, there still exists a deviation.

In Fig. 5 other important process characteristics are reported :

- the CO-conversion remains unchanged at different times-on-stream;

- the carbon mass balanced is close to 100 %, which indicates that all
  the carbon from the converted feed leaves the reactor and transfer
  section and is analyzed by the analytic set-up. Moreover, this is
  true irrespective of the time-on-stream at which the analysis is done;

- the growth factor for the C_2-C_{12} hydrocarbons does not change with
  time-on-stream.

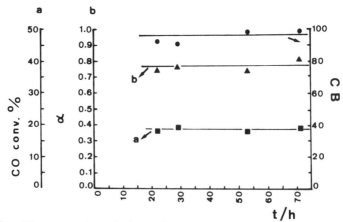

FIG. 5 : CO conversion, hydrocarbon chain growth factor (α) and carbon
material balance (CB) on a Co-on-alumina catalyst at 200 °C for
different times-on-stream (t)

The results of Fig. 4 and 5 allow to conclude that the literature results (3,4) which claim that high selectivities in the diesel range can be obtained have been confirmed but <u>only for non-steady-state conditions</u>. It is remarkable that the catalyst requires an extremely long induction period (> 70 hours) before steady state is reached. It is also clear immediately that when in a batch reactor cumulative sampling is done after 48 hours (4), a deviation from the PDL-formalism of the products is to be expected.

REFERENCES

1. M.E. DRY, in "Catalysis-science and Technology", eds. J.R. Anderson and M. Boudart, Vol. 1, Springer-Verlag, Berlin, Heidelberg, New York, 1981, p. 159.

2. P.A. JACOBS and D. VAN WOUWE, J. Molecular Catalysis, <u>17</u>, 145 (1982).

3. D. VANHOVE, L. MAKAMBO and M. BLANCHARD, J. Chem. Res. (S) <u>335</u> (1980); J.C.S. Chem. Comm. <u>605</u> (1979); J. Chem. Res. (M) <u>4119</u> (1980).

4. P. STRUYF, P.A. JACOBS and J.B. UYTTERHOEVEN, in "Energy Conservation in Industry", Eds. H. Ehringer, G. Hoyaux, P.A. Pilavachi, D. Reidel Publ. Comp., Dordrecht, 1983, p. 334.

5. For a review of the subject : P.A. JACOBS, in "Catalysis by Zeolites", Vol. 5, Studies in Surface Science and Catalysis", Elsevier, 1980.

VALORISATION DES RESIDUS DE DESASPHALTAGE PAR HYDROCONVERSION EN PRESENCE DE CATALYSEURS FINEMENT DIVISES

P. Chiche and J. Gaget
Centre d'Etudes et Recherches de Charbonnages de France
B. P. 2, F-60550 Verneuil-en-Halatte

P. Giuliani and Y. Jacquin
Institut Français du Pétrole
B. P. 311, F-92506 Rueil-Malmaison Cedex

Résumé

Le problème majeur de l'industrie du raffinage dans les prochaines années est la valorisation des résidus lourds, de plus en plus abondants, de distillation atmosphérique et sous vide des pétroles bruts.

L'IFP a développé un procédé de désasphaltage qui sépare de tels résidus en une huile désasphaltée susceptible d'être traitée en raffinerie classique et un asphalte, riche en impuretés telles qu'asphaltènes, métaux et hétéroéléments, et dont la valorisation a été recherchée par hydroconversion catalytique de façon à augmenter le rendement global en distillat.

Après des essais de laboratoire qui ont montré les bonnes performances de catalyseurs en suspension et entraînés provenant d'un précurseur soluble ou d'un catalyseur solide finement broyé, on a réalisé quatre essais d'une centaine d'heures chacun dans une installation pilote continue sur une charge d'asphalte fluxé par du "light cycle oil".

Des résultats très satisfaisants ont été obtenus, même si les conditions de fonctionnement de l'unité sont imparfaites à certains égards, tels par exemple qu'une conversion des 500^+ en 500^- de plus de 65 % et des asphaltènes de plus de 70 %, des taux d'élimination du soufre et des métaux respectivement supérieurs à 60 et 90 %, et une formation d'insolubles inférieure à 0,5 %.

1. INTRODUCTION

Jusqu'à ces dernières années, les raffineries européennes parvenaient à satisfaire les besoins du marché des produits pétroliers en fractionnant le pétrole brut par distillation éventuellement complétée d'un traitement catalytique, aboutissant ainsi à des fractions répondant à des spécifications précises des utilisateurs. Les fractions non distillables étaient employées comme combustibles industriels, essentiellement en France pour la production d'électricité par EDF.

Or l'évolution du prix du pétrole et du contexte économique européen a eu d'importantes répercussions sur l'industrie du raffinage, le problème majeur des années à venir consistant à valoriser les résidus, de plus en plus abondants, de distillation atmosphérique et sous vide des pétroles bruts.

La transformation des fractions lourdes est rendue difficile par la présence de deux familles de constituants : métaux - nickel et vanadium essentiellement - et produits de masse moléculaire élevée - asphaltènes - qui provoquent une détérioration rapide des catalyseurs de craquage et dont il faut assurer la séparation.

Parmi les nombreux schémas de traitement intégrant la conversion des résidus lourds en distillats moyens et légers, l'Institut français du Pétrole (IFP) a opté pour un procédé de désasphaltage qui sépare, par précipitation au moyen d'un solvant paraffinique - coupe pentane -, le résidu considéré en :

. une huile désasphaltée suffisamment purifiée pour être traitée par les procédés classiques de raffinage

. un extrait asphaltique ou "asphalte" qui contient la majorité des métaux et la totalité des asphaltènes.

Mais la fraction lourde ainsi séparée peut constituer, selon les cas, jusqu'à plus de 10 % du pétrole brut d'origine, si bien que l'économie globale du procédé dépend fortement des possibilités de valorisation de l'asphalte. Parmi les différentes voies envisageables à cet égard - combustion directe, oxydation partielle ... -, l'hydroconversion catalytique au-dessus de 400°C et sous pression d'hydrogène a l'avantage d'augmenter le rendement global en distillats et de réduire "le fond du baril" à une valeur très basse.

L'emploi d'un catalyseur en lit fixe, mobile ou à l'ébullition présente le risque d'un encrassement et d'un empoisonnement rapide par le coke et les métaux. Aussi a-t-on retenu la solution de systèmes catalytiques en suspension et entraînés, dont on attend la destruction des complexes organométalliques qui assurent la solubilité des métaux, la conversion des asphaltènes en fractions moyennes et légères et l'hydrogénolyse des liaisons C-S et C-N avec élimination d'hydrogène sulfuré et d'ammoniac.

La conjonction de l'expérience de l'IFP dans le domaine de la production des asphaltes et des catalyseurs d'hydrotraitement de produits lourds et de l'existence au CERCHAR d'une installation pilote continue d'hydroliquéfaction du charbon a suscité cette étude d'hydroconversion d'asphaltes, dont le déroulement a comporté les phases suivantes :

. production d'asphalte dans une unité pilote du Centre d'Etudes et de Développement industriels de l'IFP

. choix d'un solvant approprié et préparation des mélanges asphalte-solvant

. essais de sélection de catalyseurs entraînés, solubles ou en suspension

. réalisation de quatre essais sur l'unité pilote continue.

2. DESCRIPTION DES INSTALLATIONS D'ESSAIS

2.1. Installation de désasphaltage (fig. 1).

L'installation pilote de désasphaltage de l'IFP est capable de produire en continu les quantités d'asphalte nécessaires aux essais. Le mélange asphalte-solvant est soutiré à la partie inférieure de l'extracteur, le flux liquide étant réchauffé de façon à permettre de récupérer le solvant de désasphaltage dans le strippeur d'asphalte. L'asphalte liquide est soutiré à 200-250°C.

2.2. Installation d'hydrogénation (fig. 2).

L'installation d'hydrogénation du CERCHAR, d'un débit de 5 à 10 kg/h et conçue pour pouvoir opérer jusqu'à 500°C sous 400 bars, se compose des sections suivantes :
. atelier d'empâtage, où la charge à traiter est malaxée pendant une heure environ, envoyée dans un récipient de stockage, puis injectée dans le circuit des réacteurs à l'aide de deux pompes à piston montées en parallèle et opérant à tour de rôle
. circuit des réacteurs, constitué d'un préchauffeur tubulaire chauffé par effet Joule, à l'entrée duquel est injecté l'hydrogène sous pression, et de réacteurs cylindriques identiques de 10 l montés en série
. circuit des séparateurs, chaud et froid, qui divise l'ensemble des produits de réaction en trois flux principaux :
- un résidu éventuel et les huiles lourdes et moyennes
- les huiles légères et la phase aqueuse
- les gaz, épurés avant d'être rejetés à l'atmosphère
. installation de distillation formée d'une colonne à pression atmosphérique et d'un flash sous vide dont le fond est équipé d'un évaporateur agité faisant office de rebouilleur.

La viscosité élevée des charges à traiter et leur forte teneur en soufre ont nécessité le renforcement de certains circuits de chauffage et l'addition d'un système de lavage des gaz.

2.3. Appareillages d'essais de catalyseurs.

Ces essais ont été réalisés soit dans un autoclave de 250 cm^3, soit en système ouvert dans un réacteur tubulaire de 200 cm^3 vide ou garni de catalyseurs.

3. CHOIX D'UN SOLVANT ET PREPARATION DES MELANGES

L'asphalte, de point de ramollissement voisin de 150°C, doit être fluxé par un solvant afin que la viscosité de la charge soit compatible avec le fonctionnement de l'installation d'hydrogénation. On a choisi à cet effet un produit disponible en grandes quantités et de faible valeur marchande : le gas-oil de craquage catalytique ou "light cycle oil" (LCO) dont les caractéristiques sont indiquées tableau I.

Une première charge à 65 % d'asphalte s'est révélée trop visqueuse, de sorte que les essais réels ont été réalisés sur une charge "surfluxée" à 49 % d'asphalte et 51 % de LCO (tableau II), la dilution étant réalisée directement à la sortie du strippeur (cf. fig. 1).

4. ESSAIS DE CATALYSEURS ENTRAINES EN AUTOCLAVE ET EN MICROPILOTE

Une première série d'essais a montré qu'un catalyseur hétérogène sous forme de billes d'alumine de faible diamètre imprégnées de cobalt, de nickel et de molybdène permettait d'atteindre, dans certaines conditions, un taux de démétallation de près de 90 % et un taux de désulfuration voisin de 60 %.

Des résultats intéressants ont également été obtenus avec des complexes organosolubles de molybdène, éventuellement associés à des particules charbonneuses provenant des dépoussiéreurs de centrales thermiques au fuel, et dont le rôle est d'éviter l'encrassement du réacteur en fixant les précurseurs du coke et les impuretés métalliques.

Les essais ont montré (tableau III) la supériorité par rapport à un catalyseur de raffinage classique de tels complexes qui conduisent à une conversion notable des asphaltènes en hydrocarbures valorisables et dont les performances quant à la désulfuration et surtout la démétallation sont encore accrues par l'addition de particules charbonneuses.

On a également observé que, toutes choses égales par ailleurs, la réduction de la pression d'hydrogène affecte peu la désulfuration, mais diminue l'hydroconversion des asphaltènes et la démétallation et accroît notablement le taux d'insolubles, tandis qu'une baisse de concentration en métal actif augmente la formation d'insoluble et altère la désulfuration sans guère modifier le taux de démétallation.

5. ESSAIS DANS L'INSTALLATION PILOTE

Après un essai dit "hydraulique" destiné à vérifier l'aptitude de l'installation à traiter la charge envisagée, quatre essais ont été réalisés avec un débit d'hydrogène de 1 m^3 TPN/kg de charge et une vitesse volumique horaire nominale de 0,4 dans le deuxième réacteur. La moitié inférieure du premier réacteur sert à l'échauffement de la charge depuis la température de sortie du préchauffeur jusqu'à la température de prétraitement. La moitié supérieure est maintenue à température constante. Le second réacteur est à la température de réaction.

Deux systèmes catalytiques ont été expérimentés :
. un sel de molybdène soluble dans la charge (catalyseur C) introduit à raison de 500 ppm de Mo métal par rapport à la charge, associé dans l'un des essais à des particules charbonneuses à raison de 2 % par rapport à la charge.
. un catalyseur CoMo/Al$_2$O$_3$ de texture adaptée à l'hydrotraitement des grosses molécules et broyé inférieur à 12,5 μm (catalyseur D) ; la concentration utilisée correspond à 500 ppm de Mo et 120 ppm de Co par rapport à la charge.

La pression a été en règle générale égale à 200 bars, à l'exception d'un essai en présence du catalyseur C où elle a été réduite à 175 ou 150 bars.

Les tableaux IV et V indiquent les conditions d'essai et les performances obtenues pour chaque marche.

Les meilleurs résultats sont obtenus avec le catalyseur supporté broyé CoMo/Al$_2$O$_3$ (catalyseur D), qui conduit à des taux plus élevés en HDS, HDM (hydrodémétallation) et HDA. Les performances fournies pour le catalyseur C sont toutefois très élevées, et il présente l'avantage supplémentaire de pouvoir être introduit à l'état liquide dans la charge.

L'addition de particules charbonneuses apporte une amélioration de la conversion de 500$^+$ en 500$^-$ aux bas niveaux thermiques, mais aux dépens du rendement en liquides C$_4^+$, et facilite la filtration des insolubles.

Il semble possible d'opérer sous 175 et même 150 bars, mais il faudrait pouvoir mesurer la pression partielle réelle d'hydrogène au cours d'essais avec et sans recyclage d'hydrogène.

Par rapport aux essais de laboratoire en autoclave, on note en pilote des performances très analogues en démétallation, mais un taux de conversion plus élevé et une désulfuration plus poussée, due probablement à une plus faible pression partielle d'hydrogène sulfuré.

6. CONCLUSION

Bien que les données rassemblées sur les caractéristiques des produits ne doivent être considérées que comme indicatives en raison des conditions de marche de l'unité - durée limitée, fonctionnement sans recyclage de gaz ni de solvant, présence de catalyseur dans le résidu ... -, les résultats acquis en pilote continu confirment, en les améliorant même, les bonnes performances des catalyseurs très divisés, en suspension et entraînés, observées au laboratoire dans l'hydroconversion des charges très lourdes riches en métaux et en asphaltènes.

Les performances observées se caractérisent principalement par les points suivants :

- hydrodémétallation $>$ 90 %
- hydrodésulfuration $>$ 60 %
- conversion des asphaltènes $>$ 70 %
- conversion de 500^+ en 500^- $>$ 60 %
- rendement en produit liquide
  par rapport à la charge $>$ 88 % en poids
                                         $>$ 95 % en volume
- formation d'insoluble par
  rapport à la charge $<$ 0,5 %

Ces valeurs mettent en évidence surtout une démétallation très forte, ainsi qu'une conversion importante avec une formation réduite de coke. Cela prouve la saturation rapide des radicaux issus des réactions de craquage grâce aux systèmes catalytiques mis en oeuvre.

La présence de particules charbonneuses augmente la conversion aux bas niveaux thermiques, diminue les rendements en produit liquide et favorise la filtration des insolubles.

L'emploi d'une pression totale comprise entre 150 et 175 bars est possible.

- TABLEAU I -

CARACTERISTIQUES DU SOLVANT SERVANT DE FLUXANT

(LCO ou "light cycle oil")

Densité à 20°C (g/cm^3)	0,9795
Indice de réfraction à 20°C	1,572
Viscosité à 20°C (cP)	4,48
Viscosité à 40°C (cP)	2,66
Soufre (% en poids)	3,44
Azote total (ppm)	750

Distillation ASTM

Point initial	(°C)	181
5 % vol.	(°C)	220
10 % vol.	(°C)	228
20 % vol.	(°C)	247
30 % vol.	(°C)	254
40 % vol.	(°C)	260
50 % vol.	(°C)	266
60 % vol.	(°C)	277
70 % vol.	(°C)	281
80 % vol.	(°C)	295
90 % vol.	(°C)	322
95 % vol.	(°C)	340

- TABLEAU II -

CARACTERISTIQUES DE LA CHARGE EXPERIMENTEE

Composition		49 % d'asphalte Safaniya
		51 % de fluxant (LCO)
Densité à 20°C (g/cm^3)		1,056
Viscosité à 50°C (cP)		1760
Viscosité à 100°C (cP)		113
Viscosité à 150°C (cP)		12
Carbone Conradson (% en poids)		23,4
Asphaltènes au nC$_7$ (% en poids)		16,4
Analyse élémentaire		
Carbone	(% en poids)	83,59
Hydrogène	(% en poids)	8,20
H/C atomique		1,18
Soufre	(% en poids)	5,47
Nickel	(ppm)	62
Vanadium	(ppm)	190
Distillation semi-préparative (10 plateaux théoriques)		
0-200°C	(% en poids)	1,53
200-350°C	(% en poids)	42,55
350-500°C	(% en poids)	6,27
> 500°C	(% en poids)	49,22
Pertes	(% en poids)	0,43

- TABLEAU III -

ESSAIS DE LABORATOIRE AVEC CATALYSEURS ORGANOSOLUBLES

Nature de l'essai	Thermique sans catalyseur	Catalyseur classique CoMo/Al₂O₃ broyé sulfuré	Catalyseur organo-soluble A	Catalyseur organo-soluble A	Catalyseur organo-soluble B	Catalyseur B + 1 % de particules charbonneuses	Catalyseur organo-soluble B
Teneur en métaux	0	500 ppm Mo	500 ppm Mo	200 ppm Mo	500 ppm Mo	500 ppm Mo	500 ppm Mo
Charge traitée				Asphalte fluxé			Fluxant LCO seul
Conditions opératoires							
Température (°C)	411	421	419	418	418	418	418
Durée (h)	2	2	2	2	2	2	2
Pression initiale (bar)	100	100	100	100	100	100	100
Résultats							
Insolubles toluène (% en poids)	10	< 0,3	< 1	< 0,3	< 1	< 0,3	< 1
HDS (%)	7	30,3	36	30	39,5	40,5	98
HDA (%)	27	16,7	36	34	40	35,5	
HDV (%)	10	53	80	73	87	96,5	
HDNi (%)	30	30	51	28	64	86,5	
H/C atomique	1,2	1,22	1,33	1,29	1,30	1,33	1,44
(charge non traitée : 1,22)							(1,23)

HDS, HDA, HDV, HDNi : taux d'élimination du soufre, des asphaltènes, du vanadium, du nickel.

85

- _TABLEAU IV_ -

ESSAIS EN PILOTE AVEC CATALYSEUR ORGANOSOLUBLE C

	Catalyseur C seul							Catalyseur C + particules charbonneuses			
Référence de la marche	A	B	C	D	E	F	G	A	B	C	D
Températures											
Sortie préchauffeur	T_1	T_1	T_1	T_1	T_1	T_1	T_1	T_1	T_1	T_1	T_1
1er réacteur (moyenne)	T_2	T_2	T_2	T_2	T_2	T_2	T_2	T_2	T_2	T_2	T_2
2e réacteur (moyenne)	T_2	$T_2+25°C$	$T_2+38°C$	$T_2+52°C$	$T_2+38°C$	$T_2+38°C$	$T_2+52°C$	T_2	$T_2+25°C$	$T_2+38°C$	$T_2+52°C$
Pression totale (bar)	200	200	200	200	150	175	175	200	200	200	200
Durée (h)	22	18	16	18	36	30	32	23,5	24	24	26
Consommation H_2 (%)	0,69	1,66	1,85	2,35	1,60	1,66	2,39	0,42	1,56	1,80	1,98
Conversion 500⁻ en 500⁺	9,8	23,9	44,6	64,1	46,0	47,8	64,5	24	37	54	65
HDS	38,8	51,6	63,1	69,3	62,5	59,3	76,4	37	52	64	71
HDN	n.d.	n.d.	n.d.	n.d.	55	56	60	n.d.	n.d.	n.d.	n.d.
HDNi	58	72	82	82	76,7	71,3	93,6	65	75	86	91
HDV	75	88	94	93	92,4	88,0	98,3	76	90	95	98
HDA	56,0	60,1	67,3	78,7	51	61	77	56	61	70	80,6
Insolubles au toluène	0,43	0,35	0,50	0,41	0,41	0,53	0,56	1,12	1,36	1,44	2,0
Réduction de viscosité (50°C) entre charge et liquide C_4^+ (cP)	>13	>54	>132	>251	>104	>114	>320	>13	>63	>160	>255

HDS, HDN, HDNi, HDV, HDA : taux d'élimination de soufre, de l'azote, du nickel, du vanadium et des asphaltènes.
n.d. : non déterminé.

- TABLEAU V -

ESSAIS EN PILOTE AVEC CATALYSEUR CoMo/Al$_2$O$_3$ BROYE D

Référence de la marche	A	B	C	D
Températures				
Sortie préchauffeur	T$_1$	T$_1$	T$_1$	T$_1$
1er réacteur (moyenne)	T$_2$	T$_2$	T$_2$	T$_2$
2e réacteur (moyenne)	T$_2$	T$_2$+25°C	T$_2$+38°C	T$_2$+52°C
Pression totale (bar)	200	200	200	200
Durée (h)	24	24	24	26
Consommation H$_2$ (%)	0,94	1,65	2,08	2,51
Conversion 500$^+$ en 500$^-$ (%)	15,2	30,9	44,4	58,8
HDS (%)	n.d.	64,7	72,7	84,1
HDN (%)	n.d.	n.d.	56	65
HDNi (%)	n.d.	73	81	93,5
HDV (%)	n.d.	91,2	95,5	99,5
HDA (%)	n.d.	52,8	60	81
Insolubles (%)	n.d.	0,6	1,0	1,8
Réduction de viscosité (50°C) entre charge et liquide C$_4^+$ (cP)	n.d.	> 66	>169	>279

Signification des abréviations : voir tableau IV.

DESASPHALTAGE AU SOLVANT

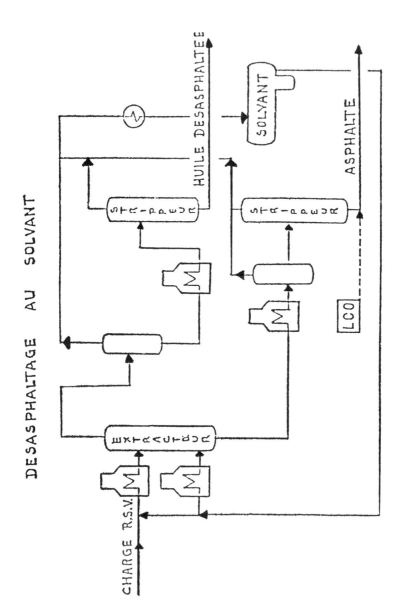

Fig.-1-

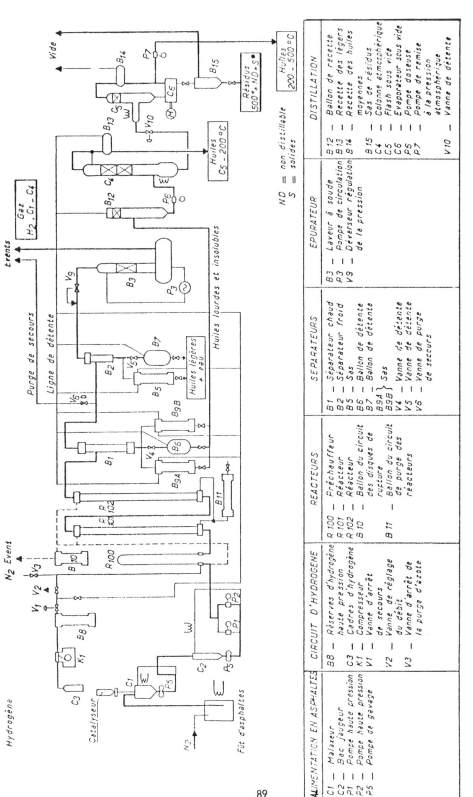

Fig. 2 _ SCHEMA DE LA BOUCLE D'HYDROGENATION DES ASPHALTES

89

KINETICS OF FERROUS SULPHATE LIQUID PHASE OXIDATION BY THIOBACILLUS FERROOXIDANS UNDER CONTINUOUS AND BATCH GROWTH CONDITIONS

M. Adami, C. Creo, A. De Angelis, G. Di Giorgio, D. Ferri, G. Levi, P. Palazzolo and M. Vian

ENEA-Casaccia, I-00100 Rome

SUMMARY

The aim of the present study is to investigate the kinetics of biological desulfurization in batch and continuous cultures to select the best operational parameters and to optimize the efficiency of the system.

For this purpose several bacterial strains of Thiobacillus ferrooxidans have been tested by factorial experiments carried out at different temperature, pH, initial ferrous and ferric sulphate concentration, and carbon dioxide substrate values. In this way, kinetc constant values were calculated.

Furthermore, several steady state growth experiments have been carried out with chemostat apparatus.

INTRODUCTION

In the majority of industrialised countries, according to the present direction taken by energy policies, one of the strategic objectives is the securing of the supply and diversification of primary sources. Thus coal will continue for many years to play an important rôle in providing for energy needs. A considerable part of the world's coal reserves, however, has such a high level of sulfur content that it cannot be used directly; a well known example is that of the sub-bituminous coal mines of the Sulcis-Iglesiente region of Sardinia, which contain up to 8% of total sulfur, of which about 50% is in the inorganic form of pyrite and 50% in organic form. (Table I)

Fixed Carbon	20.3%	S_P	3%
Volatile Matter	36%	O_2	13%
Ash	40%	CO_2	6%
C	37%	Moisture	4%
H_2	3%	L.C.V.	3286 Kcal/Kg
S_T	6%		

TABLE I

Average indicative analysis of crude coal from the mine of Nurax-Figus

Among the best-known or developing processes for the reduction of the level of sulfur in coal, or for the destruction of SO_2 in the smoke, the oxidising leaching of metallic sulphides by means of an acid solution of ferric sulphate is particularly important.

The studies made by Meyers are already well known; in these the leaching of the pyritic sulfur contained in the coal takes place according to the reaction

$$FeS_2 + 4.6\ Fe_2(SO_4)_3 + 4.8\ H_2O \longrightarrow 10.2\ FeSO_4 + 4.8\ H_2SO_4 + 0.8\ S$$

In the process suggested by Meyers, the reactant $Fe_2(SO_4)_3$ is regenerated by means of oxidation by air under pressure. One interesting alternative is provided by the possibility of regenerating the reactant by biological treatment. As has been known for some time, the microorganisms of Thiobacillus genus possess the possibility of growth in the absence of light in a completely inorganic medium. This detail, known as chemoautotrophy, makes it possible to carry out two vital functions under these conditions: to provide energy from the metabolic oxidation of a reduced inorganic compound, a reduced valence inorganic sulfur or ferrous ion, and to use CO_2 as the principal and only source of carbon according to the cycle of pentose phosphates, or Calvin's cycle.

Despite the numerous studies which have been made on this subject it has not yet been established with certainty according to what mechanism the oxidation of the iron takes place. It can be described by the following reactions

$$2\ FeSO_4 + \tfrac{1}{2}\ O_2 + H_2SO_4 \xrightarrow{\text{T.f.}} Fe_2(SO_4)_3 + H_2O$$

$$Fe^{++} \xrightarrow{\text{T.f.}} Fe^{+++} + e^-$$

Numerous experiments have shown the capacity of Thiobacillus ferrooxidans to oxidise metallic sulfur directly, according to the following pattern

$$FeS_2 + \tfrac{1}{2}\ H_2O + 15/4\ O_2 \xrightarrow{\text{T.f.}} \tfrac{1}{2}\ Fe_2(SO_4)_3 + \tfrac{1}{2}\ H_2SO_4$$

and elementary sulfur to sulphuric acid

$$S + 3/2\ O_2 + H_2O \xrightarrow{\text{T.f.}} 2\ H_2SO_4$$

91

The tendency of Thiobacillus ferrooxidans to grow in a strongly acid medium (pH 1.5 + 3) makes it highly interesting from the viewpoint of industrial application, because it does not require expensive treatment for the sterilisation of the medium. Thus on the theoretical basis at least there is a possibility of using a biochemical process to eliminate the pyritic fraction of the sulfur contained in bituminous or sub-bituminous coals. The process can, in theory, be carried out by two different methods
- indirect method:
chemical leaching of the pyrite contained in the coal

$$FeS_2 + 4.6\ Fe_2(SO_4)_3 + 4.8\ H_2O \longrightarrow 10.2\ FeSO_4 + 4.8\ H_2SO_4 + 0.8\ S$$

biological regeneration of the reactant

$$2\ FeSO_4 + \tfrac{1}{2}\ O_2 + H_2SO_4 \xrightarrow{T.f.} Fe_2(SO_4)_3 + H_2O$$

this process can theoretically be carried out in two separated stages (chemical stage and biological stage) or in one single stage.
- direct method:
direct biochemical leaching of the iron and the pyritic sulfur

$$FeS_2 + \tfrac{1}{2}\ H_2O + 15/4\ O_2 \xrightarrow{T.f.} \tfrac{1}{2}\ Fe_2(SO_4)_3 + \tfrac{1}{2}\ H_2SO_4$$

The purpose of this present study is the kinetic analysis of the biological regeneration phase of the reactant, i.e. of the oxidation of the ferrous sulphate to ferric sulphate in the presence of Thiobacillus ferrooxidans, so as to provide the necessary data, at the next stage, for the devising and development of a complete process for the reduction of pyritic sulfur contained in sub-bituminous coal.

ISOLATION AND   CULTURE   OF THE STRAINS

For the experimental tests, strains of Thiobacillus ferrooxidans from various sources were used. Some of these strains were isolated from samples of water and mud taken from various sulphuric sources of central Italy. Others were isolated from core-sampling carried out on the coal deposits in the Sulcis mine in Sardinia. Other strains were provided by the Microbiological Institute of the University of Rome.
The water samples were centrifugated at 10,000 rpm for 20'; the samples of mud and earth were kept in agitation for 2 hours in acidified water (pH 2.3) and were then centrifugated at 10,000 rpm for 20' after filtration of the surnatant.
For each sample, strains of Thiobacillus ferrooxidans were isolated by inoculating the pellets obtained after centrifugation in the 9K growth medium, and incubated at a temperature of 28°C.

Preservation tests of the strains were carried out by means of refrigeration at +4°C in acidified water; by means of freezing in liquid nitrogen
and preservation at −80°C and by means of gradual freezing up to −80°C.

Viability tests carried out after 30 and 90 days of preservation show that
in the case of preservation at −80°C, the lag time is very long, while in
the first case there was an immediate resumption of metabolic and catalytic
activity.

From the comparison of the growth and oxidation patterns of the ferrous
ion, carried out in 200 ml flasks in the same conditions (growth medium: 9K
Silverman and Lundgren, T: 28°C, pH: 2.4), no significant differences appeared between the various strains selected and collected.

The ascertaining of bacterial growth was carried out by analysis of the
proteic nitrogen according to Lowry's method, using a Beckman 35 spectrophotometer at 750 nm. The concentration of total iron in the solution was determined by atomic absorption (Perkin Elmer 5000); the concentration of ferrous
ion was ascertained by titration with $KMnO_4$; the concentration of ferric ion
was calculated from the difference. The sulphate ion was determined by tur-
bidimeter in the form of $BaSO_4$, using a Beckman 35 spectrophotometer at
450 nm.

BATCH CULTURE

The functional relationship between the growth-pattern of the biomass and
the main operational parameters in the most significant range for an overall
process of desulphurisation of coal, has been analysed by means of a special
ly designed apparatus made up of 12 vessels each of 5 liters useful volume.

The vessels are immersed in three thermostatic baths; the agitation is
carried out by aeration at 300 Nl/h per vessel , by means of three porous
plugs, placed near the bottom of each vessel. The air line makes possible
mixing with CO_2 in excess.

The tests were planned through a factorial experiment, in four factors
at three levels, fractionated into 27 tests according to the method of con
founding the effects. The values of the levels of each factor are given in
Table II.

FACTORS			LEVELS		
			0	1	2
A	T	(°C)	28	32	36
B	$[Fe^{++}]$ (g/l)		2.95	8.84	17.68
C	$[Fe^{+++}]$ (g/l)		5.59	11.18	22.36
D	CO_2 (Nl/h)		0	15	30

TABLE II

As established by Silverman and Lundgren, the growth of Thiobacillus ferrooxidans in flasks is logarhythmic

① $$x = x_o e^{\mu t}$$

x = biomass concentration at time t (mg proteic N/l)
x_o = initial biomass concentration
μ = specific growth rate (h^{-1})
t = time (h)

The growth rate is thus

② $$\frac{dx}{dt} = x_o\, \mu\, e^{\mu t}$$

hence

③ $$\mu = \frac{1}{x}\, \frac{dx}{dt}$$

The specific growth rate is a function of the substrate, the temperature, the pH, etc... Various kinds of models have been suggested to express μ in relation to the parameters of the medium. According to the model of enzymatic kinetics suggested by Michaelis-Menten, and also used by Monod, under constant temperature and pH, the specific growth rate can be expressed in relation to the limiting substrate by

④ $$\mu = \frac{\mu_M \left[Fe^{++}\right]}{K + \left[Fe^{++}\right]}$$

μ_M = maximum specific growth rate
K = Michaelis-Menten's constant

For a very low $\left[Fe^{++}\right]$, μ is proportional to $\left[Fe^{++}\right]$; for very high $\left[Fe^{++}\right]$, i.e. in non-limiting conditions, μ tends towards the value μ_M and becomes constant. In these conditions ④ can be integrated between x_o and x, and thus

⑤ $$\ln x = \ln x_o + \mu_M t$$

The constants of ④ can easily be calculated in linear form

⑥ $$\frac{1}{\mu} = \frac{K}{\mu_M} \frac{1}{\left[Fe++\right]} + \frac{1}{\mu_M}$$

Since the oxidation rate of the iron is proportional to the growth rate of the biomass

⑦ $$\frac{d\left[Fe^{++}\right]}{dt} = - \frac{d\left[Fe^{+++}\right]}{dt} = - \frac{1}{Y} \frac{dx}{dt}$$

Y = biomass produced per gram of oxidised Fe^{++}

94

If $\left[Fe^{++}\right]$ is not limiting, and if Y is constant, ⑦ can be integrated, and thus

$$\text{⑧} \qquad \ln\left\{\left[Fe^{++}\right]_o - \left[Fe^{++}\right]_t + \frac{x_o}{Y}\right\} = \ln\frac{x_o}{Y} + \mu_M\, t$$

which expresses the relation between oxidation, time, and the initial quantity of the biomass.

The experimental data obtained do not seen to follow Michaelis-Menten's model ④ sufficiently closely.

As can be seen from figure 1, the data obtained, in the range of values tested for $\left[Fe^{++}\right]$, follow a more or less linear pattern; in this first stage of the experiment, therefore, it was decided to adopt, for initial purposes, a linear model of the type

$$\text{⑨} \qquad \mu = A + B\left[Fe^{++}\right]$$

By calculating the linear regression by the least squares method, the value of the constants is shown to be

$$A = 0.033$$
$$B = 0.034$$

In order to analyse the results of the factorial experiments, and define the pattern of the μ_M in relation to the initial conditions of the medium, μ_M and maximum specific productivity σ_M were calculated

$$\text{⑩} \qquad \sigma_M = -\frac{1}{x}\frac{d\left[Fe^{++}\right]}{dt}$$

by graphic derivation of the growth-pattern and the corresponding oxidation pattern.

Y was calculated on the basis of

$$\text{⑪} \qquad \sigma = \frac{\mu}{Y}$$

by using the slope of the linear regression of the values previously obtained for μ_M and σ_M, the resulting value was

$$Y = 0.773$$

In figure 2 are recorded the values obtained for μ_M in relation to the initial value of T, $\left[Fe^{++}\right]$, $\left[Fe^{+++}\right]$ and CO_2.

In the temperature range used for the experiment, μ_M decreases distinctly above 28°C, thus confirming the data recorded in the literature on the subject

Similar results have been shown in relation to the initial concentration of Fe^{+++} ion, which when above 5.5 g/l, strongly inhibits the specific growth rate, reducing it to zero for values of 22 g/l.

On the other hand, in certain results recorded in the literature, an enrichment of the air with carbone dioxide also produces inhibiting effects. In the experiment pure CO_2 was used at 99.95%, but it cannot be entirely

ruled out that other compounds, even if only present in traces, may appear
in the solution and create inhibiting effects.

This and other aspects linked to the enrichment of the air with CO_2 will
be the object of further study.

It has not been possible to make tests with different initial pH values,
and it was therefore not possible to evaluate the influence of the pH on μ_M
because the pH is not an independent variable, but is obviously closely lin
ked to the initial $\left[Fe^{+++}\right]$ value.

CONTINUOUS CULTURE

Growth tests in continuous culture were carried out by means of a New
Brunswick Scientific Microferm Fermentor MF 107, with mechanical agitation
and aeration at a temperature of 28°C.

From the balance equation of the biomass for the chemostat

(12) $$r_x \, V = F \, x$$

r_x = biomass growth rate   (mg prot. N/lh)
V = useful volume (l)
F = flow (l/h)
x = biomass concentration (mg prot. N/l)

hence

(13) $$\mu = \frac{F}{V} = D$$

and μ is equal to the reciprocal of the mean holding time.

The experimental data are given in figure 3.

By analysing the results according to the Lineweaver-Burk equation, fi-
gure 4, it is clear that the relation between μ and $\left[Fe^{++}\right]$ follows fairly
closely the model of Michaelis-Menten (4).

The calculation of the constants gives the values

$$\mu_M = 0.238 \ h^{-1}$$
$$K = 0.66 \ g/l$$
$$Y = 1.23 \ \text{mg proteic N/g} \ Fe^{++}ox.$$

CONCLUSIONS

Thiobacillus ferrooxidans is capable of carrying out a vigorous catalytic action in relation to the oxidation of acid solutions of ferrous sulpha
te. The specific growth rate of the microorganisms depends considerably on
the temperature and the concentration of ferric ions in the solution.

The discontinuous growth tests produced little significant results
in comparison   of kinetic analysis of the growth and oxidation patterns, and the interpretative model given by Monod seems not to be valid.

In the growth tests under continuous steady state conditions, it seems
that the model of Monod can be applied with sufficient accuracy   and that
this model can thus be used to define, in quantitative terms, the relation

between the specific growth rate and the concentration of ferrous ions in the solution.

The data obtained from the experiments described can therefore be used to design the experimental plant to investigate the whole process for bituminous coal desulphurization.

REFERENCES

1. J.E. Dutrizac, R.J.C. Mac Donald, Minerals Sci. Eng. 6 (2) 59-100,(1974)
2. R.A. Meyers et al., U.S. Department of Commerce (1976)
3. A.R. Colmer, M.E. Hinkle, Science 106 253, (1947)
4. L.D. Owen, Design and analysis of industrial experiments, pub. Oliver and Boyd (1956)
5. M.P. Silverman, D.G. Lundgren, J. Bacteriol. 77 642-647 (1959)
6. L. Toro et al., Giornate genovesi di metallurgia, Maggio 1983
7. L.E. Murr et al., Metallurgical applications of bacterial leaching and related microbiological phenomena, Academic Press (1978)
8. A.E. Torma, Advances in Biochem. Eng. 6 2-37 Springer Verlag (1977)
9. D.W. Tempest, Methods in Microbiol. 124 A 111-121 (1973)
10. F. Kargi, Enzyme Microbiol. Technol. 4 13-19 (1982)
11. F. Kargi, Biotechnol. and Bioeng. 24 749-759 (1982)
12. N. Lazaroff et al., Appl. Environm. Microbiol. 43 924-938 (1982)

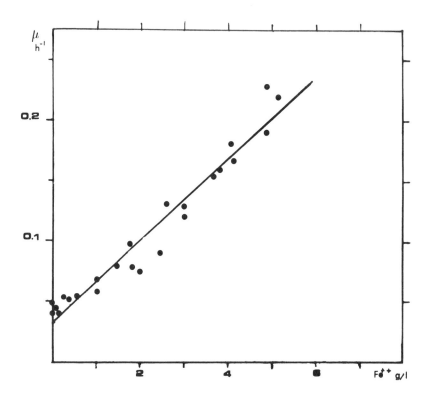

fig. 1

Relationship between specific growth rate   and Fe^{++} in batch cultures

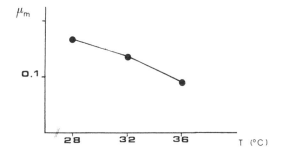

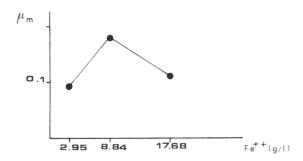

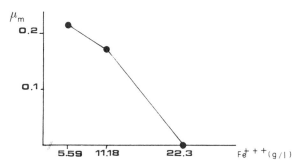

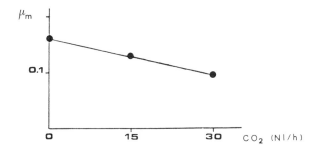

fig. 2
Effect of T, Fe^{++} , Fe^{+++} , and CO_2 on the specific growth rate

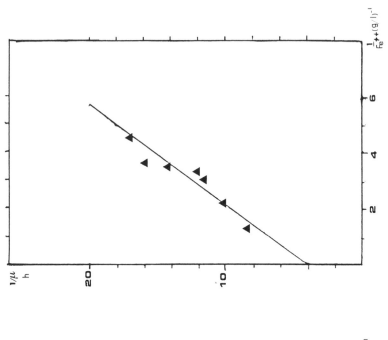

fig.4 – Specific growth rate versus Fe^{++} in continuous culture as calculated in according to Monod model

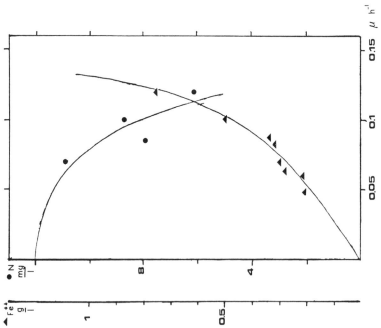

fig. 3 – Relationship between specific growth rate and Fe^{++} from steady state experiments

PEAT HARVESTING MACHINERY FOR OPERATION ON SMALLER BOGS

E. Kinsella

National Board for Science and Technology
Shelbourne House, Shelbourne Road, Dublin 4, Ireland

Summary

A contract (No. EEB-5-190-EIR(H)) between the Commission
of the European Communities and the NBST was entered into
in December 1981 for the development of a peat harvester
which would be suitable for smaller peat bogs. The
original design was based on an auger, which, it was
hoped, would extract the peat, at the same time subjecting
it to a degree of maceration. The peat would then be
extruded on to a spreader arm, which when full, would
deposit it on the bog surface for air drying. The machine
built to this design worked so well in initial tests that
a number of models were sold to interested farmers.
Operation on bogs of different characteristics (surface
vegetation, degree of decomposition, submerged obstacles)
showed, however, that the machine, as designed, was not
suitable for general application. A digger boom,
delivering into a macerator, was substituted for the auger;
the machine with these attachments has worked well.

1. INTRODUCTION

Ireland, the only EEC country in which peat fuel makes a
significant contribution to national energy requirements, has,
for generations depended on peat for part of its fuel supplies.
Up until well into the present century, peat was produced manually
by farmers, mainly for their own domestic requirements, with,
occasionally, small quantities for local sale. In 1946 a state
body (Bord na Mona) was established for the mechanical production
of peat fuel, mainly for electricity production. This is a large
scale operation, employing masive high-cost machines and
requiring very extensive bog areas for economic production.

With the change in energy situation since 1973, it became
necessary to consider the possibility of mechanical peat
harvesting on the many hundreds of small bogs which exist
throughout the country. Plainly, what was required was a light,
but sturdy, machine, capable of being driven by a conventional
farm tractor (less than 100 Kw). The capital cost would
necessarily be moderate and the target was about 9,000 ECU - the
large machines used by Bord na Mona cost about 350,000 ECU.

Several different designs have been developed, with varying
degrees of success. One of them is described in the present paper.
The contract was administered by the NBST and the machine, with its
several modifications, was built by the Shamrock Machine Turf
Company, a firm which has for many years been producing larger peat
harvesting machinery.

Design Concept

In the harvesting of sod peat, the following steps are
necessary

1. Excavation - it is desirable to excavate to some depth so that
   the highly decomposed, good quality peat at lower levels can be
   recovered.

2. Mixing - the good-quality peat should be mixed with the less
   decomposed material which exists near the surface.

3. Maceration - the peat should be macerated so as to randomise
   the disposition of the fibres. This gives the sods mechanical
   strength in all directions; an increase in density, and more
   rapid and irreversible drying.

4. Extrusion - the soft material must be extruded in a "ribbon"
   of suitable cross section on to a spreader arm.

5. Sod forming - the "ribbon" must be divided into pieces of
   suitable length.

6. Drying - when the spreader arm is completely full, the
   divided ribbon is deposited on the bog surface for air drying.

There seemed to be good prospects for combining operations (1),
(2), (3) and (4) into one in the design of an auger which would
excavate, mix, macerate and extrude, in one process.

Operation

Mark 1 machine

Auger screw: length 1.5 m
             dia   250 mm
             pitch 200 mm

Sod-belt speed   1.4 m/s
         length   4 m
Sod cross-section   130 cm^2

Output calculation   65 m^3/hr (corresponding to 14.4 tonnes/
                               hr at 25% moisture content)

Tractor power   60 H.P.

In practice, a great deal of material oozed out of the screw near
the top, but this was corrected by fitting side-shields. The
calculated output was achieved but not continuously, due to frequent
blockages at the top by heather and fibres etc. Occasionally the
screw encountered timber and other obstacles in the bog, on one
occasion breaking a bevel gear, indicating the necessity of overload
protection, e.g. a shear-pin device.

Some potential customers who inspected the machine in operation were satisfied with the performance, but demanded a 50% larger output. This led to the development of the Mark 2 machine

Mark 2 machine

Auger screw: length 1.8 m
             dia   325 mm
             pitch 240 mm

Spreader length   6 m
Sod cross section   130 cm^2
Output   65 m^3/hr., but capable of 90 m^3/hr.
Tractor power   142 H.P. (104 kw)

In practice, the machine worked well when cutting through a fairly uniform bog. However, if the peat at the top was unusually dry the soft peat underneath was unable to push the dry peat through the spout, and was merely "churned" by the auger. The spout was increased from 15 cm to 20 cm diameter and a small auger was fitted to help clear it. This worked well.

Following promising demonstrations on a local bog, the Shamrock Machine Turf Company received far more orders than they could possibly accept, and in response to requests for higher outputs, they created the Mark 3 machine, which was similar to the other two except for the auger, which was increased to 465 mm dia. It was fortunate that they could only accept three orders, since difficulties were experienced when the machines went into production in different areas of the country. These difficulties were similar to those experienced in the unmodified Mark 1.

The company then found themselves in a very awkward position, and their only option was to substitute a digger boom with macerator for the auger, in order to satisfy the customers requirements. Indeed the modified machines with the digger boom and macerator worked very well.

Economic Appraisal

It is estimated that the cost of the peat cutting attachment will be about 10,000 ECU. Providing the machine can operate for 100 days a year on a bog of 80 per cent moisture, an output of approximately 12 tonnes per hour, and approximately 75 to 80 tonnes per day can be achieved. In the operator's opinion an output of 7,500 tonnes per annum is possible, with yields of 23 to 25 tonnes per hectare during a good cutting season.

It is reasonable to assume a 'profit' margin of 5% on peat valued at 137 ECU per tonne. Accordingly, the machine's capital cost would be recovered in less than one year. The 'profit' margin is low due to high handling and transport costs and the competitive price of coal and factory produced briquettes.

Conclusion

While the original intention (to develop a reasonably priced harvesting machine which could be driven by a conventional tractor) has been fulfilled, it has been a disappointment that the central feature of the machine (the auger) has not been made to work within the contract period. The company are, however, resolved to proceed with the development of the augur excavator at their own expense.

A minor bonus which has emerged is that the auger machine is extremely good for forming drains, with some recovery in the form of sod peat of the material removed.

Mark 1   Field Trials

Mark I

under construction

(i) Sod spreading arm

(ii) Auger

METALLURGY

Presentation by Rapporteur
Prof. Dr. J. M. Schissler

Institut National Polytechnique de Lorraine
F-54042 Nancy Cedex

The fabrication of any metal object requires the use of complex processes which rely upon high thermal flows. This constitutes a major economic problem. It is however possible to seek energy savings in this vast field within the process of manufacturing the solid object.

Metallurgical studies developed under the heading of "the application of energy saving technologies" can be classified in three groups :

1. Research in connection with the formation of the solid product from the liquid state

2. Research in connection with reducing the number of phases in the manufacturing cycle for the piece

3. Research in connection with the selection of new alloys or with the assembly of members made therefrom while ensuring a given level of mechanical characteristics.

These research approaches correspond to the following investigations :

Approach I :

- lubrication by slags of the continuous casting of steels (ARMINES)

- reduction in energy requirements for converting liquid aluminium to semi-fabricated rolled products (THE BRITISH ALUMINIUM COMPANY).

Approach II :

- Economy storage in forged parts (REGIE NATIONALE DES USINES RENAULT - R.N.U.R. - SOCIETE DES ACIERS FINS DE L'EST - S.A.F.E.)

- Energy savings achieved by hot shakeout and heat treatments of castings : application to S.G. cast iron (CENTRE DE RECHERCHES DE PONT-A-MOUSSON - INSTITUT NATIONAL POLYTECHNIQUE DE LORRAINE - L.A. 159).

Approach III :

- Development of bainitic nodular iron for the construction of speed gears for the car industry (FIAT AUTO SpA)

- Engineering with adhesives : testing and design (AERE HARWELL).

1. The application of new processes such as continuous casting yields not inconsiderable savings in energy. ARMINES advanced a theoretical analysis of lubrication by molten slag which makes it possible to improve the continuous casting of steel. This research has clearly shown the importance of the choice of slag on the basis of the following variables :

-   keeping surface defects to a minimum

-   rupturing of the lubricating film

-   wear of the ingot mould

Monitoring of all these factors makes it possible therefore to proceed to the rolling stage directly after the continuous casting, thus eliminating or reducing all the expensive operations necessitated by these defects.

In the research in connection with the obtention of the solid body, the study on the "thin strip casting technique" has identified a considerable saving of energy. Investigated by the BRITISH ALUMINIUM COMPANY, this process makes it possible to produce sheet obtained by continuous casting of the molten aluminium between two cooling cylinders.

This operation is of considerable interest because it eliminates all the intermediate phases which are normally required in the "D.C. Casting/hot rolling process" type of manufacturing cycle.

A comparative study of the two processes based on the industrial production of six different products highlighted the energy savings provided by this new process. The percentage saving achieved varied between 27.89 and 37.66 % according to the type of alloy used.

A lower rate of saving – 8.12 % – has been recorded in the case of an alloy which requires a thermal homogenisation treatment. This clearly demonstrated the incidence on energy consumption of the intermediate phases of the manufacturing cycle.

2. Energy savings by reducing the number of operations in the manufacturing cycle for the piece also constitute a most important field of research.

The REGIE NATIONALE DES USINES RENAULT and the SOCIETE DES ACIERS FINS DE L'EST investigated the manufacturing cycle for forged steel pieces.

Two phases were investigated :

-   elimination of rolling, by forging the pieces from cast bars

-   reduction or elimination of the thermal treatment after the forging operation.

The use of steel bars manufactured by centrifugal continuous casting (c.c.c.) or horizontal continuous casting (h.c.c.) made it possible to show that after hot-working, the pieces could meet the strength and industrial use tests.

Since these pieces are subsequently subjected to a series of thermal treatments, the investigation carried out by the two companies showed the possibility of applying the thermal cycle directly from the "forge-hot" state.

This new operation thus allows of avoiding cooling followed by the need to raise the piece again to a high temperature. This energy saving was achieved in the case of three different thermal treatments (three types of steel with a different type of treatment).

The overall saving thus achieved was :

- in respect of the rolling operation : 14.10^6 kWhE for 7 000 tonnes of steel,

- in respect of the thermal treatment : 70.10^6 kWhT for 50 000 tonnes of steel.

A saving of energy can also be achieved in foundry work. An investigation carried out by the CENTRE DE RECHERCHES DE PONT-A-MOUSSON and the INSTITUT NATIONAL POLYTECHNIQUE DE LORRAINE (L.A. 159) shows the promise offered by new processes.

Since the thermal treatment of a casting calls for a phase in which a high temperature is maintained, the new process eliminates the energy consumption required to raise the temperature. This is made possible by using the "hot de-moulding" (knocking-out) process. The piece, removed from the mould at high temperature, is immediately transferred to the phase in which it must be maintained at high temperature. The thermal cycle then continues in the normal manner.

The investigation of spheroidal graphite cast iron treated by these new cycles shows that their mechanical characteristics vary but little from those of cast irons produced by the classical process.

All the thermal treatments can be applied using this method, including the bainitic treatments.

Hot de-moulding considerably improves the hardenability of the alloy, and this characteristic may lead to a saving in alloying elements. This improvement varies as a function of the period for which the piece is maintained at high temperature.

The saving of energy obtained by applying hot knocking-out varies as a function of the time for which the piece is maintained in the hot state. The investigation shows that for a period of one hour at 1 000°C, the saving in energy may be 44 % of the amount of energy expended for an identical cycle which includes a temperature-raising phase.

3. The third research approach comprises two categories of work.

FIAT applied a bainitic treatment to spheroidal graphite cast iron. This cast iron so treated was compared with a carbo-nitrided steel to determine the advantages associated with the use of the spheroidal graphite cast iron.

Bainitic spheroidal graphite cast iron which has been given shot-peening treatment exhibits mechanical characteristics inferior to those of steel. Spheroidal graphitic cast iron in the ferritic state can be more easily machined and there can be a saving in tool costs. After machining, a bainitic treatment causes deformation which may be considerable and can lead to rejection of 50 % of the pieces.

This investigation has shown that while the usefulness of the spheroidal graphite cast irons given a bainitic treatment was clearly demonstrated, it was also necessary to define clearly the bainitic treatment itself, the machining cycles and the mechanical characteristics desired.

AERE HARWELL carried out studies into the use of light materials assembled by special adhesive techniques. Reduction in weight of the materials used in the automobile industry provides a saving in energy. Research was concentrated on the formulation of test methods capable of providing data about the adhesives.

The application of new tests derived from those employed in high-technology sectors like the aerospace industry has yielded information on the adhesives.

This investigation also made it possible to formulate a method of forecasting the strength of the adhesive bond.

This research project developed methods for assessing the materials and clearly showed the need for further studies. This would be amply justified if one remembers that a 10 % reduction in the weight of a vehicle reduces its operating consumption of energy by about 5 %.

This whole set of projects has made it possible to identify several types of energy saving. The percentage savings are considerable, and lie at all levels of production of metal items as well as in certain areas of use.

The importance of the research carried out and the breadth of the fields studied give a clear indication as to the approaches which merit exploration so as to achieve a reduction in the energy cost of the product, either during its manufacture or when it is in use.

ECONOMY STORAGE IN FORGED PARTS

M. Volmi, R. El Haik, L. Backer and F. Lardet

Regie Nationale des Usines Renault (R.N.U.R.) and Societe des Aciers Fins de l'Est (S.A.F.E.)
8–10 avenue Emile Zola, F-92109 Boulogne Billancourt (Usines à Hagondange – 57301)

I - INTRODUCTION

The industrial manufacturing processes for forgings were established
to maintain a high standard of performance and guarantee a high degree of
product reliability.The manufacturing and treatment cycles involved entail
a high energy input.

The current economic situation has caused us to review the possibility
of optimizing the energy balance.Research work was, therefore, aimed at
reducing the amounts of material and energy going into each manufacturing
operation, while maintaining the utilization properties of the parts.

Research was directed towards the reduction or suppression of certain
phases in the manufacture of a part, without this having an effect on the
properties of the part.

The two following main avenues were explored :
- suppression of the rolling process with the parts being forged directly
  from cast bars.
- reduction or suppression of heat treatment after forging.

Three of these new treatments cover all our forging applications :
- direct isothermal annealing,
- direct conventional annealing,
- direct water or oil quenching.

II - SUPPRESSION OF THE ROLLING PROCESS AND FORGING FROM CAST BARS

A rough cast bar has, in a given structural condition, low, non-uniform
mechanical properties (toughness , tensile strength, fatigue) owing to
grain size, absence of metal compactness, segregation, etc.....

Hot reducing by rolling then forging makes it possible to eliminate
these drawbacks and enhance mechanical properties.Correct forging does,
moreover, produce a fibering condition which helps to improve matters
further in the event of stresses applied in the direction of the fibres.

Our knowledge of the evolution of mechanical properties as a function
of the reduction ratio shows that this evolution is asymptotic and that,
beyond a certain critical reduction ratio the energy spent is practically
wasted.

There are, therefore, families of forgings where hot reducing of the
stressed area is enough to obtain this optimum condition by forging
directly from a non-rolled blank.It is to verify this idea that tests have
been conducted using suitably-sized products.

2.1 - METHOD OF OBTAINING CAST BARS

Two alternative technologies exist to produce these products :
- Vertical centrifugal continuous casting (C.C.C.) whereby bars of a
  minimum diameter of around 90mm can be produced.This product which has

a correct surface condition is suitable for forging.Figure 1 shows a C.C.C. casting facility and macrographies on the cross-section of a 16 CD 4 steel.

- Horizontal continuous casting (H.C.C.), whereby products of diameters more in keeping with the requirements of the automotive industry (30 to 90mm) can be produced.However, the conditions in which the cast bar is removed cause circular folds on the surface in a "pitch pattern" and make it unsuitable for direct forging (although certain parts would be geometrically apt if the "residual defect" after forging was eliminated by machining).

The H.C.C. steel makers are currently making every effort to reduce this "peculiar condition".

2.2 REMARKS ON THE FORGING PROCESS FOR THIS PRODUCT

Numerous vertical forging machines are still fed with billets which are cold cut and heated in a gas-fired or induction furnace.It was not possible with the products in this study (32 C 4 $\emptyset$ 46, 30 CD 4 $\emptyset$ 59, 40 CD 4 $\emptyset$ 75, 16 CD 4 and 37 C 4 $\emptyset$ 90) to obtain correctly cold cut billets.Here, only sawing would guarantee a suitable cutting quality with no subsequent defect on the forging.However, the induction heated bar feed of the multiple station, horizontal forging machine permits high temperature cutting of the billet ($\sim$ 1200C°).Some development is still going on to reduce or even eliminate a minor shearing burr found in various sized folds on the forging (these residual defects are normally eliminated by machining).

2.3 STUDY OF UTILIZATION PROPERTIES OF PRODUCTS

2.3.1. - Mechanical properties on test specimens

These tests are conducted on forged billets for various reduction ratios from 0 to 10 ($\mathcal{T} = \frac{So}{S}$ where "So" is the initial billet section and "S" is the final section).

The study which concentrated more especially on resilience, both longways and crossways, and tensile strength properties R, E, A% and Z% in the quenched and tempered condition for 1000 MPa, confirmed the fact that, on 16 to 40 CD 4 and 32 C 4 steel, these properties increase fairly rapidly between the cast condition (reduction 0) and reduction ratios in the region of 3 to 4, where they stabilize and become similar to the values obtained on conventional rolled products.The graphs in figure 2 show how these properties evolve.

2.3.2. Tests on parts obtained with C.C.C. bars

We felt that it was better to conduct fatigue strength tests on actual parts.Such tests made it possible to monitor the behaviour of the material during the different stages of production (forming, machining, quality of structures after thermochemical or heat treatment) and also to ensure that no uncontrollable defect or deformation impaired the quality of the part prior to it being bench tested for endurance.

The first two parts chosen, a wheel hub made from a 37 C 4 steel quenched and tempered for 1000 MPa and the differential crown wheel made from a case hardened 16 CD 4 grade, were obtained from a 90 mm diameter C.C.C. metal.

These fairly big axisymmetric parts adapt quite well to forging from 90mm diameter cast bars.As illustrated in the photos in figure 3, the areas of maximum stress (toothed area of the bevel crown wheel - photo 9242 and the plate and hub/plate junction on the wheel hub - photo 9241)

112

are areas where the hot reducing operation is the most intense during forming and they concern the most compact section of the initial billet. In the central area of the part, where the hot reducing operation is less effective, traces of the central part of the billet can be found.However, this less compact area is eliminated when the bore is machined.

Endurance tests were run on a bench which reproduces the most severe stress conditions to be found on a vehicle.Results were satisfatory and behaviour was.similar to that of production parts.

This product was incorporated in our production, for both these parts, following a large scale test (5 to 10,000 parts) which proved satisfactory.

These results encouraged us to continue developing the product on other parts of a similar geometry and approval is being sought for a differential cylindrical crown wheel using a 30 CD 4 grade (a ring-shaped part with a large centre piece punched out) and a 61 tooth crown wheel for an agricultural tractor.This part, in a 25 CD 4 grade steel, is a bulky part ($\sim$ 50 kg) and is obtained from a sawn billet made from a 165 dia. cast bar.

2.3.3. Tests on parts obtained with H.C.C. cast bars

As already mentioned, the current surface quality of the H.C.C. bars has precluded any thoughts of a large scale forging of parts (tests on several batches of pinions had to be abandoned).

However, a small trial batch has been initiated for the wheel hub with a 40 CD 4 $\emptyset$ 75 steel, to enable an appraisal of the "internal" quality of this product (as machining eliminates all traces of the defects caused by the circular folds on the cast bar).Fatigue findings proved satisfactory.

III. - REDUCTION OR SUPPRESSION OF HEAT TREATMENT AFTER FORGING

Rough parts made by hot forging are cooled down to ambient temperature after the forging operation before being subjected to a heat treatment to regenerate the steel by refining the metal grain (heating above the AC3 transformation point).

The metallurgist's wish to limit grain coarsening when forging (avoiding subsequent regeneration) has partly been answered with the arrival of new steels known as "micro-alloy" steels (low content of Nb, Ti or V, approximately 0.10% added).

As recent work has shown us that a relatively coarse grain is not necessarily detrimental to a part's mechanical strength (durability, impact strength, etc....) provided that the substructure is fine, we thought it interesting to adopt that approach which allows conventional steels to be used, thus avoiding the added cost of specific grades.It does therefore appear possible to heat treat a part as it leaves the forging machine using the heat available in the part.

3.1 REMARK ON THE CHOICE OF COOLING CYCLE

These remarks cover the two types of annealing mentioned.There are temperature/time diagrams for each grade of steel which makes it possible to predict what the micrographic structure of a steel will be at ambient temperature for a given cooling cycle, whether it be via transformation of austenite under isothermal conditions (T.T.T. diagram) or via continuous cooling (T.R.C. diagram).

These diagrams, intended to determine cooling cycles on materials which are normally regenerated, will be used to choose the appropriate cooling process for a part straight from the "forging heat", bearing in

mind that the hot deformation of the part brings about a certain
refinement of the structure.

3.2 REMARKS ON GRAIN REFINEMENT DURING HOT DEFORMATION

The metal billet is heated to a high temperature (~1200° C) before
forging and although this temperature is held for a short period only, the
austenite grain obtained is coarse.

When the part is being formed, the austenite grain which appears is
only as a result of the recrystallization mechanism during and immediately
after deformation.

The result of recrystallization is dependent upon a number of factors:
billet heating temperature, deformation temperature, the mode and rate of
deformation, deformation speed, the time the deformation temperature is
held after deformation, the shape of the part (areas of different
bulkiness and with different deformation rates).

There are, therefore, a number of difficulties involved in obtaining
a well-defined austenite grain size in a part under these conditions.

3.3 REMARKS ON PRODUCT MACHINABILITY

The production process of a hot forged part necessarily includes a
machining operation.This operation may be the last one before assembly.
In that case, heat treatment (annealing, quenching and tempering) to
produce the desired utilization properties, is carried out on rough
forgings (e.g. connecting rods, steering knuckle etc.....).In other cases,
the treatment can produce forgings with a structure suitable for machining (isothermal annealing for example).This is true of gears where the
quality treatment (quenching case hardening or carbonitriding) is executed as a final operation on the machined part.

When developing direct treatments after forging, it is important to
ensure that the product has good machinability, as well as studying its
mechanical properties.

The acceptance factor for the machine shop is obviously how significant trial batches perform in the workshop.However, the direct treatment
cycle is developed first of all on samples - a test specimen under
laboratory conditions - before being tested on parts in a workshop.The
following test developed ten or so years ago at the R.N.U.R. laboratory
is used to evaluate machinability on small-size samples.

Machinability factor D 0.20 (MATHON - RENAULT)

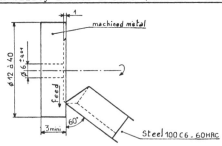

The test is conducted as shown in the above diagram.A reduced cutting
capacity tool in 100 C 6 steel is used; this enables facing tests to be
run with complete tool wear at diameters of between 6 and 40mm.The machined profile which should be a plane if the tool did not wear, gives the
retraction of the tool tip through wear as a function of the machined
diameter.The machinability factor D 0.20 retained is, therefore, the
machined diameter corresponding to a retraction of 0.20 mm under

114

specified cutting conditions.The machinability factor D 0.20 is in
relation with the cutting speed actually used.If the machinability
factor D 0.20 increases , the cutting speed will increase by approximately the same amount but it will increase in different degrees for each
type of machining operation.

A STUDY OF THE MAIN DIRECT TREATMENT CYCLES AFTER FORGING

For these new heat treatments of parts processed straight from the
"forging heat": direct isothermal annealing - direct conventional annealing and direct quenching, figure 4 shows, on a comparison basis, the
diagrams of the new cycles we are considering substituting for the
conventional cycles in current use.

4.1 DIRECT ISOTHERMAL ANNEALING (ANNEALING FOR MACHINING GEARS)

4.1.1. Conventional isothermal annealing of 30 - 35 CD 4 steels.

Industrial isothermal annealing operations executed under optimum
conditions are only "pseudo-isothermal"(semi-continuous & semi-isothermal).
Attempts are made to control the cycle on batches of parts to comply
"as best as possible" with the cooling processes imposed by the T.T.T. or
T.R.C. transformation diagrams.

Despite this peculiarity, these treatments have for years permitted
machining shops to supply ferrite-perlite structured products of the
right morphology with hardly any hardness scatter.

4.1.2. Direct isothermal annealing

After important preliminary work, an optimized cooling cycle was able
to be defined with two isothermal stages at 825°C and 650°C.Pilot
facilities with two fluidized bed furnaces contributed to the satisfactory
manufacture of batches of transmission gears in 30 CD 4 and 30 CD 4 R
(high resulphuration grade) (fig. 5).It was possible with this treatment
cycle to produce, with excellent repeatability on all parts, a coarse-
grained ferrite-perlite structure perfectly suitable for machining and
restorable when the part undergoes the final quenching carbonitriding
treatment (fig. 6).Furthermore, checks made on the various batches show
that there is very little difference between them with respect to hardness.

Finally, dimensional checks following thermochemical treatments of the
parts showed that there was no uncontrollable deformation to be feared
with this cooling technology.Figure 7 gives the MATHON-R.N.U.R. D 0.20
machinability measurements, which show the improved machinability of the
coarse grain, an improvement which adds to the improvements due to the
higher sulphur content (the 30 CD 4 R for instance).These results were
confirmed by the excellent way in which the 3000 gears built by the
workshop responded to machining.

All these results encourage us to continue work to industrialize
this cooling cycle.However, for different reasons (installation layouts,
forging machine rates etc....), fluidized bed furnaces have not been
retained for industrial development.

Work has been done to develop better suited equipment, capable of
coping continuously with forging machine rates (from 2 to 6 tons of parts
per hour) while moving "as close as possible" to the new direct "ISO"
annealing cycle.

Numerous cooling cycle tests have been conducted with preheated
"box-furnaces" and have given satisfactory results (fig. 8 presents a
cooling cycle and the structure obtained).

These "box-furnaces", in a carrousel configuration, used in sufficient
numbers to cope with the production of parts (300 to 500 kg of parts per
"box") could be a possible solution.However, another more satisfactory
approach has been adopted.The cooling cycles obtained with the " box -

furnace" have enabled a "heat-insulated tunnel furnace" with several heating and cooling zones to be designed with a furnace maker.It is in the process of development.

4.2 DIRECT CONVENTIONAL ANNEALING AFTER FORGING

For low strength parts of 600 to 800 MPa, normalizing is the quality treatment applied to ensure properties of that level on grades such as AF 60 or 45 M 5.Our connecting rods are currently made from 45 M 5 and so the study on direct annealing after forging began on that grade (fig.4).

The treatment consists in taking each part as it leaves the forging machine at a temperature of approximately 1100°C, lowering its temperature fairly quickly to 800 - 850°C to avoid any risk of the grain, refined by the forging operation, becoming coarse again by a stay at too high a temperature.Then its ferrite-perlite structural transformation must be carried out at between 800 and 550°C, within the time-frame prescribed by the T.R.C. diagram for the 45 M 5 grade,which is about 15 minutes.This would appear difficult to achieve by mere cooling of unit parts in still air.

The cooling process must, therefore, be slowed down.The "direct" cooling procedure thus defined has enabled us to obtain parts of a correct, uniform hardness and a ferrite-perlite structure of a peculiar morphology but one which is acceptable for machining (fig. 9).These parts were, moreover, subjected to tension compression fatigue tests and their behaviour was satisfactory and similar to that of production parts.

4.2.1. Installation of pilot test equipment at the forges and industrialization

One of the main difficulties which has been resolved for the pilot tests, was to install test equipment (heat-insulated cooling tunnel) at the different subcontracted forges, to be able to run the cooling cycle as defined, from the first to the last of several thousand parts (volume necessary to follow-up machining on an industrial scale).

Before starting connecting rod production, the tunnel should be pre-heated and the enclosure brought to an "optimized temperature profile" for the cooling cycle to be carried out on parts (fig. 10).

Following satisfactory results on pilot batches, industrialization of this technology was initiated for the connecting rod and bearing cap with our main subcontractor, whose high production rates will enable a rapid amortization of the equipment installed (a tunnel furnace with several electrically heated zones and a fan to expel hot gas for a correct control of the cooling cycle).

4.2.2. Direct annealing:application on R9 Frt. steering knuckle (AF60)

Initial developments carried out at the SAFE on the connecting rod have made it possible to consider applying direct annealing to this important, high-volume part using a cooling procedure fairly close to the one applied for the 45 M 5.

Using the "box-furnaces", the cooling processes studied enabled batches of parts to be built for testing.The R9 front steering knuckle is a safety critical part which must meet the requirements of various behavioural tests.

Two of the batches successfully underwent endurance and "global impact"tests on the steering arms.These results allow us to undertake full scale tests to evaluate machining behaviour and the installation of direct cooling equipment tailored to this part (heat-insulated tunnel furnace with several zones) is being reviewed.

4.3 DIRECT QUENCHING AFTER FORGING

The idea of directly quenching a part after forging to save on the heating operation to produce austenitization before quenching is not new, but difficulties of a technological nature had until now curbed its development. Improvements in the mechanization of forging equipment, the installation of better suited heating facilities combined with a more reliable pyrometry (induction heating of billets) mean a better control of the "heat line" in the production process of forgings.

Previous work showed that direct quenching after forging could produce products with properties of an equivalent standard to that obtained by the conventional treatment.

The study was first of all oriented towards a part which accounts for a high level of tonnage in our production: the steering knuckle in 20 MB 5. Research work, therefore, was continued on parts and test pieces to examine how this steel reacts to direct water quenching.

The steering knuckle is a safety critical part which must meet quality requirements involving the three following aspects:
- hardness (1000 MPa) obtained by quenching and tempering
- good impact strength (resilience)
- durability.

Tests proved that the coarser grain inherent in direct quenching does not adversely affect product quality, as the substructure remains relatively refined. The resilience of this material when quenched and tempered is already naturally high and the slight drop registered with direct quenching guarantees a sufficient impact strength for parts even at low temperatures, according to the study conducted on the resilience transition temperature (fig. 11).

Durability proved to be very satisfactory on the steering knuckle and the uniformity of results may be accounted for as follows :
- direct water quenching of unit parts under identical conditions.
- the better hardenability of this material when directly quenched which gives less hardness scatter.
- lesser decarburization and a surface condition which is less disturbed as there is no second heating operation prior to quenching.
a full scale test on 10,000 parts confirmed that the "heat line" of this technology is well under control. Machining follow-up in the workshop gave satisfactory results.

4.3.1. Additional advantages of the better hardenability with direct quenching

The better hardenability observed with the 20 MB 5 led to us initiating similar tests with a less expensive grade, the 20 M 5. Results on the steering knuckle also proved satisfactory.

Furthermore, other products are affected by the improved hardenability and this means that even more economical production processes can be contemplated for some parts. There are two interesting examples of parts which were originally oil quenched and tempered for 1000 MPa and which have proved satisfactory when directly quenched with the change in grade :
- the ball-joint housing (37 B3 Pb oil quenched) can be changed to 20 M5S with direct water quenching.
- the wheel hub (37 C 4 oil quenched) can be made from a 20 MB 5 grade with direct water quenching.

The additional saving involves both the material and the quenching medium.

4.3.2. Installation of direct quenching facilities

Each forge reviewed the possibility of installing the appropriate equipment.Depending on the production rates specific to each subcontractor, industrialization using this technology may be a short or medium term prospect.Under these conditions, the ball-joint housing was able to be rapidly applied in production.

V COST EXERCISE AND ENERGY SAVINGS

Action taken to reduce energy consumption during heat treatment and the possibility in certain instances of being able to use less expensive grades will generate lower cost prices for all the parts covered in this study.The cost exercise will have to take into account the capital expenditure necessary for these new technologies and the additional operations which will, in some cases, have to be included in the process eg sawing billets on cast bars).Furthermore, some of the existing facilities stand to have lower utilization rates (treatment furnaces, etc)

However, we can, from a review of each area studied in which industrialization has been achieved or is a possibility, put forward the following figures, as an overall estimate of potential energy savings:
- energy saving on rolling operation: 14.10^6 kWhE for 7,000 tons of steel.
- energy saving on heat treatment: 70.10^6 kWhT for 50,000 tons of steel.

Obviously these technologies applied to hot forgings manufactured in Europe will lead to significantly greater energy savings.

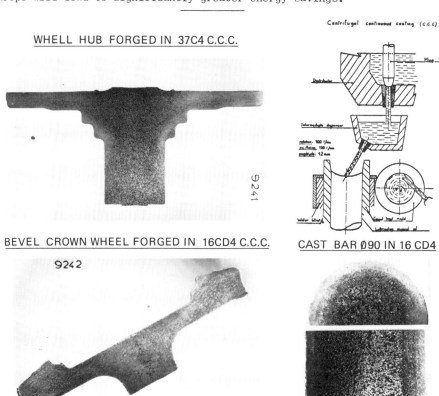

WHELL HUB FORGED IN 37C4 C.C.C.

Centrifugal continuous casting (c.c.c)

BEVEL CROWN WHEEL FORGED IN 16CD4 C.C.C.

CAST BAR Ø90 IN 16 CD4

Fig. 3

Fig. 1

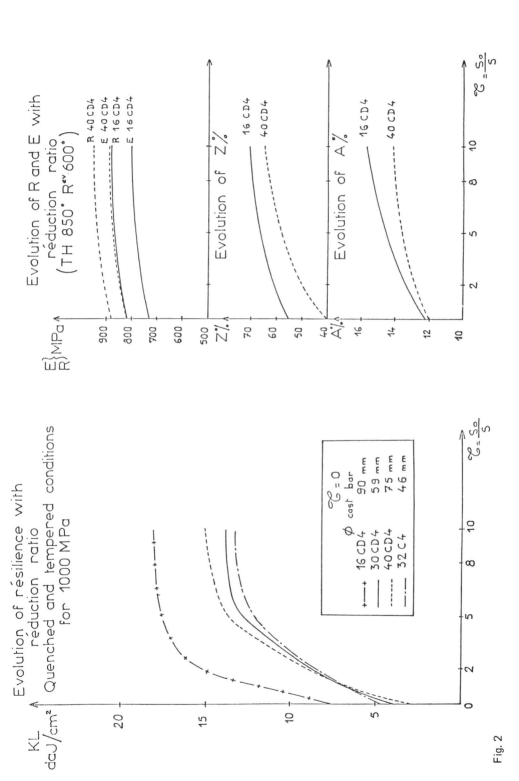

Fig. 2

119

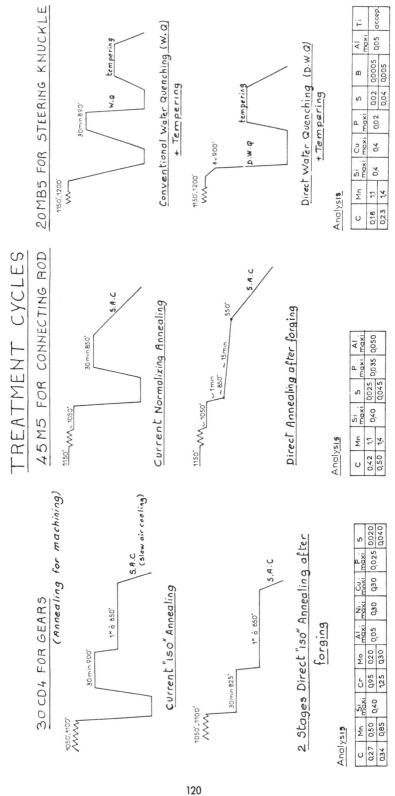

TREATMENT CYCLES

45M5 FOR CONNECTING ROD

Current Normalizing Annealing

1150° ∿∿∿∿∿ ~1050°   30 min 850°   S.A.C

Direct Annealing after forging

1150° ∿∿∿∿∿ ~1050°   ~1 min ~850°   ~15 min   550°   S.A.C

Analysis

C	Mn	Si maxi	S	P maxi	Al maxi
0,42	1,1	0,40	0,025	0,035	0,050
0,50	1,4		0,045		

20MB5 FOR STEERING KNUCKLE

Conventional Water Quenching (W.Q) + Tempering

1150°-1200° ∿∿∿   30 min 890°   W.Q   tempering

Direct Water Quenching (D.W.Q) + Tempering

1150°-1200° ∿∿∿   e.~900°   D.W.Q   tempering

Analysis

C	Mn	Si maxi	Cu maxi	P maxi	S	B	Al maxi	Ti
0,18	1,1	0,4	0,4	0,02	0,02	0,0005	0,05	accep.
0,23	1,4				0,04	0,005		

30CD4 FOR GEARS
(Annealing for machining)

1050°-1100° ∿∿∿   30 min 900°   1" à 650°   S.A.C (slow air cooling)

Current "ISO" Annealing

1050°-1100° ∿∿∿   30 min 825°   1" à 650°   S.A.C

2 Stages Direct "ISO" Annealing after forging

Analysis

C	Mn	Si maxi	Cr	Mo	Al maxi	Ni maxi	Cu maxi	P maxi	S
0,27	0,50	0,40	0,95	0,20	0,05	0,30	0,30	0,025	0,020
0,34	0,85		1,25	0,30					0,040

Fig. 4

120

FLUIDIZED BED
TEMPERATURES 825°C AND 650° C

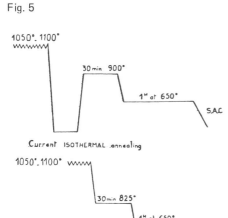

Fig. 5

DIRECT ISOTHERMAL ANNEALING on 3ᵗʰ GEAR
B.V. 354 in 30 CD4 and 30 CD4R
2 full scale' tests on 3000 parts (14 batches)
Machinability D 0,20

30 CD4 : S. 0,030	
Hardness HB	D. 0,20 (mm)
179	19,03
187	18,81
192	19,15
200	18,78
207	16,51
223	17,08

30 CD4R : S. 0,073	
Hardness HB	D. 0,20 (mm)
187	21,18
202	19,11
217	19,13

Grain Structure : ferrite (α) 7.9
perlite (P.L) 3.7

Production Isothermal Annealing on 30 CD4
D 0,20 : 17,03 mm (183 HB) S. 0,033
Grain Structure : ferrite (α) 8-9
perlite (P.L) 7-8

Fig. 7

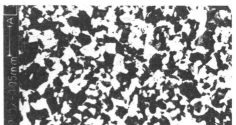

1050°. 1100°

30 min 900°

1ᴴ at 650°

S.A.C

Current ISOTHERMAL annealing

1050°. 1100°

30 min 825°

1ᴴ at 650°

S.A.C

Direct Isothermal annealing after forging with 2 stages

Fig. 6

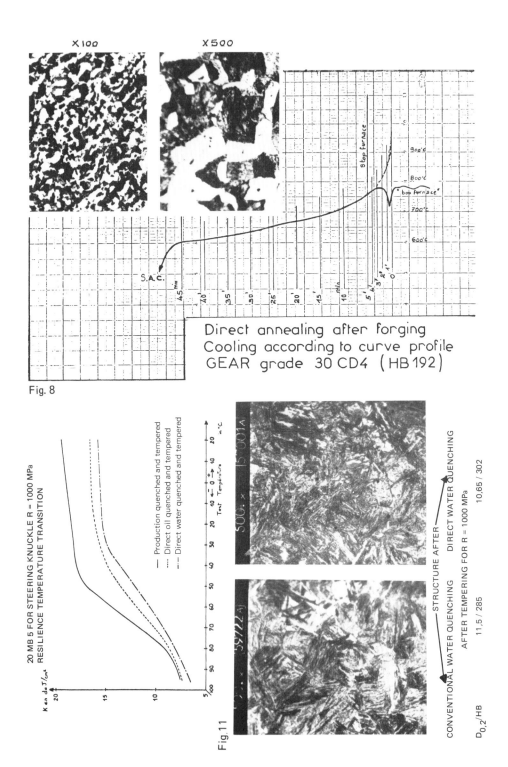

×100   ×500

S.A.C.

Stop furnace

900°c
800°c
"bab furnace"
700°c
600°c

Direct annealing after forging
Cooling according to curve profile
GEAR grade 30 CD4 (HB 192)

Fig. 8

20 MB 5 FOR STEERING KNUCKLE R = 1000 MPa
RESILIENCE TEMPERATURE TRANSITION

— Production quenched and tempered
···· Direct oil quenched and tempered
–·– Direct water quenched and tempered

K en daJ/cm²

Test Temperature n °C

Fig. 11

CONVENTIONAL WATER QUENCHING   DIRECT WATER QUENCHING

STRUCTURE AFTER

AFTER TEMPERING FOR R = 1000 MPa

$D_{0,2}$/HB   11,5 / 285   10,65 / 302

122

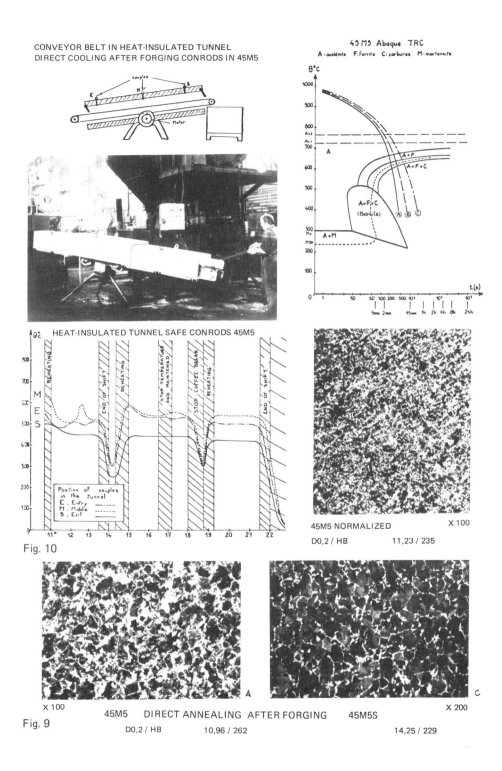

CONVEYOR BELT IN HEAT-INSULATED TUNNEL
DIRECT COOLING AFTER FORGING CONRODS IN 45M5

45 M5 Abaque TRC

A : austénite F : ferrite C : carbures M : martensite

HEAT-INSULATED TUNNEL SAFE CONRODS 45M5

Position of couples
in the tunnel
E . Entry   ——
M . Middle   ----
S . Exit

Fig. 10

45M5 NORMALIZED   X 100
D0,2 / HB   11,23 / 235

X 100   A

45M5   DIRECT ANNEALING AFTER FORGING   45M5S
Fig. 9
D0,2 / HB   10,96 / 262   14,25 / 229

X 200   C

DEVELOPMENT OF BAINITIC NODULAR IRON FOR THE CONSTRUCTION OF SPEED GEAR FOR THE CAR INDUSTRY

M. Baffigi, S. Corso and F. Rabezzana

Fiat Auto S.p.A., C. G. Agnelli 200, I-10125 Torino

Summary

One potential application of alternative materials for the manufacturing of automotive components, is the utilization of spheroidal casr iron for vehicle power line components where high specidic pressures and flexural load stresses are involed.

This report intented to analyse the industrial feasibility and possible problems connected with the use of spheroidal cast iron for gear applications (bevel gears for a rear drive differential) in replacement carbonitrided 18 CrMo 4 steel.
In order to grant mechanical and dynamic characteristics similar to steel, to spheroidal cast iron bevel gears, it was necessary to treat the machined parts with ferritization, austempering and shot-peening processes.
The use of spheroidal cast iron resulted in a 75% saving on tool cost during the machining stage.
However, considerable problems rised up concerning deformations of the finished parts, with scraps amounting to about 50 % of total production.
The survey has made it clear that if cast iron is to be used for gear applications, further efforts are needed to align both the heat treatment and machining cycles with the characteristics of the new material.

Introduction

The development of alternative materials for the manufacturing of automotive components has followed two main trends in the past few years : reducing the alloying elements in hardening and tempering and casehardening steels, and replacing hardening and tempering steels with spheroidal cast iron.
One potential application, which seemed impossible up to a few years ago, is the utilization of spheroidal cast iron for vehicle power line components where high specific pressures and flexural load stresses are involved.
The development of improved manufacturing techniques, heat treatment methods and casehardening processes has permitted to impart to spheroidal cast iron such mechanical and wear resistance characteristics very similar to those found in casehardening steels used for gear manufacturing.
The major advantage obtained by using spheroidal cast iron in place of casehardening steels are: improved machinability, energy saving in the manufacturing of blanks and reduced part weight.

In view of these potential benefits, a development and testing program was undertaken concentrating on crown wheel and pinion gears of a rear drive vehicle differential, currently made from carbonitrided 18 CrMo 4 steel. This program was designed to define and compare both cast iron heat treatment cycles and the types of casehardening cycles apt to confer to cast iron functional properties very similar to casehardening steel, as well as the machinability of cast iron compared to gear steel.

1. Heat Treatment Cycles and Mechanical Characteristics

In order to confer to spheroidal cast iron the functional characteristics suitable for the specific application of gear manufacturing it is necessary to treat it with a ferritization process designed to reduce the pearlitic content to < 5 % and to guarantee constant deformation after the bainitic austempering treatment.

The cast iron used was of the Gh 65-48-05 type with the following percent chemical composition: C=3.87 %; Si=2.65 %; Mn=0.4 %; Ni $\leqslant$ 1.5 %; Mg=0.3%; S=0.012 %; P=0.02 %.

The mechanical characteristics of the cast blank meet the UNI 4544 standard : surface hardness HB=240÷280 kg/mm^2; spheroid density= 390 n°/mm^2, spheroid diameter= 15-30 μm.

Two separate ferritization cycles were tested :

HIGH TEMPERATURE

- Heating to 900°C for 5 hrs
- Cooling at 780°C for 1 hr
- Cooling at 630°C for 1 hr
- Cooling at 427°C for 1 hr
- Cooling in still air

LOW TEMPERATURE

- Heating to 740°C for 7 hrs
- Cooling in still air

Expansions after the ferritization treatment, as measured by dilatometric analysis, were as follows :

- 0.54 % after the high temperature cycle
- 0.35 % after the low temperature cycle

The CCT curves (Fig. 1) were determined for spheroidal cast iron in order to define the cooling rate and austenite/bainitic transformation temperature to be applied in the austempering process.

The following parameters were used in the austempering cycle :

- Heating to 910°C for 2 hrs
- Quenching in oil at 235°C
- Maintaining at 235°C for 2 1/2 hrs
- Cooling in air

Expansion measurements taken after heat treatment revealed that the sum of final expansions was practically the same whether the high temperature or low temperature ferritization cycle was applied (0.78 % and 0.79 % respectively).

For the ferritization treatment it was decided to adopt the high temperature cycle, as the larger deformations which take place during the ferritization stage can be eliminated during the machining of parts, and the subsequent hardening stage causes only deformations due to the austenite/bainite structural transformation.

The steel used for the tests was the 18 CrMo 4 type and was carbonitrided by applying a cycle similar to that used for standard production gears :

- Heating to 880°C for 2 hrs
- Diffusion at 880°C for 1 hr 20 min
- Stabilization at 830°C for 1 hr
- Oil quenching at 120°C
- Tempering at 180°C for 2 hrs

The carbonitriding depth was 0.5 to 0.7 mm. The mechanical properties of spheroidal cast iron compared with those of carbonitrided steel (Tab. I) shows that the core strength and surface hardness of cast iron are similar to those of steel and are within the limits (even though near minimum values) set by manufacturing specifications.

2. Toughness and Fatigue Limits

The dynamic properties of spheroidal cast iron were compared with those of carbonitrided 18 CrMo 4 steel in the following tests :

. 3-point bending fatigue test : The specimen tested simulated a gear tooth. The data were processed using the Stair Case statistical method. For this test, a 10 ton MTS electro-hydraulic machine was used. The values recorded at the completion of the test were 299 ± 244.5 N/mm^2 for carbonitrided 18 CrMo 4 steel, and 155 ± 127.4 N/mm^2 for bainitic spheroid cast iron.
The comparison of the 3-point bending fatigue limits for the two materials clearly indicates that bainitic spheroidal cast iron cannot replace steel as a gear material without undergoing subsequent hardening treatments, as its low fatigue limit value would cause an early failure of the gear tooth.

. Measured resilience: This test was made using an AMSLER pendulum IZOD with maximum available energy of 235 J. The specimen shape can be considered as a large module gear tooth as its dimensions (thickness and tab to specimen body junction radius) are comparable with those found in gears.
The test results, summarized in Table I, show the low toughness of cast iron in comparison with steel.
The maximum σimpact stress values for cast iron are 130 % lower than steel values. This means that between two gears of the same dimensions made from the two materials tested, the one made from bainitic spheroidal cast iron will fail under much lower stresses than those normally withstood by carbonitrided steel.

Moreover, a 18.7 joule energy is sufficient to break a cast iron specimen, against the 86.5 joules required to break a steel specimen (a 360 %
increase).

3. Surface Hardening of Bainitic Spheroidal Cast Iron

The strength properties of the cast iron must be improved by means of sur
face treatments such as shot- peening and rolling to obtain the desired
strength. These treatments produce structural changes in the surface layers
and permit to achieve dynamic characteristics similar to those found in
carbonitrided steel.
The operating conditions of the two surface treatment were as follows :

SHOT-PEENING :   - pellet $\emptyset$ 110 shot, 170 shot
                  - pellet material   casehardened steel
                  - intensity   6 Almen A; 16 Almen A
                  - air pressure   55 N/mm^2; 60 N/mm^2

ROLLING   :   - pressure   5000 N, 9000 N
                  - No. of turns   3

The steel and cast iron specimens were tested for 3-point bending fatigue strength (to determine the σ_D value), while the quantification of
the amount of compressive stresses due to the surface hardening treatments
was made by measuring the residual stress using a SIEMENS type SMD 2000
machine.
The results are summarized in Table II.
By relating the dynamic component σ_a of the fatigue limit as a function
of shot-peening intensity and rolling pressure, the diagram shown in Fig.
2 can be obtained. This indicates that shot-peening has a grater effect
on improving the fatigue strength of cast iron than rolling does, and
the dynamic componend for the 16 Almen A shot-peened specimens is similar
(6 % lover) than those for carbonitred steel.
The different fatigue performance of shot-peened and rolled specimens is
confirmed by the fractographic study of the broken pieces. Fig. 3 shows
the results of a scanning microscope analysis which indicate that in the
shot-peened specimen the crack originates at a deeper level than in the
rolled specimen. Moreover, if the measured residual stress values are
plotted against the σ_a values (Fig. 4), the importance of the compression treatment becomes even more apparent; in particular, the following
points can be noted :

- the σ_a values increase with the increasing of compression stress values;

- the maximum σ_a value for cast iron specimens ($\simeq$ 6 % lower than the
  values for carbonitreded steel) is obtained with a maximum compression
  stress value of -248 N/mm^2. This value approaches that of carbonitrided steel (-284 N/mm^2).

Having established the superior performance of 16 Almen A shot-peening over other surface treatment methods, a number of specimens thus treated were selected to determine the toughness parameters typical od instrumented resilience (Table I).

The results obtained indicate that treated cast iron yields higher values than non-treated cast iron ($\geqslant$ 65 %) but in any case lowere ($\leqslant$ 22 %) than the values obtained from carbonitrided steel.

4. Comparison of laboratory machinability tests

A set of laboratory tests was designed to simulate different types of machining operations (with their related problems) which would permit to establish a comparison among the various test materials in a short time and at low costs, and would supply preliminary indications on the correct use of the new material in production.
The following materials were tested :

- ferritic spheroidal cast iron (pearlitic $\langle$ 5%). average HB=145 (143-148)

- ferritic/pearlitic spheroidal cast iron   . average HB=201 (178-255)
- austempered annealed 18 CrMo 4 steel   . average HB=152 (149-156)

The two machining operations most suitable for a machinability evaluation of the bevel gears for a rear drive vehicle differential, are milling and drilling.

4.1. Milling Operation

The evaluation of cast iron machinability was made by means of milling tests using modular cutters made from 5 % Co high speed steel (diameter $\emptyset$ = 70 mm, No. of teeth Z = 12).
The test procedure consisted in cutting 3 mm deep and 250 mm long grooves with one return stroke with the cutter sliding on the machined surface. (cutting speed = 55 m/min).
This sequence was repeated a number of time corresponding tO 100 minutes machining. The wear of each cutter tooth was measured at regular intervals. The analysis of the machinability test results indicates that in the milling operation ferritic cast iron is 40 % better than pearlitic cast iron in terms of tool wear (Fig. 5). The tools used to machine pearlitic cast iron show a greater scatter of the wear values measured; by reference to the percentage ratio between deviation and average, the value is 12 % for ferritic cast iron and 35 % for pearlitic cast iron. When the comparison is made between the two cast iron varieties and steel (at 35 m/min speed), it can be seen that pearlitic cast iron has an advantage over steel of about 100 %, while ferritic cast iron reaches the 200 % level.

4.2. Drilling operation

To evaluate the performance in drilling operations of cast iron materials in comparison with 18 CrMo 4 steel, tests were performed using 8.5 mm dia. twist bits with cutting speeds varying between 30 and 50 m/min and with

0.34 to 0.15 mm/turn feed, using a 5 % emulsion coolant. The comparison was made counting the number of holes drilled until the average wear of cutters was V_B = 0.3 mm.

The drilling test showed the advantages of ferritic cast iron over both pearlitic cast iron and steel.

The advantage of ferritic cast iron over the pearlitic variety was in the order of 400 % for the same number of holes up to a tool wear level of V_B = 0.3 mm (Fig. 6). Under the same machining conditions, the bits used to machine the steel material chipped after 40 holes; thus ferritic cast iron would have a 1500 % advantage over steel. However, these cutting conditions are not acceptable for steel material. Other tests were performed with reduced feed rates, and under these new conditions the difference in productivity of pearlitic cast iron over steel was 130 %.

5. Comparison of machinability at the industrial level

The comparison of production machinability between ferritic spheroidal cast iron (greater machinability advantages) and austempered annealed 18 CrMo 4 steel (the currently used material) was made by machining 1300 bevel gear pairs made from spheroidal cast iron (Fig. 7).

The results obtained from machining the two materials under evaluation confirmed the laboratory test results (Tab.III).

These results were quantified in terms of tool saving and sharpening costs amounting to a 75 % reduction or Lit. 270 per gear pair.

6. Checking Deformation

One lot of 200 bevel gear pairs was treated with the ferritization process described above and then machined with the same parameters used for machining steel material.

Dimensional measurements were taken on this lot to check deformations after hardening.

The gear pairs were then austempered and measured again for a further dimensional checking.

Crown wheels had varying deformations up to 0.5 mm on the housing seat diameter. However, even though these deformations are considerably large, they are sufficiently constant and it is felt that the desired design dimensions can be achieved by calibrating the blank machining cycle. The pinions had the same dimensional anomalies noted for the crown wheels with the same chance of correction in the machining stage, but they are more critical with regard to the straightening of the stem. Fifty percent of the parts produced cannot be recovered through the straightening operation because of elastic resilience; the remaining 50 % require a time which is double the time currently needed, and even then the required tolerances cannot be achieved.

To overcome this problem it appears that austempering with a locking fixture is necessary to prevent the occurrence of large deformations and to reduce to a minimum the straightening operation, which proved to be very critical in the industrial process.

Conclusions

Considering these results, it can be stated that the characteristics of spheroidal cast iron, austempered and shot-peened, are inferior to those of casehardened steel currently used for gear manufacturing.
The machinability tests performed on a large lot of bevel gear pairs made from spheroidal cast iron have permitted to quantify the savings obtainable in terms of tool costs, but at the same time they indicated the occurence of critical deformation on the finished parts, which can be only partially eliminated with the straightening operation.

For these reasons, the use of spheroidal cast iron in the field of gear manufacturing is possible provided that the necessary changes are made in the heat treatment and machining cycles.
The work done, however, served to highlight a wide range of possible uses of surface hardening cycles, that could be successfully employed for components requiring a high fatigue strength. These possibilities must be examined at the design engineering level so that the design of a new product can be made taking into account the dynamic-mechanical properties of spheroidal cast iron.

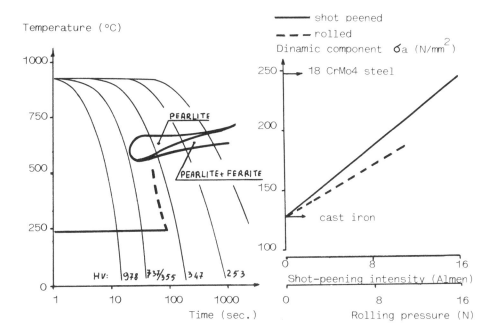

Fig. 1 - CCT diagram   Fig. 2 - Dinamic component

Shot-peened   Rolled

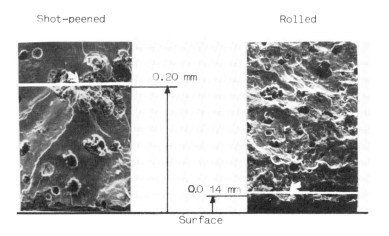

Fig. 3 - Scanning microscope analysis

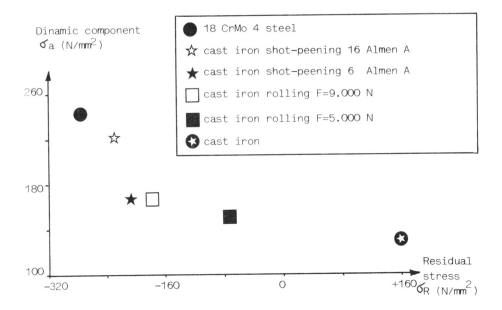

Fig. 4 - Dinamic component in relation to residual stress

18 CrMo 4 steel
cast iron ferritic matrix
cast iron ferritic/pearlitic

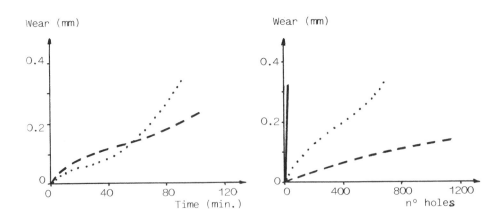

Fig.5 - Milling operation   Fig. 6 - Drilling operation

Fig. 7 - Bevel gears

Tab. I - Mechanical, thoughness and dinamical properties of steel
and cast iron

Materials / Characteristics	Bainitic spheroidal cast iron	Shot-peened cast iron 16 Almen A	18CrMo 4 carbonitred steel
Core strenght (N/mm^2)	1365		1400
Surface hardness (HRc)	57	–	60
Structure	Bainite , martensite, residual austenite and graphite nodular		Sup.=Martensite Heart=Bainite and martensite
Tensil stress (N)	18.500	30.000	42.000
Break energy (J)	18.7	24.7	86.5
Maximum impact stress (N/mm^2)	1.000	1.800	2.325
Striking time (m/sec)	0.32	0.32	0.65

Tab. II - Dinamical properties of steel and cast iron

Materials	Treatment	Surface Hardening	Fatigue limit σ_D * (N/mm^2)	Residual stress σ_R (N/mm^2)
Spheroidal cast iron	Austempering	–	155.8+127.4	+ 143 10
		shot-peening 6 Almen A	213+173	– 241+49
		shot-peening 16 Almen A	282.7+231.3	– 248+10
		Rolling F=5.000 N	183+150.2	-78.4+20
		Rolling F=9.000 N	211+172.4	-215.6+29
18 CrMo 4 steel	Carbonitred	–	298+244.5	– 240+20

$\sigma_D = \sigma_m$ (medium stress) $\pm$ σ_a (dinamic component)

Tab. III - Comparison of machinability at the industrial level

Piece	Operation	Cast iron		18 CrMo4 steel	
		Productivity	Wear (mm)	Productivity	Wear (mm)
Crown wheel	Roughing boring	250÷300	0.5÷0.7	80÷100	1.5
	Facing	250	0.2	100	0.4
	Drilling, boring-tapping	1300	–	500	–
	Rough gear cutting	1300	0.4÷0.5	180	0.9÷1
	Finish gear cutting	1300	0.2	200	0.5
Bevel pinion	Facing	3200	–	1600	–
	Turning	400	0.4	200	1
	Rough gear cutting	1300	0.4÷0.5	200	0.9÷1
	Finish gear cutting	1300	0.2	300	0.4

LUBRICATION BY SLAGS OF THE CONTINOUS CASTING OF STEELS

Ch. Niggel and E. Felder

ARMINES – Centre de Mise en Forme des Matériaux – Ecole des Mines de Paris
ERA CNRS 837 – Sophia Antipolis – F-06565 Valbonne Cedex

SUMMARY
We have coupled a semi-empirical model of the slag melting process above
the meniscus with the previous developped thermohydrodynamical model /1/.We
obtain a good estimation of the thermal flux extracted by the mold for
low and high viscosity slags. Moreover the theoretical influence of the casting speed and the slag viscosity on the consumption and friction are quali-
tatively in good agreement with the industrial observations. All these results have been obtained under the assumption of a stationary mold. But the
numerical integration of the dynamic equation of the film demonstrates that
mold oscillations do not seem have a great influence on these aspects of
the continuous casting.

I. INTRODUCTION

1.1. Economical impact of the study

The figure 1 presents the economical interest of the study : the continuous casting provides a substantial energy saving for the manufacture of
slabs, which can be increased by a good formulation of the slags able to
produce slabs with good surface aspect ; moreover this study could make
easier the choice of slags for the continuous casting of alloys, for example special steels, which must be still now casted into ingots. For this,
we aim to predict the influence of the slags properties on the heat flux
extracted by the mold, the friction between the mold and the steel shell
and the defects of the casted product.

1.2. Previous work

The figure 2 describes the geometry of the system. We have presented
earlier the thermomechanical analysis of the slag flow between shelland
mold below the meniscus (part 2 of /1/) which for a given slag flow rate Q_L
provides the heat flux profile and the slag thickness distribution : below
the meniscus the flow rate Q_L increases with casting speed and viscosity,
but increases, is maximal, of value Q_L^M , then decreases as the initial slag
thickness h_O increases (figure 3) ; comparison of the analysis with experiments suggested that low viscosity slags flow at maximal flow rate Q_L^M, but
that the melting of high viscosity slag above the meniscus controls its flow
rate. The study was then developped in order to improve these results /2/.

2. ANALYSIS OF THE SLAG MELTING PROCESS ABOVE THE MENISCUS

2.1. The model

A thermal analysis was built in the study report n° 2 /2/, and provides the results of figure 3 : the melting flow rate Q_F is a decreasing function of the liquid slag thickness and the slag viscosity, but the liquid
slag thickness above the meniscus is of an order of magnitude greater than
its value below the meniscus, in good agreement with industrial observations /6/.

The study has been developped under three major assumptions :
- the melting flow rate is limited; a first model assumes that its maximal value follows the empirical relationship.

$$Q_F \leq Q_F^M = 1.15 \ 10^{-7}/\eta \ (1400°C)$$

A second model assumes that the liquid slag flows above the meniscus for a pressure drop between the slab middle and the walls which cannot exceed a critical value Δp_C ; this value would be fixed by the flow properties of the solid powder (part 3 of /2/) but is not easy to predict theoretically ; a semi-empirical fit of the results provides the value $\Delta p_C = 0.0175$ Pa ; it seems difficult to explain this very little value of the critical pressure drop which leads to results near the first empirical model (cf. figure 7).
- the flow rate of the system is :

$$Q = Min \ \{Q_L^M, \ Q_F^M\}$$

- if $Q < Q_L^M$ h_0 takes its minimal value; it is interesting to remark that the second possible value seems near the depth of some slags incrustations in slabs and appears as an instable solution, responsible of surface defects in slabs casted with slags of too high viscosity.

2.2. Comparison with experiments

As casting speed or viscosity increases, the slag thickness and consumption increases, is maximal, then decreases (figures 4-5), in agreement with the measurements of slag consumption in industrial plants /3/. More quantitatively the figures 6 and 7 demonstrates that the model provides a good estimation of the heat flux profile and the mean heat flux extracted by the mold under low and high viscosity slags.

3. INFLUENCE OF THE MOLD OSCILLATIONS

In practice, the mold oscillates, with a speed of the form

$$U(t) = U_0 \cos \omega t$$

We have improved the previous model in order to study the influence of the mold oscillations. With the notations of /1/, the slag flow rate is now :

$$q = - \frac{h^3}{\eta_0} \ [\frac{\partial p}{\partial x} - \rho g] \ G_1(S_3) + h \ [V - U(t)] \ G_2(S_3) + h \ U(t)$$

The film thickness h follows the dynamic equation :

$$- \frac{\partial h}{\partial t} = \frac{\partial q}{\partial x}$$

The numerical integration of this equation starting from the previous static solution demonstrates that the slag thickness at the meniscus oscillates slightly around the static value and that the slag thickness under the meniscus is almost constant (figure 8).

4. CONCLUSIONS

The main conclusions of the study are the followings :
- the mold oscillations do not seem have a great direct influence on these aspects of the continuous casting.
- the model provides a good estimation of the solidification process of the steel for low and high viscosity slags ; it suggests an explanation for some surface defects due to too high viscosity slags whose flow rate is controlled by the melting rate.

- the figures 9 and Table I make a comparison of low and high viscosity slags from two differents points of view : the viscosity of optimal slags seem decreasing as the casting speed increases, for at high speed viscous slags induce high mold surface temperature, perhaps responsible of high wear, (figure 9), too thin liquid film (table I), generating high friction /5/ and too thin shell, proper to breakouts.

We think that this theoretical analysis of the slag lubrication will be able to improve the control of continuous casting and the choice of slags proper to minimize surface defects of the slabs, the breakouts of lubricant film and the mold wear.

REFERENCES

1. FELDER, E. and NIGGEL, Ch., Lubrication by slags of the continuous casting of steels. Proc. Contractors Meeting (Metallurgy) Brussels 22 Oct. 1982
2. FELDER, E. and NIGGEL, Ch., Lubrication by slags of the continuous casting of steels . Progress Report Nos 2-3 a.4 (Nov. 1982 - April a. Dec. 1983)
3. NURI, Y., OHASHI, T., MIYASAKA, N., SHIMA, K. and USCHIDA, Y. Consumption behavior of powder during continuous casting. 98th ISIJ. Meeting (Oct. 1979) Lect. N° 5703.
4. LARRECQ, M., WANIN, M., MANGIN, M., and NICOLAS, M. Résultats d'exploitation de la lingotière de coulée continue de 900 mm. de la Sollac (Sept. 1981)
5. MAIRY, B. and WOLF, M. On the importance of mould friction control in continuous casting of steel. Fachberichte Hüttenpraxis Metallweiterverarbeitung. 20 (1982) 222
6. RIBOUD,P. and LARRECQ, H. Private communication.

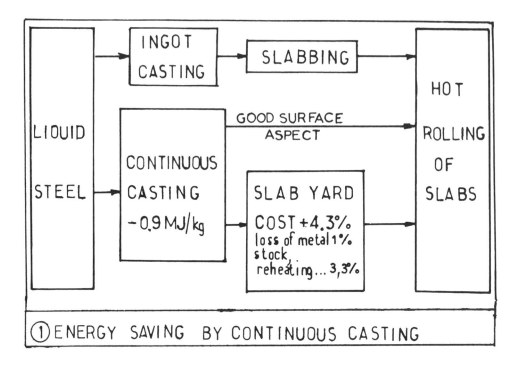

① ENERGY SAVING BY CONTINUOUS CASTING

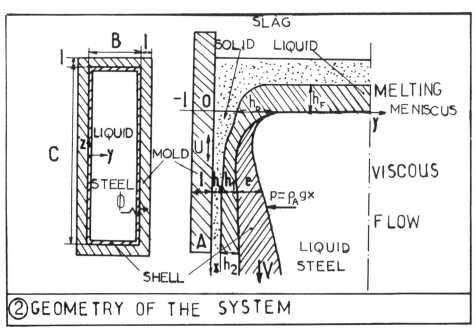

② GEOMETRY OF THE SYSTEM

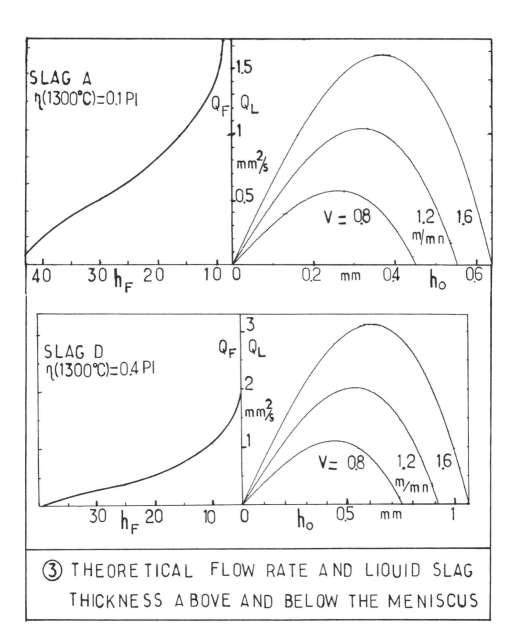

SLAG A
$\eta(1300°C) = 0.1\,Pl$

Q_F Q_L

$mm^2\!/_s$

$V = 0.8$ 1.2 1.6
   $m\!/_{mn}$

40   30 h_F 20   10   0   0.2 mm 0.4 h_o 0.6

SLAG D
$\eta(1300°C) = 0.4\,Pl$

Q_F Q_L

$mm^2\!/_s$

$V = 0.8$ 1.2 1.6
   $m\!/_{mn}$

30 h_F 20   10   0 h_o 0.5 mm 1

③ THEORETICAL FLOW RATE AND LIQUID SLAG
THICKNESS ABOVE AND BELOW THE MENISCUS

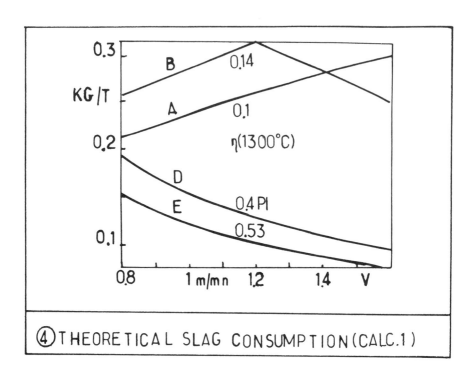

④ THEORETICAL SLAG CONSUMPTION (CALC.1)

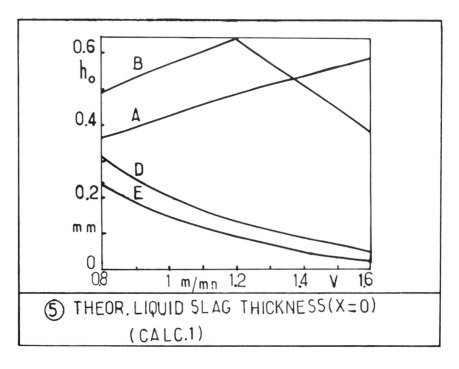

⑤ THEOR. LIQUID SLAG THICKNESS (X=0)
(CALC.1)

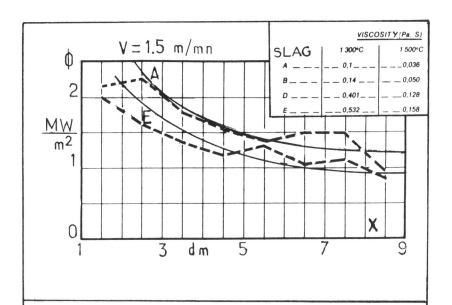

V = 1.5 m/mn

| SLAG | VISCOSITY (Pa. S) | |
	1 300°C	1 500°C
A	0,1	0,036
B	0,14	0,050
D	0,401	0,128
E	0,532	0,158

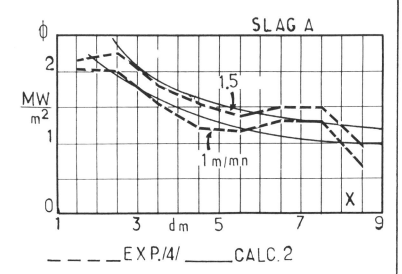

SLAG A

_ _ _ _ _ E X P. /4/ _____ CALC. 2

⑥ THEORETICAL AND EXPERIMENTAL
INFLUENCE OF SPEED AND VISCOSITY
ON THE HEAT FLUX PROFILE

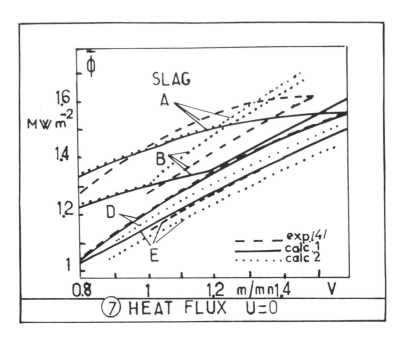

⑦ HEAT FLUX   U=0

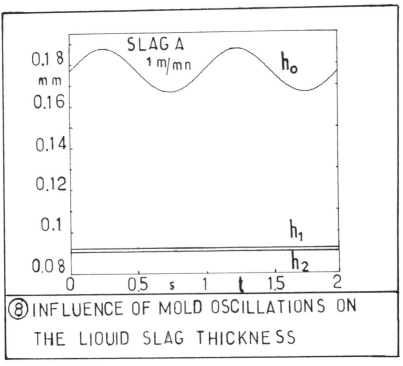

⑧ INFLUENCE OF MOLD OSCILLATIONS ON

THE LIQUID SLAG THICKNESS

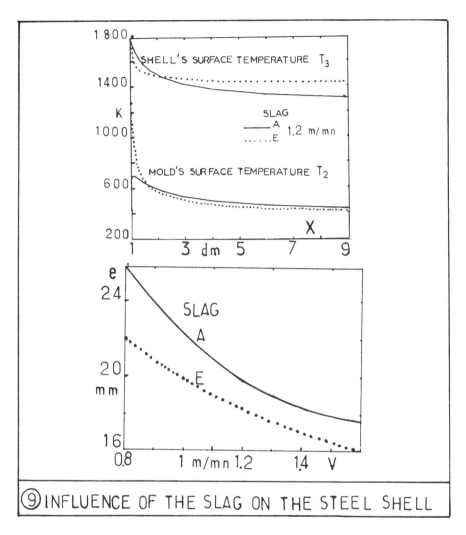

⑨ INFLUENCE OF THE SLAG ON THE STEEL SHELL

SLAG	CALC. 1		CALC. 2	
	V_c m/mn	h_o^M mm	V_c m/mn	h_o^M mm
A	1.77	0.63	1.18	0.48
B	1.25	0.66	1.	0.56
D	0.48	0.87	0.53	0.93
E	0.38	0.96	0.45	1.07

TABLE 1 OPTIMAL SPEED ($Q_L^M = Q_F^M$)

ENERGY SAVINGS ACHIEVED BY HOT SHAKEOUT AND HEAT TREATMENTS OF CASTINGS: APPLICATION TO SG CAST IRON

C. Bak and R. Bellocci
Centre de Recherches de Pont-à-Mousson, B.P. 28, F-54700 Pont-à-Mousson

J. M. Schissler and C. J. Saverna
Institut National Polytechnique de Lorraine,
L. A. no 159 – Parc de Saurupt, F-54042 Nancy Cedex

Summary

Obtaining a controlled matrix structure in SG Cast Iron parts requires
heat treatments. In order to save energy during this heat treatment
the elimination of the re-heating step was considered throuqt the hot
shakeout of the parts in the autenite temperature range (i.e. around
1000°C) directly followed by the thermal cycle.
This study has demonstrated the feasibility of the hot shakeout of
sand castings. It is possible to carry on austenitic holdings (homogenizing, annealing), right after the hot shakeout and all matrices
can be produced (by continuous cooling or austempering) just as with
conventional heat treatments.
The mechanical properties measured are close to or sometimes much
better (e.g. pearlitic matrix) than those obtained through classical
treatments.
With hot shakeout an increase in hardenability was observed, which
can be valued in the production of pearlitic or bainitic matrices,
and which can result in the saving of expensive raw materials
(alloying additions).
This technique applies to mass productions on specific equipment
enabling continuous heat treatment.

1. INTRODUCTION

Under the pressure of competition between the various materials (cast
iron, cast steel, forged steel, aluminium), one of the present trends
developing in mechanical properties requirements which can only be
attained through the control of the matrix structure.
    In the general case of a classical production, the matrix consti-
tuents, after the cooling down of sand castings, are ferrite pearlite and
graphite. Amounts of ferrite and pearlite depend on both the thickness of
the casting and the chemical composition of the cast iron. In most cases,
the achievement of a given structure starting from this as cast state
requires the reheating of the part to a high temperature in order to aute-
nitize the whole volume of the part. This process, together with the
controlled cooling which produces the desired structural transformation,
constitute the basic heat treatment of cast iron.
    It should be noticed however that the heat treatment of casting,
which aims at improving the mechanical properties of the alloy, cannot be
just considered a simple adjustment from classical heat treatments used
for wrought alloys. Factors against such a parallel are structural and
technological. A casting has a chemically heterogeneous structure which
reflects its solidification history. Moreover it requires a shakeout step,
at a temperature close to room temperature, prior to any reheating.
    In order to partially or wholy save the energy consumption that repre-
sents the heating phase of parts, a new process has been considered. This
one consists in the hot shakeout of parts in the austenitic range (between
900°C and 1000°C) and in subjecting these to the controlled cooling appropriate for obtaining the desired structural transformation (ferritic,

pearlitic or bainitic). This new technique is called heat treatment or thermal cycle with energy saving, as opposed to conventional heat treatments or thermal cycles.

The attainment of the objective for this work, represented by the proof of energy savings obtained be means of a non conventional heat treatment, depends on the feasibility of the hot shakeout operation on one hand, and on the non alteration of mechanical and geometrical properties of parts by this hot shakeout on the other hand.

As a first step, the work was focused on the improvement of high temperature shakeout of sand castings.

In the second place, this phase was followed be the identification and determination of all experimental parameters to be checked in the perspective of a subsequent comparative study. This has led to the definition of conventional thermal cycles and of energy saving thermal cycles applied on previously selected test parts. The results obtained at the end of a very large comparative study were transposed to the case of a real part, in order to set up bases for the research of an appropriate industrial technology.

2. METHODS AND INVESTIGATIONS

The comparative study was carried out from 2 cylindrical specimens with different massiveness in order to predict the bahaviour of a part with variable cross section subjected to an energy saving heat treatment. The various heat treatments were carried out in an installation comprising fluid bed furnaces, whichever was the temperature. Fluidized beds are very homogeneous temperature-wise and very flexible, and enable a good reproducibility of heat exchanges during austempering.

Each of the 3 following matrices : ferrite, pearlite or bainite, could be obtained owing to the application of 5 different thermal cycles, called A, B, C, D, E on figure 1. These were 3 energy saving thermal cycles (A, B, C). and 2 conventional cycles (D, E).

The course of the thermal cycles was traked by thermal analysis carried out 2 mm below the surface and in the core of the specimens. Classical means of investigation (optical microscope, microprobe, X-rayon ....) were used for a complete structural study. Mechanical properties (UTS, YS, elongation, KV , HB) were tested after each cycle for all 3 structures considered. In the case of thicker specimens (80 mm D.) case and core properties were both determined.

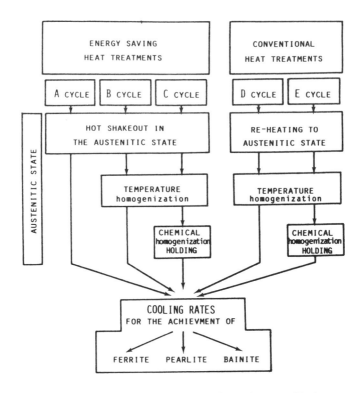

Figure 1 - Steps of the 5 thermal cycles studied

3. MAIN RESULTS

Some essential points were brought out during this research, some being confirmations necessary for the working base and others being new results.

3.1 Feasibility condition for the hot shakeout process

The heat treatment of castings after hot shakeout is first of all bound with the obtaining of a clean casting skin in the case of pouring in a sand mould. Moreover this result should be reached in a very short time, without the risk of deformation or marking of the parts.

Among conventional moulding techniques, only the chemically bound sands are suitable for this type of application. The castings may be carried out in snap flask moulds, but in considering the high cost and mechanical strength of this sand, the casting in shell mould seems better adapted.

The combination of hot shakeout and new foundry process as the V process or the casting on polystyrene lost-pattern, which use a sand without binder, is especially promising in this field.

3.2 Heat treatment achievable after hot shakeout

Until now, in some productions of cast iron parts, the use of a shakeout in the temperature range of 750-650 °C had only for object to ensure the obtaining of more or less fine pearlitic matrix.

The viewing of heat treatments described in figure 1 shows that the obtaining of all matrices is possible after hot shakeout, by adapting the colling rate (continuous coolings or austempering) as in the case of conventional heat treatments. Besides, it is possible after hot shakeout to proceed to isothermal holdings in the austenitic field ; thermal or chemical homogenizing holding, annealing, etc....

3.3. Level of energy savings attainable by heat treatment after hot shakeout

- Case of heat treatments in the austenitic field In order to quantify the energy consumptions due to the use of heat treatments in the austenitic field, treatments corresponding to thermal cycles A to E in figure 1, we have considered a plant including a gas furnace the all thermal characteristics of which are known (1).

We have supposed that the charge of the furnace, charge of 190 kg, is constituted by parts similar to our specimens, 80 mm diameter, on which we have applied the thermal cycles marked from A to E.

For each thermal cycle, the knowledge of different treatment phases (initial temperature, holding temperature in the austenitic field, time of temperature increase phase and holding time) and of different powers required for temperature increase and for temperature holding, have allowed to evaluate the energy consumptions (in MJ) relative to each of phases (table I).

In this definite case, the whole energy consumptions required for the obtaining of the austenitic phase according to the different thermal cycles are entered in the last line of table I. By taking as a reference the thermal cycle E, which is the austenizing cycle consuming the most energy, and by giving it the coefficient 100, the energy consumptions relative to each high temperature cycle evolve as shown in table II.

gas furnace, charge of 190 kg constituted by 80 mm.D rurners	A	B	C	D	E
	Energy saving cycle with shakeout at 1000°C			Conventional cycle with reheating	
Initial temperature	1000°C	1000°C	1000°C	20°C	20°C
Holding temperature in austenitic phase	/	1000°C	1000°C	1000°C	1000°C
Time of temperature increase phase	/	/	/	27 mn	27 mn
Power required for temperature increase	/	/	/	188 kW	188 kW
Q1 : Energy consumed in temperature increase phase	OMJ	OMJ	OMJ	304 MJ	304 MJ
Time of holding phase at 1000°C	/	20 mn	80 mn	20 mn	80 mn
Power required for holding phase at 1000°C	/	78 kW	78 kW	78 kW	78 kW
Q2 : Energy consumed in temperature holding phase	OMJ	93 MJ	374 MJ	93 MJ	374 MJ
Q1 + Q2 : Energy consumption required for obtaining austenitic phase according to the different thermal cycles	OMJ	93 MJ	374 MJ	397 MJ	678 MJ

Tableau I

	A	B	C	D	E
	Energy saving cycle with shakeout at 1000°C			Conventional cycle with reheating	
Energy saving compared in function of heat treatment in the austenitic field	0	14	56	58	100

Tableau II

3.4 Development of mechanical properties after hot shakeout

Generally, whatever may be the heat treatment mode, conventional or with energy saving, and whatever may be the thermal cycle, the tensile strength (R), the yield strength (Re 0,2 %) ant the hardness (HB) increase when the solidification structure of cast iron becomes finer (core from 80 mm dia to 18 mm dia). In parallel, the elongation (A) and the impact strength (kV2) have a tendency to lightly decrease.

In the case of ferrite cas irons, obtained at 700°C by austempering from the temperature of 1000°C, the level of mechanical properties between the energy saving thermal cycles and the conventional thermal cycles is very close (tableau II). However, the transition temperature, fairly higher in the case of energy saving thermal cycle, is decreasing as a function of the holding time in austenitic phase.

- The pearlitic cas irons, obtained bu quenching from 1000°C in a fluidized bed a room temperature, show a more pronouced particularity (table IV). The tensile strength (R), the elastic limit (Re 0.2 %) and the hardness (HB) obtained after energy saving thermal cycles increase for a constant elongation. In particular, these mechanical properties measured in the core of runners with 80 mm dia show an improvement of 25 % with regard to those measured after conventional cycles. For massive parts, the mechanical properties obtained after hot shakeout seem to show an optimum for the use a thermal cycle including a holding time of aroud 30 to 40 minutes at 1000°C (cycle B). With respect to the thinner parts, still after hot shakeout, the optimum would be obtained at the end of a temperature holding higher than or equal to 1 hour. This could be experimentally verified on parts.

- The mechanical properties of a 2.5 % Ni and 0.5 % Mo bainitic cast iron obtained at 360°C after austempering from 1000°C have been observed only on the 18 mm dia specimens. The values measured in the massive parts (80 mm dia) were disturbed by the presence of porosities bound with the addition of alloy elements.

A certain development is nevertheless appearing. Except for the hardness, all mechanical properties are optimal for the conventional heat treatment (table V). Notwitshtandig, after hot shakeout and holding time at 1000°C for 1 hour (cycle C), the mechanical properties observed are very close from the on observed after conventional heat treatment. The difference recorded is ranging about 2 % for the tensile and elongation.

All these tests let appear that in a spheroidal graphite cast iron, whatever may be the matrix studied, the working of an energy saving heat treatment through high-temperature shakeout allows the achievement mechanical properties very closed and, in some cases, higher (pearlitic matrix) than those observed at the end of a conventional heat treatment.

TABLE III – Mechanical Properties of SG Cast Iron with a ferritic matrix (unalloyed cast iron)

OA : Outer Area C : Core	R (MPa) Ø 18	R (MPa) Ø 80 OA	R (MPa) Ø 80 C	Re 0,2 (MPa) Ø 18	Re 0,2 (MPa) Ø 80 OA	Re 0,2 (MPa) Ø 80 C	A % Ø 18	A % Ø 80 OA	A % Ø 80 C	KCV (J/cm2) Ø 18	KCV (J/cm2) Ø 80 OA	KCV (J/cm2) Ø 80 C	HB Ø 18	HB Ø 80 OA	HB Ø 80 C
Cycle A	452	438	435	320	325	309	19,5	23,3	21,6	16,2	16,6	15,6	167	168	153
Cycle B	456	443	435	325	329	311	19	20	20	15,8	16,8	16,5	170	161	150
Cycle C	459	441	432	310	332	306	21,5	19,3	20	17,5	18,1	17,9	164	156	145
Cycle D	452	427	425	326	315	302	21,7	23	21,3	16,2	18,5	18,2	150	153	145
Cycle E	442	426	408	310	318	300	19,5	20,6	19	17,3	17,3	16,6	150	157	131

TABLE IV – Mechanical Properties of SG Cast Iron with a pearlitic matrix (unalloyed cast iron)

OA : Outer Area C : Core	R (MPa) Ø 18	R (MPa) Ø 80 OA	R (MPa) Ø 80 C	Re 0,2 (MPa) Ø 18	Re 0,2 (MPa) Ø 80 OA	Re 0,2 (MPa) Ø 80 C	A % Ø 18	A % Ø 80 OA	A % Ø 80 C	KCV (J/cm2) Ø 18	KCV (J/cm2) Ø 80 OA	KCV (J/cm2) Ø 80 C	HB Ø 18	HB Ø 80 OA	HB Ø 80 C
Cycle A	1060	1006	902	780	678	606	1,7	6	5,7	2,98	2,70	4,62	363	330	313
Cycle B	1204	1042	947	840	715	653	2,8	5,3	5	3,27	2,78	2,64	360	350	315
Cycle C	*	986	822	*	667	593	*	5	6		3,72	3,37	522	313	290
Cycle D	1078	713	658	684	425	424	4	7,5	5,7	4,05	5,48	5,58	309	235	230
Cycle E	1090	891	752	744	577	515	1,25	6,3	6	4,36	4,66	4,30	306	270	250

* partially martensitic matrix

TABLE V – Mechanical Properties of SG Cast Iron with a bainitic matrix

(COMPOSITION : 3,45 % C – 2,5 % Si – 2,45 % Ni – 0,46 % Mo – 0,050 % Mg)

OA : Outer Area C : core	R (MPa) Ø 18	R (MPa) Ø 80 * OA	R (MPa) Ø 80 * C	Re 0,2 (MPa) Ø 18	Re 0,2 (MPa) Ø 80 * OA	Re 0,2 (MPa) Ø 80 * C	A % Ø 18	A % Ø 80 * OA	A % Ø 80 * C	KCV (J/cm2) Ø 18	KCV (J/cm2) Ø 80 OA	KCV (J/cm2) Ø 80 C	HB Ø 18	HB Ø 80 * OA	HB Ø 80 * C
Cycle A	994			744			6,5			6,1	6,9	7,2	345	277	
Cycle B	994			684			6,9			7,5	6,5	7,1	335	321	
Cycle C	1024			705			8			10,5	6,8	7,5	340	307	
Cycle D	1042			757			8,2			9,3	7,5	8,9	308	279	
Cycle E	1028			678			9			10,8	7,7	8,5	315	268	

* properties lowered by the presence of porosity

3.5 Evolution of hardenability after hot shakeout

The hot shakeout involves an improvement of hardenability for ductile cast iron. This characteristic were revealed in several ways (figure 2).

We have plotted in figure 3 the energy consumed in austenitic phase for each of thermal cycles depending on the hardenability (% of martensite recorded at half radius of 80 mm dia runners) and in figure 4 the energy consumed in austenitic phase depending on the tensile strength (R) measured on the 80 mm dia pearlitic runners. Figure 2a represents the martensite percentage recorded at half-radius and at half-height for 80 mm dia specimens water-quenched after the use of different thermal cycles marked A to E, depending on the holding time at 1000°C.

In parallel, figure 2b represents, always as a function of the holding time at 1000°C and of thermal cycles with high temperature A to E, the hardening height measured from the end of a 18 mm dia specimen quenched in fluidized bed at 20°C.

The case of thermal cycle A applied to a 80 mm dia specimen shows a behaviour similar to the conventional thermal cycle marked D. Except for this case, the hardenability is clearly higher for the thermal cycles used after hot shakeout. At the end of this last one, the hardenability increases with the holding time in austenitic phase. However, for more massive parts, there is an optimum holding time (40 min in our case) beyond which this hardenability decreases (figure 2a). This is furthermore corresponding to the evolutions of mechanical properties noted on pearlitic matrices. In the same context, the evolution of hardenability between the conventional thermal cycles D and E is practically nil.

All these phenomena are bound with the existence of 2 parameters : the evolution of segregations during the thermal cycles on the one hand and the size of austenitic grain on the other hand.

3.5.1 Evolution of segregations

After solidification of cast iron and partitioning of alloy elements, we note the existence of a very sharp concentration profile of elements in the area of eutectic cell joint. Thereby, at a first time, the hardenability remains localized at the "peak" level. This hardenability will be extended to the lateral areas only after a high temperature holding time allowing the diffusion of segregated elements. In parallel will take place a progressive decrease of concentration for elements initially located at cell joint. The hardenability will remain acquired as long as the required minimum level of alloy elements will be maintened. On this side of this level the areas involved would be no more hardenable. This mechanism described in figure 5 is perfectly illustrated be the curve ABC'C of figure 2a.

3.5.2 Size of austenitic grain

Indirect observations show that the size of native austenitic grain directly derived from the solidification is clearly higher tham the size of regenerated austenitic grain obtained by heating from a ferrito-pearlitic structure. It is perfectly proved that the size of austenitic grain has a direct influence on the incubation time of reactions (2). With coarse grains correspond higher incubation times, therefore a higher hardenability.

Both phenomena, independant from each other, which are the evolution of local chemical compositions and the size of austenitic grains, contribute depending on different mechanisms, to the increase of hardenability observed in the case of energy saving thermal cycles.

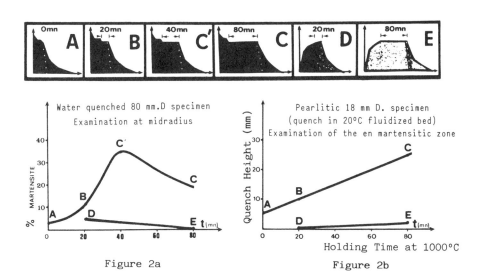

Figure 2a

Figure 2b

Figure 2 - Influence of thermal cycles on the hardenability of SG Cast Iron

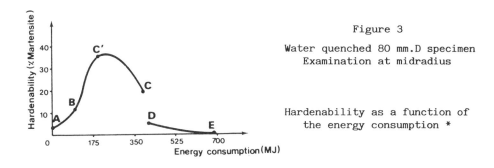

Figure 3

Water quenched 80 mm.D specimen
Examination at midradius

Hardenability as a function of
the energy consumption *

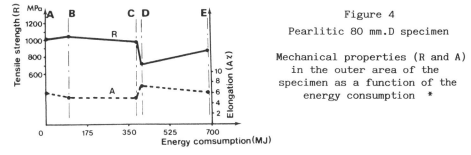

Figure 4

Pearlitic 80 mm.D specimen

Mechanical properties (R and A)
in the outer area of the
specimen as a function of the
energy consumption *

* Energy consumption required fot obtaining the austenitic phase in the
various thermal cycles of Figure 2.

151

The use of a heat treatment after hot shakeout allows then to minimize the addition of alloying elements, which would have been necessary in the case of conventional thermal cycles in order to obtain a similar hardenability. It is a very interesting characteristic for obtaining bainitic and pearlitic matrices.

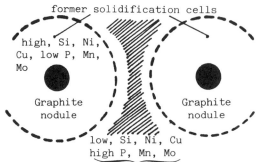

Figure 5a

Segregation of alloying elements in relation with the solidification structure

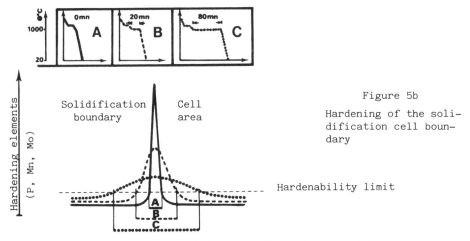

Figure 5b

Hardening of the solidification cell boundary

Figure 5 - Influence of the high temperature thermal cycle on segregations

4. FIELD OF APPLICATION

The heat treatment technique after hot shakeout applies first of all to mass production on highly specialized site. It requires specific and independant installations for transfer of moulds and castings after the pouring as also a hot shakeout equipment adapted to the part and to the moulding technique used. For the latter, the recommended technique is either the shell moulding or the uncombined sand casting. In all cases, the heat treatment after hot shakeout is a continuous heat treatment.

When the pearlitic and bainitic matrices are wanted, the application of this new technique of heat treatment is particularly well adapted.

5. CONCLUSIONS

All this work has allowed to reveal the interest for the use of a heat treatment immediately after the hot shakeout operation.

The feasibility conditions of hot shakeout operation and the main characteristics of cast iron have been investigated after different thermal cycles. Particularly, it has been demonstrated that the use of an energy saving heat treatment allow in all cases to obtain mechanical properties very close and sometimes clearly higher (pearlitic matrix) than the one observed after a conventional heat treatment.

This new process shows not only a certain interest at the level of energy savings, but it also shows an essential interest at the level of consequences which result from this on the metal. After hot shakeout, we note a considerable increase of cast iron hardenability. This characteristic allows to consider the minimization of allowing element addition in the cast iron ; this raw materials saving adds to the existing energy saving. The increase of hardenability has been explained at the scientific level and this new heat treatment technique finds an application particularly well adapted for the obtaining of matrices with hardening structure.

Finally, the use of heat treatment technique after hot shakeout has shown that it applied to mass productions, moulded in chemically bound sand (shell) or in uncombined sand, and that it requires automatized and specific installations which allow the continuous heat treatment.

REFERENCES

1. PRINCE, J., MINGAUD, J.L., SOLA, J. (1979). Paramètres influençant le bilan énergétique des fours en exploitation. Traitement Thermique n° 134, p. 43 à 45.
2. CONSTANT, A. et HENRY. (1982). Les principes de base du traitement thermique des aciers. Traitement Thermique, n° 164, p. 10.

REDUCTION IN ENERGY REQUIREMENTS FOR CONVERTING LIQUID ALUMINIUM TO SEMI-FABRICATED ROLLED PRODUCTS

T. J. Dennis

The British Aluminium Company plc Technical Department
Chalfont Park, Gerrards Cross, Bucks. SL9 OQB, U.K.

Summary

Examination of the conventional DC casting-hot rolling route for the production of semi-fabricated rolled products from liquid aluminium has confirmed that it is an energy intensive process. The alternative processing routes of thin strip casting should consume less energy because they dispense with the scalping. preheating and hot rolling operations of the conventional route.

A total energy audit of six typical rolled products produced by both routes was undertaken to determine the potential energy savings. These audits included the effect on energy of scrap generated irrecoverable metal losses and yields for each product in addition to the process energy per tonne at each stage of manufacture.

It was confirmed that product energy savings of up to 37% were possible using thin strip casting methods. These savings were less than expected because of increased cold mill passes and long high temperature homogenising anneals which partially offset the energy gains obtained from the processes eliminated.

The energy requirements of both processing routes for all six products selected were related to a typical product mix of 40.000 tonnes per annum. It was established that the potential energy saving using the thin strip casting route to achieve this output would be approximately 25% or 0.316×10^6 GJ per annum.

The annual energy savings for roll cast products amounting to 90% of the mix chosen was 0.246×10^6 GJ. The savings related to the 1982 total output of these products in the UK would have been 1.052×10^6 GJ and in the EEC 9.738×10^6 GJ.

A further saving on capital plant expenditure compared with that required for producing 36.000 tonnes per annum by the conventional route was calculated to be £45M

1 Introduction

1.1 The bulk of the semi-fabricated rolled products manufactured by the aluminium industry in the past has been produced by the conventional DC casting-hot rolling process. The apparently high energy requirement associated with this route compared with the other alternative processes for the conversion of liquid aluminium to rolled products initiated this detailed assessment of the potential energy savings.

Five alternative processes were considered worthwhile investigating. These were continuous thin strip casting using (1) roll caster (2) block mould caster (3) fixed mould caster (4) spray casting-rolling and (5)

pellet compacting by rolling. The first of these processes is well
established on a production basis with machines manufactured by Scal
Engineering. Hunter Engineering and Alusuisse installed throughout the
world. The four other processes. however. are not used extensively and
the processes concerned must be fully investigated before their consideration for bulk production.

From the point of view of reduced energy consumption these alternative
manufacturing routes are particularly attractive because they eliminate the
energy intensive scalping. preheating and hot rolling processes of the conventional route. Figure 1. illustrates the possible reduction in the
number of processes.

In addition to reducing the energy input because of a reduction in
manufacturing processes. however. the alternative methods should give rise
to less scrap and. therefore. less scrap remelting should be required per
tonne of product produced. Scrap remelting also gives rise to increased
melt losses which can be considerable for certain types of scrap such as
sawing swarf and scalpings particularly if associated with the higher
magnesium aluminium alloys.

To establish the amount of energy required to produce a tonne of a
given product. therefore. consideration must be given not only to the
energy input at each stage of manufacture in the process used. but also
the energy requirement for remelting scrap and replacing irrecoverable
metal

The amount of scrap generated and melt losses incurred are directly
related to the number of processing stages. the type of scrap produced and
the aluminium alloys and tempers involved.

1 2 For the purpose of the investigation six rolled products were considered covering a typical range of alloys tempers and forms. These were
1200 soft temper and 3003 H24 temper foilstock coil used for thin gauge
foil and container foil respectively. 1200 H14 and 5251 H34 temper sheet.
3103 H18 corrugated S12 profiled sheet and 2024 T3 clad sheet.

The following work programme was undertaken:
(a) Examination of the conventional DC casting-hot rolling method of
production and the alternative methods of continuous thin strip casting
using moving moulds (roll and block) fixed horizontal mould. spray
casting-rolling and pellet compacting techniques.
(b) Establishment of equipment used. capital costs and processing details
of both the DC casting-hot rolling and continuous thin strip casting
methods of production for the six products chosen for investigation.
(c) Determination of yields. scrap generated and melt losses incurred in
both the DC casting-hot rolling and thin strip casting methods of manufacture for the six products specified.
(d) Determination of the total energy input of the DC casting-hot rolling
and appropriate thin strip casting methods of production for each stage of
processing of the products concerned.
(e) Obtain samples of products produced by the thin strip casting process
for simulated cold rolling and property determination to establish the
necessity for additional heat treatment or other operations.

2. Examination of the DC casting-hot rolling and thin strip casting
methods of manufacture
The considerable differences in plant and energy requirements of the
conventional and non conventional routes for producing semi-fabricated
products from liquid aluminium are best seen by comparing the DC casting-
hot rolling process with the established roll caster method of thin strip
casting.

155

The roll caster method was chosen in preference to the other alternative methods because it was established on a production basis and capable of producing 6mm thick strip in the first five alloys of the typical product mix detailed in 1.2. The remaining product 2024 clad T3 sheet cannot to date be produced on a production basis by any process other than the conventional DC casting-hot rolling method. It is thought likely that the spray casting-rolling technique could probably be developed for this product and. therefore. a detailed examination of the energy requirements of this process was also undertaken.

2.1 Description of DC casting-hot rolling process
(a) Melting and casting - Rolling blocks for this process are either cast at a smelter or at the plant producing the semi-fabricated rolled product.
    In the case of the six products chosen for this investigation. the 1200 and 3103 alloys are cast at a smelter and the 3003. 5251 and 2024 alloys at the casting shop of the rolling mill plant concerned.
    The energy benefit of casting at the smelter is obvious because liquid metal from the reduction cells can be used for part of the charge compared with 100% solid ingot and scrap which has to be remelted at the rolling mill. The resultant energy saving. therefore. is considerable using liquid smelter metal. but will apply to both conventional and non conventional methods of processing and in both cases only a holding furnace is required.
    Solid scrap ingot and hardeners. however. constitute the charge at the rolling mill casting shops and it is customary to use an oil fired melting furnace for converting the solids to liquid metal and alloying to the specification required. Degassing and cleaning of the metal is achieved by using a BACO fumeless in line degassing unit between the holder and DC casting machine. This unit reduces the hydrogen content of the metal to an acceptable level and also removes inclusions. To maintain the correct casting temperature of the metal. however. it is also necessary to heat this unit using gas burners.
    Metal is then fed via launders into the vertical moulds of the semi-continuous casting machines and casting carried out at the rate of two to five blocks at a time depending upon the capacity of the filtering equipment and the size of the blocks being cast. Blocks of 1200. 3003 and 3103 alloys are cast 510mm thick. but 5251 and 2024 alloys are cast 410mm thick. Blocks cast at the smelter are cast two in the length and those at the rolling mill casting shop in single lengths.
(b) Scalping - If required by the end product concerned cast blocks from both smelter and rolling mill sources are machined on their two major surfaces to remove casting imperfections and undesirable structure.
(c) Preheating - The next process in the DC casting-hot rolling route is preheating prior to hot rolling. Rolling blocks are charged into a batch pusher type gas fired preheating furnace. These furnaces are capable of heating 25 blocks each of 6 tonne weight from room temperature to 610°C and also to maintain that temperature. The temperature used and the "soak" times depend upon the products concerned. Deep drawing 3003 material requiring fine grain size high elongation values and good temper letting down properties in the final foil. have to be homogenised for long periods at a high temperature. The similar European alloy 3103 used for profiled cladding sheet. however. only has to be heated to the hot rolling temperature to give the properties required for building products.
(d) Hot breakdown mill rolling - After preheating the rolling blocks are discharged at the required rolling temperature on to the hot line tables

prior to breakdown rolling in a two high single stand 3.000H.P. reversing mill. This mill reduces the block thickness to 25mm or thinner plate in 9 to 20 passes. depending upon the alloy and the entry and exit thickness required at the hot strip mill.

The outgoing plate temperature from this breakdown mill can vary from 450 to 320°C depending upon the product concerned

The next operation in the hot line is to shear the nose and tail end scrap of the hot rolled blank. This squares the end of the blank for subsequent rolling at the hot strip mill. but also removes laminated metal. The hot rolled and sheared blank can be edge trimmed if necessary at the entry trimmer of the hot strip mill. but this was only found necessary for 5251 and 2024 alloys.

(e) Hot strip mill rolling - The final hot rolling process is carried out in a three stand. four high. tandem hot strip mill powered by 4.000H.P. motors on each stand. This mill reduces the blank to thicknesses of from 4.0 to 2.5mm depending upon the alloy and thickness of the final coil and sheet product. If necessary the hot rolled coil can be further edge trimmed before coiling on a drum mandrel using a steel belt wrapper

The hot rolled coil product for the purpose of this investigation can be compared directly with the products of alternative continuous strip casting processes. Subsequent processing to achieve the final product form temper and dimensions. therefore. will be similar for materials from both processes except for additional cold rolling passes and heat treatment operations required for the thicker strip cast product.

2.2 The roll caster thin strip casting process

The initial processes for melting and holding for each of the products concerned are similar to those described for the conventional route. This process also requires the use of a system for cleaning and degassing the metal and this can be of the BACO fumeless in line degasser type.

The casting process is entirely different. however. and requires strict control of temperature to $\pm$ 5°C of the required casting temperature.

Details of this method of production were obtained by witnessing the operation of a Scal 3C Jumbo caster (see Figure 2). In this process liquid metal of the alloy concerned is transferred via a launder to a refractory nozzle extending the full width of the coil to be cast and placed immediately in front and between two internally water cooled rolls positioned one above the other (see Figure 3) De-mineralised water was used for this purpose and the energy content of obtaining this was included in the audit.

The water cooled rolls were 960mm in diameter and over 2.000mm long to permit the casting of this width strip down to 6.0mm thickness. although production had been standardised at 8.0mm thickness for the casting witnessed. The large diameter rolls and efficient internal water cooling permitted casting speeds of 1.4m per minute or a weight of 2.7 tonnes per hour to be achieved when casting 1200 alloy 1.500mm wide by 8.0mm thick. Metal solidification in the roll gap was extremely rapid (10mm per second) giving rise to a super saturated solid solution of the alloy concerned and different property characteristics from those of the same alloy produced by the DC casting.

The metal solidified prior to the minimum roll gap and a hot reduction of up to 40% was possible before the strip left the caster. The rolls and caster. therefore. were designed to permit this deformation over a wide range of alloys.

Lubrication of the rolls during casting was brought about by two traversing lubricators which automatically sprayed graphite suspended in water along the roll length.

The issuing cast strip controlled to close thickness tolerances was at a temperature of approximately 380°C and passed through an upcut shear (for shearing the required coil weight) to a tight drum upcoiler. Coils are removed before the leading edge of the next coil reaches the coiler.

All of the five products selected are being regularly produced using this method. but as the alloy content of the alloys increases. the casting speeds have to be reduced. The wider solidification range of 5251 alloy containing 2.25% magnesium necessitates using 50% of the casting speed of 1200 alloy of low alloy content.

2.3 Spray casting-rolling process

The wide solidification range of 2024 alloy would reduce the casting speed of the roll caster process to an unacceptable level. In view of this the spray casting process. although not used for producing 2024 clad material on a production basis. shows considerable potential.

A processing method using the spray casting technique was. therefore. formulated to give an end product of 2024 alloy clad on each side with 99.5% purity alloy. 1.25 metres wide by 2.0mm thick. This product could then be used as a reroll for producing 1.0mm thick T3 sheet (See Figure 4)

The first operation envisaged would be to first spray cladding on the belt to give 5% of the total thickness and then to spray core 2024 alloy followed by a further cladding layer of 5% to give a total thickness of 2mm. Such an arrangement could be fed by two 7.5 tonne electric channel furnaces working alternatively and capable of tilting to deliver a constant rate of metal. These furnaces would be fed by an oil fired 20 tonne reverberatory furnace. A one tonne coreless induction furnace could provide sufficient material for the 5% cladding required and this furnace would feed two electric resistance holding furnaces of 0.5 tonne capacity.

For the width of material 1.25 metres and deposition rate of 5 tonnes per hour a set of three sprays for each layer will be required each spray covering one third of the width of the coating. The coating would be deposited on a belt passing over and driven by water cooled rollers. Thickness will be set by the belt speed which will be 0.145 metres per second for a 3mm deposit. One major drawback with this method is the necessity to overspray at least 10% of the total width to ensure uniformity of thickness in the resulting reroll after hot rolling. giving rise to large quantities of scrap. The strip would be over 90% dense at this stage prior to feeding into a hot rolling mill for consolidation and reduction to 2mm coils.

3. Determination of yields. scrap generated and melt losses incurred

It will be seen from the description of the conventional and non conventional routes in 2.0 for six selected products that the DC casting-hot rolling process produces a thinner reroll product than the roll caster method for the five alloys produced by this route. The thicker strip cast material necessitates at least one and up to three additional cold rolling passes with increased energy consumption. scrap arisings and melt losses thus partially offsetting the energy savings of eliminating scalping. pre-heating and hot rolling of the conventional process.

After cold rolling the roll caster product to the same gauge as the hot rolled product. subsequent processing is mainly the same for the products selected. However. in the case of alloys that have to undergo critical forming operations such as 3003 container foil the metallurgical investigation associated with this contract confirmed that it is necessary to introduce an homogenising anneal to produce the required properties in the roll cast product.

In the case of spray casting. the reroll 2024 clad product is 2.0mm in thickness compared with the 5.00mm thickness of the hot rolled product and therefore requires less cold mill passes to achieve the final sheet thickness.

Complete processing schedules were compiled. therefore. for the six products selected for both the DC casting-hot rolling and thin strip casting methods of production. Determination of the scrap generated at each manufacturing stage and melt losses incurred on remelting. enabled the yields for each product by the different processing routes to be calculated.

The yields for each of the six products by conventional and non conventional routes for comparison purposes were calculated together with the scrap generated and melt losses incurred per tonne of product produced.

These findings applied to a typical product mix of 40.000 tonnes of the six products selected. confirmed an improvement in yield of 7.5% using the thin strip casting routes giving a reduction in scrap and melt losses of 7230 tonnes per annum.

4. Determination of the energy input at each stage of manufacture
4.1 DC casting-hot rolling route

Using improved metering equipment for oil. gas and electricity consumption at the smelter and rolling mill plant a comprehensive energy audit of all the processes used in the production of the six selected products was carried out.

The work involved recording the actual energy consumption as the products concerned were being processed through the individual items of plant in order to obtain the energy expended per tonne of product produced.

It was then possible to determine from these figures. using the previously calculated yields for each of the products concerned. the total process energy per tonne of end product produced.

In addition. of course. the energy associated with irrecoverable metal losses and the induction melting of swarf and scalpings as a separate operation also had to be included in the total energy audit.

The energy required to replace metal irretrievably lost was reassessed with the experience of modern smelter technology and found to be 243 GJ per tonne.

4.2 Thin strip casting routes
(a) Roll caster route - This route was used for the following products:-
1200 soft temper foilstock. 3003 H24 temper foilstock. 1200 H14 sheet. 3103 H18 profiled sheet and 5251 H34 sheet. Discussions with the equipment manufacturers which included both Hunter and Scal Engineering together with the purchase and processing of three continuous strip cast coils to foil-stock. permitted the determination of the energy requirements of this method of processing for each of the products concerned.

The energy of the additional cold rolling passes necessitated by the thicker gauge of the rolled cast products compared with the hot rolled thickness of the conventional process was also calculated. In the case of 3003 alloy it was also necessary to include the energy of an homogenising anneal of the coil after roll casting to prevent coarse grain developing on subsequent annealing. For the same reason it was not possible to anneal 1200 material until it had received at least 30% cold work after casting.

The process energy and metal loss replacement energy associated with the production of the five products selected. were calculated and included in Table I for comparison with the DC casting-hot rolling route.

159

It will be seen that the reduction in energy compared with the conventional route extended from 27 to over 37% for all the products except 3003 which only gave an 8.12% improvement for the reasons given above.
(b) <u>Spray casting-rolling route</u> - This method of processing has not been used on a production basis for producing 2024 clad sheet. It was felt. however, that it's ability to thin strip cast alloys having a wide solidification range and the possibility of spray casting the cladding. should be investigated in view of the considerable energy consumption of the conventional method of producing this product.

In view of the considerable experience of Swansea University College staff in the use of the spray cast process. particularly Professor A R E Singer. who developed the method. it was agreed that they should carry out an energy audit of the hypothetical process advanced by the writer. This was satisfactorily completed and enabled the energy consumption of using this method for the production of 2024 clad T3 sheet to be calculated for comparison with that of the DC casting-hot rolling method.

The large reduction in process energy of approximately 30%. however. was considerably offset and reduced to 16.1% by the large metal loss included in the energy audit. This was due primarily to the metal loss associated with 10% overspray which also increased the scrap generated. In addition. the melt loss of the melting and holding operation also seemed excessive at 5% and 2% respectively for 2024 and 99.5% purity alloys particularly in view of the fact that induction furnaces were proposed for holding and melting of cladding material. Development of the process should enable a considerable reduction in these losses to be achieved with further energy savings.

4.3 Energy savings applied to a typical product mix

The energy savings per tonne of product produced were applied to a typical rolling mill product mix of 40.000 tonnes per annum. It was established that the use of the thin strip casting routes could give rise to a total potential energy saving of approximately 25% or 3 million therms per annum compared with the DC casting-hot rolling route. (See Table I)

5. Comparison of Capital Equipment costs for conventional and continuous strip casting processes

A comparison of capital equipment cost for producing reroll coil by conventional and non conventional methods need only consider the differences in cost of scalping preheating and hot rolling equipment for the former process and the cost of the number of roll casters needed to match its output.

The cost of melting equipment will be the same in both cases. but an homogenising furnace will be required to produce similar properties in the roll cast 3003 foilstock for containers as those obtained by the conventional method. In addition the cost of buildings required to house the respective plant must be considered.

It was calculated that four casters would be needed to give 47 422 tonnes of reroll required and to provide adequate maintenance time.

It was established that the conventional method would require £55.5M of equipment and the roll caster method £10.5M giving a saving of at least £45M for the production of equivalent quantities of material.

6. Energy saving of roll caster route related to UK and EEC markets

It was established that for the 36.000 tonnes per annum mix of work selected that the average energy saving per tonne when produced by the roll caster method was <u>6.82 GJ</u> or 0.246×10^6 GJ per annum.

This saving related to the same mix of work for the UK would give rise to a total energy saving of 1.057×10^6 GJ per annum and for the EEC 9.738×10^6 per annum.

7. Conclusions

The main objective of this work was to establish a less energy intensive process than that of DC casting-hot rolling for the conversion of liquid aluminium to semi-fabricated rolled products. The thin strip casting technique achieves this aim and the potential energy savings. together with other significant findings. are as follows:-

7.1 The roll caster thin strip casting process is established for the production of 1200 soft temper and 3003 H24 temper foilstock coil. 1200 H14 temper sheet. 3103 H18 temper profiled sheet and 5251 H34 sheet.

7.2 The spray casting-hot rolling process is proposed for the processing of 2024 T3 clad sheet. but has not yet been developed to the production stage for this product. The process has considerable potential for energy saving. however. and is well worthwhile further development.

7.3 Thin strip casting and subsequent conventional processing can give rise to substantial product energy savings of up to 37% compared with the conventional DC casting-hot rolling method for the products examined.

7.4 The main factors contributing to this reduction in energy are (i) the elimination of the scalping. preheating and hot rolling processes. and (ii) the improved yields and subsequent reduced scrap remelting. giving rise to lower metal losses with corresponding metal replacement energy savings.

7.5 The extent of the energy savings using thin strip casting is reduced by the additional cold rolling passes required by some of the products to achieve the hot rolled thickness of the conventional process. In addition the introduction of continuous strip cast coil homogenising to overcome the metallurgical effects of rapid solidification and achieve the required properties in the final 3003 H24 foilstock. gave a combined reduction in potential energy savings of 3.7%.

7.6 The energy savings of the thin strip casting route when applied to a typical rolling mill product mix of 40.000 tonnes per annum results in a reduction in energy of approximately 25% or 315.517 GJ which is equivalent to 3M therms.

7.7 The energy savings when restricted to the 36.000 tonnes of roll cast products at factory level amount to 0.246×10^6 GJ.

7.8 The UK annual saving for the production of the same products by the roll cast method would be 1.057×10^6 GJ.

7.9 The EEC annual saving for the production of the same products by the roll cast method would be 9.738×10^6 GJ.

7.10 The saving in capital expenditure by using roll casters instead of the conventional hot line route for the production of 36.000 tonnes per annum of rolled products amounts to £45M.

TABLE I   COMPARISON OF TOTAL ENERGY REQUIREMENTS OF DC CASTING/HOT ROLLING AND THIN STRIP CASTING ROUTES FOR AN ANNUAL OUTPUT OF 40.000 TONNES OF SEMI-FABRICATED ROLLED PRODUCTS

Product	Tonnes per Annum	GJ/Tonne		GJ/Annum		Saving	
		DC/ Hot Roll	Thin Strip Cast	DC/ Hot Roll	Thin Strip Cast	GJ per Annum	%
1200 Soft Temper Foilstock	15 000	18.450	11.502	276 750	172 530	104 220	37.66
3003 H24 Temper Foilstock	5 000	22.370	20.554	111 850	102 770	9 080	8.12
1200 H14 Temper Sheet	6 000	20.656	13.629	123 936	81 774	42 162	34.02
3103 H18 Temper Profiled Sheet	5 000	21.843	15.752	109 215	78 760	30 455	27.89
5251 H34 Temper Sheet	5 000	36.842	24.914	184 210	124 570	59 640	32.38
2024 Clad T3 Sheet	4 000	108.417	90.927	433 668	363 708	69 960	16.13
Grand Total	40 000	30.99	23.10	1 239 629	924 112	315 517	25.45

N.B.   1KWH - 0.012 GJ (assumes generating efficiency of 30%)

162

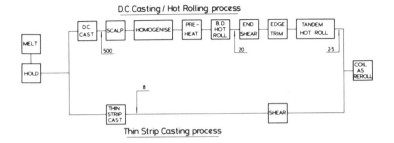

D.C. Casting / Hot Rolling process

Flow diagram comparison of the conventional D.C. casting/hot rolling and thin strip casting routes.

The numbers indicate typical metal thickness in m.m.

FIGURE 1

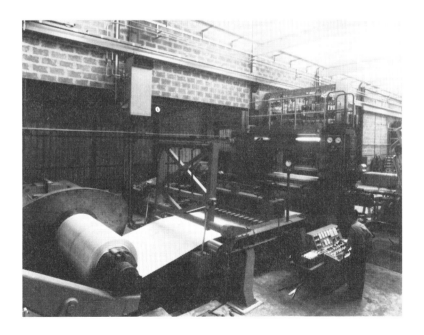

FIGURE 2

163

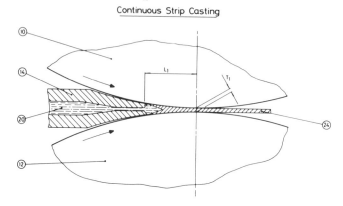

Continuous Strip Casting

10-12	Rolls
14	Feed Nozzle
20	Liquid Metal
24	Cast Strip
L_1	Distance between Nozzle and Roll Gap
T_1	Roll Gap

FIGURE 3

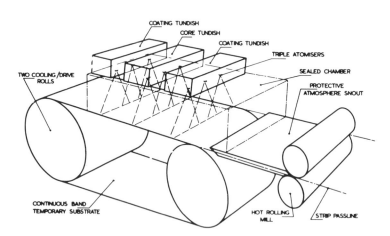

Notional layout of a 3 layer Spray Rolling installation.

FIGURE 4

ENGINEERING WITH ADHESIVES: TESTING AND DESIGN

A. C. Patterson and P. McGeehin

Materials Engineering Centre
AERE Harwell, Didcot, Oxon OX11 ORA, U.K.

Summary

The aim of the work has been to produce new design techniques for joining lightweight materials in the automotive industry. The activities have been jointly funded by the European Commission and a group of 18 companies. Emphasis has been placed on the use of structural adhesives and how to design using this means of fastening.

Two computer programmes have been produced which are for the use of designers. These programmes take account of the extensive yielding of adhesives which is necessary in order to predict the strength of joints. The materials information for use in conjunction with this analysis has not been readily available and test methods have been developed to provide the information.

Characterisation of environmental durability of various adhesives has been undertaken with a range of surface treatments exposed to different levels of humidity and temperature.

A programme of testing on real components has been started to investigate how to link failure predictions to appropriate design standards for fatigued load cases and to focus the work in an applied way.

1. INTRODUCTION

This work has been undertaken in the forum of the Composite-Metal Jointing Working Party which has been sponsored by the European Commission's Energy Conservation R&D Sub-Programme.

The commission is providing 47% of the funding and the balance is obtained from the members of the Working Party, who each pay the same membership fee. There are currently 18 members of the Working Party, summarised in Table I. As can be seen, major European companies in the aerospace, automotive and raw material supply sectors are represented, together with two UK Government Departments (Industry and Defence).

The work is undertaken by the Materials Engineering Centre at Harwell on behalf of the members, and it is managed by four-monthly meetings at which progress and technical difficulties are discussed, and future actions agreed.

2. OBJECTIVE

The central technical thrust of this programme has been to develop proven design procedures for structural joints between composites and metals, giving emphasis to the use of structural adhesives. Joint geometries and materials have been chosen to reflect specific potential applications found in vehicles.

The impact of lightweight composite materials on the automotive industry to date has been modest. This has been largely due to two factors. Firstly, the high cost of both the raw materials and their associated manufacturing techniques and secondly the inability to mesh components into an existing established design concept based on metallic components, particularly where structural joints have to be made. Adhesive bonding technology is important in both of these areas, since new second generation adhesives have enchanced tolerance to the production environment and also much faster cycle times for manufacture. However, the lack of both design methods at the concept or feasibility stage and suitable data for adhesives has hindered their introduction.

This project has approached the problem in three main areas:-

(i) Materials testing - for properties as a function of environmental ageing and surface treatments which provides data for:

(ii) Engineering design studies - which have produced two computer programmes based on continuum mechanics for use in design.

(iii) Component tests - to focus the fundamental work on how it can be applied on real joints and to establish appropriate design criteria.

In addition an evaluation of non-destructive inspection techniques is being carried out with a view to providing a rapid means of indicating production problems on the assembly line.

3. METHODS OF INVESTIGATION

The work programme is divided into four main areas:

3.1 Materials Evaluation

Materials testing underway at present is specifically aimed at providing design data for prediction of ultimate strength, fatigue life, creep resistance and of environmental ageing (time, temperature and humidity). The work has involved developing and improving existing test methods and techniques such as the Thick Adherend Shear Test. Many different techniques have been used and compared for their ability to produce useful data, particularly on resistance to environmental attack of the adhesive joint. The fundamental approach is to consider the adhesive as a material in its own right. Just as with other materials which may be used in a structural sense the characteristic stress/strain relationships are essential in order to predict performance. This is particularly true in view of the fact that most modern adhesives have a non-linear stress/strain characteristic relationship and rely to a large extent on this plasticity to achieve the desired performance.

Adhesives have been selected of various types, namely:
   One and two part epoxide.
   Toughened acrylic.
   Urethane.
   Nitrile phenolic.
   Epoxy film.
In all, ten different adhesives are being studied. The tests
which these adhesives have been subjected to are as follows:

3.1.1 Thick Adherend Shear Test

The thick adherend shear test produces the full non-linear shear
stress/shear strain characteristic which is required for the inelastic
stress analysis. An illustration of the test specimen is shown in
Fig 1. The adherend can be either steel or aluminium since the result
of the test are the properties of the adhesive itself. The use of
steel minimises the error in the test. Ten different adhesives have
been characterised at $-40^{\circ}C$, $20^{\circ}C$, $50^{\circ}C$, $100^{\circ}C$ and $150^{\circ}C$.

Considerable development has been undertaken in optimising this
test which relies on very accurate measurements of distortion across
the bondline. Typical results are shown in Fig 2 which illustrate the
yielding behaviour of an adhesive at different temperatures.

3.1.2 Lap Shear Tests

These tests have been utilised in order to give comparative data
on durability on studies with different adhesives and surface treatments.
It has been recognised that they do not give a good quantitative
information useful in design. Both single and double lap specimens
have been used and a combination of steel, aluminium, CFRP/GRP and 40% E
glass polyester SMC adherends have been studied.

The adhesives under consideration have been tested after
manufacture and again after ageing for three and twelve month periods in
environments of 100%RH at room temperature and an elevated temperature.
Three surface treatments have been examined:

   (i) Aerospace etching surface treatments
   (ii) Abraded finish
   (iii) A contaminated oil smeared surface.

3.1.3 Boeing Wedge Test

The need is clearly present for an accelerated durability test and
the Boeing Wedge Test offers the possibility of going some way towards
this. The geometry of the test is shown in Fig 3: a wedge is driven
between the adherends to produce a crack. The specimen is then
exposed to an environment of 95% RH at $55^{\circ}C$ and the crack growth
monitored as a function of time. Metal adherends are used since they
are more suited to this test and they also exhibit the most severe
interface degradation in moist environments. The use of this test has
been particularly useful in investigation of the use of silane adhesion
promoters.

3.1.4 Impact Peel Tests

Reported work on impact of metallic adhesive specimens has found little change in the strength of the new generation toughened adhesives at high strain rates as compared to static strengths. However, the stress analysis suggests that this may be due to the fact that the adhesive becomes not only stiffer but more brittle at high strain rates and that these two effects counteract each other. This has particular relevance to impact on composite adherend because the higher peel stresses set up could cause adherend failure. A programme of testing has been set up to investigate this phenomenon.

3.2 Engineering Design

Engineering design procedures are being developed in order to be able to predict the performance of adhesive bonds over a range of geometries and operating conditions. The aim has been to disseminate this technology by producing "user friendly" computer codes which accept the materials data generated in the materials testing.
A literature survey of existing design techniques for adhesive bonding revealed that the continuum mechanics approach was most likely to provide a design technique which could be widely applied. The technique can take account of different materials, geometries, adhesives and thermal effects.
Two computer codes are being developed which can tackle a range of design problems. The two codes are named BISEPS-TUG (Bonded Joint Inelastic Strength Prediction Suite - Tubular Geometry) and BISEPS-LOCO (Bonded Joint Inelastic Strength Prediction Suite - Lap Joints Combined Loading). The main features of these codes are as follows:

3.2.1 BISEPS-TUG*

This computer programme predicts the strength of coaxial tubular joints. It can use a non-linear adhesive characteristic to estimate the shear stresses and strains in the joint. It is capable of doing this for torsional load or axial load although for axial load small peel stresses are present which are not taken into account. The range of features offered by the code are as follows:

. Axial or torsional load
. Thermal stresses
. Non linear adhesive behaviour
. Profiled adherend geometry
. Variable glue line thickness

3.2.2 BISEPS-LOCO*

This code can analyse sheet to sheet bonds with combined tensile, shear or bending loads. The code is unique because of its capability for performing non linear analysis of both tensile and shear stress within the adhesive fully interacting. The code could in principle be applied to a very wide range of problems. Its main features are as follows:

. Sheet to sheet bonds
. Tensile shear or bending applied loads

---

*To be Registered as Trade Marks of the UKAEA

. Thermal stresses
. Anisotropic adherends
. Peel and shear stress/strain prediction
. Non-linear analysis

3.3 Component Testing

Component testing of model joints has been undertaken in order to focus the attention of the programme on problems which are of genuine concern. The specifications of the components have been provided by the sponsors from the automotive industry. This testing programme has taken full account of the fatigue loading spectrum and temperature extremes. In this way suitable design criteria can be established and verified. The testing programme has focussed on four different joint specifications, namely, those of composite front wheel driveshafts, composite truck propshafts, truck chassis brackets and hinge attachments for door panels.

3.3.1 Sub-Project One - Torsional Applications

The spectrum of composite-metal torsional joints which may be needed ranges from small driveshafts of ~25mm diameter and 300mm length to truck propshafts of ~100mm diameter and several metres length. In order to cover the spectrum of sizes and materials likely to be used in these applications two model components have been selected. The first is a small front wheel driveshaft where space constraints are tight and temperatures may be high. The second is a truck propshaft where the emphasis is on vibrational modes where composites can have both weight advantages and eliminate the need for central bearings.
The specifications have been provided by the Working Party members and include consideration of fatigue spectrum, space constraints, length, temperatures and whirling frequency. Consideration of these specifications has lead to the selection of two composite materials for the two types of component. The first is a +/-45° carbon fibre composite for the driveshaft application and the second is a +/-45° glass fibre composite, with axial carbon fibre added to increase bending rigidity, for the propshaft component.
Testing has been undertaken of several designs of end fitting in fatigue and statically at a range of temperatures. The analysis has been able to produce an improved design in which the limitations on performance are now in the adherends themsleves and extremely promising results have been obtained.

3.3.2 Sub-Project Two - Bracket Components

In this component area consideration is given to the application of composite materials in a bracket type component where a joint can take bending, shear and tensile loading. The various joining options cover both mechanical fastening and adhesive bonding including combinations of these two methods.
The cost of moulding inserts and the poor fatigue performance of mechanical fixings make this method less attractive for composites than for metal-metal joints. On the other hand the extreme modulus mismatch between, for example, a glass composite and steel makes the load distribution through the adhesive bond very uneven unless due consideration is given to designing the joint carefully. In addition,

the poor performance of adhesives against peeling stresses make the use
of combined mechanical and adhesive fastening desirable in some cases.

Two components were selected as representations of the problem.
A truck chassis bracket as used to mount fixtures such as the battery,
fuel tank, cab and suspension was selected. It is subjected to
considerable peel loading and hence a combined mechanical fixing and
adhesive bonding may be required. A second component is the hinge
attachment to a glass fibre SMC moulded hatch-back door. Here
adhesive bonding alone will suffice to make a joint. The advantages
of doing this came from avoiding the additional cost of moulded inserts
in the SMC and improved strength from the bonded hinge attachment.

Sample components have been moulded in SMC and testing has been
undertaken at a range of temperatures. The performance of the bonded
hinge attachment in particular has been very promising and a method of
manufacturing the joint rapidly by quench bonding has been utilised.
Fig 4 illustrates a part of the door hinge attachment being tested.

3.4 Quality Assurance

Adhesives can be difficult materials to control in a manufacturing
environment. Regular tests may be necessary to ensure that the
manufacturers specification is achieved. Unfortunately inspection of
adhesively bonded joints is inherently difficult and requires
substantial development.

The approach taken within this project was to review the techniques
which may be applied to the problem and to assess their potential. Some
of the sonic techniques examined give a degree of success, however,
they are slow and laborious. A technique which has higher potential
for rapid assessment is a new method of dynamic thermography. This
has now been shown to be feasible for some geometrical and material
combinations and holds promise for the future. However, the nature
of the problem makes a complete solution unlikely without substantial
development.

4. MAIN RESULTS

The programme has provided an insight into the difficult area of
jointing which so often forms the limitation on design efficiency.
Progress has been made in specific areas on materials testing, design
and on NDT methods.

4.1 Materials Evaluation

The techniques used in the evaluation of shear stress/strain
characteristics have been sensitive to minute displacement inaccuracies
and an experimental technique using an adapted extensometer has been
developed at Harwell.

The Thick Adherend Shear Test (TAST) has been found to be a much
more sensitive indicator of adhesive performance than is the case for
the more traditional lap shear tests and in particular it provides
designers with information in a form which allows designers to
exercise their judgement.

4.2 Engineering Design

It has proved possible to predict optimum joint performance using

170

continuum mechanics techniques, and to use computer codes for design purposes.

BISEPS-TUG, a design computer program for tubular co-axial adhesive joints has been released to industrial sponsors.

The development of an advanced computer code for designing sheet to sheet bonds has been successful and a version of the code BISEPS-LOCO is being prepared for release.

4.3 Component Testing

Early results from the fabrication and testing program have now been obtained.

It has proved possible in some cases to use processes compatible with rapid cycle times and achieve high performance from the adhesive joints. Correct design of the joints has often moved the first mode of failure to the component itself rather than the joint.

4.4 Quality Assurance

Non-destructive testing of adhesive joints has proved to be a difficult objective to fulfil.

Thermography has proved to have potential in some cases, but this is dependent on geometry and material combinations.

5. CONCLUSIONS AND PROSPECTS

The project has achieved substantial successes in developing methods for materials evaluation and improving design techniques. The potential for the application of adhesives to improve jointing techniques has been clear for some time. The project has provided a step towards linking this potential to its realisation by providing design tools.

Joining technology needs further research before full user confidence is achieved. It has been clear during the project that as one question is answered, another takes its place. The prospects for the areas examined during this project would seem, however, to be very encouraging, and further work is envisaged.

6. ECONOMIC ASSESSMENT

The work is directed towards reducing the weight of road vehicles and aircraft cost effectively. Its major economic justification arises from the reduction in fuel costs which will follow. It has been shown that a 10% reduction in road vehicle weight reduces fuel consumption by approximately 5%. Over the life of a vehicle, this is a significant saving. In the case of the specific components being considered in this project, weight savings of around 50% over existing metal designs are envisaged.

Table I

Industrial Members of the Composite/Metal
Jointing Working Party

Aerospace Industry	Automotive Industry	Materials Suppliers
Rolls Royce	British Leyland	Alcan International
Westland Helicopters	Fiat	British Petroleum
	Ford	Ciba-Geigy
	PSA	Elf Aquitaine
	Renault	W R Grace
	Volvo	Permabond
	Volkswagen	Shell

UK Government Departments

Department of Industry
Ministry of Defence

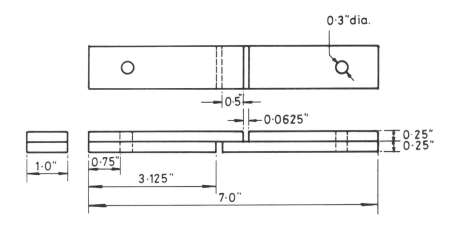

FIG.1. MODEL THICK-ADHEREND SINGLE LAP SHEAR SPECIMEN

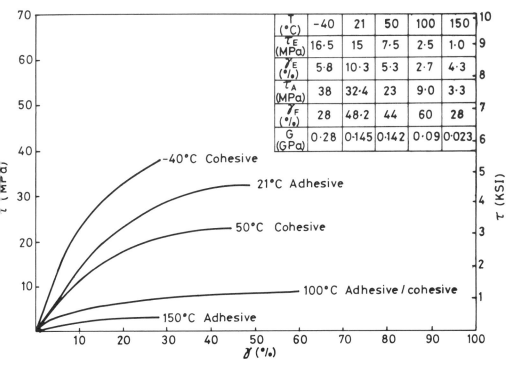

(°C)	−40	21	50	100	150
τ_E (MPa)	16·5	15	7·5	2·5	1·0
γ_E (%)	5·8	10·3	5·3	2·7	4·3
τ_A (MPa)	38	32·4	23	9·0	3·3
γ_F (%)	28	48·2	44	60	28
G (GPa)	0·28	0·145	0·142	0·09	0·023

FIG.2. THICK ADHEREND SHEAR TEST.

173

Aluminium or stainless steel wedge.

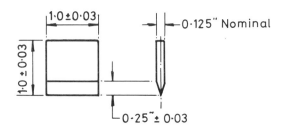

Wedged crack extension specimen

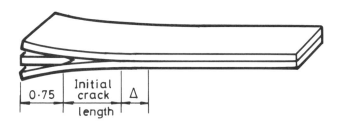

Δ = crack growth after exposure

FIG. 3. GEOMETRY OF THE BOEING WEDGE TEST.

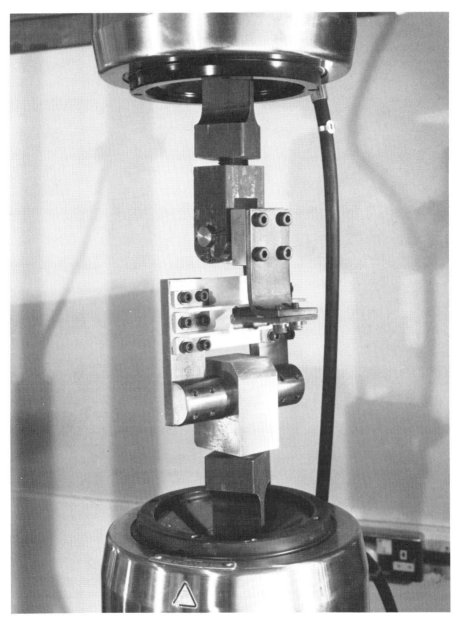

Figure 4   Door hinge attachment being tested

175

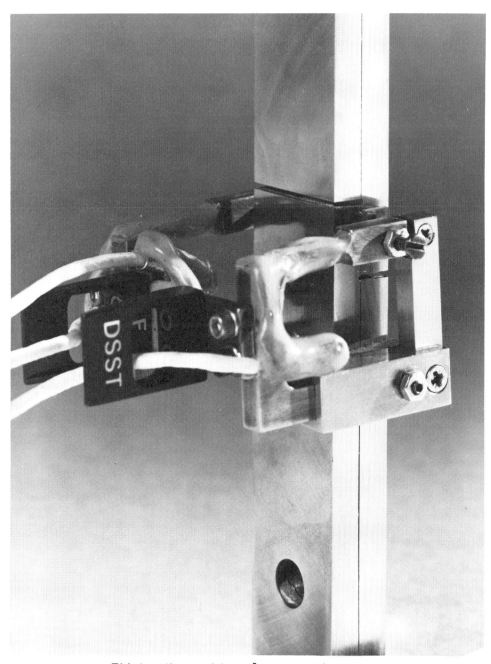

**Thick adherend lap shear specimen
with extensometer mounted**

Figure 5

Chairman: Dr. A. Rossi

Rapporteurs:
Dr. J. Carrasse (Energy Management and Textile Industry)
Dr. P. S. Rogers (Cement and Glass Ceramic Industry)
D. A. Reay, M.Sc. (Food Industry and Microwave Applications)

ENERGY MANAGEMENT

Presentation by Rapporteur
Dr. J. Carrasse
SYNTEC-Ingénierie
F-75008 Paris

Besides R & D efforts on energy saving technologies applied to specific industrial processes, considerable attention must be paid to a comprehensive analysis of energy needs and energy uses in complex factories or in complex industrial sites.

Five Community contracts are running in this energy management sector :

LISSACEC, an electrical peak surveying and reducing equipement
by ACEC, Charleroi, Belgium :

In most electricity tariffs for industrial use, there is a monthly power charge related to the maximum 15 minutes offtake recorded during the month. This maximum offtake, referred to as the peak, ought to be kept at the lowest possible value in order to minimize the average cost of electrical energy.

The LISSACEC equipment has been developed to this end. It surveys the energy consumption of a well chosen set of loads in a factory, over every 15 minutes, in order to shed some appropriate loads at appropriate moments and to re-energize them later on, under some preset conditions.

No interference with the production scheme is allowed in the process. Loads suitable for such a treatment involve as a rule an accumulation of energy under whatever form, heat in an oven or compressed air in a reservoir for instance.

All the surveying and managing actions taken by the LISSACEC are carried out automatically, owing to a built-in computing programme and to a full battery of input and output interfaces.

Among several types of shedding characteristics, the spindle characteristics has been finally chosen, for its superior versatility. Results obtained have led to the conclusion that the use of such an equipment could bring substantial savings on the electricity bills, and extended uses of the LISSACEC are planned for the months to come inside the Charleroi workshop of ACEC.

EXODUS : a program for the economic evaluation of energy exchanges between factories in industrial sites
by SCK/CEN, Belgium :

Most industrial sites, parks or regions have been planned and built in the cheap energy decades. As a result there are many energy exchange, cascading or integration opportunities available on these sites.

179

The aim of this project is to develop a general applicable computerized methodology to identify and evaluate such potential energy saving opportunities.

A computerized model, called EXODUS (energy exchange optimization in industrial sites) has been written; it contains essentially three parts : a simulation, an analysis and a synthesis.

The simulation model is the essential part of the programme and allows in three successive runs the calculation of the energy intensities, annual energy consumptions and of the associated annual costs.

The analysis module identifies potential exchanges and checks them in an improved simulated model.

Finally the synthesis module compares the performances of two energy schemes and evaluates energy savings, energy costs savings, additional costs and pay-out times. In addition different static schemes can be combined into a dynamic scenario and the effects of evolutions of industrial energy consumption or of industrial activities can be evaluated.

In the near future the model will be tested on three selected industrial sites. One of them, situated in the maritime-industrial region of Ghent-Terneuzen has been selected to compare the micro-economical approach of this study with the regional economical approach of the Ghent University project.

Modelling of regional total energy problem for a maritime industrial region by the University of Ghent, Belgium :

The aim of this project is the elaboration of a regional total energy system (RTES) : an integrated energy model of all kinds of heat/energy supply and demand will be developed, tested on the maritime-industrial region of Ghent-Terneusen. A mathematical optimizing model will be conceived for a regional total energy system with emphasis on inter-facing between this model and the inter-factory model developed by SCK/CEN.

Micro and macro-economic aspects on regional level will be integrated in a normalised method for further possible use in other countries of the Community.

Estimation of energy and cost savings arising from the rationalisation of milk assembly operations by the Agricultural Institute of Dublin, Ireland

The objective of this study was to quantify the energy and cost savings which could be made in a milk assembly operation by :

- rationalising catchment areas between different enterprises,
- reducing the frequency of collection, and
- using computerised routing techniques.

A mathematical model of the transport component of the milk assembly operation was developed which related costs and energy requirements to the general features of a given assembly operation, in particular average volume of milk per stop and average number of stops per sq. km.

For the study of routing techniques, four commercial computer routing packages were selected and tested.

It was found that the size of trucks with which milk from an area can be collected most economically can be affected by any change in the milk assembly operation for the area, but the economies of milk assemblies are such that even dramatic changes in the relative costs of fuel will not cause major alterations in the best size of truck for a given assembly operation or in the fuel requirement.

Less frequent collection of milk involves higher costs and energy requirements on farms, but there is however a reduction in the cost and energy requirements of assembly (about 20 % of total transport fuel saved per additional day delay).

Before studying the use of computerised routing techniques, great care must be taken not to underestimate :

- the amount of time and effort required to install a package,
- the expertise required to obtain useful routes from a package.

Let us note as a conclusion the high interest of these remarks for every project including the development of a complex computerised model.

Industrial building design criteria by FIAT Engineering SpA, Torino, Italy

LISSACEC, AN ELECTRICAL PEAK SURVEYING
AND REDUCING EQUIPMENT

P. Guillaume and P. Berger
ACEC
Avenue Emile Rousseau, B-6000 Charleroi

Summary

In order to reduce the monthly power peak which directly influences the
amount of the electricity bills of industrial customers, ACEC has developed an automatic peak surveying and controlling equipment, called LIS-
SACEC.
The action of this equipment is a shedding one; it consits in integra-
ting the sum of the energy offtakes of a certain number of well chosen
loads over every 1/4 hour, and in issuing adequate management orders to
them. This is of course carried out in accordance with the own requirements of every single controlled load and should in no way interfere with
the production schemes.
The basic functioning principles of the equipment are outlined, as well
as the interfaces with the outside. Results obtained in a typical workshop situation are given as examples of what to expect from the LISSACEC
system.

1. PURPOSE

In its most simplified version, the single line diagram of the electrical
energy distribution in a factory is as shown by fig. 1.
A connection to a power grid feeds n parallel connected loads, the individual
powers being P_1, P_2...P_n.
The power taken from the grid is at every moment the sum of the n single
powers, all of them being random functions of time varying for their own sake,
as illustrated by fig. 2a.
The maximum power level reached by the whole set over a given lapse of
time doesn't as a rule match the single maxima, since those individual maxima
are not synchronous, but only some of them, or possibly only one of them.
The value of the maximum power reached by the whole exerts a direct influence on the amount to be paid monthly for the electricity consumption. It
must be pointed out that most formulas used for the invoicing of industrial
customers are of the binomial type, i.e. they include two terms, one proportional to the power offtake (kW) and the second proportional to the consumed
energy (kWh).
The number of kW which is actually used in such a formula is as a rule the maximum offtake of a whole factory over a certain lapse of time, usually a quarter of an hour, during every reference period considered for the invoicing,
one month for instance.

As an order of magnitude, the cost of the electrical power in 1983 amounts to 400 belgian francs/kW monthly, regardless of how many hours the maximum offtake of kW has been actually used during the month.

Obviously, the maximum offtake, referred to as the peak, ought to be kept at the lowest possible value in order to minimize the average cost of electrical energy.

LISSACEC is an equipment designed by ACEC to this end. Basically, it records during every 15 minutes interval the sum of energy consumptions of a given set of loads and issues suitable management orders to some of the loads under survey, according to a built-in computing program which presets the value of the total peak not to be exceeded.

2. ACEC LOAD SHEDDING AND PROGRAMMING EQUIPMENT

Some choices have to be done as a prerequisite, within a given set of single loads, as to the acceptability of their being cut off, at which moment, under which conditions, etc... upon orders issued by an automatic load management system.

Loads suitable to such a treatment ought to be related to uses involving an accumulation of energy, under whatever form: ovens accumulating heat, or compressors filling air reservoirs are typical loads of that kind.

The single appliances to be admitted into the management game have as a rule requirements of their own related to their nature and to their specific use; due recognition of such requirements is an obviously compulsory preliminary step, to be translated into inputs to the computing program of the equipment.

The ACEC designed electrical loads management system allows for much versatility and safety and, moreover, it allows a large number of loads to be kept under control.

In accordance with the programmed instructions, the LISSACEC apparatus builds up decisions and takes actions such as :
a. to ensure the start or the stop of an equipment automatically, at preset times as fixed in a daily or weekly built-in time-table,allowing for modifications of various kinds, and which can be programmed up to one year beforehand
b. to ensure the switch-off of some so-called "unloadable" lines upon a remote issued order, or as a result of an internal computation of the system, in order not to exceed a given value for the consumption peak directly involved in the tariff structure
c. to ensure the priority reswitching on some lines previously shedded as a result of an external order (thermostat for instance, or any other control device) or of an internal computation of the operation time
d. to keep a just switched-off line at cut-off over a preset lapse of time, or to prevent a just re-energized line to be again too soon switched off, all of this in accordance with the specific requirements of the loads involved in the game (for instance : not to restart before some lapse of time a just switched off motor, or reversely not to switch off again too soon a just re-started motor)

The principles of the actions taken by the LISSACEC, and their result on the peak of a set of loads appears on fig. 2b.

3. DETAIL OF THE FUNCTIONS

3.1. Type of characteristics :

Several types of unloading characteristics have been investigated before the final choice of the one which has been judged most appropriate to satisfy the purpose. Let us just mention some of them :

. the threshold characteristics - with straight parallel lines
                                - with straight converging lines

. the zones characteristics - zones between straight parallel lines
                             - spindle shaped zone
(illustrated by fig. 3).

A set of simulations have been carried out with the help of a computing program. Although those simulations have shown that, among others, threshold characteristics with straight parallel lines were quite appropriate to manage a given set of loads, only the spindle shaped characteristic has been finally retained, owing to its superior versatility.

The spindle shaped characteristic has an adjustable hysteresis, namely :

. above the upper curve, unloading actions are carried out
. inside, i.e. between the upper and the lower curve, no unloading actions occurs, no matter how it was reached, either before or after an unloading action
. below the lower curve of the spindle, no unloading action takes place and the previously cut-off loads are in turn progressively re-energized

The hysteresis prevents switch-on, switch-off actions to be carried out too frequently, such actions being detrimental to the durability of the operating circuits breakers, contrarily to a simple slope control characteristics.

3.2. Reduction of the peaks of consumed energy :

The equipment integrates the consumed energy over every 15 minutes period and cuts off some loads whenever the total of the integration exceeds the preset value related to its internal characteristic at the considered moment.

The internal characteristic of the equipment which, if exceeded, results in an unloading action strongly influences its performances (fig.3). The chosen characteristics is of the so called "trend type", which enables the equimment to unload from the very beginning of the period. Owing to this, the totalized consumption can be kept throughout the period noticeably lower than with a threshold characteristic. Moreover, the point representing the cumulated energy can at every moment go down back below the lower curve of the characteristic, and so allowing previously cut-off loads to be progressively re-energized, an action which lightens the stresses they have to bear.

3.3. Dead band :

The characteristic has a dead band at the end of the integration period, in order to avoid automatic readjustments of the allowable cumulated energy level in the event of very small oversteppings. As a matter of fact, if by the end of integration period the actual value of cumulated energy exceeds the preset value in spite of the unloading actions carried out by the equipment, this new value of the 1/4 h energy peak will be the basis of the monthly invoicing and will become the new not to be exceeded preset value. The microprocessor computer of the LISSACEC will automatically readjust its characteristic on the new basis.

If sensitivity of the equipments to oversteppings occuring by the end of the period is infinitely great, every overstepping, no matter how small it could be, will result in a raise of the characteristic which will lead to less and less frequent unloading orders issued to less and less numerous loads. This would be an unlimited drift.

The purpose of the dead band is thus to decrease the sensitivity of the automatic readjustment, so as to make it occur only by straightforward oversteppings.

4. PROGRAMMING OF THE LOADS WITH THE LISSACEC EQUIPMENT

a. The equipment includes a <u>clock-calendar</u> unit which offers the following features :
   . the calendar is based on the standard week
   . the clock calendar is able to take into account the leap-years, and summer and winter time as well
   . the operation conditions can be changed according to season (summer/winter) in the programming
   . exception days can also be taken into account

b. The loads control can be done through the equipment, either :
   . by hand (switch-on switch-off, excluding every programmed operation)
   . in a half-automatic mode (switch-on and switch-off by hand, followed by automatic shedding and re-energizing)
   . automatically (switch-on and switch-off of the loads according to program only)

5. PROTECTION OF THE PROCESS

The equipment offers two kinds of protection of the controlled industrial process :
The first one is based on the operation durations and time intervals; it guarantees :
. minimum operation duration of any load after re-energizing
. minimum allowable cut-off duration after switch-off
  or :
. maximum allowable cut-off duration after swtich-off
. required operation time percentage for each period
. timing of the re-energizing operations
The second takes into account orders issued by the independent protective devices related to each controlled load. An order can be received from a single protection or from several protective devices arranged into a group.

6. INTERFACES WITH THE OUTSIDE

a. Alarms :
The following alarms are available :
. overstepping of the cumulated allowable level at the end of the period
. at every moment, danger of overstepping the cumulated energy allowable level at the end of the period; this alarm enables the operators to avoid an overstepping at the end of the integration period by voluntarily switching off some loads

b. Readjustment of setting point :
It is possible to manually readjust the setting point (increase-decrease) every month.

c. <u>Printer</u> : (optional)
The printer delivers the following information :

. total of cumulated energy from the beginning of the period
. total of cumulated energy at the end of the period
. value of the aimed energy limitation
. identification of the switched-off or re-switched-on loads

. identification of the order responsible of any operation
. day/hour/minute of every operation

7. MODULARITY OF THE EQUIPMENT

The whole set of possibilities is programmed as functional subroutines :
Subroutines are called by a master program which can be modified by the user,
for every load and at every moment in the course of current operation. A
change in the program is carried out with the help of a teletype supplied by
the equipment.
The number of controlled loads of the standard version can be increased
by adding to it interface input and output cards.
As a variation to its use for controlling electrical energy consumption,
the equipment can also control consumption of any fluid, provided flow measurement facilities are available.

8. COMPONENTS

The following components are set up inside a single cabinet :
. a stabilized feeding system
. a microprocessor computer
. optional extension cards
. output interface relays
. terminal blocks
. a teletype
. signalising lamps
. switches for alarms resetting and for setting the equipment off for every
single load
. (optional) : a printer to be laid nearby

9. FUNCTIONAL DIAGRAM

Please refer to fig. 4.

10. RESULTS

It ought to be reminded that reducing by 1 kW the power level reached
during the peak fifteen minutes period of the month results in a saving of
400 bf (figure valid in 1983). All factors varying proportionally, that gives
an idea of the monthly amount to be saved in a factory having, for instance,
a peak power level of 10,000 kW.
A LISSACEC equipment has been set up inside an ACEC workshop provided
with six ovens; the rated powers of the ovens are as follows :

Load	Power	Life number (on LISSACEC)
1. Ovens 35 (operation level A)	100 kW	08
2. Oven 35 (operation level B)	200 kW	16
3. Oven 38	50 kW	32
4. Oven 34	170 kW	28
5. Oven 15	180 kW	2
6. Oven 13	60 kW	4

Figures 5.1 and 5.2 show actual examples of actual results achieved by the
control equipment.

For instance, the load shedding control device brings the 1/4h peak down to 297 kW on may 16th from 12.30 to 13.00, instead of 333 kW, which would have been the recorded value without any shedding action.

Similarly, on May 19 from 13.15 to 14.30, 285 kW instead of 358 kW.

In both cases, the preset power level amounted to 292 kW.

The lowest monthly saving resulting from the two quoted examples amounts to (350 - 295) x 400 = 22.000 bf/month.

This amount represents more than 15% of the power term in the monthly invoice related to the loads considered.

CONCLUSION :

This result is an incentive to look after other sets of loads suitable for a similar treatment inside the ACEC workshops.

It is planned to install several other LISSACEC equipments within the next months, with a first careful aim of saving 100.000 bf monthly on the peak charges.

Fig. 1.

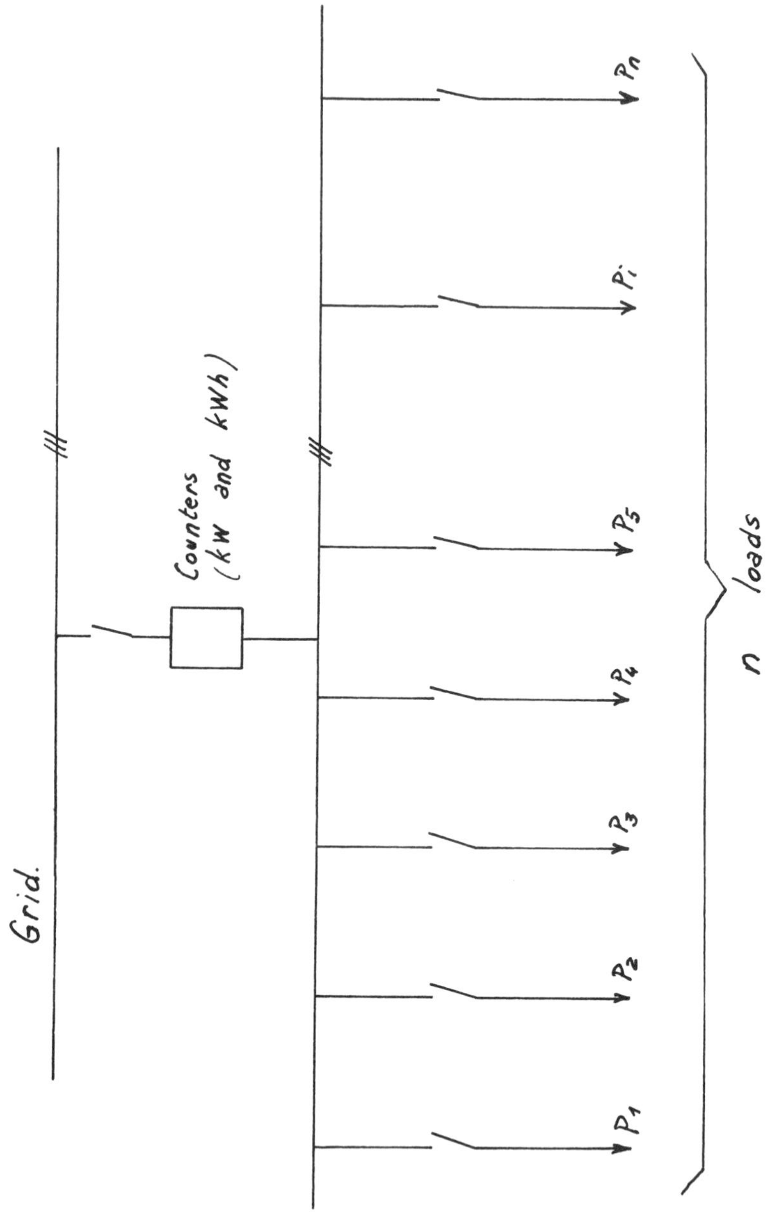

Grid.

Counters
(kW and kWh)

P_1 P_2 P_3 P_4 P_5 P_i P_n

n loads

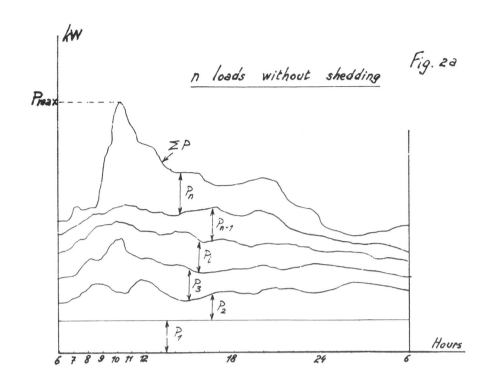

Fig. 2a

n loads without shedding

P_{max}

ΣP

P_n

P_{n-1}

P_i

P_3

P_2

P_1

Hours

6 7 8 9 10 11 12   18   24   6

kw

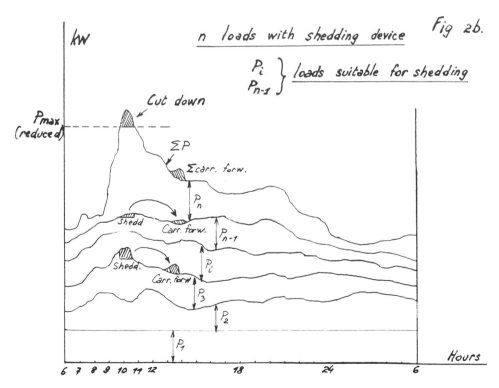

Fig 2b.

n loads with shedding device

P_i
P_{n-1} } loads suitable for shedding

kw

P_{max}
(reduced)

Cut down

ΣP

Σ carr. forw.

P_n

Shedd.   Carr. forw. P_{n-1}

Shedd.   Carr. forw. P_i

P_3

P_2

P_1

Hours

6 7 8 9 10 11 12   18   24   6

Fig 3.

Shedding characteristics

1. Threshold based

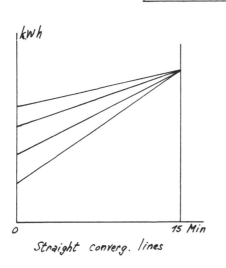

Straight converg. lines

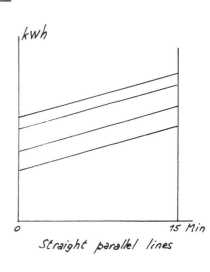

Straight parallel lines

2. Trend based

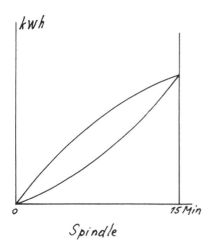

Spindle

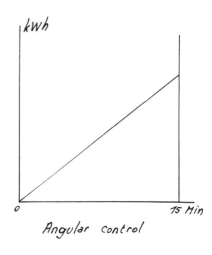

Angular control

Fig. 4

Shedding equipment. Block diagram

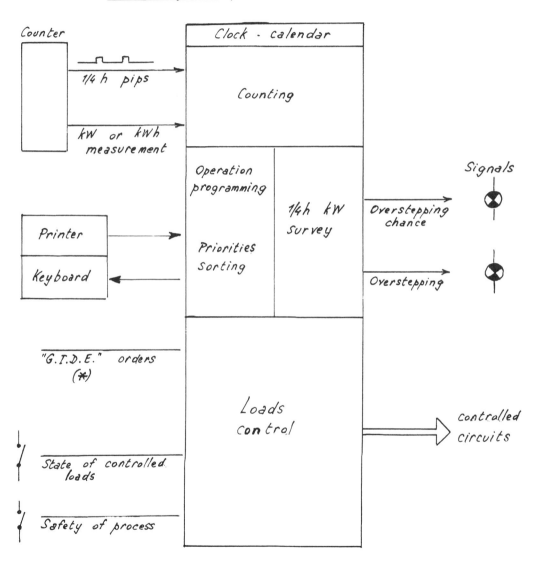

* Gestion Intégrée Décentralisée d' Energie
(outside shedding equipment)

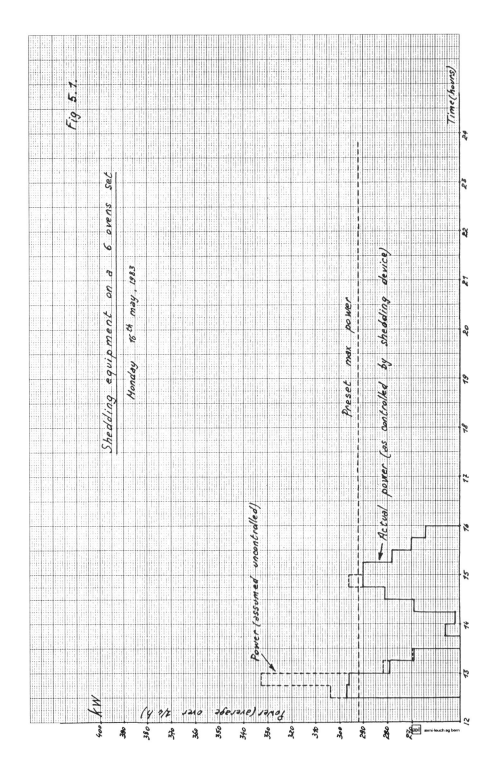

Fig. 5.1.

Shedding equipment on a 6 ovens set

Monday 16th may, 1983

Power (assumed uncontrolled)

Preset max power

Actual power (as controlled by shedding device)

kW

Power (average over 1/4 h)

Time (hours)

400
390
380
370
360
350
340
330
320
310
300
290
280
270

300

asmi-leuch ag bern

12   13   14   15   16   17   18   19   20   21   22   23   24

192

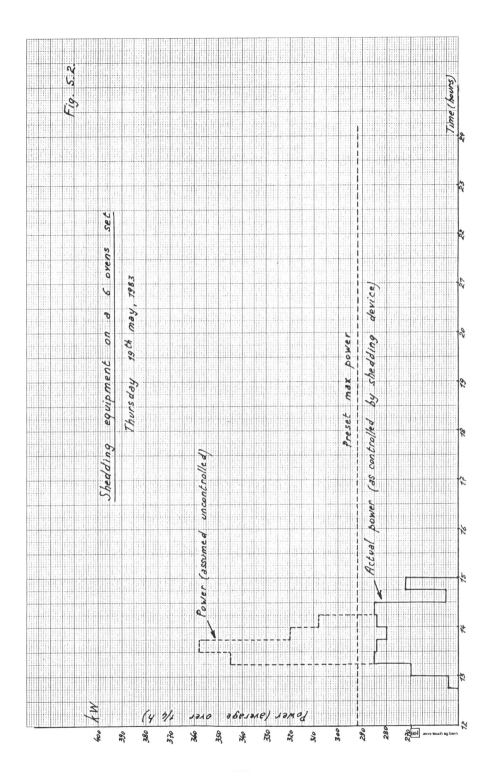

Fig. 5.2.

Shedding equipment on a 6 ovens set

Thursday 19th may, 1983

Power (assumed uncontrolled)

Preset max power

Actual power (as controlled by shedding device)

Power (average over 1/4 h)

kW

Time (hours)

EXODUS: A PROGRAMME FOR THE ECONOMIC EVALUATION OF ENERGY EXCHANGES BETWEEN FACTORIES IN INDUSTRIAL SITES

G. Wouters, E. Pastuer, W. Wegener, F. de Greef, J. Hermans and G. Spaepen

S.C.K./C.E.N.
Boeretang 200, B-2400 Mol

Summary

The present study has two objectives. Firstly, to develop a general-ly applicable selection model to identify sites with a high poten-tial for energy exchange and integration opportunities. The model also gives a first estimate of potential energy and costs savings and of associated economical benefits for the user and the country. The second objective is the demonstration of the validity of the model at different pilot sites. This second task is being carried out in co-operation with local authorities.
A selection and evaluation model has been developed and has been im-plemented on an IBM 4341/2 computer. The computer programme EXODUS (energy exchange opportunities in industrial sites) has been con-ceived as a modular and interactive system.
A first version of the model has been made operational and has been tested on some example test cases. During the first quarter of 1984, the model will be tested at two pilot sites located in the Province of Antwerp. An extended and modified version will be developed in 1984 and will be further tested at several pilot sites. In addition, a comparative study is planned between the micro-economical EXODUS model and the regional-economical RTES model. This last model is being developed by a Belgian-Dutch research team under another CEC contract.

1. INTRODUCTION

As a result of modern urbanization philosophy, industrial activities are being concentrated at industrial sites, parks or regions. Most of these industrial sites have been planned and built during the cheap ener-gy decades. Energy exchange or integration opportunities were not con-sidered at the time since they were not economically viable.
In recent years, much progress has been made in improving process or in-plant efficiency. But once all beneficial in-plant energy rationaliza-tion measures have been exploited, huge quantities of waste energy are still being discharged into the environment. In principle, this residual energy is freely available to any potential user. In addition, the re-use of this waste energy will in any case result in a reduction of the pri-mary energy input into the system. Also secondary effects on industrial competitiveness, on pollution control and on employment should be of interest to the community. Hence interfactory energy exchange should be as much the concern of governments and local authorities as of private companies involved.

2. PROJECT SCOPE AND OBJECTIVES

The first aim of the project is to develop a generally applicable computerized methodology designed to identify and evaluate technical and economical feasibility of interfactory energy exchange or integration opportunities in existing industrial sites. In an extended version the model should also be able to define the optimum energy profile for new factories to be added to the site.

A second objective is to test the developed methodology at three different pilot sites, in collaboration with local authorities. At two pilot sites the micro-economical optimization model will be evaluated as such. At the third site and in addition to the micro-economical optimization, a comparison will be made with a regional energy optimization model, taking into account the interactions between local and regional economical interests. The regional energy optimization model is being developed under CEC contract EEB-3-171-B, by SSRP (Seminarie voor Survey en Ruimtelijke Planning) of the University of Ghent and by TERP (Toegepaste Economie en Ruimtelijke Planning) a private Dutch consultancy company. The present report describes only the development and testing of the micro-economical model.

The project is being executed in two phases. In the first phase a preliminary version of the model has been developed and is being tested at two industrial sites. Data collection for the two test sites is going on and testing of the model will be finished in the first quarter of 1984. In the second phase, planned during 1984, the final and extended version of the model will be developed and further be tested at different pilot sites.

3. DESCRIPTION OF THE WORK

3.1. Selected methodology

The computerized model EXODUS (energy exchange opportunities in industrial sites) has been developed as a modular and interactive sytem. An interactive procedure has been selected to give maximum flexibility and initiative to the programme user. The model has been considered as a design aid, giving the programme user all necessary information on identified exchange opportunities. The design decisions have to be made by the user. Therefore the model does not contain an optimization algorithm and it does not make a selection between exchange opportunities autonomously. The decisions have to be made by the programme user, taking into account technical and non-technical constraints involved in interconnecting individually managed and operated plants. The model then evaluates the energy and cost savings associated with the different strategies introduced by the programme user.

3.2. Computer programme description

3.2.1. Model flow sheet

The EXODUS model has been written in FORTRAN 77 for use on an IBM 4341/2 computer, running under VM/SP. The model is constituted by three main modules, which can be run independently. Extensive documentation is available to the user via "help" commands. The three essential steps carried out by the EXODUS model are : the simulation, the analysis and the synthesis step. Each step corresponds with a main programme module. The interaction between the three modules is clearly illustrated by the general model flow sheet given on Figure 1. This figure gives also decision points where user intervention is required.

The essential functions carried out in the three modules are :
- for the simulation module : modelling of a given energy conversion and energy use system by means of a network of unit operations and streams. This module provides the energy and cost data needed by the analysis and synthesis modules for selection and evaluation of feasible exchange opportunities;
- for the analysis module : identify technically and thermodynamically feasible energy exchanges and calculate operational characteristics of required exchange units and estimate potential energy savings;
- for the synthesis module : evaluation of the micro- and macro-economical profits associated with energy exchange projects. Prior to this economical evaluation, different energy use situations may be combined into scenarios allowing the evaluation of evolving systems.

3.2.2. Simulation module

The purpose of this module is to provide relevant energy and cost data to the analysis and synthesis modules for a given energy use scheme. The calculations are based on a network of unit operations and streams. The unit operations represent any installation or system in which energy is converted, distributed, stored or consumed. Streams represent the energy flows between unit operations. Eight different types of unit operations can be used, for each of which different component options can be selected. A list of available unit operations is given on Figure 2. A process function corresponds to each unit operation. Process functions describe the relationship between input and output streams for the actual installation. This relationship is described for the three following simulation levels : intensities, annual consumption and annualized costs. The library of unit operations and process function subroutines is gradually expanded as new systems are required. To adapt process functions to the specific requirements of an installation, operational values of up to ten process parameters can be introduced. If no values have been given, the programme assigns normalized values to the default variables. Since the EXODUS model is not designed as an analytical engineering tool, but as a preliminary selection and evaluation tool, simulations are being carrried out for only those items which are essential to a preliminary evaluation. The simulation module successively calculates energy intensities, annual energy consumption and annualized costs. Energy intensities are calculated for a steady-state situation in which all end users simultaneously demand maximum energy loads. Intensity calculations allow definition of peak loads and of installed equipment capacities. In a second run respectively annual use patterns, operating hours, load factors and annual energy consumptions are being calculated. Finally annualized costs are determined. Energetic and non-energetic costs are calculated separately. Energetic costs are related to quantities of energy supplied, waste energy removed or waste energy recovered. Non-energetic costs are related to capital costs, maintenance and other exploitation costs and to depreciation costs. All costs are evaluated as annualized present values after taxation and are calculated for a given exploitation period and starting year. Time value of money is taken into account by means of a general inflation rate and by specific inflation rates per company, energy source or exploitation unit.

3.2.3. Analysis module

The purpose of this part of the model is to identify feasible energy exchange opportunities, to define operational characteristics of the exchange unit and to give a first estimate of associated energy savings. The analysis is carried out for a given energy use scheme and is based on the data provided by the simulation module.

Three integration options can be selected for analysis :

1. direct energy exchange between unit operations or groups of unit operations with compatible energy use patterns;
2. indirect energy exchanges with an intermediate storage option. In this option compatibility between energy use patterns is no longer required;
3. integration of energy conversion and distribution systems. In this option opportunities for centralized energy conversion systems can also be analysed.

In the first version of the programme only the first option is made available. The other two options are under development.

The analysis module contains five essential steps :

1. select analysis level : in addition to the choice of an analysis option, a selection has to be made of the energy source and the energy levels to be analysed;
2. energy offer : an inventory is being made of all waste energy streams available at the site for energy exchange, conversion efficiencies of the waste energy streams to the specified energy sources and levels are taken into accounts;
3. energy demand : a similar inventory is being made of all energy inputs meeting the specified requirements;
4. compatibility controls : for all possible combinations between offer and demand streams a series of compatibility controls is being carried out. Also operational characteristics and energy saving potentials for projected exchange units are estimated in this step;
5. ordering of identified exchange opportunities according to the estimated savings potentials.

3.2.4. Synthesis module

The ultimate aim of the synthesis module is to compare the performance of two energy use schemes or of two evolving schemes (scenarios). The comparison is made on total energy purchased on energy costs, on non-energetic costs and on capital costs. However before this final evaluation is being carried out, different stationary energy use schemes can be combined into evolving scenarios. For instance, evolutions in industrial energy use or in industrial activities at the site could be evaluated by scenarios. A gradual realization of energy exchange opportunities or of integration projects could also be simulated in scenarios.

3.4. Testing of the model

Each step of the model was tested on some simplified test cases. Figure 3 gives an example of a test case and illustrates also the schematic representation used by the simulation calculations.

Tests on three real industrial sites are planned in 1984. Data collection has been started at two industrial sites but no further results can be reported yet. Testing of the model for these two sites should be finished in the course of the first quarter of 1984.

EXODUS

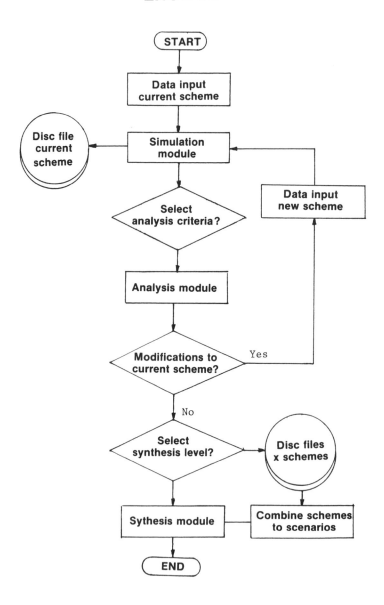

Figure 1 : General programme flow sheet

PROCESS FUNCTION CODES	DESCRIPTION OF UNIT OPERATION
PF 1000	End user
PF 2000	Transformer (general)
PF 2001	Boiler-single fuelled
PF 2002	Boiler-dual fuelled
PF 2200	Compression heat pump
PF 2401	Steam turbo generator
PF 2411	Gas turbine generator
PF 2501	Combined production, back-pressure steam turbine
PF 2506	Combined production, intermediate take-off turbine
PF 2511	Combined production gas turbine
PF 2901	Air compressor – open cooling circuit
PF 2902	Air compressor – closed cooling circuit
PF 3000	Stream splitter – distribution unit
PF 4000	Stream combiner – mixer
PF 5000	Supply unit – source
PF 6000	Recuperator unit (general)
PF 6101	Heat exchanger
PF 6304	Compressor heat pump
PF 7000	Sink (environment)
PF 8000	Storage unit

Figure 2 : List of available process functions for unit operations

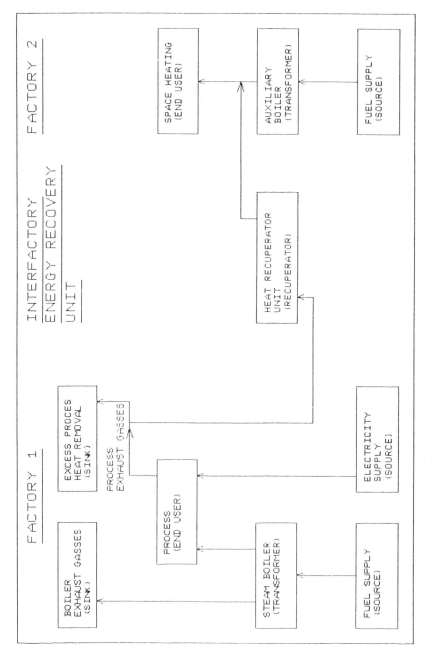

Figure 3 : EXODUS : SCHEMATIC REPRESENTATION OF AN INTERFACTORY ENERGY EXCHANGE AS USED BY SIMULATION CALCULATIONS

MODELLING THE REGIONAL TOTAL ENERGY PROBLEM STARTING FROM A PILOT-STUDY FOR THE MARITIME-INDUSTRIAL REGION OF GHENT-TERNEUZEN

G. Allaert, M. Anselin, F. Tahon and M. van Handenhoven

Rijksuniversiteit te Gent
Seminarie voor Survey en Ruimtelijke Planning
Onafhankelijkheidslaan, 17-18
B-9000 Gent

A. INTRODUCTION

Objectives of the study

Up to now energy-measures in most countries have only a national dimension. The real regional dimension is absent, therefore the team has chosen for the elaboration of a regional total energy system (RTES), where for a diversified urbanised/industrialised region an integrated energy-model of all kinds of heat/energy supply and demand will be developed.
The model will cover the necessary procedures and parameters for an RTES, and will show how micro- and macro-economic aspects on regional level can be integrated, harmonised and evaluated.
In order to show a practical application, the model will be applied and tested on the maritime-industrial region of Ghent-Terneuzen – the aim is to come to a standardised/normalised method for further use in other regions of the E.C. The study will run parallel with stage 1 & 2 of the S.C.K./C.E.N. study concerning the optimum energy exchange between factories in an industrial site (april 1983 – medio 1984).

Work program-tasks

The program is conceived in two stages :
stage 1 (May-Dec. 1983) : construction of mathematical optimizing models for a regional total energy-system
1.1. Theoretical introduction, conceptions, difference between a R.T.E. S. and a classical T.E.S., criteria for the delimitation of a R.T.E.S. (scale of a region, proximity, degree of polarisation of activities and population, constraints, etc.)
1.2. First joint compatibility-evaluation of the inter-facing between the two SCK/C.E.N. – S.S.R.P./T.E.R.P.-models.
1.3. Concretisation of the working hypothesis on the region Ghent-Terneuzen : elaboration of the energy-space-model.
1.4. Second joint compatibility-evaluation of the inter-facing between the two S.C.K./C.E.N. – S.S.R.P./T.E.R.P. models and decision on the structure of stage 2.

stage 2 (Jan.-May 1984) : final construction of a regional total energy system (tentative programm)
2.1. Grafting of the energy-space model on the geo-information-system (G.I.S.)
The energy-space-model (integrated) is fit for use in regional energy planning in relation to physical, economic and social planning.
2.2. Construction and testing of the energy-space-model on the G.I.S. of Ghent-Terneuzen. Evaluation, ev. adaptation of the model.
2.3. Elaboration of a standard R.T.E.S.-model
   - procedural and material aspects
   - advantages and potential contributions of the R.T.E.S. to the E.C.-energy policy
   - criteria for further application in other/similar regions of the E.C.

2.4. Final evaluation of the applied models of S.C.K./C.E.N. and S.S.R.P./
T.E.R.P. to a <u>micro-macro integrated energy-saving-model</u>.

The research programm will be carried out jointly by the "Seminarie voor
Survey en Ruimtelijke Planning" (S.S.R.P.) of the University of Ghent
(Belgium) and the "Buro voor Toegepaste Economische en Ruimtelijke Plan-
ning" (T.E.R.P.) in Amersfoort (the Netherlands).

B. <u>SOME DEFINITIONS USED</u>

The objective of the research program is the solution of <u>regional total</u>
<u>energy-problem</u> by means of integrated optimising models.
All items of energy optimization are located by geographical x, y, z-
coordinates.
As a region is here considered a <u>city-region</u> comprising : the core
(C.B.D. and town-centre), the residential areas, industry estates,
the peripherical areas, the commuter-zone.
In this city-region the intensity and diversity of the activities
diminish by the distance to the epicentre.
As an RTES means the optimisation of primary and secundary energy-con-
sumption by integration of all kinds etc. of demand and offer of energy
within a definitive region, it is normally requested that there should
be a <u>great variety of productions</u> c.q. <u>consumptions of energy</u>.
A polarised, multi-functional city-region is an appropriate area.

C. <u>FRAMEWORK OF THE RTES-MODEL</u>

The starting point of the modelling of the Regional Total Energy System
(RTS) is the elaboration of different energy-scenario's. Every energy-
model is namely based on a concept of the development now and in the
future of the energy situation (supply and demand; ressources and
techniques). In many cases the future of the energy situation is based
on political goals, on economic goals, on social goals.
Between these goals there are several constraints : geographical, geo-
logical, etc.
It is therefore necessary to start with an elaboration of different
energy-scenario's (seen as level : world, country, regions and as item:
oil - gaz - nuclear - coal - others ...) rather than to start with a
model based on the situation today. The RTES has namely to be a
<u>dynamic future oriented model</u>.

In the whole discussion round scenario's there are two types :
1. <u>P.E.S.</u> (Prospective Energy Scenario's).
   The evolution of the situation today in a future perspective is an
   example herefore : trend scenario.

2. <u>C.E.S.</u> (Contrast-Energy-Scenario's)
   Here we work with different basic ideas on different levels : on the
   level of the physical planning, economic planning, social planning
   (facet planning idea) and we look about the consequences of the
   facets on the energy (demand-supply).

<u>Is is the facet-sector combination of the C.E.S.</u> that will be used in
the RTES-modelling because it is the best way to make relations between
components of the R.T.E.S. in a matrix-modelling interrelationship.
The character of that matrix-modelling interrelationship of energy production and consumption is elaborated in point D . Energy production

and consumption matrix on a regional level.

The information on energy-production and consumption is based on a street-aggregation-level concerning the collection of information and on a grid-level concerning the modelling.
Both information levels are based on the so-called G.I.S. (Geo-Information-System) approach.
With the GIS-approach the RTES can be linked on a physical space model (spatial supply-demand optimization) and on a micro & meso economic model (optimal supply network and technico-economic optimization).
After the confrontation of both models there is a feedback to the C.E.S. (Contrast Energy-Scenario's).

Framework of the RTES-Model   (Figure 1)

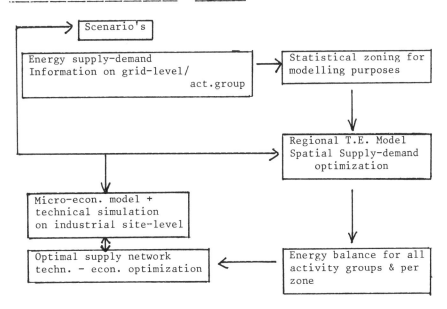

D. ENERGY PRODUCTION AND CONSUMPTION MATRIX ON A REGIONAL LEVEL

In order to be able to develop a regional total energy system a regional model is required.
This means that such a model is constructed not only on the basis of technical and economic data concerning demand and supply but also on the basis of activities with their specific spatial location and land use.
The most simple form to represent the model structure is a matrix (see figure 2) of rows and columns. The main part of the matrix shows on one hand the activities and the demand side using the energy sources (columns), and on the other hand the supply elements are shown consisting of all kinds of resources including energy(rows).

Figure 2

			Activities									import/export	Balance
			zone A					zone B					
			energy	industry	agriculture	built space	etc.	energy	industry	agriculture	built space	etc.		
Supply elements	zone A	resources (incl land-use), energy, investments, environment												
	zone B	resources (incl land-use), energy, investments, environment												
	Transport													

The rest of the matrix is used to express the relationship between zones in terms of transport of resources (including transport of energy) and in terms of input/output.

As explained above, the transportation network is optimized in a technical-economic submodel. This submodel is calculating the exact energy production, consumption and transport in the network combined with investment and exploitation figures. The results of these calculations are integrated in the optimization structure on an aggregated level.

The aggregation takes place on the level of activities and on the level of geographical zones. Concerning the geographical zones the system works as follows : the network is coded on the level of nodes, links, segments and blocks; this linear system is transformable to grids (500 x 500 m) and the grids are then combined to energy zones.
This combining & aggregation procedure is based on grouping of activities with their appropriate energy use.
The algorithm of the model is based on optimization theory with multiple goals. The goal functions are:minimizing energy costs, maximizing port activities (f.i. coal),minimizing balance of payment impacts, minimizing pollution problems.

E. CASE-STUDY : THE MARITIME-INDUSTRIAL REGION GHENT-TERNEUZEN

The trans-border region Ghent-Terneuzen forms an integrated multifuncti-
onal city-region, grown since several centuries by a number of physical,
geographical, political and economic determinants. The maritime canal
Terneuzen-Ghent is the backbone of this region.
Ca. 400.000 people live in this area, with more than 170.000 jobs.
The M.I.D.A. itself occupies some 30.000 people : a petro-chemical industry, a fertilizer-plant, an integrated steelmill, different metal-
and assembly plants, 3 grain-elevators, 3 electricity-works, cokery,
etc.
As the sealock and the canal are accessible for ships up to 70.000 tdw.,
the maritime traffic amounts some 31 mln. tons in 1983.
This Ghent-Terneuzen region has been practically the only still quick
growing M.I.D.A. in North-Western Europe, notwithstanding general economic recession.

F. STATE OF THE ART : MANAGEMENT OF THE REGIONAL DATA BASE

Starting point is the existing infrastructure of the area that is digi-
tized in such a way that automatic data processing and geographical
representation by means of plotting is possible.
In order to make this possible a number of files is created : the
coordinates-file, the file of all blocks and the segments-file. The
coordinates-file consists of the Lambert-coordinates of every node in
the street-pattern, the block-file gives the successive nodes that form
a block, and the segment-file contains all the necessary data to find
the final relation between an address and the spatial situation.
The total area is divided in different types of zones :
- housing areas and mixed areas
- industrial areas
- services areas
- open areas and recreational areas
- areas for other land use.

The delimitation of zones has to be corresponding with blocks. This
means also that the smallest spatial elements are blocks. Due to the
existance of the coordinates-file it is easy to combine blocks or
spatial locations to grids of 500 x 500 m.
Each square in the grid corresponds with an element of the above-men-
tioned matrix used for optimization.
Most of the data as far as they are published, are known per street
or per address, namely :
- the detailed heat demand per dwelling and building;
- the number of dwellings/buildings per street;
- the number of industries and their respective number of working places;
- survey-figures of energy production and energy use in bigger industries.

By means of the segment-file all these detailed data can be geographi-
cally located and represented and easily processed for further calculations.
In cases where individual data are not published or not free for use
statistical data per municipality are applied (fig.3.), agricultural
data, green-houses, working places, office and shopping area, type of
heating, etc. These data are then distributed over the different zones
used for modelling.

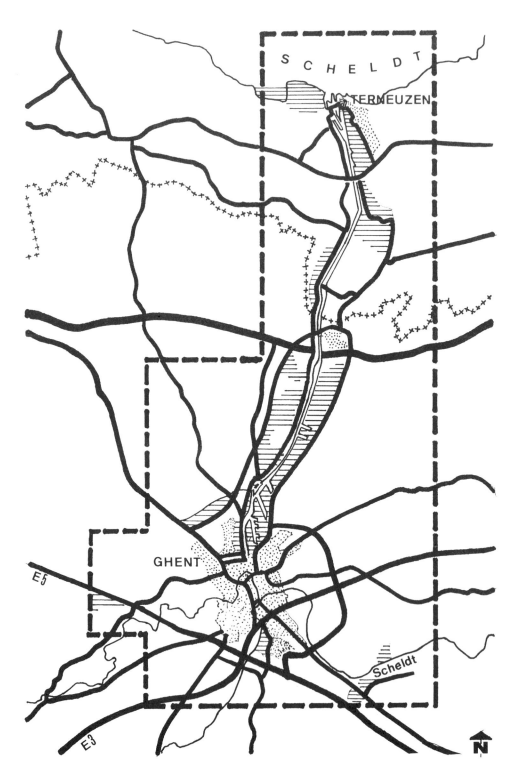

SCHELDT

TERNEUZEN

GHENT

E5

E3

Scheldt

N

ESTIMATION OF ENERGY AND COST SAVINGS ARISING FROM THE RATIONALISATION OF MILK ASSEMBLY OPERATIONS

P. Herlihy, M. Butler and E. Pitts

The Agricultural Institute
19 Sandymount Avenue, Dublin 4, Ireland

Summary

A mathematical model of the transport component of the milk assembly operation is developed which relates the cost and energy requirements of milk assembly to the parameters of a given assembly operation, in particular the average size of supplier and the density of suppliers. A major feature of this model is that it allows an optimal truck size to be calculated and this allows the effects of changes in truck size to be incorporated in subsequent analyses. This model is used to estimate the likely fuel and cost savings in the transport operation from the rationalisation of catchment areas between collection agencies. It is also used to estimate the savings in fuel and cost in the transport operation due to less frequent collection of milk. These savings are compared to the increased fuel use and costs on farms due to less frequent collection.
       The application of computer routing techniques to the milk assembly operation is also considered. Four commercial routing packages were selected and tested on two problems, one theoretical and one practical. Some of the special features of the use of computer packages in the milk assembly area were considered.

1. INTRODUCTION

The assembly of milk is a major economic activity. The total cost of assembling milk in the EC is of the order of DM3 billion annually and about five hundred million litres of fuel are used in the transport operation
       (a) The dairy processing industry in the EC is a mixture of co-operatives and private enterprises which have developed over the years in a free market. Each of these enterprises has a catchment area from which it collects milk. In a number of cases these catchment areas overlap or depart in some other way from the pattern of catchment areas which would minimise transport costs. In this study we consider the problem of the likely level of savings in fuel and costs which would result from the removal of anomalies of different types. In particular the dependence of these savings on the parameters of the catchment areas being considered is explored.
       (b) On a modern dairy farm milk is stored in refrigerated bulk tanks and collected by bulk tanker. With good farm hygiene milk can be collected as infrequently as every third day. Less frequent collection usually gives fuel and cost savings in the transport operation. However it means that more milk has to be stored for longer on the farm which means increased costs and fuel use on farms. In recent times (1) there has been a move to less frequent collection. In order to estimate the effect of changes in the frequency of collection the estimated on-farm costs are compared with the estimated saving in the transport operation.
       (c) Computer routing packages are a valuable tool in many distribution/ assembly systems. These techniques are not used extensively in the milk

assembly area.   The reasons for this are considered and the performance of
a number of computer routing packages compared on two assembly problems.
    Central to considering the first two topics above is a model of the
cost and fuel requirements of the transport component of the milk assembly
operation.   This model has to be very general and capable of handling the
large variations in the parameters of the milk assembly operation which
occur between different regions of the Community.

2. The model of the transport component of assembly systems

    In this study we restrict attention to centralised assembly operations
where the primary responsibility for assembling the milk is that of some
one agency usually the processor.   The basic unit of such a collection
system in our model is the route.   The route involves collecting milk at a
number of stops (sometimes milk from more than one farm will be collected
at one stop) and bringing it to the plant.   The time spent in collecting a
route can usefully be divided into five components, i.e.

(i)   the time spent driving from the plant to the first stop
        and from the last stop to the plant,
(ii)   the time spent on the public road driving between stops,
(iii)   the time spent actually loading milk at stops,
(iv)   the time involved in a stop, other than that involved in
        actually loading milk, i.e. manoeuvring into and out of
        the premises and initiating and terminating the loading
        operation, taking samples, slowing down and accelerating,
and (v)   the time to turn the truck around at the plant including
        queuing, weighing, unloading and administration.

    In the situation where there is a fixed pattern of routes which is
reported in each period the total time spent collecting from an area can be
calculated based on the five components above

$$\text{Time spent collecting} = \text{number of time periods} \times \left[r.\frac{(DO + DI)}{S} + \frac{(N-r) \cdot AD}{S} \right.$$

$$\left. + \frac{N.D}{LP} + N.AS + r.TO \right] \quad \dots\dots (1)$$

where
N   is the total number of stops
r   is the number of routes
AD   is the average inter-stop distance
S   is the average road speed of trucks
D   is the average amount collected per stop
AS   is the average non loading stop time at farms
DO   is the average distance to first supplier
DI   is the average distance from last supplier to plant
TO   is the average turnaround time for a truck
LP   is the loading rate at farms

    In calculating the fuel used on the transport operation relationships
of the following type (2, 3) are used.

fuel consumption per km travelled $= \alpha_1 + \alpha_2 W + \alpha_3 W^2$ .... (2)
fuel consumption per stop $= \beta W$ .... (3)
fuel consumption per hr of idling $= \gamma + \delta C$ .... (4)

where W is the weight of the truck plus the load and C is the capacity.
    In calculating the fuel used it is necessary to take into account the
changing load on the truck.   In terms of the components considered above,
the fuel consuming activities are:

(i)   fuel used driving to first stop (truck empty)
        fuel used driving from last stop (truck full),

208

(ii)   the fuel used driving between stops (truck filling),

(iii)   the fuel used in stopping and accelerating to cruising speed at each stop (truck load increasing),

(iv)   the fuel used in idling at stop (independent of truck load),

and (v)   does not normally involve any significant fuel consumption for the truck.

If Wo is the unladen weight of a truck and UC is the average final load then the average load is (Wo + UC/2). The estimated fuel consumption of a fleet of trucks of capacity C based on equations (2), (3) and (4) is

$$\text{Total fuel consumed} = \text{number of time periods} \times$$

$$\left\{ r \cdot DO(\alpha_1 + \alpha_2 W_0 + \alpha_3 W_0{}^2) + r \cdot DI \left[\alpha_1 + \alpha_2 (W_0 + UC) + \alpha_3 (W_0 + UC)^2 \right] \right.$$

$$+ AD(N-r) \left[\alpha_1 + \alpha_2 (W_0 + \frac{UC}{2}) + \alpha_3 (W_0{}^2 + UC.W_0 + \frac{UC^2}{3}) \right]$$

$$\left. + N\beta (W_0 + \frac{UC}{2}) + (\frac{ND}{LS} + N.AS) (\gamma + \delta C) \right\} \qquad \text{.... (5)}$$

where the parameters have the same meaning as in equation (1).

In calculating the costs of a transport system it is standard procedure to consider it in two components. One component covers these costs which can be considered fixed and do not depend on the actual use to which the truck is being put. These costs are incurred even when the truck is stationary and includes depreciation and wages. These costs can be expressed as a cost CF per hour. The other costs are those variable costs incurred when the truck is used and includes fuel, tyres and mainten- ance. These costs are usually expressed as a cost per km travelled. In this model there is an unusually detailed calculation of fuel consumed and it was decided to use this as the measure of variable costs so that variable costs are calculated as a cost per litre of fuel used. This is likely to give a more accurate assessment of the variation in variable costs from one milk assembly situation to another where the number of stops is a significant factor affecting fuel consumption and maintenance require- ments. This is totally omitted in the standard treatment.

Both fixed and variable costs increase with truck size (4). A detailed study of this variation was undertaken which took into account the impact of the tanks and the metering equipment on cost and available payload. Based on this analysis the relationships used were:

fixed costs per hour in IR£ = $5.6 + 0.24C$

variable costs per litre of fuel used IR£ = $\begin{cases} 1.2 - 0.05C & (C < 10 \text{ tonnes}) \\ 0.7 & (C \geqslant 10 \text{ tonnes}) \end{cases}$

3. Distances in the model

Equations (1) and (5) give the total time spent collecting in an assembly operation and the total fuel consumed. They involve AD, the average distance between stops, DO, the distance to the first stop, and DI, the distance from the last stop to the depot. To use these equations it is necessary to have some method of estimating these distances.

To do this we consider a simple routing strategy where trucks drive to the start of a route and then visit stops minimising distance until the addition of the milk at the next stop would cause the truck's capacity to be exceeded. The truck then returns to the depot. This seems close to the routing strategy used in practice. In actual routing situations a truck may collect a supplier or two on the way out or back but this does not affect the broad structure of routes. Given this strategy it can be shown that the number of routes is the next highest integer to ND(C-D/2).

Calculation of the average interstop distance is based on theoretical work (5) which gives the result that if stops are distributed at random in regions of area A the length Q(n) of the shortest tour passing through all n points is on average given by

$$Q(n) = K \sqrt{A} \sqrt{n} \qquad \dots \ (6)$$

when n is large. K is a constant independent of A and n and has a value of about 0.75 (6, 7).

This result is for the situation where there are straight line links between the stops. To allow for the greater road distance between stops a factor of 1.28 (8) was used. A further refinement of equation (6) was introduced which ensured that the length of minimum tour approached the total length of road in the region for very large n. This correction can be important in very dense systems. The estimate of interstop distance used in the model is got by dividing Q(n) by n-1.

To calculate DO and DI the distances to the first supplier and from the last supplier to the depot it is assumed that these points are distributed randomly in the region. In this case the expected values of DO and DI depend on the distance of the region being considered from the depot, the size of the region and to some extent on its shape. This problem has been widely discussed. The model could cope with a rectangular region an arbitrary distance from the depot and is discussed in (6).

4. Use of transport model in study

An interesting feature of the model as formulated is that the dependence of both time spent collecting and fuel used on the capacity of the trucks used appears explicitly. The size of truck used is a key decision variable. In the study it is assumed that the size of truck used in any situation is such as to minimise total cost. In estimating the effects of any changes the costs and fuel consumption before and after the change are each estimated for the size of truck which is then optimal. This approach avoids the problem of estimating the effect of a change on the basis of fixed truck size when part of the effect of a change can be to alter the appropriate size of truck to use.

In using the model it is reasonable to use typical values for some of the technical parameters, e.g. loading/unloading rates, which are reasonably representative of the situation in the Community as a whole. Some of the features of the milk assembly operation, however, vary widely from region to region in the Community, in particular the average amount of milk collected per stop and the number of stops per sq km. In the case of these two parameters results were calculated for the range of values of these parameters found in the Community.

5. Rationalisation of catchment areas

There are two basic types of rationalisation. Any rationalisation in practice will be a combination of these two basic types.

In a type I rationalisation (figure I) the milk from a district was going to one processing plant before the rationalisation and goes to a different one after the rationalisation. Savings arise if the plant to which the milk is delivered after the rationalisation is nearer than the one to which it was being delivered before the rationalisation.

Table I shows, based on the model, how the cost savings from a type I rationalisation vary with the distance of the two plants from the district being transferred and with average volume of the milk per stop in this

district.   This is for the situation where there is one stop per sq km.
The percentage cost savings are slightly lower when the density of stops
per unit of area is lower and slightly higher when the density of stops is
higher.   The pattern of fuel savings from a type I rationalisation is
similar to the pattern of cost savings but the savings are about one third
higher.

TABLE I: Percentage savings in transport costs from a type I
rationalisation

Distance to original destination km	Distance to new destination km	Milk collected per stop (tonnes)						
		0.0625	0.125	0.25	0.5	1.0	2.0	4.0
20	10	7	9	11	16	20	22	22
30	20	4	7	10	14	15	16	18
40	30	4	6	10	11	12	14	15
50	40	4	6	8	8	10	12	13
60	50	4	6	7	8	9	11	12
70	60	3	5	6	7	9	10	11
80	70	3	4	5	7	8	9	10
90	80	3	4	5	6	7	8	9
100	90	3	4	5	5	6	7	8

One stop per square km on average

   A type II (figure I) rationalisation occurs where two processors are
collecting from a district and one withdraws leaving all the milk from the
district to be collected by the other.   The savings result from the fact
that a truck need now travel a shorter distance to collect the same amount
of milk.   Table II shows the percentage savings in total transport cost of
milk collection from a district from a type II rationalisation when both
plants are equidistant from the district.   There is a dramatic reduction
in the percentage savings as the amount of milk collected per stop
increases.   These results are for the case where there is one stop per
sq km.   The percentage savings increase as the density of stops decreases
(by a factor of 1.5 when there is only one stop per four square km).
As the density increases the savings decrease (by a factor of about 1.5
when there are four stops per square km).   The pattern of percentage fuel
savings from a type II rationalisation is similar to that for costs but are
at least one third higher.   In the case of distinctly large suppliers,
i.e. two tonnes per stop or more, percentage fuel savings can be twice the
percentage cost saving.
   The figures in Table II refer to the situation where each plant is
collecting half of the milk from the shared district.   In the situation
where one processing plant is receiving the bulk of the milk and the other
withdraws, ceding its share of the milk, the saving per tonne of milk ceded
is greater.   This saving is on a smaller volume of milk so that the percentage saving per tonne in the district will be fairly similar to the case
we have been considering.   The results from the model are for a uniform
production pattern for milk throughout the year but a moderate level of
seasonality of product should not significantly effect the results.

Type 1: RATIONALISATION

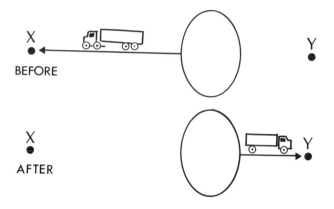

BEFORE

AFTER

Type II: RATIONALISATION

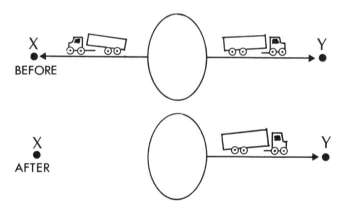

BEFORE

AFTER

Fig. 1: TWO BASIC TYPES OF RATIONALISATION

TABLE II: Percentage savings in transport costs from a type II rationalisation

Distance from both plants km	Milk collected per stop (tonnes)						
	0.0625	0.125	0.25	0.5	1.0	2.0	4.0
10	13	12	10	8	5	3	1
20	12	11	9	6	4	3	1
30	12	10	8	6	4	3	1
40	12	10	8	6	4	2	1
50	11	9	7	5	4	2	1
60	11	9	7	5	3	2	1
70	10	8	7	5	3	2	1
80	10	8	7	5	3	1	1
90	10	8	6	5	3	1	1
100	10	8	6	4	2	1	1

One stop per square km on average

6. Effect of frequency of collection

On the modern dairy farm milk is stored in refrigerated bulk tanks. With good hygiene, collection as infrequently as once every three days is feasible. Less frequent collection involves increased on-farm costs and energy usage since more milk must be stored for longer. Less frequent collection however tends to result in reduced milk transport costs and fuel usage. The net effect of less frequent collection depends on the balance between the on-farm effects and the effects on the milk transport operation.

FIGURE II: Fuel savings in transport operation in going from every second day collection to every third day collection in litres per tonne

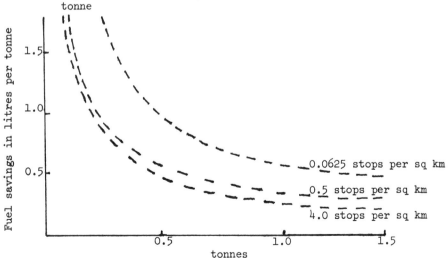

0.0625 stops per sq km

0.5 stops per sq km

4.0 stops per sq km

Average daily output per stop

Figure II shows, based on the model*, how the fuel savings in the
transport operation, in going from every second day to every third day
collection, depend on the parameters of the region being considered.
These savings relate to the case where the district being considered is
30 km from the plant.   If the district is nearer the savings are somewhat
smaller; if it is further away they are somewhat larger (about 20 per cent
larger at 50 km).   A detailed analysis of the likely increase in on-farm
energy requirements indicates that only the ambient temperatures in the
region has a major effect on the additional on-farm requirement for energy
and that provided that the average ambient temperature is below 20° the
additional energy requirement should be less than the equivalent of 0.2
litres of diesel per tonne of milk produced.   Comparing this figure with
figure II it is clear that every third day collection is more energy
efficient than every second day collection.

The pattern of cost savings in the transport operation from a change
to every third day collection is similar to the pattern of fuel savings, i.e.
they are lower the greater the density of stops and the daily output per
stop.   The increased on-farm costs per tonne of milk produced does not
vary much with these two parameters.   Thus net gains from a switch to
every third day are less in regions with a high density of large suppliers.

The on-farm costs are sensitive to the rate of interest.   Every third
day becomes financially attractive compared to every second day collection
only if the average volume per stop is less than 0.3 tonnes in the case of
high interest rates and high density of suppliers.   In the case of low
density and low interest rates it is attractive even in areas of high
average daily output per stop.

7. Use of computer routing packages

The problem of finding what pattern of routes minimises the total distance
required by a fleet of trucks to service a set of customers is common to
many economic systems.   Because of the complexity of the problem little
progress has been made in developing exact solution procedures.   However
there has been considerable progress in developing procedures which give
good though not necessarily optimal results.   These procedures are the
basis of numerous computer routing packages, many of which are marketed
commercially and are used routinely and successfully in many organisations.

From our enquiries it would appear that routing in milk assembly by the
use of computer packages is comparatively rare in the Community.   Even the
largest buyer of milk in the Community (the Milk Marketing Board for
England and Wales) is only using its computer package for monitoring, in a
general way, the efficiency of its present operations in primary milk
assembly.   A number of enterprises in Germany, Holland and France are
using computer packages.   (One large Dutch firm, however, which had
installed a package in the mid 1970s has ceased using it.)   So far as we
can ascertain no firm is using a package for regular routing in Denmark,
Ireland or Belgium.

A possible reason for the lack of widespread use is the stability of
routes in milk assembly where each supplier is collected with regularity.
Thus schedulers are not under time pressure in designing routes and can
refine the routes they derive over a considerable period.

---

* In this analysis it is assumed that the pattern of stops in a district
  does not change.   To the extent that the change to every third day
  collection makes impractical the use of mobile tanks by smaller
  suppliers, the analysis would have to be adjusted.

To investigate the routing efficiency of commercial packages the results from a number of them were compared on two problems, one theoretical and one practical. A solution to the practical problem was also obtained from two experienced schedulers. The results indicate that the output of three of the packages (VSPX, ROUTEMASTER and PARAGON) gave a similar level of routing efficiency and that this was about six per cent better than that achieved by the schedulers. The indications were that a further improvement of two per cent could be obtained by adjusting the output from the packages using an interactive facility now available with some packages. One would expect the initial solution produced by the schedulers for an area with which they were familiar to be somewhat better than for an area with which they were unfamiliar, as in this test. Also in practice they would have the chance to refine the routes they are using. In addition the percentage cost savings due to improved routing will be somewhat less than the actual reduction in route length. Thus the level of cost savings from operating packages seem likely to be less than five per cent. These savings have to be set against the considerable expense of purchasing and operating a routing package. A further inhibiting factor in the use of computer routing packages for milk assembly is that frequently an enterprise has a non-standard feature in their assembly operation, e.g. use of trailers, mixed frequency of collection or multiple depots.

At present a generation of routing packages is being developed which have improved routing procedures. At present these packages are restricted in the size of problem they can handle. In the future, these new procedures may provide the basis of routing packages which will find widespread use in the milk assembly area.

8. Conclusions

It is necessary to differentiate between two types of rationalisation of milk assembly. One type is where milk is taken to a nearer processing point after the rationalisation. In this case the saving is broadly proportional to the difference in distance and the order of magnitude of savings is about one per cent of transport costs per km reduction. However the percentage saving increases with milk collected per stop and in areas with large suppliers it can be twice this figure while in areas with small suppliers it can be about half the above figure. The percentage fuel savings behave in a similar way and are about one third higher.

The second type of rationalisation is where two processors are collecting from the same area and one withdraws. If the two processors are equidistant from the area the percentage of total cost saved is smaller the greater is this distance. The variation of percentage savings with size of supplier is the opposite to that in the previous type of rationalisation, i.e. the percentage savings tend to be less in areas with large suppliers. In areas with large suppliers cost savings of only a few per cent can be expected while in areas with small suppliers savings in excess of 10 per cent are not unlikely. In this case also the percentage fuel savings tend to be about one third higher than those for costs.

Less frequent collection of milk involves higher costs and energy requirements on farms. There is however a reduction in the cost and energy requirements of transport. The absolute saving per tonne transported is less for regions of more intensive milk production. Provided all producers have bulk tanks the additional requirements, per tonne, on farms do not depend on the intensity of milk production in the area. Thus the net savings per tonne from a change to less frequent collection are

greatest in the less intensive regions. In times of high interest rates
the overall cost advantage of less frequent collection can be questionable
in areas of high milk production intensity. Less frequent collection
normally results in a net saving in direct energy (20 per cent of total
transport fuel saved per additional day delay is the order of magnitude of
the saving).

Because of the stability of routes, current computer packages do not
offer major advantages in the routing of milk assembly. Improved routing
procedures currently being incorporated into commercial routing packages
may lead to more widespread use of computer routing packages in milk
assembly in the future.

ACKNOWLEDGEMENTS

The authors wish to thank Dr. J.P. Stöckl, Technische Universität München,
who supplied us with the data for one of our test problems.

REFERENCES

1. K.H. HAISCH, J. BETZ and U. HUCK (1980). Die milcherfassung in der
   Bundesrepublik Deutschland im Zeitvergleich 1973-1978. Deutsche
   Molkerei Zeitung 1466-1472
2. CLAFFEY, P.J. (1971). Running costs of motor vehicles. National
   Co-operative Highway Research Program Report 111, Washington
3. RENOUF, M.A. (1981). An analysis of the fuel consumption of commercial
   vehicles by computer simulation. TRRL Supplementary Report 973,
   Transport and Road Research Laboratory, UK Department of the Environment,
   Crowthorne
4. Irish Management Institute (1983). Irish transport and distribution
   handbook 1982/83, Dublin
5. BEARDWOOD, J., HALTON, J.H. and HAMMERSLEY, J.M. (1959). The shortest
   path through many points. Proceedings of the Cambridge Phil. Soc.,
   55:299
6. EILON, S., WATSON-GANDY, C.D.S., CHRISTOFIDES, N. (1971). Distribution
   management; mathematical modelling and practical analysis. Griffin,
   London
7. GOLDEN, B.L. (1977). A statistical approach to T.S.P. Networks 7:
   209-225
8. BESSE, H. (1979). Der Einsatz eines Tourenoptimierungs programms für
   die Milcherfassung einer Molkerei als Teil der Kurzfristigen
   Produktionsprogrammplannung. Kieler Milchwirtschaftliche Forschungs-
   berichte

CONTRIBUTION TO THE IMPROVEMENT OF INDUSTRIAL BUILDING DESIGN CRITERIA AIMING AT A RATIONAL UTILIZATION OF ENERGY FOR SPACE HEATING, ON THE BASIS OF AN INVESTIGATION CARRIED OUT ON EXISTING PLANTS

Dr. P. Immordino

FIAT Engineering SpA.
Via Belfiore 25
I-10125 Torino

1. INTRODUCTION

At present, the energy consumptions for space heating of the indu-strial buildings are an important amount of the total energy balance in the industrial countries.

Several energy saving investigations carried out on industrial plants emphasized important inefficiencies in space heating.

Said inefficencies may be reduced through a better design of the "building-systems".

At present, an organic, comparative and critic collection of data on the actual behaviour of the "building-system" is not available.

2. OBJECTIVE

The investigation aims to determine criteria both for design of new industrial buildings and for retrofit on existing ones.

The reference to experimental data on "building-systems" behaviour is the peculiarity of the research. In fact the data will result not only from theoretical evaluations or laboratory tests but they will derive from experimental investigations on industrial buildings carried out in actual conditions.

3. WORK PROGRAMME

The project aims at examining deeply the "building-systems" perfor-mances for the most significant industrial typologies through a critic census of the said typologies, experimental survey on existing buildings and use of physical and mathematical models.

The organic and critic collection of gathered information is aimed at limitation and rationalization of energy demand for space heating both in new industrial buildings and in existing ones.

3.1 Stages of this project

The project will be subdivided in the following stages:

a) critical census of the main building and installation typologies and their classification according to their use and to the climatic and environmental conditions.
Fiat group is ready to make all information relevant to its indu-

strial plants available on the purpose of carrying out said investi
gations.

b) Identification of criteria for the comparison of different "building-systems" performances.

c) Experimental investigations to single out the actual performances
of typical industrial buildings.
This phase requires specific experimentation and analysis especially for:
- thermal stratification
- wrong use of heating media
- heat losses
- air flows
- management
- correlations between buildings and energy systems
- correlations between building envelope characteristics and natural lighting
- sectoring of the working areas with different requirements of air
changes.

d) Development of physical and mathematical models to correlate the per
formances of typical buildings with their characteristic parameters.

e) Check of these models accuracy in accordance with the experimental
results of phase 3.

f) Final evaluations (technical, energetic and economical) and development of criteria applicable both to design of new industrial buildings and to retrofitting.

4. PROGRESS

The stages a) and b), pointed out in the previous section 3.1, were
completed.

The stage c) is under progress.

Nineteen industrial buildings of eight different factories were investigated.

The investigations/researches concerned different building shapes:
- big building
- medium building
- small building

Valuations on following matters were carried out, according to the
exprimental fuel consumptions and complying with UNI Standards:
- Heat losses through different items of building envelope
- Machineries and equipments heat
- Air charges

Also, termographies were taken into account to carry out qualitative
valuation on the heat flow uniformity.

5. FIRST EVALUATION OF INVESTIGATED PARAMETERS

A significant spread of figures has been arising, which demonstrates that, at the present stage of the industrial building technology and maintenance, a conscious energy saving behaviour is not always performed.

Therefore it seems possible to locate technical areas where building technologies, equipment design and maintenance criteria may receive some common, energy saving aimed guide line.

TEXTILE INDUSTRY

Presentation by Rapporteur
Dr. J. Carrasse
SYNTEC-Ingénierie
F-75008 Paris

A large proportion of the energy requirements of the textile industry are concentrated in the finishing sector. About 50 % of the energy consumed per ton of fabric by this sector is used in the wet processing stages of desizing, scouring, bleaching, dyeing, etc.

Opportunities for energy savings can be seized in different ways, e.g. by shorter processing times, lower processing temperatures, using less water, combined processing stages, elimination of intermediate drying between successive wet processes. The two projects on the textile industry under the Commission's R and D Programme investigate such means of energy savings :

Industrial application of continuous wet-on-wet treatment of fabric webs
by the Netherland Organisation for Applied Scientific Research TNO :

The possibility of impregnating wet fabrics directly, thus avoiding the energy-expensive intermediate drying stage is being investigated by TNO.

Two methods have been tested in Dutch textile mills :

–   impregnation of a wet cloth on a pad in a modified way : a pad is often used to impregnate dry fabric. Wet fabrics can also be impregnated in a pad, the concentration of the solution being adjusted. TNO determined the optimal values of this concentration as a function of impregnating conditions : type of cloth, speed, initial water content of the cloth, type of substance. The determination of this function, called "parameter" by TNO, is first carried out with a small length of cloth. Once the parameter is known the condition can be calculated for a uniform impregnation of a lot of the same fabric. A large number of "parameter" determinations were carried out by TNO on a full scale laboratory pad. In addition similar experiments were performed with an industrial pad in a Dutch textile mill.

–   impregnation of a weth cloth by means of engraved rollers :
    In this method some solution of the bath is applied to the fabric by means of the engravings of the roller, the fabric having no contact with the bath. Satisfactory results were obtained on a semi-technical printing machine and the process proved to be much less dependent of the working conditions. A final conclusion will be drawn after a few tests in industry have been carried out.
    It is of interest to note that the progress of this investigation is regularly discussed with representatives from industry.

<u>Low energy preparation processes for textiles</u> by the Shirley Institute :

The objective of the project was to develop a sequence of optimum low-energy pathways for the preparation of cotton and polyester/cotton fabrics. Energy consumption of up to 30 GJ/tonne of fabric processed is not uncommon. From the work carried out in the project, the authors recommend a process which consumes a maximum of 7 GJ/tonne.

The recommended process depends upon the use of a steam purge unit. Fabric runs counter-current to the flow of steam, which displaces air in the fabric. On immersion of the purged fabric into the preparation solution, there is instantaneous and uniform impregnation. This is an essential feature of rapid processing at this stage : reaction at 40°C for 5 hours produces acceptable results, and the only significant energy requirement is for washing-off and drying. To maximise reductions in energy and water consumption, the three separate processes of desizing, scouring and bleaching were combined into a single process.

The steam purging unit had been patented by the Shirley Institute and a full-scale equipment is now being manufactured. Many finishing companies have expressed an interest in this equipment and the process for fabric preparation.

INDUSTRIAL APPLICATON OF CONTINUOUS WET-ON-WET TREATMENT OF FABRIC WEBS

Ir. R. B. M. Holweg
Fibre Research Institute TNO
97 Schoemakerstraat, NL-2628 VK Delft

SUMMARY

The impregnation of a fabric is often carried out on a pad. For this process use is made of a dry fabric. If use could be made of a wet fabric, energy savings could be obtained as a result of the omission of a drying stage.
The investigation deals with an impregnation process, frequently carried out in the textile finishing industry. It includes the impregnation of a dry fabric with a resin to make the fabric crease resistant. It has been examined in which way this impregnation can be carried out in practice without applying a preliminary drying stage.
The following methods have been tested in Dutch textile mills:
- impregnation of wet fabric on a pad in a modified way;
- impregnation of wet fabric by means of engraved rollers.
Before padding wet fabric it is necessary to determine parameters. These parameters enable the calculation of the conditions to obtain a uniform impregnation of a batch of fabric.
The parameters depend on the type of chemical, fabric and on the fabric speed.
The impregnation process using engraved rollers is significantly less dependent on different factors such as type of fabric.

1. INTRODUCTION

In manufacturing a dyed or a printed fabric from grey material the fabric is subjected to a multiplicity of treatments. The four main characteristic treatments are: impregnating, reacting, washing and drying. They are often performed in the sequence shown in Fig. 1. This sequence of treatments is repeated several times during the manufacturing of a dyed or a printed fabric. In each sequence of treatments the fabric is impregnated with different types of chemicals. The reacting and washing conditions differ as well. In most cases the fabric is dried after each sequence of treatments.

Fabric → Impregnating → Reacting → Washing → Drying →

Fig. 1   Sequence of treatments carried out several times in a textile finishing mill

When a large batch of fabric is impregnated with a resin or a dyestuff, the impregnation is carried out on a pad. To avoid inferior results it is necessary to dry the fabric first.

The pad, shown in Fig. 2, consists of a trough and a squeezing device. The solution of water and chemicals to be applied to the fabric are put into the trough. By means of rollers the fabric is guided through the trough, after which the excess solution is squeezed off.

In this way some thousands of metres of fabric are dyed continuously. If wet fabric could be impregnated continuously on a pad energy savings could be obtained by omitting the drying stage.

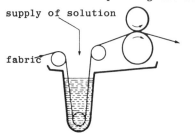

squeezing device

supply of solution

fabric

Fig. 2 Principle of a pad

In some cases wet-on-wet impregnation, which consists of impregnation of wet fabric with a solution, is already applied. This refers to treatments which are carried out discontinuously, and to continuous treatments where lowcost chemicals are applied and where the accuracy of the application is not very important. However, it would be of interest to be able to impregnate wet fabrics reliably in a continuous manner in more difficult situations.

There are several methods which would be suitable. In advance of this investigation in 1978 and 1979 a research project, supported by the Commission of the European Communities, dealing with wet-on-wet impregnation of fabrics, was performed (contract no. 392-78-EENL).

In this research project three different methods were tested and compared in the laboratory. From the experiments it could be concluded that the most promising and simple way to impregnate wet cloth is the method using engraved rollers. However, it is also possible to impregnate wet cloth on a pad.

The above mentioned project was continued by considering an impregnation process, carried out in industry, which started with the use of dried cloth. It was examined in which way the impregnation could be carried out in practice without applying a preliminary drying stage.

2. DESCRIPTION OF THE INVESTIGATION

The investigation under consideration can be divided into the following three stages:
1. An enquiry was made in the textile industry with respect to the type of impregnation processes to be performed with wet fabric without intermediate drying. One of these processes was selected and studied in detail.
2. Pilot or full-scale experiments were performed in the laboratory of the Fibre Research Institute TNO. Three different methods to impregnate wet cloth were tested, including a method which had not yet been tested previously. In this way experience was gathered to enable the performance of the selected impregnation process in practice, without applying a preliminary drying process.
3. Two methods were tested in industry. The results of the usual procedure were compared with the results obtained by impregnating wet cloth.

3. ENQUIRY AND SELECTED PROCESS

3.1. Enquiry

From an enquiry made in the Dutch textile industry it was concluded that textile finishing mills are interested in applying the following chemicals to wet fabric without previously drying the fabric: resins, optical brighteners, softeners, water repellent compounds and dyes.
Moreover, it became clear that the above mentioned chemicals would be applied to wet cloth if a reliable and accurate method would be available. In particular for dyeing processes a high accuracy is needed.

3.2. Selected process

The process selected in the present investigation is the impregnation of fabrics with a resin. This process, carried out frequently is of general interest.
The aim of the resin impregnation is to make the cloth crease resistant. After the (dry) cloth has been impregnated with the resin the cloth is dried and next treated at a high temperature to fix the resin to the fibres of the cloth. A resin frequently used was selected.
In impregnating fabrics with a resin a number of different chemicals are applied at the same time. From these chemicals the catalyst is a very important one, because it is needed for the fixation of the resin to the fibres of the cloth. For this purpose magnesium chloride is often applied. In the experiments the selected resin and magnesium chloride have been applied.

The chemical solution applied to fabrics in order to obtain a crease resistant finish is almost colourless. A green dyestuff is added to the impregnating solution to enable a visual inspection of the process during the experiment.

So, the following chemicals are applied in experiments:
- a resin
- magnesium chloride
- a green dyestuff.

In general in each mill a large number of specialized products are manufactured. Therefore, it is of interest to study the effect of cloth type in the wet-on-wet impregnation. In the investigation three different cloths have been involved: light print cloth, poplin and work clothing. Details on the composition and the weight of these fabrics are given in Table I.

Table I   Composition and weight of the fabrics

Fabric	Composition	Weight per square metre (bone dry)
Light print cloth	100% cotton	0.10 kg
Poplin	100% cotton	0.12 kg
Work clothing	35% cotton 65% polyester	0.25 kg

225

4. PILOT AND FULL-SCALE LABORATORY EXPERIMENTS

4.1. Introduction

The following methods by means of which wet cloth can be impregnated were
selected to be tested in the laboratory:
- impregnating wet fabric on a pad in a modified way;
- impregnating wet fabric by means of engraved rollers;
- impregnating wet fabric by means of foam, which method has not yet been
  tested.

4.2. Experiments on the pad

A pad is usually used to impregnate dry fabric. However, wet fabric may
also be impregnated on a pad, if some precautions are taken. Both the
starting concentration of the solution in the trough of the pad and the
concentration of the solution supplied to the trough during the impregnation have to be adjusted. For the adjustment of these concentrations a
parameter has to be determined. In the preceding investigation a method
was developed to determine this parameter. In this method a (relatively)
small length of fabric is impregnated without supplying a solution to the
trough of the pad which is followed by analyzing samples of the bath. The
parameter depends on the type of chemical and fabric and on the impregnating conditions.
In the present investigation a number of parameter determinations were
carried out, using the three types of fabric and impregnating them with a
solution containing the resin, the dye and magnesium chloride. The effect
of the initial moisture content of the wet fabric and the effect of the
fabric speed were examined.
These determinations were carried out with a pad on a technical scale,
which is represented in Fig. 3. Some of the results obtained will be discussed.

Fig. 3
Pad used in the laboratory experiments

Fig 4. shows the results of two experiments with the poplin cloth in
which only the initial moisture content of the fabric differed. The values found for the parameter (PAR) of the dyestuff and magnesium chloride
are plotted against the initial water content of the wet fabric (R_I). According to theoretical considerations the values of PAR of each chemical
should be on a straight line where the tangent of incline is 1. So there
appears to be a fairly good agreement between theory and practice.

4.3. Impregnation of wet fabric by means of engraved rollers

Experiments with engraved rollers were performed on a semi-technical printing machine, which is shown in Fig. 6. Modifications of the printing machine were introduced to make it more suitable for the impregnation of wet cloth.
Fig. 7 shows a diagram of the arrangement, in the case of the impregnation of wet fabric by means of an engraved roller.

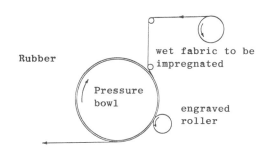

Fig. 6 Printing machine

Fig. 7 Diagram of the printing machine for wet-on-wet impregnation

A solution containing the same chemicals as used in the experiments with the pad was applied to the wet cloth. The way this solution is applied is schematically represented in Fig. 8. The solution to be applied is put into the trough. By means of a rubber roller the solution is applied to the engraved roller. The excess solution on this roller is scraped off with the aid of a doctor blade and next the solution is applied to the fabric. Rollers which are engraved by the milling technique are suitable for wet-on-wet impregnation. Fig. 9 shows part of a roller engraved in this way. The roller used has the following engraving characteristics:
- 40 holes/cm
- depth of holes 100 µm.

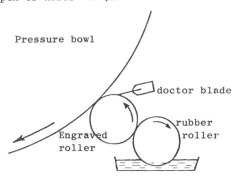

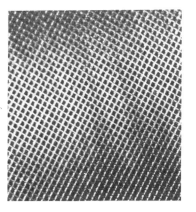

Fig. 8 Scheme of the application of solution with the engraved roller

Fig. 9 Surface of a roller engraved by the milling technique

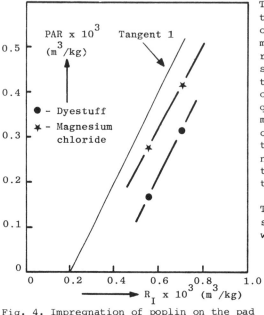

The correlation between PAR and the initial moisture content is of great interest. The initial moisture content of a wet fabric to be impregnated may vary slightly. The correlation means that additional determinations of the parameter are not required. Considering the mathematical description of the process it may even be said that the starting concentration need not be changed in practice when the initial moisture content of the fabric varies.

The effect of fabric speed is shown in Fig. 5 in the case of work clothing.

Fig. 4. Impregnation of poplin on the pad
Effect of the initial moisture content of the fabric (R_I) on the parameter (PAR)

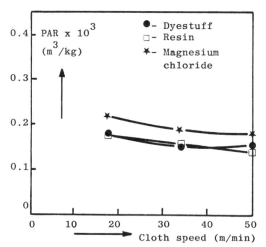

Fig. 5
Impregnation of work clothing on the pad
Effect of fabric speed on the parameter (PAR)

Note
The values of PAR are corrected values which would have been found when the initial moisture content of the fabric in each experiment would have been exactly $0.450 \cdot 10^{-3}$ m³/kg

When a solution is applied to one side of the fabric the penetration of the solution into the fabric is of interest. This is satisfactory in the case of print cloth and poplin. For work clothing a roller is required which can supply a larger amount of solution.

The effect of process variables is dealt with in the description of the industrial experiments. It is only pointed out that the pressure between the printing roller and the cloth should be controlled accurately. It influences the amount applied.

4.4. Impregnation of wet fabric by means of foam

By means of foam a solution can be applied to wet fabric by adding only a small amount of water.

A foam is obtained by adding a foaming agent to the solution containing the chemicals to be applied. Next air is blown in the solution and the air and the solution are thoroughly mixed. This is performed on a special machine.

Experiments have been carried out on a semi-technical installation, enabling the application of foam to fabric by means of two methods, shown schematically in Fig. 10 and Fig. 11. Fig. 10 shows a diagram of the method by means of which foam is applied to a rubber roller after which the foam is applied to the fabric. Fig. 11 shows a diagram of the application of foam by means of the vertical slit method. The foam in the slit has a subatmospheric pressure, which results in penetration of the foam into the fabric passing the slit.

The foam applied in the experiments composed of a resin, magnesium chloride, a green dyestuff and foaming agents. In the experiments a wetted poplin cloth was used.

From the experiments performed it may be concluded that wet fabric can be impregnated reasonably well by foam using each method. A rather homogeneous impregnation across the width and an adequate penetration are obtained.

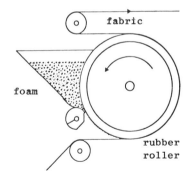

Fig. 10 Foam application with a roller

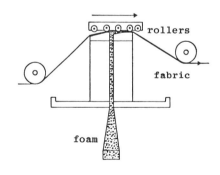

Fig. 11 Foam application with a vertical slit

5. FULL SCALE EXPERIMENTS IN INDUSTRY

5.1. Introduction

After completion of the laboratory experiments the following methods were
selected to be tested in Dutch textile mills:
- impregnation of wet fabric on a pad in a modified way,
- impregnation of wet fabric by means of engraved rollers.

The method using foam was not evaluated in industry, because it would be
necessary to develop an application technique and a suitable recipe to
obtain optimum results. The recipe determines the foam characteristics,
which influences the application.

5.2. Impregnation of wet fabric on a pad in industry

For the impregnation of wet fabric on a pad an industrial installation
was available consisting of a heavy duty squeezing device and a pad which
is shown in Fig. 12. The wet fabric was squeezed off as well as possible
on this installation and then impregnated in one continuous operation.
First parameter determinations were carried out on the installation. The
parameters were determined of the same fabrics as used in the laboratory
experiments. The fabrics were impregnated too with the same solution containing a resin, magnesium chloride and a green dyestuff. However, the
fabric speed was not varied and was in all experiments 50 m/min.

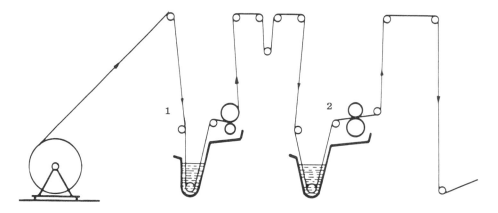

Fig. 12 Scheme of the industrial padding installation
1. Heavy duty squeezing device   2. Pad

The results of the determinations show higher parameter values compared
with those obtained on the pad used in the laboratory experiments. The
industrial pad slightly differs from the laboratory pad used. The trough
of the industrial pad contains a larger amount of solution; moreover the
diameter of the roller in the trough is larger. The established deviations in the parameter values may be attributed to the differences mentioned.

By means of the parameter values found the conditions for a continuous, uniform impregnation of the fabrics were calculated. Next batches of wet fabrics with lengths of several hundreds of metres were impregnated with a continuous supply of solution to the trough. During the impregnation bath samples were taken and next analyzed. It appeared that the concentration of the chemicals in the bath remained fairly constant during the passage of the fabrics (within 1% for the dye and the chloride, within 2% for the resin). This means that the wet fabrics were impregnated homogeneously.

5.3. Impregnation of wet fabric with engraved rollers in industry

By means of engraved rollers wet fabrics were impregnated on an industrial installation, used for the application of small quantities of solution to dry fabrics (Dutch patent no. 160891, November 6,1981). This installation consists of four identical units. Each unit includes a trough, an engraved roller, a rubber and a metal roller (cf. Fig. 13). Solution from the trough is applied to the rubber roller by means of the engraved roller. The solution put on this roller is applied to the fabric. This application method differs from the one used in the laboratory (compare Fig. 13 and Fig. 8).

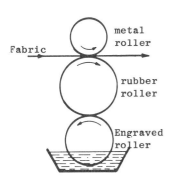

Fig. 13. Scheme of the industrial installation used to impregnate wet fabric by means of engraved rollers

A number of experiments have been carried out on the installation. In the experiments the amount of solution applied to the wet fabrics under different conditions was determined. Moreover, it was examined whether the impregnation was homogeneous. In the experiments the three types of fabric mentioned in Table I were wetted and next impregnated on the installation the troughs of which were filled with a solution containing green dye and sodium chloride. For practical reasons resin and magnesiumchloride were not applied. After the impregnation the fabrics were dried. From the experiments it was concluded that the amount of solution applied in ml/m^2 is rather independent of the type of fabric, the fabric speed and the water content of the fabric before impregnation (cf. Table II). The amount of solution applied slightly differs from the amount of solution applied to a dry fabric. Furthermore, it appeared that each individual unit applied almost equal amounts.

To check whether the application was homogeneous the dried, impregnated fabrics were examined with a spectrophotometer. From these measurements it appeared that the impregnation is fairly equal along the length and the width of the fabric. Both sides of the fabric differ not much.

Table II

Impregnation of fabrics on the industrial installation with engraved rollers

Fabric	Squeezing off before impreg- nation	Fabric speed (m/min)	Amount applied per square metre (ml)
Light print cloth	moderate	20	38
	heavy	20	38
	heavy	40	38
	heavy	60	38
Poplin wet	heavy	20	36
dry	-	20	43
Work clothing	heavy	20	40

6. ECONOMIC EVALUATION

The amount of energy which can be saved when fabric is impregnated wit-
hout a preliminary drying depends upon several factors (e.g. on the ma-
chine running hours).
Annually the savings may be Dfl. 150,000,-- per mill.
The investments which depend on several factors as well may amount to
Dfl. 200,000,--.

7. CONCLUSION

By means of engraved rollers wet fabrics can be impregnated in the best
way. In using this method the application only slightly depends on different factors (e.g. type of fabric).
The method using a pad is more complicated and a number of preparations
need be made before a batch of wet fabric can be impregnated in this way.

LOW ENERGY PREPARATION OF COTTON AND COTTON BLENDS

J. G. Roberts and B. C. Burdett

Shirley Institute, Didsbury, Manchester M20 8RX, U.K.

Summary

The objective of the project outlined in this paper was to
develop a sequence of low-energy pathways for the preparation
of cotton and polyester/cotton fabrics. Surveys of current
practice show that energy requirements for fabric preparation
range between 10 and 30 GJ/tonne of fabric processed.
Investigations carried out in the project have lead to a process
that consumes a maximum of 6.9 GJ/tonne. The recommended
process depends upon steam purging the loomstate fabric prior
to the fabric entering the preparation solution where
instantaneous and uniform impregnation occurs. In addition,
the three separate processes of desizing, scouring and bleaching
have been combined into a single-stage process. It is thus
possible to achieve acceptable preparation of cotton fabrics at
room temperature with reaction times of only a few hours. From
laboratory trials, a storage (reaction) time of 5 hours is
recommended for batchwise processing. Overall, the only
significant energy requirement (6.9 GJ/tonne) is for washing
and drying. In addition, machinery is much simplified, requiring only a steam purge pad-batch unit, and a washing and drying
range.

1. INTRODUCTION

The objective of the project was to develop a sequence of
optimum low-energy pathways for the preparation of cotton and
polyester/cotton woven fabrics.

The final stages of production of textile materials are
application of colour by dyeing or printing and the application of
special finishes to impart properties desirable for the end use of
the material. However, before any of these processes can be
carried out, textile fabrics require preparation. The latter
consists of a series of energy consuming processes that may require
upwards of 30 GJ/tonne of fabric processed.

In the conventional preparation of cotton and polyester/cotton
woven fabrics the following sequence of processes is carried out:

1. Singeing

In the singeing process, surface fibres are removed by passing
the fabric through a gas flame. The energy requirement is consequently low and is of the order of 0.3 to 0.4 GJ/tonne of fabric
processed. As fire is a risk in this process it is normal for the
fabric to be passed directly into a quench bath which is frequently
used as the impregnating step for the next process, namely, desizing.

2. Desizing

To remove size from a fabric it must either be swelled in

233

water or broken down by acid or enzyme. Sizes are polymeric
materials that are applied to strengthen and lubricate fibres during
weaving. The most common sizes are starch based; synthetic sizes
such as polyvinyl alcohol or polyacrylamide are also used. Synthetic sizes are generally soluble or are highly swollen in water and
thus do not require to be degraded. However, starch and starch
derivatives do require breaking down to render them soluble.
Whichever method is used to remove the size, the appropriate
reaction is time and temperature dependent so that, in practice,
a period of heating or a longer dwell in the cold is necessary.
Such a delay may be followed by either a washing-off process or
the next stage of preparation. If washing is carried out, an energy
use of about 5 GJ/tonne is required.

3. Scouring

Scouring is an alkaline treatment that saponifies amd removes
fats and waxes and solubilises pectic cell-wall material in the
cotton fibre. It is this stage that drastically affects the
wettability of the fabric. In processing polyester/cotton fabrics
the level of alkalinity must be controlled so that the polyester is
not significantly hydrolysed. Again this process is time and
temperature dependent and the way in which it is carried out varies
from approximately 24 hours in the cold to one or two minutes at
$110^{o}C$. In most cases scouring is followed by washing-off to remove
the impurities.

Scouring can be a high-energy process consuming about 5 GJ/
tonne. Subsequent washing-off requires a further 5 to 6 GJ/tonne.

4. Bleaching

Although, at this stage, fabric is now cleaner and wettable
it is coloured. Oxidative bleaching is carried out to improve
the ground colour of the fabric and to provide a uniform base
for subsequent processes. The chemical most commonly used is
hydrogen peroxide though sodium hypochloride and sodium chloride
are also used; hydrogen peroxide was used throughout the project.

As with scouring, the bleaching process is carried out on a
wide variety of machines with equally widely differing time and
temperature characteristics. Hence the energy requirements are
similar and may amount to 5 GJ/tonne. Washing-off is an important
part of the processing and is again found to require about 5 GJ/
tonne. This energy requirement is very dependent on the water
consumption in the process and can also be significantly influenced
by the use of a heat exchanger to recover heat from the effluent.

5. Drying

The final washing-off is followed by drying. This latter
stage is usually carried out on cylinders and varies in energy
requirement between 1.9 and 3.7 GJ/tonne. This variation is, in
part, a reflection of variation in fabric width, weight and moisture content.

This sequence of preparation stages, converts an inherently
coloured, sometimes dirty, unwettable material into an absorbent,
clean and white fabric ready to be dyed or printed and finished.
Overall, the preparation process makes a significant contribution
to the energy consumption in a dyeing and finishing works where
cotton or polyester/cotton fabrics are processed. Water

consumption is not insignificant either. Upwards of 30 G/J tonne are used in processing such fabrics.

In order to determine the above energy contents of individual stages in the preparation sequence, surveys were conducted of typical preparation processes in textile mills processing cotton or polyester/cotton fabrics. Three such examples are given in Table 1, together with the energy content of energy consuming stages and the total energy use. It is clear from this information that modifications in the separate stages resulting in reduced energy consumption are highly desirable, provided production rates and fabric quality do not suffer.

It was envisaged that processing could be achieved with a very low energy use. Hence, it was thought desirable to eliminate all heated processing with the exception of the singeing process, final washing-off and drying. An overall energy use of about 6 GJ/tonne would then be possible. From the work carried out in the project a preparation process consuming a maximum of 6.9 GJ/tonne of fabric is recommended (Table 2).

2. METHODS OF INVESTIGATION

To achieve low energy use in preparation, three broad areas of experimentation were carried out, namely,

a. steam purging
b. combined desizing, scouring and bleaching, and
c. catalytic or activated bleaching.

2.1 Steam Purging

A significant factor in all preparation reactions is the poor wettability of the fabric in the early stages of processing. If air can be displaced from interstices within the fabric, either by applying steam or vacuum, then a fabric can be fully wetted-out on immersion in a solution. The fabric should have no further contact with air during the intervening period between the original air displacement and immersion.

Steam purging of fabric enables air to be displaced by steam and the method is used primarily to enable complete wetting-out to occur when impregnating textile materials. The principle of the method is described in British Patent No. 1,468,028.

In a steam purging unit, the fabric passes vertically down an insulated chamber where it meets a counter current flow of steam, which displaces air in the fabric. The fabric outlet of the unit, the probe, dips into a trough containing the impregnating solution where impregnation is instantaneous and uniform throughout the width and construction of the fabric. During much of the period of the project various modifications of the unit have been evaluated, particularly the seal contained within the probe. A line diagram of the final laboratory equipment is shown in Figure 1; full-scale equipment based upon this laboratory unit is now being manufactured under licence by Sir James Farmer Norton International Ltd. Many textile finishing companies have expressed an interest in this equipment and the process recommended for fabric preparation.

Typical improvements in pick-up of impregnating solutions by unprepared (loomstate) cotton fabric is from 35-40% by conventional padding to 85-100% when steam purging precedes impregnation. Thus, thorough wetting-out of loomstate fabric is possible, and this factor was important in determining reaction times of applied preparation solutions as well as their composition.

TABLE 1

Energy Use in Typical Preparation Processes
as Determined by Survey

Energy Consuming Processes	Energy Use (GJ/tonne)
1. Scour (pad steam)	6.2
Wash-off	5.5
Bleach (pad steam)	6.2
Wash-off	5.5
Dry	1.9
	25.3
2. Rope-kier scour, bleach	
and wash-off	7.0
Dry	3.7
	10.7
3. J-box scour, bleach	
and wash-off	8.1
Dry	2.0
	10.1

TABLE 2

Recommended Preparation Process for
Low-Energy Consumption

Energy Consuming Processes	Energy Use (GJ/tonne)
Steam purge, followed by cold combined desize, scour and bleach	Negligible
Wash-off	5.0
Dry	1.9
	6.9

2.2 Combined Desizing, Scouring and Bleaching

To maximise reductions in the consumption of energy, as well
as water, it appeared logical to combine all the three preparation
stages (desizing, scouring and bleaching) into a single-stage
process. A single washing-off stage and a drying stage would then
be the only significant energy consuming stages. If, in addition,
the single preparation reaction could be carried out at ambient

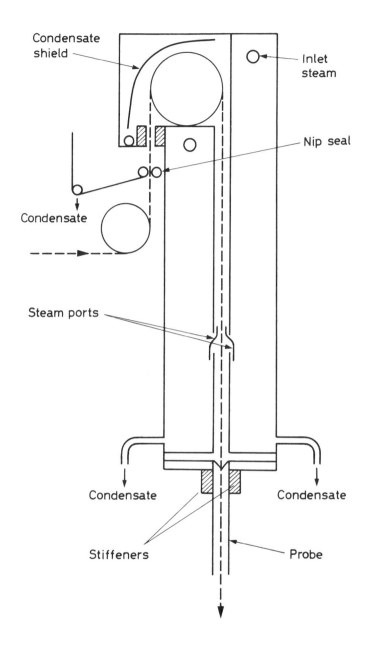

Fig. 1 LABORATORY STEAM PURGE UNIT

temperature, then the energy requirement would be at an absolute minimum. It was also hoped to reduce chemical costs by using a combined preparation process.

Many combined processes have been reported in the literature and almost all of them have been based upon the use of hydrogen peroxide, which is the basis of the work reported here. Reduction in water and steam consumption have been reported (1-4), and fabrics have been prepared that have good tensile strength, excellent degree of whiteness and high wettability (1,3,5). However, many combined preparation processes on cotton fabrics have failed, particularly in continuous processing, because of inadequate seed, wax and size removal (1,6).

These problems have been overcome by steam purging fabric prior to preparation because this has ensured maximum pick-up of the preparation solution by the fabric. Hickman had noted that maximum pick-up of liquor favours seed removal (7). Steam purging also eliminated the need to include special auxiliary chemicals to aid desizing, scouring and bleaching in the combined process. Many other single-stage processes do include special chemicals (1,3,5,8,9).

Application of the chemical compositions was carried out predominantly from aqueous solution. Preparation of fabric by foam application was not completely successful, though the results were sufficiently encouraging for the technique to be developed in future work.

To determine the more effective preparation procedure from aqueous solution in terms of time and temperature, and thus energy consumption, cold-pad followed by cold-batch storage procedures were investigated as well as cold-pad followed by short steaming times.

2.3 Catalytic or Activated Bleaching

Hydrogen peroxide may be used for both desizing and bleaching. However, for optimum effectiveness the conditions of use are different for the two processes. In bleaching there must be a balance between the addition of alkaline activator (sodium hydroxide) and of stabilizer (sodium silicate). On the other hand, oxidative desizing uses a comparatively unstable system, allowing more free radical formation which favours size degradation rather than bleaching (8). Peroxo anions, such as peroxodisulphate, will interact with hydrogen peroxide to form free radicals and thus produce a more effective reaction.

On this basis, sodium peroxodisulphate was used, and its effect evaluated, in the work reported here. This compound was found to have a beneficial effect on fabric preparation, particularly 100% cotton. In the absence of peroxodisulphate, fabric whiteness was lower, and fat and wax removal less effective.

Other compounds were investigated as activators, but only sodium peroxodisulphate brought about controlled activation which was beneficial to fabric preparation.

3. MAIN RESULTS

Ideally, prepared cotton and polyester/cotton fabrics should have the following properties:
high whiteness value, or a value sufficient for the next stages of processing,
low fluidity i.e., minimised chemical damage,
complete seed removal,

low residual size,

good absorbency or wettability, and

low residual fat and wax.

An assessment was made of the effect that each component of the preparation bath had on individual fabrics in terms of the above properties.

3.1 Preparation of Cotton Fabrics

As stated earlier, steam purging was carried out to aid impregnation of the fabric which was a 7 oz seedy loomstate 3:1 twill fabric sized with 10% starch and tallow. Typical experimental conditions and results are given in Table 3.

Overall, whiteness (Taube) values were increased by the presence of sodium silicate and sodium peroxodisulphate, and with increasing time and concentration of hydrogen peroxide. Poor absorbency (high values in the table) was obtained in the presence of peroxodisulphate and by increasing the concentration of sodium hydroxide. On the other hand, absorbency improved if the concentration of hydrogen peroxide and the reaction temperature were both increased. Residual starch was reduced in the presence of sodium silicate and by increasing the concentration of sodium hydroxide; the latter also increased seed removal. However, seed removal was inadequate with all treatments. In addition it was appreciated that all results were affected by the temperature at which the fabric samples were treated in the final washing-off procedure. The temperature was therefore increased from 55°C (as used in the earlier experimental work in order to minimise energy consumption) to 95°C. None of the treatments gave the same level of preparation as the conventional three-stage process.

Improved preparation was obtained when the concentration of hydrogen peroxide was increased (to 50 ml/l) and when the samples were stored for 5h at a reaction temperature of 65°C. However, seed removal was still inadequate. Although the properties of the fabric had improved, the change in the time and temperature had considerably increased the energy consumption. Consequently, a relatively long (e.g. 5h) cold process or a short (e.g. 5 min) steaming (100°C) process was required.

The complex interactions between the components, or variables, outlined above gave rise to the use of a central rotatable plan for the experimental work(10).Initially it was decided to develop a cold batch process; in the laboratory, reaction conditions consisted of a 5h storage time at 40°C. The latter was used to simulate the heating that occurs in full-scale batch bleaching operations.

After carrying out a series of preliminary experiments, to determine the relative contribution of each of the four components to the whiteness values of the prepared fabric, it was possible to design the full experimental plan. The concentration range that was used for each of the four components is given below:-

hydrogen peroxide, 35%	22.0 – 98.0	ml/l
sodium hydroxide	1.0 – 39.0	g/l
sodium silicate	10.5 – 29.5	g/l
sodium peroxodisulphate	5.0 – 15.0	g/l

The plan dictates that each of the four variables is used at five different levels of concentration within the given range, and that 31 experiments are carried out based upon given permutations of

TABLE 3

Combined Desizing, Scouring and Bleaching of Cotton Fabric

Hydrogen Peroxide, 35% (ml/l)	39		39		39		39	
Sodium Hydroxide (g/l)	25		25		25		25	
Sodium Silicate (g/l)	–		12		12		–	
Sodium Persulphate (g/l)	–		–		2		2	
Reaction Time at								
Ambient Temperature (h)	5	24	5	24	5	24	5	24
Whiteness (Taube)	58	64	64	72	68	78	61	67
Absorbency (s)	5.4	4.3	4.3	5.5	6.7	18.3	10.1	8.6
Fat and Wax (%)	0.43	0.42	0.44	0.41	0.38	0.42	0.46	0.47
Starch Equivalent	3.50	2.84	2.13	2.32	2.09	2.92	2.41	2.35

Hydrogen Peroxide, 35% (ml/l)	19.6		19.6		19.6		19.6	
Sodium Hydroxide (g/l)	40		40		40		40	
Sodium Silicate (g/l)	–		20		20		–	
Sodium Persulphate (g/l)	–		–		2		2	
Reaction Time at								
Ambient Temperature (h)	5	24	5	24	5	24	5	24
Whiteness (Taube)	50	54	52	61	57	69	55	56
Absorbency (s)	11.9	13.3	7.8	7.9	4.9	8.4	15.3	13.4
Fat and Wax (%)	0.36	0.31	0.35	0.33	0.32	0.34	0.42	0.36
Starch Equivalent	1.55	1.56	1.48	0.90	1.42	1.68	1.93	1.68

these concentrations. Each of the 31 experiments included magnesium sulphate (0.1 g/l) to simulate water hardness, and Sandogen CBN (Sandoz) (6 g/l), an emulsifier to aid removal of impurities in the washing-off process. It was immediately observed that it was necessary to use higher concentrations of hydrogen peroxide and sodium peroxodisulphate than hitherto.

Analysis of the properties of each of the prepared cotton samples gave the following range of results:

Whiteness (Taube)	69.5	–	95.5
Fluidity	4.24	–	2.32
Seed Removal	34	–	99%
Residual size (starch)	1.6	–	0.35%
Absorbency	1.8	–	$<$ 1s (with water)
Residual fat and wax	0.384	–	0.170

The values on the right hand side of each range indicated that it was possible to obtain commercially acceptable results. However, it was necessary to obtain a computer analysis of the significant effects and two-dimensional contour diagrams before an optimum recipe could be predicted.

Analysis of significant effects confirmed the complexities of the interactions and indicated that; whiteness was dependent upon peroxide, sodium hydroxide and silicate; fluidity upon peroxide, sodium silicate and peroxodisulphate; seed removal upon peroxide and sodium hydroxide; fat and wax upon sodium hydroxide and silicate. Absorbency and residual starch could not be analysed for significant effects because the values of these two properties were not sufficiently wide spread.

From the total data, the following optimum recipe was obtained:

hydrogen peroxide, 35%	90	ml/l
sodium hydroxide	30	g/l
sodium silicate	30	g/l
sodium peroxodisulphate	5	g/l
together with, magnesium sulphate	0.1	g/l
Sandogen CBN (Sandoz)	6	g/l

This predicted recipe was confirmed experimentally and demonstrated clearly that it was possible to prepare a 100% cotton fabric to commercially acceptable standards. However, although the energy requirements for the total process is at a minimum (6.9 GJ/tonne) and the water consumption has been drastically reduced, the concentration of chemicals, and therefore costs of chemicals, has increased.

The alternative preparation conditions i.e., cold pad followed by a short steaming process, was investigated. Again a central rotatable plan was used for the experimental work, but a fifth variable, time, was added. Although the experiments were successfully carried out and acceptable preparation was possible, the following must be noted:

1.   The use of more energy than the previously described procedure.

2.   The results were sensitive to small changes in values of the variables, particularly time.

For these reasons, the cold pad, cold storage preparation procedure is recommended.

3.2 Preparation of Polyester/Cotton Fabrics

Work carried out on a 50/50 polyester/cotton fabric (4oz, having a mixed size of maize soluble starch, polyvinyl alcohol and acrylic) was sufficient to indicate that acceptable preparation could be achieved by a combined single stage process. The most satisfactory results were obtained when sodium silicate was replaced by an organic stabiliser (1 g/l). A reaction time of 1h at either ambient temperature or 60°C produced satisfactory preparation; at 60°C the fabric had a better prepare than from the conventional process: e.g. whiteness value was 87 (average value) as against 79, with residual starch at a value of 0.060% in both cases. Acceptable size removal can be difficult to achieve on polyester/cotton fabrics because of the use of different mixtures of synthetic sizes. This can be overcome by using either organic stabiliser (as above) or using a pretreatment in cold water when sodium silicate is used as the stabiliser.

4. CONCLUSIONS

The project has clearly demonstrated that acceptable low-energy preparation of cotton and polyester/cotton fabrics can be obtained. Using a steam purge unit followed by a combined single-stage process, it is recommended that cotton fabrics be stored at ambient temperature (40°C in the laboratory) for 5h. The only significant energy use occurs in washing-off and drying, and amounts to 6.9 GJ/tonne. In comparison to conventional processing this represents a large reduction in energy consumption and leads to economies in textile preparation. Economies in machinery requirements can be made because only pad-bath, batching frame, washing range and drying facilities are required.

REFERENCES

1. DICKINSON,K., KINDRON, R.R. and CURZONS, P., Text. Chem. Col., 14 (1982) 126.
2. DICKINSON, K., J. Society Dyers and Colourists, 95 (1979) 119.
3. COOK, F.L., Text. Chem. Col., 14 (1982) 10.
4. STUHLMILLER, M. and LEHMANN, H., Textile Praxis Int., 37 (1982) 524.
5. CARRON, H., Teintex, 45 (1980) 23.
6. EVANS, B.A., Text. Chem. Col., 13 (1981) 254.
7. HICKMAN, W.J., Int. Dyer, 160 (1978) 600.
8. DICKINSON, K. and THOMPSON, T.J., Amer. Dyestuff Reporter, 69 (1980) 19.
9. BISHOP, B.J., Amer. Dyestuff Reporter, 68 (1979) 37.
10. COCHRAN, W.G. and COX, G.M., Experimental Designs, 2nd Edn., John Wiley and Sons.
    DAVIES, O.L. (Ed.), The Design and Analysis of Industrial Experiments, 2nd Edn., 1978, Longmans.

CEMENT AND GLASS CERAMIC INDUSTRY

Presentation by Rapporteur
Dr. P. S. Rogers
Department of Metallurgy & Materials Science
Imperial College, London, S. W. 7., U. K.

The cement, glass and ceramic industries are all large consumers of energy, particularly since in each case the production methods involve high-temperature processes. It is therefore very profitable to look for savings in energy consumption, since even a small percentage saving in fuel costs represents a substantial saving in overall cost.

In this session there are two papers which deal, in different ways, with energy saving in cement manufacture, a paper which describes how steelmaking slags may be used in the cement industry, and finally a paper which describes how energy may be conserved in the manufacture of glass-ceramics from industrial by-products.

The first paper which is reported here is from P. Corompt and M. Launay of the Commissariat à L'Energie Atomique at the Centre d'Etudes Nucléaires de Grenoble, and N. Musikas and B. Douailler of the Societé des Ciments d'Origny : *'Investigations on raw materials preparation, transfer and baking in a cement factory to optimise energy consumption'*.

Fuel costs represent about 30% of the total costs for cement manufacture. One of the contributions to this energy consumption is the overbaking (over-firing) which is found necessary to compensate for the fluctuations in composition which are encountered in the raw mill that is fed to the kiln. The objectives of the work have been two-fold :
  (a) to develop a method for analysing the preparation circuits for the raw mill,
  (b) to develop a method for monitoring the passage of material through the kiln.
The investigations have been carried out at the partially-automated cement works near Bayonne in South West France. The study has been effected by making use of radioactive and fluorescent tracers. The main results may be summarised taking the stages in the manufacturing circuit in turn.

A study of the raw mill preparation circuits was carried out to determine their mixing capacities. Marked cement-mortar blocks, as simulated rocks, were added to the quarried material which provided the feed to the grinder. The results of this tracer study were obtained in the form of pulse responses of the raw mill preparation circuit from the quarry, to the grinder and thence to the homogenisation silo. It was found that there were variations of ± 25% from a set deviation in the concentrations of marker materials in the raw mill coming out of the grinder. Similar tracer studies of the homogenisation silos showed that blowing air for one hour yielded values with fluctuations of ± 3% from a set deviation, measured on a batch of 850 tonnes; the fluctuations decreasd to ± 0.75% for homogenisation over a two hour period. The results are interpreted in terms of a mathematical model for the preparation and transfer circuit which is represented by a superposition equation.

A study of kiln operation made by tracing the kiln charge showed that, while the mean residence time in the kiln was about 1½ hours at a rotation speed of 1.1 r.p.m., 10% of the charge stays longer than 4 hours, and a further 10% passes through in less than 45 minutes. This dispersion of transit speeds is thought to be related to the physical condition of different fractions, such as particle size and liquid content.

When a fresh pre-homogenisation stockpile is used, no special instructions are transmitted to the kiln operators regarding baking (or firing) conditions. The monitoring work consists of observing continuously the final 10 metres of the 60 metre long kiln by television. The more difficult of the raw mill input materials still show dust particles at the output after one hour, and a variation in the size and speed of the clinker as it travels down the slope. This monitoring is combined with regular 30 minute monitoring of free lime content of the cement clinker. Should these tests recommend, the flow rate of the raw mill is reduced by about 5%, and the composition of the feed is adjusted by suitable additions to the homogenisation silos that follow.

The authors conclude that the use of tracers has shown that there are problems associated with the   mixing of the raw materials, and that consequently steps have already been taken to make improvements to the process. They estimate that savings of up to 2% on energy consumption can be made, which would represent a saving of 0.6% on the production costs overall.

The   second paper in this group is by J.C. Grosjean, M. Hamman and R. Pazdej of IRSID, F.P. Sorrentino of Lafarge-Coppée and C.M. George and M. Verschaeve of Lafarge Fondu International : *A Study of treatment of oxygen steelmaking slag for use in the cement industry*.

The aim of this work was to study ways in which the alumina content of steelmaking slag could be increased so that the slag possessed hydraulic properties, and could thus find use in the cement industry. Such a material would be of advantage to the cement industry, since it would produce a hydraulic material without consuming extra energy; it would also contribute to reduction in steelmaking costs by giving value to a by-product. If the slag is to have hydraulic properties, then the alumina content has to be raised from the 1 to 2% in typical oxygen-steelmaking slags to about 10%. The project has investigated ways in which this increase in alumina level can be achieved. The treatment consisted of using an aluminous flux ('Camflux') in the converter or adding bauxite to the liquid slag in the slag pot after leaving the converter, or a combination of these methods.

'Camflux' is an aluminous flux produced by melting bauxite with limestone. Its addition to the converter was intended to have the dual effects of increasing the alumina content while at the same time providing lime in a reactive form. The high cost of 'Camflux' meant that it was not advisable to add sufficient quantities to attain the full 10% alumina level. However, it was considered that sufficient addition to raise the alumina level to about 3% was sensible, because this would give the advantage of more efficient refining. Three heats were made at the Usinor steelplant at Dunkerque, and the slag produced had the predicted increase in alumina content, but the metallurgical success of the trials was not conclusive because of overhigh temperatures unrelated to the trials.

The second method by which the alumina content was raised was by making additions of bauxite, to liquid in a 20 tonne slag pot (ladle), again at the Usinor steelplant. Because extra heat was required for the assimilation of the bauxite, oxygen was injected via a lance into the slag. This generated heat by the oxidation of iron from divalent to the trivalent state ; in some cases further heat was provided by making additions of aluminium metal scrap; further, in some of these cases 'Camflux' had been added to the converter. These trials produced slags with up to 6% Al_2O_3 if only bauxite was added, but there was over 10% Al_2O_3 in slag resulting from bauxite and aluminium scrap additions and the use of 'Camflux'.

Mineralogical studies of the untreated and treated slags showed that the increase in alumina content was associated with the formation of hydraulic phases, including calcium alumino-ferrites and calcium aluminates. The hydraulic behaviour was determined in strength versus time tests. The treated slag had intrinsic hydraulic properties on its own, with just 7% of gypsum added to control the hydration of aluminate phases. When mixed with 85% Portland cement, the behaviour was found to be comparable with the best blast-furnace slag cement compositions.

Analysis of the production costs by the authors suggests that the cost of producing alumina-enriched slag at the rate of 150,000 tonnes per year is about 100 FF per tonne. They consider that this cost makes mixtures with Portland cement uncompetitive with similar blast-furnace slag/Portland cement mixtures. Alternative applications, in which it is used as a binding agent for road materials or, after further optimization of its composition, as a cement in its own right, appear to be the most promising.

The third paper is by R. Margrita and H. Santos-Cottin of the Centre d'Etudes Nucléaires de Grenoble and C. Pailhes of the Laboratoire Lafarge Coppée Recherche at Viviers : *'Cyclone heat-exchangers : Establishment of a method to define and improve their performance'.*

The project described is concerned with the working parameters of cyclones in a preheater tower above a cement kiln. The preheater is provided for the thermal preparation of the input material to the kiln, by a contra-flow heat exchange between the cold raw feed descending towards the kiln and the hot gas drawn up to the top of the tower by fans. The objective of the project was to reduce the energy consumption in the preheater tower: this would be achieved by, firstly, increasing the separation efficiency of the cyclones and, secondly, decreasing the pressure drop in the cyclones.

The methods employed have been to carry out a theoretical study of the physical parameters which govern the separation of gas and solid material, and the pressure loss. A computer program was designed to show the influence of variations in dimensions of the cyclone, temperature, chemical mixture, particle size and density and flow rates of gas and solid.

In parallel with the theoretical modelling, an experimental study was carried out at the 'Le Teil' cement plant of Lafarge Coppée in Ardeche. In this work, a detection method using sodium-24 radioactive tracer was developed and used to observe the distribution of the flow of material at different levels in the preheater tower. The plant operation was also employed to collect the necessary data for the computer program.

The experimental work carried out in the plant allowed some important results to be obtained. Firstly, it was found that the retention time of the material in the cyclones is independent of the size distribution of the particles. Thus, the flow appears as a combined movement, without segregation of particle sizes. This observation conformed with the computer model, because the separation of dust is not mainly due to centrifugation. Indeed, a phenomenon known as 'decantation' occurs when heavily laden gases (1 kg solid per 1 kg gas) enter a cyclone. Secondly, the flow rates of material in different parts of the preheater tower and of particles carried by gases from the kiln were measured, as a means of calculating the separation efficiency of the cyclones. The values for pressure loss and separation efficiency of the cyclones calculated by the computer were in accord with the experimental results.

In the light of these results, the computer program was used to simulate modifications to the geometry of the cyclones. The application of the model indicates that improvements can be achieved by an enlargement by about 10% of the cross-sectional area of the inlet duct and outlet duct of each cyclone; this has the effect of increasing the separation efficiency by 1% and of reducing the pressure loss by 20%. The authors, in their economic evaluation, calculate that these modifications to the geometry would decrease the energy requirements and thus reduce the cost per tonne of clinker produced by 2.13 FF, which would be a financial saving of 1140 thousand francs per year in a plant producing 1700 tonnes of clinker per day. The corresponding increase in profit is not large enough to justify an alteration of a plant already working. Nevertheless, optimisation of the geometry of the cyclones in future installations should be made in line with the computer program, to achieve the maximum energy saving and profit in the newly commissioned plant.

The final paper reviewed here is by P.S. Rogers, J. Williamson, J.F. Bell and M. Campbell of Imperial College of Science and Technology, London : *'Erosion-resistant glass-ceramics made by direct controlled cooling from the melt'*.

The project has been concerned with the pilot-plant development of a process for manufacturing and evaluating a novel glass-ceramic. This material has desirable physical and mechanical properties and it can be made from low cost industrial by-product materials such as blast-furnace slags by a novel energy-saving route.

Glass-ceramics are materials which are made from silicate melts by conventional glass-forming techniques, but by heat-treatment are transformed to fine-grained ceramics of low porosity. The overall energy required to manufacture glass-ceramics is less than that needed for the equivalent sintered ceramics. Furthermore, extra energy savings can be made by adoption of the new process employed at Imperial College. With a particular combination of nucleating agents added to the melt composition, the silicate melt can be converted to a glass-ceramic during a controlled-cooling heat treatment, thus removing the necessity for first quenching to a glass and then reheating which is essential in the conventional process. This novel heat treatment programme provides a further saving in energy requirement.

A pilot-plant has been constructed and used to manufacture the new glass-ceramic, 'Silceram', on a semi-continuous basis. This plant consists principally of an oil-fired tank furnace capable of melting 100kg batches at 1450°C and two electric heat-treatment kilns. The material is formed by casting into metal moulds, sand casting, spin casting or rolling. 'Silceram' glass-ceramics have been made at the pilot-plant from a wide

range of raw materials and a corresponding range of overall chemical
compositions whose principal components are calcium oxide, magnesia,
alumina and silica.   All have added nucleating agent which consists,
chemically, of iron oxide and chromium oxide.   Blast-furnace slag has
been used as a major constituent not only because of its low cost but also
because it accelerates homogenisation of the melt.   A typical composition
which makes use of waste materials as constituents is 60% blast-furnace
slag and 40% red colliery shale with added nucleating agents.
Compositions made up from blended pure oxides and carbonates have also
been made.

The physical and mechanical properties of 'Silceram' glass-ceramics
have been determined by means of well-established techniques.   The
strength (modulus of rupture, 180 MPa) and fracture toughness (2.1 MPa m$^{\frac{1}{2}}$)
are values which correspond to those of a high-quality sintered ceramic,
and are due to the small size (about 2μm) of the pyroxene crystals which
are the principal feature of the microstructure and the almost zero
porosity.   Comparative data with other materials have been obtained,
particularly for resistance to erosion by gas-borne solids.   Tests
carried out on a sand-blasting rig have shown that only expensive ceramics,
such as alumina, have a better resistance to erosion under the test
conditions, indicating the attractiveness of the new glass-ceramic
material compared with other industrially-used materials on a cost/
performance basis.

An economic analysis of 'Silceram' indicates that, for an annual
production of 1000 tonnes in a scaled-up version of the pilot-plant batch
process, the manufacturing cost would be less than £270 per tonne.   If
the possible energy savings associated with burner recuperation and the
use of hot slag direct from the blast-furnace were incorporated in the
process design, then the cost could be reduced to below £200 per tonne.
This manufacturing cost, and the attractive mechanical properties,
indicate that commercial exploitation as a high quality industrial
ceramic is to be expected, particularly in applications where erosion-
resistant sheet or tube is required.

INVESTIGATIONS ON RAW MATERIAL PREPARATION, TRANSFER AND BAKING IN CEMENT FACTORY TO OPTIMIZE ENERGY CONSUMPTION

P. Corompt and N. Musikas

Commissariat à l'Energie Atomique
Centre d'Etudes Nucléaires de Grenoble
85 X – F-38041 Grenoble Cedex

SUMMARY

The development of a method aiming to optimize energy consumption in cement factories from analysis of the operation of the raw mill preparation and transfer circuit and identification of the kiln monitoring parameters was undertaken on BOUCAU cement factory. Tracing of materials carried out in the quarry showed up some defects affecting the mixing capacity of the prehomogenization stockpile and the homogenization silos. The analysis carried out on the kiln operation helped improvements to be made in the measurement devices necessary for clinker baking monitoring. The energy savings liable to be made would lead to a decrease of about 2 % in initial fuel consumption.

1. OBJECTIVE AND DESCRIPTION OF WORK

The cement industry is a large energy consumer. As a defective raw mill is frequently overbaked, a means of reducing this energy consumption is sought by perfecting a method enabling the causes of possible variations in the quality of a raw mill to be analysed and the influence on operation of the kiln to be determined.

The study therefore involves two steps :
- Analysing the operation of the raw mill preparation circuits to detect their defects : poor mixing of additives for exemple.
- Determining the parameters used for monitoring the kiln and reducing the influence of raw mill composition on the quality of the clinker.

This method is developed on a barely automized cement factory, with a raw mill that is difficult to constitute due to the nature of the quarries used, and a thermal balance which poses a few problems. This cement factory is located near BAYONNE in the South-west of France. Figure 1 gives the lay out diagram of this cement factory and shows the raw material transfer and preparation circuits.

2. METHODS OF INVESTIGATION

Study of the raw mill preparation circuits was carried out using tracers which enable the raw material transfers to be followed and the degree of homogeneity of mixing of an additive with the main bulk of the materials to be determined.

Having taken stock of the circuits involved in raw mill preparation in this cement factory, radiactive and fluorescent tracers were used to study:
a/ the mixing capacities of :
   . the quarry-to-grinder circuit including the prehomogenization stockpile.

. the homogenization and storage silos.
b/ operation of :
  . the raw mill grinder
  . the kiln, it being important to follow the dispersion of the charge
    during baking.
The analysis of the kiln monitoring method was carried out with the collaboration of the users.

In decreasing order of priority, the means of regulation used on this
installation are :
- Modulation of the raw mill flow-rate at kiln input. This possibility is
  regularly used if a defect in raw mill baking occurs.
- Modulation of the fuel (coal) feed-rate, which is only implemented if
  the incident persists.
- Modulation of the speed of rotation of the kiln which is used rather for
  disturbances lasting over half a day or on restart-up after the raw mill
  flow has been suspended.
- Adjustment of the flow of air through the kiln, used essentially to maintain as complete a fuel combustion as possible (gas outlet CO, CO_2, O_2
  detectors).

The measurement parameters used to monitor kiln operation are also in
decreasing order of importance.
a/ Visual monitoring of the last 10 meters of the kiln. This monitoring is
   carried out by means of a black and white television camera.
b/ Measurement of the percentage of free lime present in the clinker every
   half-hour constitutes a second warning system.
c/ The third warning parameter is constituted by the variations in the
   temperature of the gases, and of the raw mill, and of the oxygen, carbon dioxide and carbon monoxide contents of these gases permanently
   measured at the kiln input.

Thus in the cement factory studied, kiln monitoring is essentially
based on a certain pragmatism, but the method of study used will enable
guide-lines to be established for investigation and analysis of situations
to be carried out on cement factories in which the monitoring rules could
be different.

3. MAIN RESULTS

3.1 Identification of raw mill preparation circuits
The study enabled the most characteristic to be selected :
- Waterway barge transport of the materials from the quarry to the pre-
  homogenization stockpile.
- The sampling unit enabling a mean representative sample of each barge-
  load to be taken.
- The grinder
- The homogenization and storage silos.

3.2 Operation of the raw mill preparation circuits
Tracings in the quarry using marked mortar blocks simulating rocks
show that the materials in these blocks are distributed with variations in
relative concentrations of about ±25 % from a set deviation in the raw
mill flour coming out of the grinder.

The histogram in figure 2 is homothetic to the material transfer Pulse
Response. It was determined by means of an injection of marked mortar
blocks carried out in the quarry towards the end of the elaboration of the
prehomogenization stockpile.

In the same figure the tracer contents of the raw mill flour samples, of 850 tons each, taken at the two homogenization silo outputs, are also shown. Seven samples were made during the emptying of each silo. The mean values of the tracer contents of these samples are well placed on the histogram expressing the evolution of the tracer concentration of the raw mill during filling of the silos. Moreover, the tracer contents of samples relating to any one silo are distributed around their mean value presenting fluctuations of ±3 % from a set deviation for the silo which was homogenized by air-blowing for one hour, and of only ±0.75 %, still from a set deviation, for the silo which underwent homogenization for twice the length of time.

These results thus confirm the previous study of direct tracing of the charge of a silo already presented (1), which led to fears that the homogenization capacity of these silos might be too low.

The histogram in figure 2 can enable the dispersion in the whole of the raw mill flour of a material additive carried out in the quarry and given by any one prehomogenization stockpile to be evaluated by means of the following mathematical transfer model.

The raw mill preparation and transfer system should be considered to be linear but probably non-stationary in time. It is likely that the passage from one material to another disturbs the conditions of transfer slightly. Moreover, the size of the fluctuations shown by the Pulse Response (R.I.) or the homothetic histogram in figure 2 is a point in favour of this theory. If there was a single R.I. the mixing capacity of the system would be greatly defective.

The mathematical model of the raw mill preparation and transfer circuit should therefore be represented by a superposition equation and not a convolution one. An equation of this kind links the evolution in time of the parameters $e(u)$ and $s(t)$ expressing the composition of the raw mill and $q_e(u)$ and $q_s(t)$ representing the flow-rates per mass of raw mill at input e and output s respectively of this circuit by the relation :

$$s(t) \cdot q_s(t) = \int_0^t e(u) \cdot q_e(u) \cdot h(u,t) \cdot du$$

$h(u,t)$ Pulse Response of the circuit is variable in terms of the instant u of the in-quarry input for example of the flow-rate $q_e(u)$ of material in the circuit.

The family of functions $h(u,t)$ satisfies the following relationships :

$$- \int_0^\infty h(u,t) \cdot dt = 1, \forall \, u \text{ for the Pulse Responses are normed.}$$

$$- \int_0^\infty h(u,t) \cdot du = 1, \forall \, t \text{ such that, to the injection at circuit input of}$$
a range of material of constant composition $e(u)$ and flow-rate $q_e(u)$ there corresponds at the output a range of materials of equally constant composition $s(u)$ and flow-rate $q_s(u)$ once the transient regime has been established.

The distribution of fluctuations in concentration, at the output of a system, of a material, limestone, silica or marl for example, injected according to a law $e(u) \cdot q_e(u)$ can be determined from making the superposition equation discontinuous by setting down :

250

$$a_i = e\ (u_i) \cdot q_e\ (u_i),\ b_j = s\ (t_j) \cdot q_s\ (t_j)\ \text{and}\ h_{ij} = h\ (u_i, t_j)$$

The superposition equation is replaced by the matrix product:

$$b_j = \sum_i a_i \cdot h_{i,j} \cdot \Delta u$$

Two paths can be followed to evaluate the variance σ_b^2
- Determining a family of Pulse Responses h_{ij} by carrying out for example about ten tracings in the quarry at the different stages of composition of the same prehomogenization stockpile so as to be able to calculate the b_j and then the variance of their distribution.
- By elaborating, on a computer, Pulse Responses h_{ij} having the same variance σ_h^2 as that shown in figure 2 and respecting the conditions $\sum_i h_{ij} \cdot \Delta t = 1, \sum_i h_{ij} \cdot \Delta u = 1$ stated previously. Series of b_j terms can then be calculated for distributions a_i of materials introduced into the quarry and the related σ_{bj}^2 can be drawn.
    The first way is the more representative of reality but more cumbersome to implement, so we would recommend the second way, as the test carried out is reputed to give a good appreciation of the σ_h^2.
    The same method can be applied to calculate the distribution of concentration fluctuations in a raw mill composite at homogenization output from the R.I. of this silo determined by means of an instant injection of tracer according to the process already implemented in this study and exposed elsewhere (1).
    Figure 3 summarizes all the measurements and regulations performed to monitor the raw mill manufacture. The purchasing of an X-ray fluorescence sample titration device enabled a reduction to be made in the time needed for a complete analysis of the representative sample from the prehomogenization stockpile and of the samples taken at the base and top of the second and fourth homogenization silos composed from a new stockpile.
    This investment thus enables a better dosing of corrective additives to be obtained and certain homogenization cycles to be repeated.

3.3 Kiln operation
    A tracing of the kiln charge showed a mean time spent by the materials in the kiln of a little over an hour and a half when it is rotating at 1.1 revolutions per minute. These times are, however, very widely dispersed. The 10 % of materials which stay the longest spend more than 4 hours in the kiln. The 10 % which pass through the quickest spend less than 45 minutes.
    This phenomenon of dispersion of transit speeds could be linked to the physical states that the different phases of the clinker adopt : powder, liquid and paste, with variable granulometries.

3.4 Kiln monitoring mode
    In the cement factory studied, the analyses and titrations of the raw mill only serve to prepare the best raw mill that can be manufactured from the quarry vein worked. No special baking instructions are transmitted to the kiln monitors when they start using a fresh prehomogenization stockpile.
    The monitoring mode used therefore consists essentially as specified in figure 4 :
a/ of following the evolution of the televised picture of the last 10 metres of the 60 metre long kiln. The monitors know that the arrival at the kiln input of a raw mill which is more difficult to bake manifests itself one hour later at the output by the appearance of dust particles and

a variation in the size of the clinker balls and grains and in their travel speed on the slope. The televised picture can be confirmed by a direct visual examination of the inside of the kiln.
b/ of measuring the free lime content of the clinker every 30 minutes. The signs mentioned above correspond to a large rise in this content.
c/ of reducing by about 5 % for example the flow-rate of the raw mill feeding the kiln should the afore-mentioned disturbances be confirmed. In the hour which follows, the kiln operator will endeavour to restore the initial flour flow-rate, by overheating.

If the incident detected is in fact caused by a drop in raw mill quality, it can be compensated in the following silos by suitable additions.

The operating instructions provide for a mean content of free lime of 1.5 %, the maximum admissible figure being 1.8 %. But the operating conditions necessary to obtain 1.5 % make the baking system unstable. The slightest disturbance in the air supply or in the raw mill quality results in rapid rises in the free lime content. As a consequence, the operators generally have to respect heating conditions limiting the free lime content to 1.2 %, which leads to an overconsumption of fuel of about 2 %, but which avoids incidents that could cause reductions, or even temporary halts in production.

4. CONCLUSIONS AND PROSPECTS

The use of tracers has shown up problems in raw material mixing. These problems can be solved progressively.

Moreover, investments have been made since the beginning of the study.
- Evaluation of the quality of the clinker was based on its density and on its general visual aspect, which is not very accurate. It is now based on measurement of its free lime content repeated every 30 minutes.
- Only the calcium carbonate content of the sample representative of each barge-load was measured during elaboration of the prehomogenization stockpile. The composition of this stockpile was adjusted by additions based on a complete analysis of a single mean sample obtained after completion of the stockpile by addition and mixing of samples relating to each barge-load.
- The purchasing an X-ray fluorescence analysis apparatus enables the FSC, MS and MAF modules of each barge-load or addition of materials taken from the factory stocks to be determined, improving the accuracy of prehomogeniz-ation stockpile composition.
- Visual examination of the inside of the kiln is replaced by a televised picture which is consulted far more frequently.
- The presence of large stocks of quarry rocks in the factory enables the prehomogenization stockpile to be completed, according to the indications in figure 3, maintaining better control over the composition of the materials involved, which makes it much easier to obtain the required titres and modules.

5. ECONOMIC ASSESSMENT

Fuel consumption represents about 30 % of cement manufacturing costs. Perfect regulation of the raw mill composition would lead to a 2 % decrease in fuel consumption, i.e. a 0.6 % decrease in cement production costs in this cement factory.

The present trend is to go over to dry travel circuits which means losing the perfect homogenization which can be found in wet circuits. Problems similar to those dealt with here could therefore arise in cement factories lacking very good quarry veins and these problems could be approached according to the method described.

REFERENCE

1. COROMPT, P. et al. (1982). Etude par traceurs des paramètres de trans-
   fert du système régulant la composition chimique de l'alimentation des
   fours à ciment afin d'optimiser leur rendement. Energy Conservation in
   Industry - Applications and Techniques - Brussels October 1 1982. -
   Commission of the European Communities.

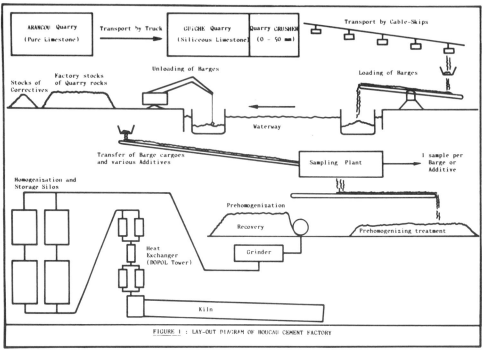

FIGURE 1 : LAY-OUT DIAGRAM OF BOUCAU CEMENT FACTORY

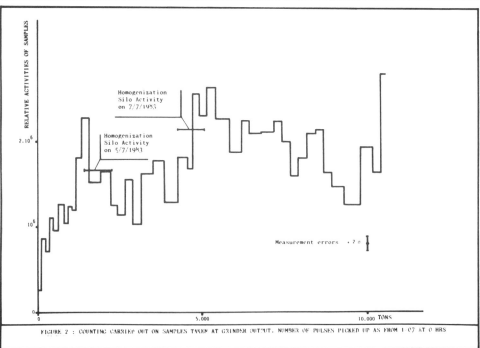

FIGURE 2 : COUNTING CARRIED OUT ON SAMPLES TAKEN AT GRINDER OUTPUT. NUMBER OF PULSES PICKED UP AS FROM 1-07 AT 0 HRS

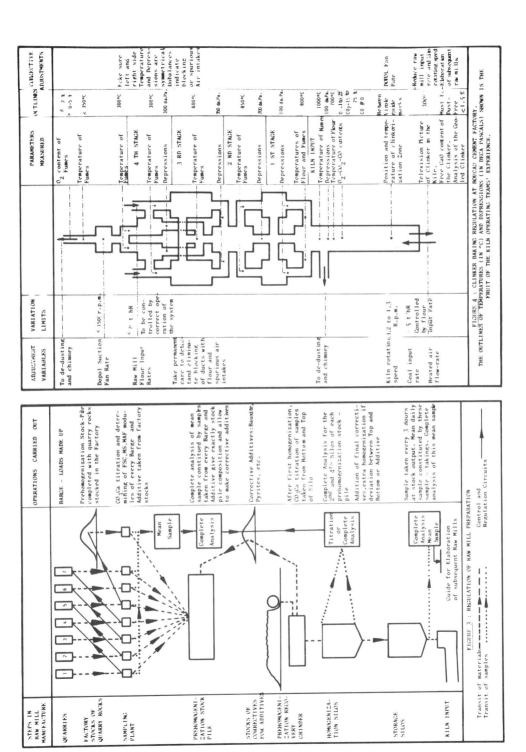

FIGURE 4 : CLINKER BAKING REGULATION AT RONCAI CEMENT FACTORY. THE OUTLINES OF TEMPERATURES (IN °C) AND DEPRESSIONS (IN DECA PASCALS) SHOWN IS THE FRUIT OF THE KILN OPERATING TEAMS' EXPERIENCE.

FIGURE 3 : REGULATION OF RAW MILL PREPARATION

Transit of materials ———
Transit of samples ·········
Control and Regulation Circuits ———

255

A STUDY OF TREATMENT OF OXYGEN STEELMAKING SLAG
FOR USE IN THE CEMENT INDUSTRY

J. C. Grosjean, M. Hamman, R. Pazdej (IRSID),
F. P. Sorrentino (Lafarge-Coppée) and C. M. George (Lafarge Fondu Int.)

IRSID, Station d'Essais
F-57210 Maizières-les-Metz

ABSTRACT

This paper gives the results of an IRSID - Lafarge-Coppée study of treatment of slag resulting from the oxygen steelmaking process, for the purpose of use in the cement industry.

The slag alumina content is increased up to 10 % by adding bauxite and injecting oxygen in the slag pot and/or by adding Camflux in the converter.

The resulting slag exhibits hydraulic properties. When mixed with Portland cement, it behaves like the best blast furnace slags, but the cost of treatment is too high to compete with blast furnace slags for such a use.

The results of the tests leave the hope that the product can be used by itself, provided its composition is optimized and regular. Tests on these grounds would require the construction of a semi-industrial unit.

I. INTRODUCTION

Oxygen steelmaking slags from the refining of low phosphorus hot metal have not yet found any large scale use, except the partial recycling in the blast furnace. These slags contain generally between 1 and 2 % alumina. If this content could be brought to about 10 %, this product should have sufficient hydraulic properties for a use in the cement industry. The use of such a product would bring an energy gain to the cement industry as it should decrease the fuel consumption during the klinker firing operation.

The addition of an alumina bearing product, such as some bauxite, to the liquid slag, would be a way to obtain such a product. The heat necessary for the melting and dissolution of the alumina bearing product could be generated by the oxidation of the divalent iron in the slag through an injection of gaseous oxygen. On the other hand, if the temperature of the slag at the end of the treatment is lower than the initial temperature, part of the sensible heat of the slag would then have been recovered.

However, the bauxite additions are limited by the available heat. And two techniques have been tested in order to increase the Al_2O_3 content of the slag :
- to increase the available heat by adding an exothermic agent in the slag pot as aluminum scraps for example ;
- to increase the Al_2O_3 content of the initial slag by adding an alumina containing flux (Camflux) in the converter.

256

A thermal balance shows that an alumina content of about 10 % can be hoped for by using a combination of these various techniques.

II. USE OF CAMFLUX IN THE CONVERTER

The composition of Camflux (produced by melting a bauxite-limestone mix) is given in Table I. It is an anhydrous product manufactured by Lafarge Fondu International. Addition of Camflux to the converter should provide an increase of the slag alumina content ; it should also act as a fluxing agent for the lime and consequently accelerate the formation of reactive slag.

The attainment of the desired high alumina content (10 %), only by addition of Camflux in the converter, cannot be considered on account of its high cost. An increase of the alumina content of 2 to 3 % however can be advantageous if it allows savings during refining. For example, an increase of the iron yield obtained by decreasing the iron oxide content of the slag.

Three heats were made with addition of five or ten kg/tonne of Camflux in the Usinor steelworks at Dunkirk. The composition of the hot metal charged, of the steel and of the slag obtained are given in Table II.

The alumina content of the slag has indead been raised. It is however not possible to make any conclusion on the metallurgical advantages of use of Camflux because the charges were not representative of normal operation on account of an uncontrolled excessive oxygen blowing, not related to the use of Camflux.

Considerable wear of the refractories was moreover noted. The high temperatures and the high iron oxide content of the slag largely explains such a wear ; a harmful effect of the Camflux can nevertheless not be excluded.

III. TREATMENT IN SLAG POT

The treatment in slag pot consists of an addition of bauxite and a simultaneous injection of oxygen. The oxidation of divalent iron into trivalent iron supplies the energy required to dissolve the bauxite. If the heat released is not sufficient, it should be possible to supply the extra energy by adding aluminum metal in the form of scrap.

III.1. Description of experimental layout

The various techniques described above have been tried in the steel shop No. 2 of Usinor Dunkirk.

In order to have a setting as simple as possible and, as a consequence, to keep the research costs level as low as possible, an existing steel ladle treatment stand has been used for the trials. However, due to this, the possibilities to make trials were reduced as the slag treatment could be done only when the converter associated to the steel ladle treatment stand was not in use.

The experimental setting is shown on Fig. 1. It is mainly composed of :
- a 20 t slag pot ;
- an oxygen lance. The outer diameter of the steel tube is 20 mm

and its length was 4.9 m for the first campaign, and 5.4 m for the next two campaigns because of the very rapid wear observed. It is covered with pure alumina (Purotab from Ker-France) and the outer diameter of the lance is 180 mm on a length of 4 or 4.5 m ;
- an oxygen line (diameter 20 x 27 mm) with various regulation and control devices : 2 manual regulating valves, 1 safety electro-magnetic valve, 2 pressure gauges. The flowrate was measured with a rotameter during the first campaign and with a sonic orifice during the next two campaigns ;
- a temperature sensor Positherm from Electronite. During the third campaign, the temperature was measured with an optical pyrometer ;
- a steel bar for slag sampling.

III.2. Test procedure and results

Eight slag pots were treated. The results are given in Table III.
For trials Nos. 1, 2 and 3, only oxygen was injected. No slopping was observed and a temperature increase of about 100° was obtained within less than 20 minutes. There was however a considerable increase of iron oxide content in some pots, probably due to oxidation of the steel at the bottom of the pots.
For the other trials, bauxite additions between 50 and 200 kg/tonne were made together with the oxygen injection. Aluminum scrap was added for trials 6, 7 and 8 to provide heat. The original content of alumina in pots 7 and 8 had been increased by adding Camflux in the converter.
The maximum Al_2O_3 content was 6 % when only bauxite was added, whereas contents higher than the desired 10 % were obtained by combining the various techniques.

III.3. Properties of the slag

Slag samples of 500 kg were taken from pots 5, 6 and 7 in order to study its properties. An untreated slag was also studied for comparison purposes.

III.3.1. Mineralogical study

The X-ray diffraction and electronic microanalyzer analysis show that alumina was dissolved and that it enriched first the calcium ferrite phase, with a formation of calcium alumino-ferrites ($C_6 A_{1.2} F_{1.8}$).Then, when the Al_2O_3/Fe_2O_3 ratio gets higher than 1.2, calcium aluminates ($C_{12} A_7$) favourable to the hydraulic properties of the product are formed. On the other hand, two phases containing no alumina : dicalcium silicate and magnesio-wustite,are present.

III.3.2. Ability of the slag to be crushed

The products obtained after treatment are very hard and their crushing requires a large energy spending. The fineness had to be limited to 3500 cm²/g for economic reasons, although wished finenesses were 3500, 4500 and 6000 cm²/g. A less fine granulometry lowers however the reactivity of the product.

III.3.3. Strength properties

The first tests showed that although the treated slag alone exhibited hydraulic properties, it was harmful to the setting when mixed with Portland cement.

A more thorough study showed that this behaviour was due to a considerable difference in the hydration kinetics of the slag containing alumina and of the Portland cement. The problem was overcome by adding a suitable amount of gypsum to the slag (7 % of gypsum for slag containing 10 % Al_2O_3), to slow down the speed of aluminate hydration.

Standard tests carried out on mixtures containing 15 % of treated slag and 85 % of Portland cement gave satisfactory results. The times of setting, expansion, handling ability, shrinkage, swelling, remained within the limits of the standard and mechanical strengths were comparable with those of the best blast furnace slags as is shown in Table IV.

IV. PILOT UNIT FOR SLAG TREATMENT

The research agreement anticipated construction of a pilot treatment plant is justified by the properties of the slag and its cost. This was essential to continue with the research because large quantities of treated slag were needed to study the following :
- regularity of the composition of the slag produced ;
- optimization of its composition ;
- improvement of the lifetime of the lances ;
- assessment by the cement industry of the sale price of the slag.

The preliminary project for the pilot plant was based on mechanization of the main functions (storage and handling of added products, handling of lances, transport and weighing of slag pots, sampling and temperature measurement, pneumatic transport of samples). The treatment and storage was moreover to be carried out under shelter.

The cost of such a plant for the treatment of more than 150,000 tonnes per year (corresponding to 1 Mt steel), was estimated as 8,750,000 FF without the cost of the building and of civil engineering work that was estimated at 4,500,000 FF (prices at June, 1983).

V. ECONOMIC ASPECT

V.1. Production cost

The cost of introducing alumina into the slag varies greatly, depending on the origin of the alumina and of the heat source, as is illustrated in Table V. Cheap heat sources (oxidation of Fe^{++} to Fe^{+++}, sensible heat of slags) are limited in quantity.

Oxidation of metallic iron that has settled at the bottom of the slag pot is not a satisfactory heat source as it is difficult to control, and as an increase of iron oxide content of the slag is detrimental to hydraulic properties. It may therefore be necessary to make use of a more costly heat source such as introducing aluminum.

Although Camflux is an expensive source of alumina, it can be used (assuming that the refractory problems in the converter are overcome) since it would decrease time of treatment in the slag pot, thus easing synchronization with the working rate of the converter.

Optimal additions for slag pot treatment have been calculated by material and thermal balances on the following assumptions, which were observed during the trials :
- the maximum content of Al_2O_3 obtained by simple addition of bauxite is 6 % ;
- thermal efficiency is 50 %.

The cost of the slag was determined by allowing for the minerals additions thus calculated, for costs of personnel incurred by the treatment of 150,000 t of slag, and of the consumption of the injection lances. The cost of producing one tonne of alumina-enriched slag appears to be about 100 FF on condition of mastering certain technologies : manufacturing lances that are subject to less wear, low temperature heat path, reduction of heat losses.

V.2. Possible uses

The properties of the slag as an addition to Portland cement are excellent ; it does not have to be quenched in water and therefore requires no energy for drying. However, its direct competitors, blast furnace slags, provide the same mechanical characteristics at lower cost.

An application that gives greater added value is therefore desirable, for example :
- as a road material binding agent : such an application could be considered on account of the mechanical properties of the slag and its intrinsic hydraulic properties ;
- as a cement : its present hydraulic properties are much weaker than those of a cement. Nevertheless, if the composition is optimized (reducing the Fe_2O_3 content and increasing the CaO content), the mechanical properties should improve. We have no information at present on the limits and a more thorough study is required to determine them.

CONCLUSION

The treatment of BOF slag has allowed its alumina content to be increased by more than 10 %. Its hydraulic properties allow it to be used as an addition to Portland cement. But, on account of the high cost of treatment (about 100 FF per tonne), a more profitable application is desirable, either as a road material binding agent, or as a cement.

Development of a more profitable system would require more thorough studies bearing on :
- analysis of regularity of the slag ;
- research on the composition that gives the best hydraulic properties ;
- reduction of treatment costs.

Such a research would require construction of a semi-industrial treatment plant able to produce considerable quantities of hydraulic slag.

TABLE I : CHEMICAL COMPOSITION OF CAMFLUX AND BAUXITE(%)

Product	Fe_{tot}	SiO_2	CaO	Al_2O_3	TiO_2	MgO	P	Mn	Cr_2O_3	H_2O
CAMFLUX	11.3	1.5	37.3	36.5	1.6	7.8	0.08	0.05	0.024	–
BAUXITE	16.2	3.5	4.8	51.9	2.5	1.1	0.08	0.10	0.15	11.0

TABLE II : RESULTS OF TESTS WITH CAMFLUX

Heat Nr	Steel shop	Steel Temperature	C steel (%)	P steel (%)	Weight of CAMFLUX (kg/t.st)	iron oxide of slag (%)	Al_2O_3 of slag (%)
95024	2	1622°C	0.030	0.008	5	21	3.8
35029	2	1648°C	0.014	0.007	10	30	3.3
34451	1	1757°C	0.031	0.013	5	25	1.8
Normal heat	/	1620 – 1650°C	0.030 0.050	0.010 0.020	0	16 – 18	0.5 – 1.5

261

TABLE III : RESULTS OF THE TREATMENTS IN SLAG POT

Slag pot Nr	CAMFLUX (kg/t.steel)	Bauxite (kg/t.slag)	Al. Scrap (kg/t.slag)	iron oxides (%) initial	iron oxides (%) final	$Fe^{+++}/Fe^{++}+Fe^{+++}$ initial	$Fe^{+++}/Fe^{++}+Fe^{+++}$ final	Al_2O_3 (%) initial	Al_2O_3 (%) final	Temperature (°C) initial	Temperature (°C) final
1	0	0	0	17.5	25.1	0.29	0.40	/	/	1615	1740
2	0	0	0	20.0	20.0	0.25	0.70	/	/	1600	1680
3	0	0	0	15.0	17.4	0.37	0.46	/	/	1595	1630
4	0	50	0	21.1	22.6	0.48	0.46	/	3.8	1600	1625
5	0	70	0	23.2	24.6	0.33	0.67	3.7	5.9	1550	/
6	0	150	20	16.4	19.4	0.32	0.52	2.8	6.0	1605	1590
7	5	155	15	18.8	26.8	0.31	0.57	3.8	10.5	/	1595
8	10	190	7.5	26.2	39.0	0.37	0.67	3.3	13.7	1015	1520

TABLE IV : COMPRESSION STRENGTH OF VARIOUS MIXTURES
OF CEMENT + 15 % SLAG (MPa)

	1 day	2 days	7 days	28 days
Portland cement	21.5	33.2	47.4	56.1
Portland cement + 15 % inert	15.9	24.5	38.4	45.4
Portland cement + 15 % treated slag	16.7	27.8	41.3	52.2
Portland cement + 15 % blast furnace slag	18.5	27.0	39.0	47.0
	20.0	20.0	42.0	52.0
	14.0	22.0	37.0	51.0
	/	23.0	/	54.0

TABLE V : COST OF ADDING ONE KG OF ALUMINA TO SLAG
ASSUMING HEAT EFFICIENCY TO BE 50 %

Alumina source	Heat source	Cost (FF/kg Al_2O_3)
Bauxite	Slag coding	0,50
Bauxite	Combustion $Fe^{++} \rightarrow Fe^{+++}$	0,70
Bauxite	Combustion $Fe \rightarrow Fe^{++}, Fe^{+++}$	1,30
Bauxite	Combustion $Al \rightarrow Al_2O_3$	1,55
CAMFLUX	NIL	2,50

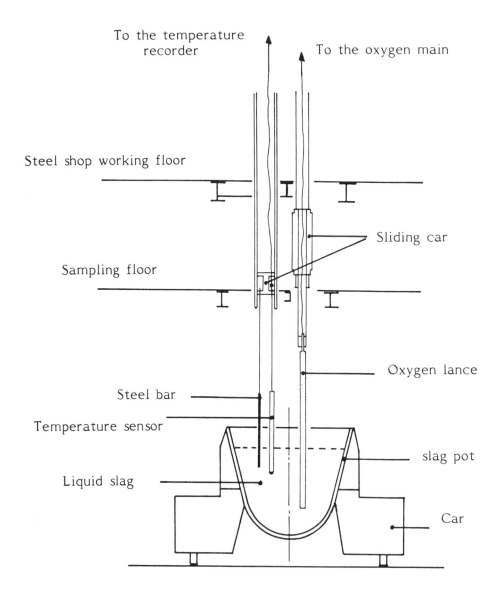

To the temperature recorder

To the oxygen main

Steel shop working floor

Sliding car

Sampling floor

Oxygen lance

Steel bar

Temperature sensor

slag pot

Liquid slag

Car

Fig. 1: Diagram of the oxygen injection experimental setting

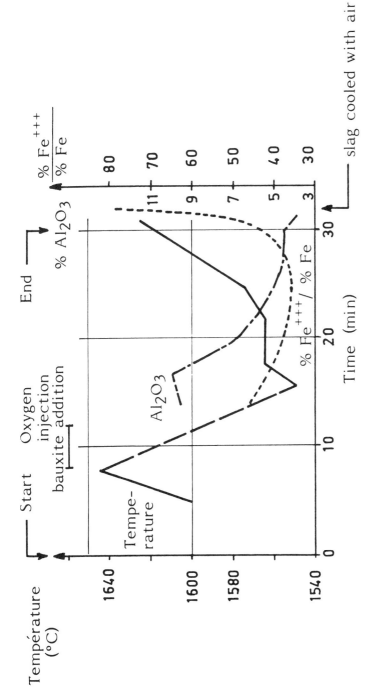

Pot # 4 Evolution during the treatment of the temperature, the alumina content and the oxidation of the slag (Oxygen flowrate : .15 m³/s)

Fig.2: Example of temperature, Al₂O₃ content, and oxydation ratio evolution during the treatment

2

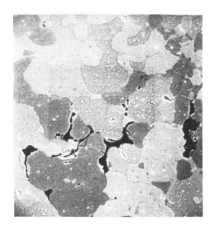 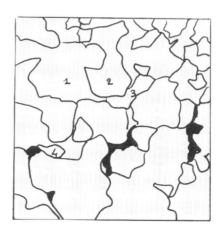

x 500

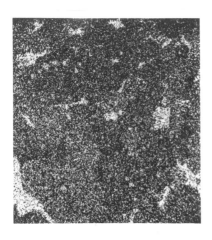 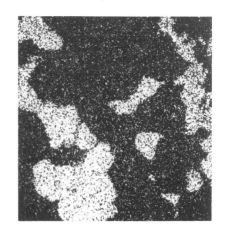

Al   Si

Fig.3: Aluminium and Silicon distribution in non treated slag (1,5% Al$_2$O$_3$)

7

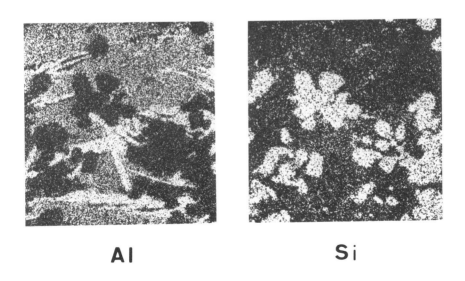

X 500

Al   Si

Fig. 4: Aluminium and Silicon distribution in treated slag (10% Al_2O_3)

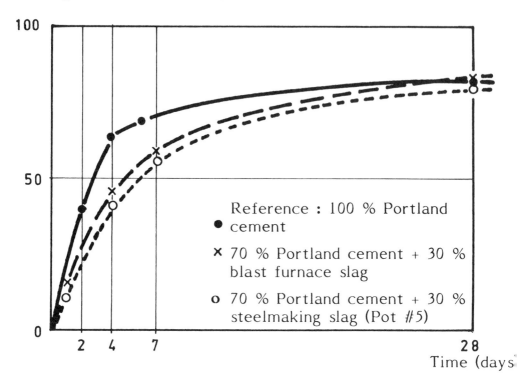

Evolution of the compression strength of samples made with blast furnace slag, steelmaking slag and Portland cement during time

Fig. 5: Evolution of the compression strength of samples made with blast furnace slag, steelmaking slag and Portland cement during time

COMPRESSION STRENGTH OF VARIOUS MIXTURES
OF CEMENT + 15 % SLAG (MPa)

	1 day	2 days	7 days	28 days
Portland cement	21.5	33.2	47.4	56.1
Portland cement + 15 % inert	15.9	24.5	38.4	45.4
Portland cement + 15 % treated slag	16.7	27.8	41.3	52.2
	18.5	27.0	39.0	47.0
Portland cement +	20.0	20.0	42.0	52.0
15 % blast furnace slag	14.0	22.0	37.0	51.0
	/	23.0	/	54.0

Fig. 6: Compression strength of various mixtures of cement + 15% Slag

CYCLONE HEAT EXCHANGERS
ESTABLISHMENT OF A METHOD TO DEFINE AND IMPROVE THEIR PERFORMANCE

R. Margrita and H. Santos-Cottin
Centre d'Etudes Nucléaires de Grenoble
C. Pailhes
Laboratoire Lafarge Coppée Recherche (Viviers)
B. P. 8, F-07220 Viviers-sur-Rhône

Summary

The study discusses cyclones situated in a preheater tower located above a cement kiln. The preheater insures the thermal preparation of the material by a counter-flow heat exchange between the stream of cold material descending towards the kiln and the hot gases being drawn upwards to the top of the tower by fans. The purpose of the study is to find means of reducing the energy consumption in the preheater tower ; energy can be saved by diminishing the electric power consumed by the fans and by better utilization of the heat furnished by the gases. The efficiency of the thermal exchange is affected by the separation efficiency of the cyclones. However there is a lack of information about the internal working parameters of these separators (separation efficiency, pressure drop, etc...) since a suitable method of investigation was not available. An experimental method has been perfected, using radioactive tracers to investigate these parameters. A computer program has been designed and evaluated by the experimental data. This program has been used to optimise the cyclone geometry for better separation efficiency and a lower pressure loss. An economic assessment of the results shows the economic impact is too small to justify alteration of a plant already in operation. However, improvment of the cyclones geometry, with the help of the computer program, should be taken into account for future installations.

1 - INTRODUCTION

The study takes place in the preheater tower of a cement plant (photograph n° 1).

In such a plant, we burn a basic material or "raw mix" (a powder of clay and limestone) that becomes clinker after it passes through :
- a multi-cyclone heat exchanger or preheater tower
- a rotary kiln , where the clinkerisation takes place
- a cooler, that permits a recuperation of the major part of the heat transfered to the clinker during the burning.

Our research concerns the cyclone heat exchanger or preheater. The purpose of this study is to gain a better knowledge of the preheater's operation (the cyclones'separation efficiency, pressure drop, retention time of the raw material particles, etc...) in order to decrease the energy consumption in the preheater tower.

The energy savings can be produced in two ways :
- a better separation efficiency in the cyclones, therefore a decrease of the material loops between cyclone levels in the tower, and consequently a better use of the heat transfered by gases to the raw material
- a decrease in the cyclones'pressure loss, therefore a decrease in the electric power consumed by the fans.

270

A theoretical study has been made in order to determine the physical mechanisms that govern the separation gas/material and the pressure loss in a cyclone. This study was then used to design a computer program calculating the separation efficiency and the pressure loss in a cyclone from the following data :
- dimensions of the device
- physical parameters of the gases (temperature, chemical composition, volume of air introduced, etc...)
- material parameters (particle size, density, flow rate of material introduced, etc...).

At the same time experimental measures have been made in a cement plant of LAFARGE COPPEE (the "Le Teil" plant in ARDECHE - FRANCE).

The distribution of the material at the different levels of the preheater tower required the development of a detection method using radioactive tracers. These measures permitted us to define the applied working conditions of each cyclone of the preheater and eventually compare the computer results with the actual measures.

2 - DESCRIPTION OF THE EXPERIMENTAL TESTS AND THE INSTALLATION

The cyclone preheater of the "LE TEIL" plant comprises two towers in parallel, each composed of four levels of cyclones (photograph n° 1).

Each level includes one cyclone, except the upper level which comprises two similar cyclones in parallel. These twin upper level cyclones insure a proper cleaning of the gases exiting the tower.

Our measures have been made on one of the two towers. The tower is constructed as shown in photo 1 and comprises :
- two upper cyclones in parallel, "C1N" and "C1S", at level number one
- one cyclone, "C2", at level number two
- one cyclone, "C3", at level number three (photo n° 2)
- one cyclone, "C4", at level number four
- a "smoke chamber" situated between the kiln entry and the duct conducting the gases towards cyclone C4.

A preheater tower permits the preheating at the raw mix before it is introduced into the kiln by a thermal exchange between the cold material, injected at its top and descending towards the kiln through a set of cyclones, and the hot gases passing through the kiln and drawn up by fans towards the top of the tower.

The cyclones insure the separation between gases and raw mix particles at each level of the preheater. Under these conditions, it would be best if each cyclone realised a perfect separation between gases and raw mix particles (separation efficiency = 100 %) such that the flow of the raw mix passes straight through the tower from top to bottom without looping between cyclones.

The measures realised on the preheater tower were the following :
- collection of all necessary data for the computer program that is the physical parameters of gases and the raw mix granulometry at the entry of each cyclone.

These measures were made by conventional means :
  . Pitot tube for measuring gaseous flow rate
  . isokinetic sampling of the raw mix to obtain the density and particle size distribution
- study of the raw mix flow rate at the different levels of the preheater and the flow path of the particles. This study required perfecting a method using radioactive tracers.

Tests were performed, by injecting at the top of the preheater tower, (at the same place where the raw mix is injected) a sample of a few grammes of a radioactive tracers and tracing its motion up to the entry of the kiln, by detectors placed at the appex of each cyclone (figure 3). The selected tracer was the raw-mix itself, a few grammes of which was activated in a nuclear reactor. The radioactive element created in these conditions is sodium 24, which has a half life of 15 hours. The iradiated quantities fluctuate between one gram and ten grams depending on the sample. A testing stand was set up on the experimental site in order to compare the radioactivity of each sample at the moment of the injection and to make necessary adjustments such that the recorded graphs of each test could be compared to each other.

Several samples of primary radioactive raw mix, having the same particle size distribution as the raw mix were injected.

When the activated material passed the probes it produced impulses which were recorded. This information permitted the drawing of curves which plotted the radioactive emmission against time.

Thus we were able to deduce the residence time of the raw mix particles in each cyclone. To determine quantitatively the radioactivity a careful calibration of the probes was necessary, to calculate the flow rates of raw mix passing through each cyclone and the cyclones'separation efficiency. The particles'sizes in the standard raw-mix injected in the tower ranged between 1 μm and 300 μm. Because of this wide range in particles size distribution several injections were made with a series of size intervals to study the specific flow of particles according to their diameter.

These size intervals were :
- particles with diameters smaller than 5 μm
- particles with diameters between 40 and 60 μm
- particles with diameters between 160 and 200 μm.
"500 - 1 000 μm" size interval :

This size class doesn't exist in the standard raw mix but we intentionally injected this particle class to calibrate the probes placed at the apex of each cyclone.

Indeed such particles have sufficient diameter to be separated from gaseous flow by all the cyclones and pass the whole tower without looping. The curves produced by probes for this size class were used as a reference for the calibration of the probes each other.

The measures using radioactive tracers are instantaneous, in order that we could consider them as representative of the average flow it was necessary to verify the permanence of the raw mix's flow with time. For this purpose we used a radioactive transmitting station (gamma rays) situated close to the pipe where we wanted to study the raw mix concentration mass'changes, poles apart, a probe receive the rays that have crossed the duct measurement volume. The signal's amplitude caught is function of the signal's amplitude transmitted, of the material, and of the mass of material crossed.

This method has been applied at the apex of each cyclone (figure 3) and permitted us to verify quantitatively the flow's steadiness during a ten minutes'time period (about the time period for a radioactive test with tracers).

3 - RESULTS - EXPLOITATION AND INTERPRETATION

31 - Particles'residence time
Among the parameters describing the straight passage of the raw mix in the cyclones, we can consider the time period "ta" corresponding with the time it took for the tracers to reach each cyclone's apex after the injection.

The following table gives values of the parameter "ta" for each cyclone of the tower and for the different tests realised.

TABLE I

Residence time ta (seconds)				
Granulometry of the radioactive samples injected (µm)	Cyclones			
	C1N C1S	C2	C3	C4
∅ < 5 µm	4,7 4,7	12,0	18,5	26,5
(40 < ∅ < 60) µm	4,8 4,7	11,7	18,0	26,0
(160 < ∅ < 200) µm	4,8 4,8	11,6	20,0	27,0
raw mix (injection 1) (1 < ∅ < 300) µm	4,0 4,1	11,6	19,0	26,0
raw mix (injection 2) (1 < ∅ < 300) µm	4,6 4,6	11,0	19,7	26,0

The table shows that there is no appreciable difference in the arrival time of the tracer at the base of the cyclone, i.e. the retention time in the cyclone, for the different granulometries studied.

The direct passage of the material through the cyclones was thus shown as an aggregate motion without significant segregation of the particles. These results tended towards the results obtained in a model of separation efficiency in cyclones.

In effect, the concentration of raw mix'particles in the gas is very high (in the order of 1 kg material per kg of gas) without a homogeneous transportation of the particles by the gas. Thus there is a tendency for the particles to be drawn to the walls of the horizontal ducts and results in a build-up of these particles. This comes from the fact that the gas flow has a limited force to entrain the particles.

Beyond a limited concentration one part of the material particles are deposited on the walls of the ducts and moves as strands. Therefore a large quantity of particles, both large and small, are thrown against the walls of the cyclone immediately at the entry. This effect benefits the separation of the gas-material and adds to the centrifugation in a proportion that cannot be neglected (we evaluate by calculation that this phenomenon contributes 80 % of the overall separation in the preheater cyclones at "LE TEIL"). This explains the identical retention times registered for all particle sizes.

Energy wise this phenomenon is interesting because it requires a low velocity of the gas at the cyclone's inlet, thus a lower pressure loss. The lower the velocity of the gas at the inlet, the higher is the separation by "decantation" and the higher are the strands of the material. The centrifugation on the other hand needs a high velocity, generating a pressure loss, in order to obtain centrifugal acceleration sufficiently high to throw as fine a particle as possible against the walls.

32 – Exploitation of the measures by radioactive tracing – Determination of the flow rates of material and separation efficiency of the cyclones

Qe and Qs are respectively the amount of material entering the cyclone and exiting the base of a cyclone. The efficiency of the device is defined by :

$$\rho = \frac{Qs}{Qe} \qquad 0 \leqslant \rho \leqslant 1$$

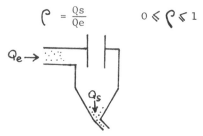

After an instantaneous injection Ao (radioactivity of the tracer, mCie) at the top of the preheater tower, the flow of radioactive activity Si and Ei measured at the base and the inlet of each cyclone are proportional to the flow of material and we have for the four devices the relationships.

$$\rho_i = \frac{Si}{Ei} \qquad i = 1, 2, 3, 4$$

Never the less for a given amount of material, Qo, injected at the top of the tower there is no conservation of this given amount of the material until the base of the tower. The raw mix is composed of a mixture of limestone-clay, which, after a certain temperature, liberates carbon dioxide, CO_2, according to the reaction called "decarbonization" : $CaCO_3 \longrightarrow CaO + CO_2$. When the raw mix finally exits the kiln after the burning cycle it is in the form of clinker with a total rate of decarbonization of the raw mix of $\tau = 0,36$. In other words 1,563 kg of raw mix produces 1 kg of clinker and liberates (0,36 x 1,563) kg of gas.

τ is also called ignition loss and includes not only the liberation of CO_2 (the largest part) but also the dehydration of the clay. For cyclones C1, C_2 and C_3 the temperatures are not sufficiently high to bring about the total phenomenon but at the level at the lower cyclone C4 the temperature attains 830°C and we estimate about $\delta = 40$ % the amount per cent of the decarbonization of the material (δ is calculated by a low of decarbonization as a function of temperature).

We assume that this 40 % decarbonization has been realised in the duct conducting the gas from the kiln to the inlet of cyclone C4. Therefore the quantity of material calculated at the entry of cyclone C4 does not go through further transformation in the cyclone itself. In other terms in the interior of cyclone C4 the separated material plus the nonseparated material equals the amount of material entering the cyclone, just like the other cyclones.

The general relation given the quantity of material entering the cyclone is :

$$E_i^* = S_{i-1}^* + S_i^* + \frac{\tau(\delta' - \delta)}{1 - \tau\delta'} S_3^* - S_4^* + X \qquad i = 1, 2, 3, 4$$

for i = 1 $S_o^* = Qo$ the amount of material entering the tower.
Consequently the efficiency of the cyclones is expressed as :

$$\rho_i = \frac{S_i^*}{E_i^*} = \frac{S_i^*}{S_{i-1}^* + S_i^* + \frac{\tau(\delta' - \delta)}{1 - \tau\delta'} S_3^* - S_4^* + X}$$

with :
Qo = amount of material (raw mix) entering the tower
E_i^* = the amount of material at the inlet of each cyclone Ci

S_i^* = the amount of material at the base of each cyclone Ci determined by the radioactive measures

$\mathcal{C}_i$ = the separation efficiency of each cyclone Ci

X^i = the amount of material coming from the kiln. This material we assume is 100 % decarbonated and is constituted of particles entrained by the gases as they passe through the kiln

$\mathcal{T}$ = the ignition loss or total rate of decarbonization

$\mathcal{S}'$ = the degree of decarbonization of the material leaving the bottom of cyclone C3

$\mathcal{S}$ = the degree of decarbonization of the material (coming from the base of cyclone C3) at the inlet of cyclone C4

$\mathcal{S}''$ = the degree of apparent decarbonization of the material at the bottom of cyclone C4.

Considering the production figures of the plant for 31/2/83 :
Clinker production in the kiln (dry process kiln with two identical towers of cyclone exchangers (photo 1) :

P = 1 706 t/j   thus 19,75 kg/s

Amount of material fed to one tower :

Qo = 61,3 t/h   thus 17,03 kg/s

Amount of dust exiting the tower :

S^+ = 1,02 kg/s   thus (0,1 kg/kg clinker)

Average amount of dust leaving the kiln and entering one tower :

X = 3,73 kg/s   thus (0,38 kg/kg clinker).

Separation efficiency of cyclones :

Top cyclones C1S and C1 N : $\mathcal{C}_1$ = 0,95

cyclone   C2   : $\mathcal{C}_2$ = 0,86

cyclone C_3 : $\mathcal{C}_3$ = 0,87

cyclone C_4 : $\mathcal{C}_4$ = 0,80

Amount of gas in the tower and its physical characteristics :

TABLE II

Physical characteristics of the gas	CYCLONES			
	C1	C2	C3	C4
Average flow at the cyclones' inlet in m3/s	21,37 x 2*	52,02	59,62	67,17
Average temperature in cyclones in °C	410	580	720	830
Dynamic viscosity in kg/ms	$3,11 \ 10^{-5}$	$3,62 \ 10^{-5}$	$4,01 \ 10^{-5}$	$4,3 \ 10^{-5}$
Volumetric mass in kg/m3	0,57	0,46	0,4	0,36

* There are 2 cyclones C1 in parallel in each tower.

Physical characteristics of the material (raw mix)

Average granulometry of the raw mix at the inlet of the cyclones

Dimension of the grains in µm	2	4	8	16	32	64	100	160	200	315
% in weight passing cumulated	4	13	32	53	69	80	83	92	96	100

TABLE III

Average volumetric mass of the material at the inlet of each cyclone :

TABLE IV	CYCLONES			
	C1	C2	C3	C4
Volumetric mass of the particles of the material in kg/m3	2 740	2 750	2 770	2 840

33 - Separation efficiency and pressure loss of the cyclones determined with a mathematical model

Two working parameters were modelized to produce the separation fonc-
tion of a cyclone's.

- Centrifugation : the particles are thrown against the walls of the
separator and separate from the gaseous mixture by centrifugal force due to
the setting into rotation of the gases in the body of the cyclone (fig. 3).
This mecanism requires a high velocity of the gas to obtain the particles
as fine as possible.

- Decantation : the grains of material are dissociated from the gas
movement with their entry into the cyclone as a result of the high concentration of the material in the gas ($\simeq$1 kg of material per kg of gas). For
an equal concentration of material entering a cyclone this form of separation is amplified by a lower gas velocity at the cyclone entry.

The pressure loss due to any singularity (knee, restriction, cyclone,
etc...) in a "conduction means"is ingeneral proportional to the dynamic pressure of the gas for any given area of reference. The coefficient of propor-
tionality is a function fo the geometry of the singularity and does not vary
with the volume of gas. It is this coefficient with which we have created
a model for the calculation of the pressure loss in cyclones.

We see that the more the geometry of a cyclone lends itself to the
creation of large swirling velocities in the central vortex of the device
(an outlet duct of small diameter for example) the greater is the pressure
drop. As, when high velocities are sought to raise the centrifugation in
dust collecting cyclones they also have high pressure losses.

We find these results in the following table which give the pressure
loss and the efficiency of separation (theoretical and experimental) for
each preheater cyclone studied.

TABLE V	Separation Efficiency (%)		Pressure loss (mm W.g)	
	Theoretical	Experimental	Theoretical	Experimental
Upper, dust collecting, cyclones C1	95 %	95 %	158	183
C2	87 %	86 %	127	90
C3	85 %	87 %	104	100
C4	82 %	80 %	107	95

We remark that the cyclones C1 which are conceived to dedust the gas
as much as possible have the best efficiency of separation but also the
highest pressure loss, the efficiency of centrifugation of these cyclones
is 73 % and their pressure loss is 160 mm w.g.

The three lower cyclones C2, C3 and C4 are larger than the cyclones
C1, and have a lower gas velocity. The consequence of this is an efficiency of centrifugation about 40 % and a pressure loss of about 100 mm w.g.

Even, thanks to the mechanism of decantation, the efficiency of these
cyclones are condiderably increased attaining 80 % to 87 %.

276

4 - ECONOMIC EVALUATION

In a counter-current exchanger we see that the optimal exchange occurs with a minimum of loops. In a cement plant preheater, the recirculations or loops are constituted of particles of the material which are not separated in the gas flow. We can improve the overall thermal exchange in the tower by reducing the material circulating between the stages of cyclones. This implies an improvement of the efficiency of the separation in the cyclones.

This constitutes our first concern with which we hope to save energy. The relation between the efficiency of separation in a cyclone and the heat energy consumed is obtained by means of a thermal model which simulates the exchanges gas-material in a preheater cyclone tower. We find that one rate per cent of improvement in separation in each stage of cyclones permits us to gain 0,5 thermies per ton of clinker produced in the kiln.

The second place where we can reduce the energy consumed in the preheater is in the pressure loss in the cyclones. In effect the higher the pressure loss the more kWh are consumed by the fans which aspirate the gases.

We found by means of the mathematical model that we could gain improvements on the two previously stated problems by modifying the geometry of the cyclones. However, a compromise has to be made since the physical mechanisms which govern the centrifugation and the pressure loss evolue in the same direction. We cannot simultaneously have a large improvement in the separation efficiency and a substantial decrease in the pressure loss.

In the case of our preheating tower, the model gives the following results
- an enlargement, of about 10 %, of the area of the inlet duct and outlet duct of each cyclone permits us to gain one rate per cent of efficiency per cyclone and a decrease of 20 % of the pressure loss. These geometrical modifications reduce the velocity of the gas at the inlet and their rotational velocity in the inner core. These consequently produce an improvement in the "decantation" mechanism, a little decrease in the centrifugation, and a decrease in the pressure loss.

Given the base of the price of coal-thermie 0,9 francs/ton and the electrical cost 0,22 Francs/kWh we gain 2,13 Francs per ton of clinker produced, thus 1 140 K Francs/year, for a plant of 1 700 t/d (assuming approximately 90 % uptime).

5 - CONCLUSION

An experimental method of measuring was created. The particularity of this method is the possibility, with the use of a radioactive tracer, to trace the flow of material in turbulent areas. The method was applied in a tower of exchange cyclones in a cement plant and thus enabled the measure of:
- the distribution of the raw mix in the preheater ensemble
- the retention time of the particles in each stage of the tower
- the recirculations of the raw mix between cyclones
- the efficiency of separation of the cyclones.

At the same time a mathematical model was created. This program calculates the efficiency of separation and the pressure loss for a cyclone. This model is based on the modelizing of physical phenomena which govern the flow of charged gases. This model was used to simulate geometric modifications on the particular cyclones used in the study.

These modifications had as a goal a decrease in the energy consumption of the preheater by reducing the pressure loss in the cyclones and increasing their separation efficiency. We found by the simulations that the gain was not sufficient to justify a modification in the installation already in operation. Nethertheless the optimisation of the geometry of cyclones, by means of the model, should be taken into account in future installations.

1 - General view of the
    preheater cyclones in
    the LAFARGE PLANT at
    LE TEIL

2 - A view of two cyclones
    in the preheater to-
    wer at the same level.
    Vertical cyclones with
    a tangential scroll
    inlet

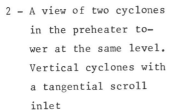

FLOW PATH OF GASES IN A VERTICAL CYCLONE WITH TANGENTIAL INLET DUCT

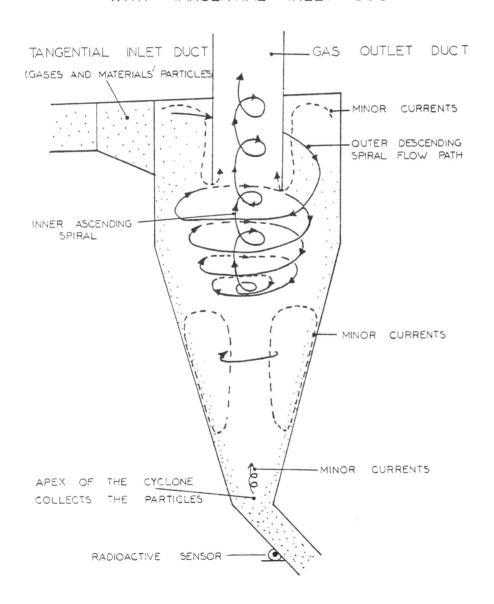

TANGENTIAL INLET DUCT
(GASES AND MATERIALS' PARTICLES)

GAS OUTLET DUCT

MINOR CURRENTS

OUTER DESCENDING SPIRAL FLOW PATH

INNER ASCENDING SPIRAL

MINOR CURRENTS

MINOR CURRENTS

APEX OF THE CYCLONE COLLECTS THE PARTICLES

RADIOACTIVE SENSOR

EROSION-RESISTANT GLASS-CERAMICS MADE BY DIRECT CONTROLLED COOLING FROM THE MELT

P. S. Rogers, J. Williamson, J. F. Bell and M. Campbell

Department of Metallurgy and Materials Science
Imperial College, London, S. W. 7 2 BP, U.K.

Summary

The objective was to develop a pilot-plant facility to produce glass-ceramic ('Silceram') by a novel process. In this, a silicate melt is converted to a fine-grained pore-free ceramic during a controlled-cooling heat-treatment, removing the need for reheating which is essential to conventional glass-ceramic processing. The new heat-treatment programme offers a substantial saving in thermal energy. Glass-ceramic has been produced at the pilot-plant principally as flat tiles, but also by casting into special shapes. These products have been made from melts whose components were pure oxides and carbonates, and also from mixtures of blast-furnace slag and colliery shale with added nucleating agent. These industrial by-products not only reduce the raw material cost but improve the efficiency of melting and refining. The new material has superior mechanical properties. The crystal size of the major silicate phase is about 2μm and the porosity is close to zero. The high strength and hardness are associated with excellent resistance to erosion by fluid-borne particles. Estimates of manufacturing cost for flat product 'Silceram' on the 1000 tonne per year scale show it to be strongly competitive with other erosion-resistant materials used industrially. The cost benefit for more complex shapes is better still.

1. INTRODUCTION

Glass-ceramics constitute a class of materials which are shaped by conventional glass-forming techniques but, during a subsequent heat-treatment, are transformed to fine-grained ceramics of extremely low porosity. The microstructure of a glass-ceramic is associated with a number of desirable properties which are otherwise difficult to achieve, notably high mechanical strength, great hardness and resistance to abrasion and erosion. Like conventional ceramics, glass-ceramics are relatively chemically inert, with the added advantage over sintered ceramics of having extremely low porosity as a result of the fusion stage of the process. This combination of properties has encouraged interest in industrial applications as constructional materials, particularly where conditions of wear due to erosion may be severe. Examples of such conditions occur at power stations in the transportation of coal and ash, at mines in the transportation of coal, spoil and ores and at steelworks in the conveying of furnace burden and slags, and in coke ovens. Other applications include the provision of pipework to convey dusts and slurries which are both mechanically and chemically corrosive. Tests so far carried out show the

280

new materials to be highly competitive with conventional materials on the basis of combined cost and performance.

The crystallisation of glasses has, in the past, been avoided by glass manufacturers, as sporadic nucleation and crystal growth leads to very poor mechanical properties.   However, if the nucleation and growth stages can be promoted in a controlled way to produce a highly crystalline material the properties can far exceed those of the parent glass.   By careful choice of the glass composition and the addition of nucleating agents this can be achieved.   In conventional glass-ceramics the glass melt is cooled to a chosen temperature in order to produce the nuclei from which the major crystalline phase will later grow.   The temperature is then raised to enable the growth of this phase, then slowly cooled to room temperature. During investigations of the effectiveness of different nucleating agents on the crystallisation of a particular range of glasses based on blast-furnace slag it was found that one particular combination, ferric oxide and chromium oxide, enabled nuclei to be formed at the temperature at which crystal growth occurs.   This meant that the process could be simplified to a single-stage heat treatment during cooling from the melt rather than the conventional two-stage treatment.   These observations provided the foundation for the development of the new ceramic material called 'Silceram'.

The adoption of this direct-cooling heat-treatment, using the programme described below, can result in energy savings of about 60% when compared with the conventional glass-ceramic processing cycle.   This follows from the removal of the necessity to provide heat for holding at the lower temperature for nucleation and then raising the temperature again for the crystallisation step.   If the new material were manufactured on a sufficiently large scale, then further energy savings can be made by using molten slag freshly produced from the blast-furnace.   Because the preferred composition for 'Silceram' manufacture contains 60% slag, then the saving in energy requirement for melting from the use of hot slag can be about 50%.   Since a major proportion of the manufacturing cost of glass-ceramics is fuel cost for melting and refining, these energy savings are of great importance.

2.   THE PROCESS

The objectives in building the pilot-plant were to understand and overcome the problems in going from the laboratory scale to a small production scale, and to produce sufficient numbers of samples for industrial testing.   The largest samples that had been made prior to this study had been about 1kg, melted in crucibles in a gas-fired furnace.   The pilot-plant is capable of melting 100kg in a batch process using an oil-fired, tilting furnace, shown in Figure 1.   The melt has to be in a shallow pool because of poor transmission of infra-red radiation through the liquid and the hearth refractory must be capable of withstanding corrosion by the melt.   Tests on various refractories showed that a magnesia-chrome satisfactorily withstood the action of the melt.   The remainder of the furnace is constructed from a high alumina refractory with outer layers of insulating bricks and fibre blanket.   The melt is held at a temperature of 1450 to 1500°C for three hours then cast into steel or sand moulds to produce flat or textured tiles and a variety of detailed shapes.   The castings are then heat-treated for three hours in electrically fired kilns at a temperature of about 900°C, and allowed to cool slowly.   The two kilns have a combined volume of approximately 0.8m³ and can hold 75kg of cast product.   During experimental runs the batch size was usually limited to 50kg to reduce wastage and shorten the procedure.

Figure 1. Melting Furnace

The composition limits of the 'Silceram' patent are shown in Figure 2, and all the successful samples produced to date lie within this range.   A smaller range of preferred compositions is also shown. (1)

A number of raw materials can be incorporated into 'Silceram' batches including blast-furnace slag, pulverised-fuel ash, coal slag and colliery shale.   The most successful materials have been made from a blend of sixty five parts blast-furnace slag to thirty five parts colliery shale, with an extra seven parts of nucleating agents and small amounts of pure oxides to correct small deficiencies in the base composition; this composition, SCR25, and the analysis of the finished product, with those of two other typical batches, are shown in Table I.

One hundred and fifty batches of twenty eight different experimental compositions have been melted and cast and the melting and casting conditions have been optimised for small-scale production.   A wide range of sample sizes and shapes have been produced and a number of companies are performing larger scale testing than has previously been possible.   The results of these tests will be reported in a later paper when they are available.

3.   PROPERTIES AND TESTING

A wide range of physical and chemical properties have been determined for 'Silceram'.   Although a large number of different compositions have been produced there is a remarkable similarity between their properties. Differences do occur when there are very large differences in microstructure, for example large crystals which tend to produce microscopic shrinkage voids or large amounts of residual glass.   Even when there are considerable differences in microstructure this does not mean that there will be any significant differences in properties.   For example, Figure 3 and 4 show the microstructures of three different materials, a pure oxide material made on the laboratory scale, SCF5, a pure oxide material made at the pilot-plant, SCR19, and a slag/shale batch also made at the pilot-plant, SCR25.

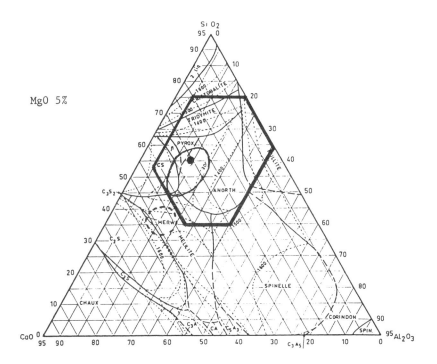

MgO 5%

Figure 2.   Phase diagram for CaO-Al₂O₃-SiO₂ system containing
5% MgO (after reference 2)

    $- - - -$ typical blast-furnace slag compositions

    ●   composition SCR25

    ———   preferred compositions

    ▬▬▬   'Silceram' patent range (reference 1)

The sample of SCF5 shows a highly dendritic structure with crystal
extensions of up to 30µm, and quite a large amount of residual glass.   The
microstructure of SCR25 shows some similarities in that there is a degree
of dendritic structure, but much more compact.   The third sample, SCR19,
has some areas of extremely fine structure with inclusions of much coarser
crystals, surrounding spinel crystals of about 2µm in size.   These areas
of coarser crystallisation are always associated with large spinel crystals,
but the reverse is not always true.

    The properties of these three materials, shown in Tables II and III,
are remarkably similar and it is likely that the other properties shown in
Table IV will be equally close.   The fact that the much finer structure
exhibited by SCR19 does not seem to affect the properties may be due to the
presence of the clusters of much coarser crystals.   If these can be removed

TABLE I

Compositions of selected 'Silceram' samples

Material	Component	Composition of batch (parts by weight)	Analysis of product (parts by weight)
SCF5	CaO	20	16
	MgO	14	10
	Al_2O_3	10	15
	SiO_2	56	59
	Fe_2O_3	3	3
	Cr_2O_3	1.3*	0.6
SCR19	CaO	27	23
	MgO	7	6
	Al_2O_3	15	14
	SiO_2	51	57
	Fe_2O_3	4	5
	Cr_2O_3	1.5*	0.9
SCR25	Slag	65	–
	Shale	35	–
	CaO	–	27
	MgO	1**	6
	Al_2O_3	0.5**	14
	SiO_2	–	53
	Fe_2O_3	4**	4.5
	Cr_2O_3	1.5*	1.1

* added as $Na_2Cr_2O_7$

** supplement to component in slag/shale

TABLE II

Modulus of Rupture

Material	Modulus of Rupture (MPa)	Specimen dimensions (mm)	Span (mm)
SCF5	180 ± 15	2 x 4 x 25	20
SCR19.5	138 ± 8	4 x 4 x 35	25
SCR25.1	149 ± 6	4 x 4 x 35	25
SCR19.5	100 to 110	10 x 30 x 120	100

then it is hoped that the properties can be further imporoved beyond those
of the laboratory material, SCF5, which has been used as standard for
comparison.

The results for SCF5 are for laboratory-made material and are included
here for comparison with material produced at the pilot-plant. The small

specimens were cut by diamond wheel from the cast tiles and the face of each to be in tension was polished, whereas the large ones were as cast. Modulus of rupture has been calculated from the breaking load in three point bending. As can be seen, the large bars of SCR19 gave a lower result than the smaller ones from the same material. However this is to be expected, since the strength properties of ceramics and glass-ceramics are determined by the presence, size and abundance of flaws in their structure and at the surface, so that the lower value is still a good result from a very much larger thickness of material subjected to stress.

TABLE III

Erosion Resistance

Material	Weight loss under test conditions (mg)	Test conditions used
		(a)
		Erodant : sand, 100-150µm, 830g
SCF5	11.7 ± 0.5	Impact angle : 90°
SCR19.5	12.3 ± 1.4	Sand flow rate : 120g/min^{-1}
		Velocity at target : 15 ms^{-1}
SCR25.1	12.5 ± 1.7	
		(b)
		Impact Angle : 45°
SCR25.1	24.4 ± 4	Sand flow rate : 190 g/min^{-1}
Cast Basalt	38.1 ± 1	Velocity : 25 ms^{-1}
		Other conditions as (a)
		(c)
SCR25.1	20.1	Erodant : sand, 100-500µm, 830g
Cast Basalt	33.2	Velocity : 13 ms^{-1}
		Other conditions as (b)

These results show that the two new materials produced in large scale at the pilot-plant, SCR19.5 and SCR25.1, are almost as resistant to erosion as the laboratory standard, SCF5, and compare very favourably with 'cast basalt' which exhibits a mass loss 55 to 65% greater. When expressed as a volume loss the value for 'cast basalt' is still over 50% greater.

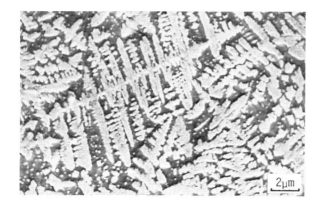

Figure 3.

Scanning electron micrograph of laboratory material 'Silceram' SCF5.

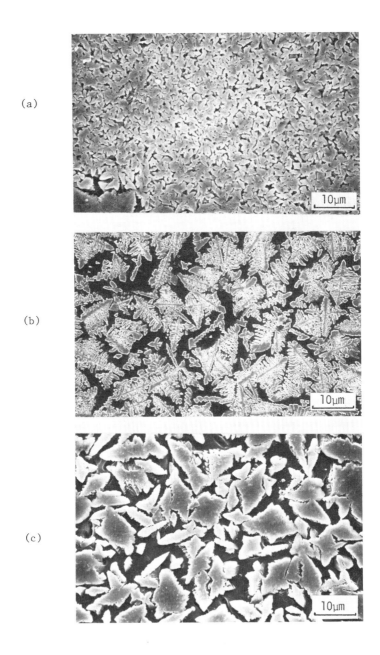

(a)

(b)

(c)

Figure 4.   Scanning electron micrographs of pilot-plant material
(a)   SCR19-1;   (b) SCR19-5;   (c) SCR25-1.

TABLE IV
Properties of 'Silceram' SCF5

Density	2.9 gcm^{-3}
Fracture toughness	$2.1 \text{ MNm}^{-\frac{3}{2}}$
Young's modulus	$95 \times 10^3 \text{ MPa}$
Compressive strength	850 MPa
Hardness (Vickers)	$7.0 \times 10^3 \text{ MPa}$
Coeff. of thermal expansion	$7.5 \times 10^{-6} \text{ K}^{-1}$
Thermal conductivity	$1.76 \text{ Wm}^{-1} \text{ K}^{-1}$
Viscosity of melt at 1450°C	6.0 Pas

4.   MANUFACTURING COSTS

In making an assessment of the potential of the material, it has been assumed that in the first instance 'Silceram' will be exploited for its resistance to erosive wear by fluid-borne solid particles.   The figures given here are estimates for the manufacture of flat tiles and sheet produced by a process similar to that operated at the pilot-plant, but on a larger scale, with consequent increase in size of melting furnace to a capacity of one tonne, and a larger number of heat treatment kilns.   The costing exercise has been carried out on an assumption of 1000 tonnes per year of finished product.   This quantity is equivalent to about 40,000 square metres of flat sheet, 1 cm thick and represents about a fifth of the U.K. market for erosion-resistant ceramics, determined on a tonnage basis.

TABLE V
Capital costs for 1000 tonnes per year production capacity

	£
Tank furnace, gas fired	24,000
Ancillary equipment, controls, etc.	5,000
Casting equipment for tiles and sheet	4,000
Heat-treatment kilns	22,000
Foundry equipment, mixers, etc.	10,000
Installation costs	5,000
	£70,000

The capital costs of plant for full-scale production, shown in Table V for 1000 tonnes per year capacity, are of course strongly dependent on the assumptions made concerning the nature of the products and the volume of production.

TABLE VI

Recurrent costs for manufacture of 1000 tonnes per year

	£
Staff costs, manufacturing, 6 persons	72,000
Staff costs, marketing, 2 persons	24,000
Services, at 25% of staff costs	24,000
Rent, 500 square metres	21,000
Gas	86,000
Electricity	12,000
Raw materials, including transport	10,000
Maintenance, at 10% of Capital Cost	7,000
Depreciation, at 15% of Capital Cost	10,500
	£266,500

The manufacturing cost per tonne of £266.50 shown in Table VI compares well with the cost of competitive materials such as cast basalt, even with the assumptions made in this analysis. Savings in fuel cost not included are those which would result from the use of recuperators in the burner supply (up to 50%). The attractiveness of the 'Silceram' is further improved by its better resistance to erosion than other ceramics of comparable cost. The advantage when both cost and performance are considered is very clear.

In order to make a complete assessment, attention must also be paid to the market for special shapes, to be used, for example, as nozzles, venturis and pipe-bends. These would be made by casting into sand moulds or shell moulds, techniques for which 'Silceram' is particularly suited. The selling price for such items is an order of magnitude higher, and the profit margin thus substantially larger.

Another potential application is in the manufacture of pipes for carrying liquids and slurries (e.g. drain pipes). Here the level of production would be as high as 100,000 tonnes per year, using continuous centrifugal casting. Some laboratory trials have been started with this application in mind.

5. CONCLUSIONS

The pilot-plant which was designed and commissioned during this project has been used to optimise melting, casting and heat-treatment conditions for the small-scale manufacture of 'Silceram'. This industrial ceramic is made by a novel process by direct-cooling from the molten condition, and is particularly suited for applications as an erosion-resistant material.

Laboratory work has shown 'Silceram' to have excellent mechanical properties and a high resistance to erosion by fluid-borne solids when compared with other ceramics in common use. Comparative tests of this kind depend upon the prevailing conditions, such as particle velocity, size and number density and angle of impact; tests under industrial conditions have shown the new material to be eroded 1.5 to 3.5 times more slowly than cast basalt, the material imported from outside the EEC area which

288

currently dominates the market. Since the cost per tonne is close to that of cast basalt, the advantage on a cost-plus-performance basis is quite clear.

The techniques for forming 'Silceram' used in the work detailed here have, for the most part, been simple casting processes using steel and sand moulds. The silicate melt used is suitable also for shaping by spin-casting and shell moulding. There is thus scope for extending the process beyond the manufacture of flat products to more sophisticated techniques: on the high cost/low tonnage side, material may be cast as special shapes such as valve seats, nozzles and elbows; on the high tonnage side, 'Silceram' may be continuously spin-cast as pipes and tubes on a scale two or more orders of magnitude greater than the tonnage assumed in the economic analysis summarized in Table VI.

If the pilot-plant development is to be translated into an industrial process, a number of questions must be answered. If production is to be on a large scale using a continuous glass-melting tank furnace, then further information on melt behaviour and refractory performance would be required. If hot slag is to be incorporated as a raw material, then the use of cyclone mixers or rotary furnaces must be considered. It is intended that the problems of large-scale melting, as well as the techniques of spin-casting and shell moulding will be examined in the continuation of this work, in parallel with industrial exploitation.

6. REFERENCES

(1).   Rogers, P.S. and Williamson, J. : Brit. Pat. 1 462 035
                                           U.S. Pat. 3 799 836

(2).   Cavalier, G. and Sandrea-Deudon, M. (1960) : Révue de
        Metallurgie, _57_, 1143 - 1157.

ACKNOWLEDGEMENTS

This work has been funded jointly by the CEC on Contract No. EE-B-4-184-UK and by the British Technology Group. We are grateful to Dr. K. Hills for his advice and support.

FOOD INDUSTRY

Presentation by Rapporteur
D. A. Reay, M. Sc.

International Research & Development Company Ltd
Newcastle upon Tyne, NE6 2YD, U.K.

Summary

The food industry is a significant user of energy in all Community
countries, and is also diverse in terms of both the type of process
used and the size of production facility.
The three projects described here cover a variety of baking and
edible oil processing facilities. Detailed audits have been carried
out in Dutch bakeries, both large and small, leading to many useful
recommendations regarding conservation measures. Process improvements
in soyabean extraction, and the use of total energy plant in edible
oil processing are also reported.

1.   INTRODUCTION

The food industry is a significant user of energy in all Community
countries. Figures available for 1981 indicate that EEC countries used
approximately 9.3 million tonnes of oil equivalent (mtoe) in the food,
drinks and tobacco sector in that year. (Note that the total energy consumption by industry in the Community was about 210 mtoe in the same period).
The preparation of food products for human and animal consumption can
involve many different processes, a large number of which are energy-
intensive in that they are based on heating or refrigeration duties. The
industry is noted for its use of significant quantities of water and steam,
and the associated large amounts of effluent.
Quantification of the energy consumption in all sectors has been
difficult because of the diverse nature of products and processes and the
wide size range, in terms of output and number of employees, of manufacturing units. This latter feature sets the food industry apart from most other
sectors, and the contrast is typified by the existance of large breweries
and canning plants on the one hand, and the local bakery behind a high
street shop on the other. One of the papers presented in this session
highlights this aspect, and it will become obvious that many and varied
approaches to energy conservation are needed or   practiced.
In common with most other subjects discussed at this Conference, the
techniques developed for, or employed in, the food industry for conservation can have a significant impact in other industrial sectors, and two of
the projects described below, the survey of savings in bakeries and the
use of total energy plant, are particularly important in this context.
All three of the projects being supported were undertaken by the
Netherlands Organisation for Applied Scientific Research (TNO). The first
project described is concerned with energy savings in bakeries, and was
managed by the Institute for Cereals, Flour and Bread. This project has
produced vast amounts of valuable data on the uses of energy in bakeries,
both large and small, and the conservation measures which can readily be
undertaken.

The Division for Nutrition and Food Research within TNO had responsibility for the other two projects. Processing of soya beans is energy-intensive, and some of the stages in their treatment, including desolventizing, toasting and drying, have received attention. The manufacture of edible oils is an area where the heat : power ratio is such that total energy packages may be attractive. The use of total energy, or combined heat and power (CHP) plant is of considerable topical interest, and the study by TNO is a model for the analysis of similar systems in other processes and sectors.

2. ENERGY SAVINGS IN BAKERIES

The distribution of bakeries in the Netherlands is such that approximately half (59%) of the output is produced in small units, where batch operations predominate. There are 3650 such small bakeries. The balance is provided by 119 'industrial' bakeries, where continuous processes can be justified. In terms of energy usage, the annual consumption of 7000 TJ is predominantly natural gas (85-93%), the balance being electricity, a significant proportion of which is for refrigeration or freezing.

In this study (1), TNO selected 7 representative small bakeries employing batch ovens and 5 industrial bakeries. (An idea of the size of the small bakeries may be obtained from the fact that 93% of them employ 10 or less staff). The small bakeries using batch production methods could save significant amounts of energy by a variety of good housekeeping, or low investment, measures. Substitution of pilot gas flames by spark ignition systems on ovens could, it is estimated, save up to 10 per cent of the total oven gas consumption, and the formal paper highlights many other energy-saving opportunities on this and other items of plant.

In bakeries with higher production rates, where continuous ovens are used, a smaller proportion of the total gas consumption is used in the ovens, (50-65 per cent), the balance being used for steam production, space and domestic water heating. Again good housekeeping would lead to significant (up to 22 per cent) savings in oven gas use in 75 per cent of ovens where indirect firing is employed - a surprising figure in 1984. Bad steam use practices and the large number of factories simultaneously operating heating and ventilation systems without heat recovery also point to a previous lack of awareness or interest in conservation. The contractor cited the recovery of heat from continuous baking oven exhausts as an attractive investment.

This project has revealed that much remains to be done in educating and persuading companies, both large and small, to practice conservation. The data produced should be of value to bakery operators throughout the Community.

3. ENERGY SAVING IN THE SOYABEAN EXTRACTION INDUSTRY

The soyabean extraction industry, which processes soyabeans to produce oil and meal, has been the subject of several energy studies. Most Community activity has centred on the Netherlands or the TNO laboratories. (West Germany and the Netherlands are responsible for over 50% of all oil seed processing in the EEC, as shown in Table 1). In the 1st Energy R&D Programme, TNO reported on heat recovery in the extraction process and in hydrogenation of the oils (2), although payback periods were somewhat in excess of 2 years at the time. The study recently completed (3) concentrates on the desolventizing-toasting and drying sections of the soyabean oil manufacturing process. (The various stages in meal and oil production are indicated in Ref.2).

TABLE 1 - SOYABEANS AND OTHER OILSEEDS PROCESSED IN THE EEC IN THE YEARS 1981 AND 1982

Country	1981 Total Oilseeds (10^6t)	1981 Soyabeans Share Percentage of Total (10^6t)		1982 Total Oilseeds (10^6t)	1982 Soyabeans Share Percentage of Total (10^6t)	
Belgium/ Luxembourg	1,5	1,3		1,8	1,6	
Denmark	0,3	0,2		0,3	0,2	
France	1,6	0,6		1,8	0,9	
West Germany	5,1	3,0		5,4	3,7	
Greece	0,4	0,2		0,4	0,2	
Ireland	-	-		-	-	
Italy	1,5	1,2		1,7	1,5	
The Netherlands	3,0	2,7		2,9	2,5	
United Kingdom	1,7	1,1		1,7	1,2	
Total	15,1	10,3	68	16,0	11,8	74

Desolventizing of the beans, now in the form of flakes, is carried out using live steam, the aim of this stage being to remove the hexane used in extraction. The subsequent toasting, which improves the meal nutritional value, is via indirect heating. Flakes are finally dried using hot air, prior to grinding. The steam usage in all these stages is high.

By combining the toasting operation (current energy use 60 kg steam/ tonne beans) with the heat conditioning step (45 kg steam/tonne beans) and using waste combustion products from natural gas for preheating, the research has shown that energy savings of about 15 kg steam/tonne beans can be achieved. More significantly, by desolventizing the flakes via indirect heating, with minimum live steam usage, drying energy demand is dramatically reduced, giving a net saving of 35 kg steam/tonne beans. The energy used in drying has been reduced by about 70%.

A comparison of energy usages in the original and new process route is given in Table 2.

TABLE 2 - STEAM CONSUMPTION (KG/TON OF PROCESSED SOYABEANS)

	Present State of Art	New Process
Heating (10°C to 70°C) and Conditioning	45	-
Toasting	-	110
Desolventizing - Toasting	140	-
Desolventizing - Only	-	90
Distillation	25	25
Meal Drying (20% to 12% moisture)	80	-
(14% to 12% moisture)	-	25
Hexane Recovery	25	25
Total	315	275

4. APPLICATION OF TOTAL ENERGY SYSTEMS IN EDIBLE OIL PROCESSING PLANTS

Total energy systems are of considerable value at sites where the demand for heat and electricity meets certain criteria. The principal feature of a total energy system is its ability to produce heat at a useful

temperature level, in addition to the generation of electricity. Thus with
thermal efficiencies in excess of 80% in some cases, a prime mover capable
of supplying the desired heat/power ratio with high utilization can prove
to be an attractive investment, (4). Prime movers include Diesel and gas
reciprocating engines, gas turbines and steam turbines, and in all cases
heat may be recovered for process use or space heating. Applications are
fairly common in the larger process industries, and installations are now
being seen in buildings such as hotels, where 40 kW (electricity) packages
have attractions.
    The study by TNO (5) has concentrated on the use of total energy
systems in the field of edible oil processing, in particular on three diff-
erant processes:
   (i)   Soyabean extraction (1000ᵗ/day capacity)
   (ii)   Soyabean oil refinery (480ᵗ/day capacity)
   (iii) Margarine manufacture (200ᵗ/day capacity)
    A detailed analysis of the energy consumption at the selected sites,
the heat/power balance and utilization profiles, and of course energy costs
was performed, and three schemes, all based on gas turbines, were costed.
A summary of the results is given in Table 3.

TABLE 3 - HEAT/POWER RATIO, ANNUAL OPERATING HOURS AND PAYBACK PERIOD OF
          GAS TURBINE TOTAL ENERGY PLANT IN 3 CASE STUDIES.

Case Study	Heat/Power Ratio	Annual Operating Hours	Payback Period of gas turbine TE-System (Years)
Soyabean extraction plant, capacity about 1000 tons per day	6.9	6600	3.3
Soyabean oil refinery, capacity about 481 tons per day	18.3	6000	5.6
Margarine plant, capacity about 200 tons per day			
a. with compressor cooling	0.7	2250	17.8
b. with absorption cooling	2.4	2250	12.8

REFERENCES

1. DE VRIES, L.W.B.M. (1984). Energy saving in the bakery by improvement
    of energy efficiency and recovery of waste heat. (Contract EEB-1-148-N).
    Proc.Int.Seminar 'Energy Conservation in Industry', Dusseldorf, 13-15
    Feb, 1984, VDI, Dusseldorf.

2. ONG, T.L. (1980). Recovery of residual heat in the extraction of oil
    seeds and in the hydrogeneration of edible oils and fats. 'New Ways to
    Save Energy'. Proc.Int.Seminar, Brussels, Oct-1979, D.Reidel, Dordrecht.

3. ONG, T.L. (1984). Energy saving in the soyabean extraction industry by
    reducing the steam consumption for desolventizing-toasting and drying
    extracted beans. (Contract EEB-1-138-N). Proc.Int.Seminar 'Energy
    Conservation in Industry', Dusseldorf, 13-15 Feb, 1984,VDI, Dusseldorf.

4. REAY, D.A. (1983). The engineering systems approach to small scale
    combined heat and power. Proc. Dual Purpose Energy Systems Symposium,
    Fawley, 17 Nov. Institute of Energy.

5.   ONG, T.L. (1984). Energy saving in edible oil processing plants by application of a total energy (TE) system. (Contract EED-1-303-N). Proc.Int.Seminar 'Energy Conservation Industry', Dusseldorf, 13-15 Feb. 1984. VDI, Dusseldorf.

ENERGY SAVING IN THE BAKERY BY IMPROVEMENT OF ENERGY EFFICIENCY AND RECOVERY OF WASTE HEAT

Ing. L. W. B. M. de Vries

Institute for Cereals, Flour and Bread TNO

P. O. Box 15, NL-6700 AA Wageningen

1. SUMMARY

Each year a total of approx. 7000 TJ of energy is used in the production of bread and confectionery in the Netherlands. Partly because production is very decentralised, up to now very little is known about the energy consumption in this particular sector.

The object of this investigation is to determine and evaluate possible ways of energy and of recovering and re-using heat in the bakery. Prime importance has been attached to those processes or places where a large quantity of energy is used or lost. A second important aspect is to point to situations where energy can be saved by very simple means.

The investigation has been subsidized by the European Economic Community, the Bakery Trade Association, and the Dutch Ministry for Economic Affairs. Supervision was in the hands of a committee in which the Netherlands Bakery Foundation, the Netherlands Foundation for Information on Energy, and the Ministries of Agriculture and Fisheries and Economic Affairs were represented. Execution was in the hands of the Institute for Cereals, Flour and Bread TNO, in cooperation with the VEG-Gasinstituut NV.

2. METHODS OF INVESTIGATION

After consultation with the supervisory committee it has been decided, to investigate energy consumption in 12 bread bakeries. These 12 bakeries were selected on the basis of statistical data on the production of various groups of bakeries, contained in "The Structure of the Bakery Industry in the Netherlands" compiled and published in 1982 by the Netherlands Bakery Foundation. Table I indicates the data used.

First of all the bakeries were divided into two main groups, viz. those with batch process ovens and those with continuous process ovens; they will be called small and industrial bakeries, respectively. Within each of these main groups the bakeries were divided into 5 groups according to the quantity of bread produced. The investigation was performed in 7 bakeries with batch ovens representing 3650 bakeries, which produce 59 % of the bread in this country. Furthermore, 5 industrial bread bakeries (i.e. with continuous ovens) were examined, representing 119 bakeries producing the remaining 41 % of the bread.

This energy study only refers to the production equipment and areas, including the office and staff facilities connected with them. In every bakery the energy consumption was measured during an uninterrupted period of seven days. The consumption of electrical energy by equipment, lighting, fans, etc. was continuously measured with kWh-meters or hour counters on each apparatus or group of

Table I. DUTCH BREAD BAKERIES DIVIDED INTO GROUPS WITH BATCH OVENS AND CONTINUOUS OVENS.

Bakeries with batch ovens			
Number of bakeries	Bread production tons flour/week	National bread production %	Number of bakeries for energy investigation
850	0 - 0.75	4½	-
1550	0.75 - 1.5	17½	1
700	1.5 - 2.5	12½	2
400	2.5 - 5.0	12½	2
150	5.0 - 15	12	2
3650		59	7
Bakeries with continuous ovens			
37	5 - 15	3	1
20	15 - 25	3½	1
14	25 - 35	4	1
18	35 - 50	6½	1
30	> 50	24	1
119		41	5

apparatuses that are always switched on and off together. The consumption of gas was continuously measured by installing per baking oven or other baking apparatus a separate gas meter. Alternatively, the gas valves of the burners were provided with relays, so that the positions of the various burner valves could be recorded.

3. RESULTS

3.1. Bakeries with Batch Ovens

In these bakeries not only the baking process is non-continuous, but also the other stages of production - e.g. mixing, dividing, rounding and fermentation. In most bakeries these operations are mechanized. All bakeries have refrigerator and/or freezer facilities. The bakeries work in one or two shifts.

After production the energy supply to the ovens is shut off. The ovens cool down and must consequently be heated up to baking temperature again each day before baking can begin.

Table 2 shows the energy consumption per 100 kg of flour of the bakeries with batch ovens that have been investigated. The energy measurements showed that, for average assortments of bread and confectionery, the energy consumption per 165 kg of bread dough (= 100 kg of flour) is the same as per 100 kg of confectionery dough or batter. For the purposes of the calculation of the energy consumption per 100 kg of flour, the amounts of flour for bread production and dough or batter for confectionery production have been added together.

Table 2.
ENERGY CONSUMPTION OF BAKERIES WITH BATCH OVENS.

BAKERY CODE	A	B	C	D	E	F	G
PRODUCTION in tons flour/week	1.56	2.12	3.02	3.26	5.33	7.34	20.37
CONSUMPTION OF ELECTRICAL ENERGY in kWh per 100 kg flour							
- mixing	1.72	1.70	1.04	1.66	1.80	1.30	1.12
- dough processing	3.90	1.28	4.10	2.86	4.80	4.76	3.24
- baking ovens	6.46	3.00	31.04	-	4.32	-	0.92
- lighting	2.94	5.74	4.12	0.68	2.60	2.72	1.60
- refrigeration-freezing	10.98	16.86	6.04	6.20	6.00	9.40	6.76
- miscellaneous	0.30	0.60	-	-	2.40	0.32	1.26
Total kWh per 100 kg flour	26.30	29.18	46.34	11.40	21.92	18.50	14.90
CONSUMPTION OF NATURAL GAS in m^3 per 100 kg flour							
- cooking + heating of tap water	1.34	0.68	1.14	0.44	1.34	0.56	0.64
- heating system	1.46	1.54	1.26	1.96	0.68	4.40	3.60
- steam production	-	-	-	-	-	-	1.60
- baking ovens	14.88	13.54	8.46	11.14	10.58	12.20	12.52
Total m^3 per 100 kg flour	17.68	15.76	10.86	13.54	12.60	17.16	18.36

3.1.1. Consumption of Electrical Energy

Table 2 gives an overview of the consumption of electrical energy of the major items of equipment and the lighting. Included in "miscellaneous" is the electricity consumption of equipment such as electric boilers, compressors, sheet washing machines, central heating pumps, battery charges, etc.

In all the bakeries the energy consumption by refrigerators and freezers is high, in most cases amounting to 50 % or more of the total electrical energy consumption. The high energy concumption of refrigerator and freezer units is largely caused by:
a) opening doors unnecessarily frequently to put away or to take out small quantities of products;
b) putting products into the refrigerator or freezer, before they have cooled sufficiently. This loads the cooling unit unnecessarily;
c) in addition, evaporation of moisture from too warm products results in an extra deposit of ice on the cooling coil, which has to be de-frosted several times a day;
d) insulation not thick enough;
e) doors that don't shut properly and insulation leakages, shoddy maintenance of the refrigeration system, such as insufficient refrigerant and fouled condensor, hence poor heat dissipation;
f) unnecessary continuous door heating.

Of the total energy consumption for cooling and freezing, 5 to 15 % could be saved by using the equipment more efficiently. By improving the insulation, savings of 0-20 % can be achieved; good, regular maintenance can bring about a saving of 5-10 %, and by reducing the operating time of the door heating a further saving of 0-15 % can be obtained.

3.1.2. Consumption of Natural Gas

In bakeries with batch ovens, 70-85 % of the total natural gas consumption is used for the baking process. It was found that a great deal of energy is lost in the ovens in periods when they have to be kept up to baking temperature although no products are being baked. Improvements in production planning could reduce, or even prevent the idling time of the baking oven, with a consequent saving in energy consumption. It was also found that energy can be saved by restricting the heat lost via the flue gas exhaust duct, and by improving the insulation of the oven.

3.1.3. Savings as a Result of Good Production Planning

To ascertain the energy consumption of the baking ovens, the energy consumption was divided into the following categories on the basis of the continuously measured energy consumption and recorded data on the temperature in the baking areas and the amounts and types of products baked.

A. Energy Losses Before Baking

At the beginning of each production day the ovens are in a more or less cooled state. The energy that has to be supplied to bring them back to baking temperature is considered "cooling losses" (see below). Energy losses between this moment and the baking proper of the first batch are the "energy losses before baking".

During the investigation it was found that all the baking ovens had reached the baking temperature before there were products ready to be baked. The energy consumption of the ovens during this idling period varied between 5 % and 14 % of the energy consumption of the ovens.

B. Energy Losses During Baking

Idling periods also occurred in the baking ovens during production, because a subsequent batch of products was not yet ready to be baked. After the bread has been baked, the confectionery is usually baked at a lower temperature. Here too it was found that the ovens were kept at baking temperature for an unnecessarily long time, although they were only used incidentally for baking confectionery.

The average energy consumption for baking 100 kg of flour for bread production and 100 kg of dough or batter for confectionery production was calculated per baking oven from the daily energy consumption recorded for the production of bread and confectionery and the amounts produced. Figure 3 shows the daily energy consumption per 100 kg of flour, by two particular ovens with baking areas of 7.3 m^2 (oven A) and 14 m^2 (oven B). The figures shows that there are large differences in the energy used per day for baking the same amount of product.

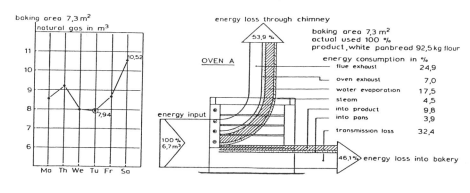

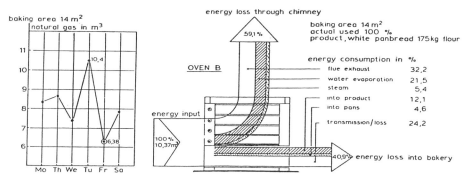

An analysis of the measurements shows that these differences can largely be attributed to loss of energy during longer or shorter periods of idling between two successive batches and only very slightly to changes in the composition of the product assortment. If the daily production in these bakeries were to be planned as it was done on the most efficient day in the investigation period, an energy saving of 24-31 % of the energy consumption for the baking proces could be achieved.

Energy balances have also been made for these baking ovens for baking a single batch of bread. The energy consumption figures quoted in the energy balances are the gas consumption of the baking oven during the baking process plus the gas consumption needed to heat the empty baking oven after the baking process back up to the original starting temperature; they do not include energy losses between batches. In this case oven A consumed 7.2 m^3 gas per 100 kg flour. According to the graph on the left hand side, the energy consumption on the most efficient day was 7.94 m^3 per 100 kg. In the case of oven B, the energy balance shows 5.92 m^2 of gas per 100 kg for the single batch; on the most efficient day 6.38 m^3 of gas per 100 kg was consumed. With both ovens, the energy consumption for a single batch is 10 % lower than the energy consumption on the most efficient day, both per 100 kg of flour. This difference is a result of energy losses between batches in the periods that the oven is maintained at the baking temperature; they are composed of transmission (into bakery) and ventilation (into chimney) losses. If, by proper planning, these idling periods are eliminated, a saving of 10 % will be achieved.

As already has been mentioned, the energy lost during idling is the gas consumption that is needed to keep the baking oven at the required temperature without the oven being used for baking, in other words to compensate for the heat wasted (transmission and ventilation losses) by the oven.

An additional saving of energy can be achieved by baking in such a way that the oven temperature at the end of baking is the same as just before entering the dough. Then it is unneceassary to heat the oven between batches; consequently, transmission losses during those heating periods are avoided. With both ovens, baking time was 30 minutes and the heating periods between batches were 15 minutes; transmission losses per unit of time are approximately the same during baking and during heating. As a result 1/3 part of the transmission losses occur during heating. As the transmission losses are 32 and 24 %, respectievely, of the total gas consumption, elimination of the heating periods will result in a saving of energy of approx. 10 %.

C. Cooling Losses

Energy lost when the oven cools down between two consecutive production days, when no energy is being supplied. The energy loss due to cooling is equal to the energy that must be supplied to the oven to bring it back up to the same baking temperature the oven was at the previous day when baking was stopped.

3.1.4. Saving in the Energy Consumption of Baking Ovens due to Technical Measures

Many gas-fired batch process ovens are fitted with pilot flames that burn continuously. The energy consumption investigation revealed that the gas consumption of these pilot flames at times when the ovens are not being used for baking is approx. 10 % of the total gas consumption of the baking ovens. By switching off the pilot flame or substitution by a spark ignition unit, a saving of 10 % of the total energy consumption of the baking oven would result.

Another source of energy loss in baking ovens is ventilation, with air passing through the oven burner section at times when no gas is being combusted. It has been found that 8-10 % of the energy supplied to the oven is lost again due to ventilation via the chimney. This loss can be eliminated by fitting a valve or baffle plate into the flue gas exhaust duct, which would automatically close off the exhaust duct when no gas is being supplied to the oven.

From the energy balances for the baking ovens, the data for which were recorded with full or almost full baking ovens, it can be seen that during the baking process approx. 20-30 % of the energy supplied is lost through the oven walls. These losses also occur at times when the ovens are not being used for baking. Better oven insulation can therefore also contribute considerably to energy saving in this sector.

The investigation also revealed that insufficient attention is paid to the setting and maintenance of the burners. A less than optimal setting will reduce the yield and hence result in loss energy. The same applies to defects and dirt in the ovens. During the investigation the average energy consumption per 100 kg of flour was measured for 2 identical baking ovens; for the one it was found to be 10 m^3 of natural gas and for the other 18 m^3 of natural gas. The high consumption of natural gas was caused by a defect in the oven's heat exchanger, which was simple enough to rectify. That is why regular, expert maintenance is so important.

3.2. Bakeries with Continuous Ovens

The bread production of the 5 bakeries with continuous ovens that have been investigated lies between 20 and 70 tons of flour per week. Dough preparation is done in batches, and the time between successive batches is planned in such a way that the processing of the dough, such as dividing, rounding and fermentation, takes place continuously; there is an uninterrupted flow of dough to the baking oven. Continuous dough preparation is not applied in Dutch bread bakeries.

After baking the loaves are mechanically de-panned using a mechanical depanner. The bread is then placed into trolleys by hand to cool down, or is transferred to a bread cooling conveyor belt using the depanner. The bread pans are force-cooled in a cooling tunnel using air from outside and are then returned to the dough moulding machine.

In the bakeries investigated bread production takes place on average 12-16 hours a day.

Table 4 shows the energy consumption per 100 kg of flour in the five investigated bakeries with continuous ovens.

From this tabel it can be seen that the average energy consumption per 100 kg of flour for bread production in the industrial bakery (with continuous ovens) is 510 MJ. In the small bakeries (with batch process ovens) the average consumption is 680 MJ per 100 kg of flour. In general the industrial bakeries used 25 % less energy to process 100 kg of flour into bread than the small bakeries.

TABLE 4. ENERGY CONSUMPTION OF BAKERIES WITH CONTINUOUS OVENS.

BAKERY CODE	H	I	J	K	L
PRODUCTION in tons flour/week	19.45	31.50	50.35	58.65	66.15
CONSUMPTION IN ELECTRICAL ENERGY in kWh per 100 kg flour					
- mixing	0.96	1.38	1.00	1.42	1.76
- dough processing	3.70	2.88	3.90	2.52	1.76
- baking ovens	0.68	1.20	2.56	2.54	3.00
- lighting	2.60	1.52	1.68	3.88	1.52
- refrigeration-freezing	4.10	3.40	1.80	2.84	0.42
- miscellaneous	1.84	2.46	3.70	3.86	2.46
Total kWh per 100 kg flour	13.88	12.84	14.64	17.06	10.92
CONSUMPTION OF NATURAL GAS in m^3 per 100 kg flour					
- cooking + heating of tap water	0.10	0.32	0.26	0.26	0.16
- heating system	0.08	2.36	4.48	6.46	3.04
- steam production	1.58	1.86	1.86	2.70	4.00
- baking ovens	6.24	7.20	6.76	8.22	7.14
Total m^3 per 100 kg flour	8.00	11.74	13.48	17.64	14.34

3.2.1. Consumption of Electrical Energy

Table 4 gives an overview of the consumption of electrical energy by the major items of equipment and the lighting. The consumption of electrical energy by the baking ovens in the bakeries H and I is lower than in the bakeries J, K and L. The higher energy consumption in the bakeries J, K and L is caused by the engines of the burner and circulation ventilators of the indirectly heated continuous ovens. The continuous ovens in the bakeries H and I are directly heated.

The energy consumption of the refrigerators and freezers is relatively lower in the industrial bakeries than in the small bakeries: 15-30 % of the total electrical energy consumption, as opposed to 50 % in the small bakeries.

The item "miscellaneous" includes consumers of electrical energy such as bread cooling conveyor belts, air compressors, sheet washing machines, central heating pumps, battery charges, electric boilers, etc. In bakery K the air compressors accounted for more than half the "miscellaneous" consumption percentage (23), and in bakery J 10 % of total electrical energy consumption, almost one half of the miscellaneous consumers, was caused by the fact that the sealing elements of the packaging machines were not switched off after use.

3.2.2. Consumption of Natural Gas

In the bakeries with continuous ovens the largest elements responsible for the consumption of natural gas are the baking process, ambient heating and the production of steam. Equipment for the production of steam is not usually found in small

303

bakeries. The steam that is used in these small bakeries is obtained by evaporating water in the baking areas of the ovens. In the case of continuous ovens steam is introduced during the baking process on the feed-in side of the ovens. The steam is generated by a steam boiler or generator located elsewhere in the bakery. The steam thus generated is also used to humidify the fermentation and proofing cabinets.

All the industrial bakeries investigated has one or more batch process ovens, which were used to bake small amounts and special products, including confectionery. Large energy losses occurred with these batch process ovens because they were used so infrequently, and consequently stood idle for much of the time. Of the total production 1.5-3 % was produced using batch process ovens; these ovens accounted for 8-10.5 % of the total baking energy consumption. Much of the energy was lost in these baking ovens while they were on stand-by and not being used for baking. The average energy consumption per 100 kg of flour is therefore very high, and varies between 950 MJ and 1600 MJ. The average energy consumption per 100 kg of flour measured for 16 batch ovens in the small bakeries was 350 MJ. Good production planning in these bakeries would possibly save 65-80 % of the energy consumption of these batch ovens, which corresponds to a saving of 6 to 7 % of the total energy consumption for the baking process in these bakeries.

In the industrial bakeries investigated 97-98 % of the production is done in continuous ovens. In all the bakeries the warming up of the continuous oven every day was planned in such a way that the oven reached baking temperature just as the first products were ready for baking, so that no energy was lost due to the oven standing idle. The production was planned in such a way that when the change-over was made from one type of pan bread to another there was no, or virtually no idling time in between baking processes. Idling periods did, however, occur when the change-over was made from panbread to rolls, buns or luxury types of bread in the continuous oven. The energy losses during these idling periods amounted to approx. 10 % of the energy consumption of the baking oven concerned.

In bakery K a second continuous oven was used for baking a relatively high proportion of rolls, buns and luxury bread types. The use of this oven for the baking of these products was extremely irregular, with the result that a great due of time the oven was standing idle and energy was lost. During the week that the investigation was carried out an energy loss of 43 % of the total amount of energy used by this baking oven was recorded, which amounts to 7 % of the bakery's total natural gas consumption. This can be avoided by better production planning.

In the industrial bakeries the energy consumption of 2 directly heated and 4 indirectly heated continuous ovens was investigated. In the case of 3 of the 4 indirectly heated ovens, it was found that energy losses occurred due to leakage in the circulation system. These losses varied between 10 and 22 % of the total energy consumption of the baking ovens. It is to be expected that such leakages occur in the case of a great many indirectly heated continuous ovens with large resultant energy losses.

In the case of one of the continuous ovens 10 % of the gas consumption could be saved by repairing a defect burner. Good, regular maintenance aimed at optimal energy consumption will do a lot to save energy.

From the energy measurements during the baking process it was found that in the case of several continuous ovens the transmission losses were 30 % or more. By improving the insulation of the ovens a considerably energy saving can be achieved.

3.2.3. Savings in the Consumption of Energy for Steam Production

In virtually all the bakeries with continuous ovens one or more steam boilers or steam generators are installed, which are situated in a central boiler house together with the central heating boilers and other boilers. Steam is used during the baking process and to humidify the fermentation and proofing cabinets. The steam is passed along conduits from the central boiler house to the various items of equipment. Automatic steam traps are installed in the conduits to trap any condensation that forms. The investigation in these bakeries revealed that a relatively large amount of condensation was discharged from the conduits, the lowest amount being 740 1/week in bakery H, and the highest amount 1710 1/week in bakery J.

In the investigated bakeries the condensate was not returned to the steam boiler but discharged to the sewer. The resultant energy losses varied between 7 % and 21 % of the energy supplied to the steam boiler. A carefully designed conduit with the right dimensions and good insulation could eliminate a large proportion of this loss.

3.2.4. Air-Conditioning in the Fermentation and Proofing Areas

In the fermentation cabinets, ambient conditions are maintained at approx. 30 °C and 80 % relative humidity, and in the proofing cabinets at approx. 35 °C and 90-95 % R.H. The discharge of steam which is used to humidify the fermentation areas, results in large energy losses. The fermentation areas, which are usually lined with non-insulated sheeting, are set up in the bakery, which has a temperature of appr. 26 °C. The desired optimal ambient conditions will be frequently upset by heat dissipation from the fermentation cabinets to the surrounding area, often strongly influenced by ventilation in the bakery, but also by excess heat due to condensation of steam and heat dissipation from poorly insulated steam and hot water pipes. Excess heat or humidity in the fermentation areas is generally removed via a ventilation system.

305

Since it is impossible to regulate the effect of humidification
by steam on the heat supply to the fermentation rooms, the air-
conditioning control equipment will start to fluctuate. To avoid
this sections of the sheeting are often removed, or windows in
the fermentation room are opened. As a result the discharge of
heat and humidity is kept in balance with the supply of heat
and humidity, which is controlled by the air-conditioning unit.
Considerable energy losses obviously ensue.

An improvement of the air-conditioning in the fermentation
area, and the consequent reduction of energy losses, can be
obtained by lining these areas with insulated sheeting and by
using water spray instead of steam to create the necessary
humid conditions. The heat that is neede to evaporate the water
will be taken from the fermentation area and will be supplemented
from the heating system. Technically speaking it will be easier
to control such a system within the set range for temperature
and relative humidity. It may be concluded that by the careful
use of steam, plus efficient design of the steam pipes as far
as their dimensions and insulation are concerned, so that condensation losses in the pipes will be reduced, can result in
savings which will vary between 6 and 16 % of the total natural
gas consumption in the bakeries investigated.

The energy consumption for heating can also be reduced in
most bakeries. In one of the investigated bakeries a reduction
of the ambient temperature from 30 $^{\circ}$C to 26 $^{\circ}$C can result in a
saving in the gas consumption of the heating installation of
473 m^3 per week. Throughout the whole heating season this represents a saving of 4 % of the bakery's total gas consumption.

Another possible way of saving energy is to improve the
ventilation and heating system. In the investigated bakeries it
was found that the ventilation system and the heating system
operated simultaneously 40-80 % of the time, so that the energy
supplied to the building by the heating system was immediately
discharged again via the ventilation system. The main reason
for this is usually the large distance between the inlet vents
for outside air and the outlet vents. Consequently the relatively
cold outside air has to travel a large distance in the building
itself, thus cooling down the building unnecessarily.

In bakery J the ventilation system of the open bread cooling
belt causes considerable movement of air in the building. During
47 % of the time that the bread cooling belt was in operation,
the heating installation was also working. It has been calculated
that if the bread cooling belt were to be encased and the ventilation system changed, a saving of 17.5 % of the total gas consumption by this bakery could be achieved.

To sum up, it can be said that in industrial bakeries with
continuous ovens a saving of 5-10 % of the consumption of electrical energy and a saving of 20-35 % of the consumption of
natural gas can be achieved by better production planning and
the introduction of technical measures.

4. RECOVERY OF HEAT

The use of economisers in the flue gas exhaust duct in continuous ovens is a sure way of recovering energy. The economisers that are now available on the market can recover approx. 55 % of the heat present in the flue gases. In the economisers the heat from the flue gases is exchanged to water. The water circuit of the economiser can be connected up to an industrial boiler for heating both tap water and central heating water. In many industrial bakeries tap water is heated by a boiler incorporated into the heating system, so that many of these industrial bakeries choose to connect the water circuit of the economiser to the return water circuit of the heating system. When calculating the pay-back period, it has been assumed that the steam humidification of the fermentation rooms will be replaced by a water spray system. This will not only bring about the energy saving mentioned earlier, owing to the use of considerably less steam, but, particularly in the summer months, more of the recycled energy can be re-used for the heating of the fermentation and proofing rooms. Recovery of heat from the flue gases of indirectly heated continuous ovens will result in a considerable saving in natural gas consumption, so that the pay-back time will be 1.5 to 2.5 years. In some bakeries heat can also be recovered from the flue gases of the steam boiler and on the central heating boiler(s), resulting in a pay-back time of 1.1 to 1.5 years.

Continuous ovens with a leak in the recirculation system use extra energy. A large part of this extra energy can be recovered from the flue gases of these ovens with the help of an economiser. If the heat that is recovered in this way can be re-used, the cost of repairing the circulation system must be weighed up against the cost of heat recovery.

ENERGY SAVING IN EDIBLE OIL PROCESSING PLANTS BY APPLICATION OF A TOTAL-ENERGY (TE) SYSTEM

T. L. Ong

The Netherlands Central Organization for Applied Scientific
Research TNO
Institute CIVO-Technology TNO
Utrechtseweg 48, NL-3704 HE Zeist

Summary

An investigation has been made into the possibility to reduce the
steam consumption in the soybean extraction process, by the following modifications:
a. combining the toasting operation with the heat-conditioning step
and utilizing waste combustion gases for preheating;
b. desolventizing the defatted flakes by means of indirect heating
and a minimum of live steam, resulting in soybean meal of low water
content which will hardly needs any drying.
In this context the optimal specific energy consumption of the operations concerned has been assessed. Besides, toasting experiments
have been carried out with a semi-technical toaster. It appeared
possible to toast soybeans in a relatively dry condition without de-
teriorating the protein and oil quality. However, it was found that
toasting had an adverse effect on the extractability of the beans.
A prudent conclusion is that by applying the new process about 40 kg
of steam per ton of beans can be saved, as compared with the present
state of art.

1. INTRODUCTION

In the EEC soybeans rank at the top of the list of oilseeds being
extracted. The amount of soybeans and other oilseeds processed in the EEC
is presented in table 1.
For the production of soybean oil and meal, soybeans are consecutively:
cracked, dehulled – in making soybean meal 49 % protein –, heat-con-
ditioned, flaked and extracted by means of hexane; the defatted flakes,
containing 30–40 % hexane, is subsequently desolventized and toasted – to
improve the nutritional value – by means of steam; finally the wet extracted meal is dried by means of hot air (see figure 1).
In this process steam is required for heat-conditioning, extraction,
desolventizing-toasting, drying and for distilling hexane out of the
oil-in-hexane solution (miscella).
In the manufacture of low-phosphorus degummed soybean oil, the
flakes – prior to extraction – are cooked at a moisture content of about
16 % and a temperature of about 110 °C – to partiallly deactivate the enzymes – and subsequently dried to about 10 % moisture and cooled to about
60 °C. These flakes are extracted in the usual way and – after desolventizing – still have to be toasted to improve its nutritional value (see
figure 1).
The aim of the research is to reduce the steam consumption in the
following process steps:
a. the toasting process by about 20 kg/ton of beans, by combining this
operation with the heat-conditioning step, and utilizing waste combustion
gases for preheating;

308

b. the <u>drying</u> process by about 30 kg/ton of beans, by desolventizing the defatted flakes by means of superheated hexane vapour, resulting in soybean meal of low water content which hardly needs any drying.

In this context it is essential to assess the optimal specific energy consumption in the processes concerned. Consequently, the optimal specific energy consumption of the following processes has been assessed:
a. heat-conditoning soybeans;
b. desolventizing defatted flakes by means of steam;
c. desolventizing defatted flakes by means of superheated hexane vapour;
d. toasting soybeans;
e. drying desolventized-toasted soybean meal.

In accordance with the pertinent research programme, the following have also been accomplished:
a. survey of the available quantity and the properties of the combustion gases from steam-boilers fired with natural gas, fuel oil and coal respectively;
b. toasting experiments with cracked beans in an experimental toaster;
c. investigation into the yield and quality of the oils extracted from the toasted beans.

2. DESCRIPTION

2.1 Assessment of the optimal specific energy consumption of heat-conditioning soybeans, desolventizing defatted flakes by means of steam and superheated hexane vapour, toasting and drying soybean meal

2.1.1 Optimal energy consumption for heat-conditioning soybeans

Heat-conditioning of cracked soybeans at 60-80 °C - prior to flaking - is necessary to plasticize the kernel particles, so good flakes can be formed. The kernel particles are flaked by passing through a set of smooth rolls travelling at different speeds. The assessment of the energy consumption for heat-conditioning soybeans was made for the standard vertical stacked kettle type and was based on the following process conditions:

   plant capacity of 1000 tons per day:
   1000 kg soybeans (12 % water) yields: 180 kg oil + 820 kg meal (15 % water)
   cracked beans entering heat-conditioner at 10 °C and 12 % moisture, cracked beans leaving heat-conditioner at 12 % moisture and at temperatures of 60 °C, 70 °C and 80 °C respectively.
The results are summarized in table 2.

2.1.2 Optimal energy consumption for desolventizing defatted flakes by means of steam

Soybean flakes are normally extracted with hexane at about 50 °C. The assessment of the energy consumption for desolventizing defatted flakes by means of steam was based on the following process conditions:
   plant capacity of 1000 tons per day:
   temperature of defatted flakes leaving extractor: 50 °C;
   hexane content of defatted flakes: 30 %, 35 % and 40 % respectively;
   specific heat (Cp) of hexane: 2,5 kJ/kg·K;
   specific heat (Cp) of soybean meal containing 12 % water: 2,0 kJ/kg·K; latent heat of hexane 330 kJ/kg,
   steam condensing on the flakes: 101,3 kPa and 100 °C;
   temperature of vapours leaving desolventizer: 70 °C, 75 °C, 80 °C and 85 °C respectively.

Nowadays, it is still normal practice to blow open steam onto the hexane-wet defatted flakes, so as to desolventize the material. The steam condenses on the flakes and the condensation heat evaporates the hexane. The energy/steam consumption for desolventizing defatted flakes, and the resulting water content of the desolventized material are shown in table 3.

2.1.3 Optimal energy consumption for desolventizing defatted flakes by means of superheated hexane vapours

The amount of heat and superheated hexane of 150 °C for desolventizing defatted flakes are shown in table 4. Operating parameters are:
- hexane content of extracted flakes: 30 %, 35 % and 40 % respectively;
- temperature of vapours leaving desolventizer: 70 °C, 75 °C, 80 °C and 85 °C respectively

TABLE 1 – SOYBEANS AND OTHER OILSEEDS PROCESSED IN THE EEC IN THE YEARS 1981 AND 1982

Country	1981 total oilseeds $(10^6 t)$	1981 soybeans $(10^6 t)$	1981 share % age of total	1982 total oilseeds $(10^6 t)$	1982 soybeans $(10^6 t)$	1982 share % age of total
Belgium/Luxembourg	1,5	1,3		1,8	1,6	
Denmark	0,3	0,2		0,3	0,2	
France	1,6	0,6		1,8	0,9	
West Germany	5,1	3,0		5,4	3,7	
Greece	0,4	0,2		0,4	0,2	
Ireland	–	–		–	–	
Italy	1,5	1,2		1,7	1,5	
The Netherlands	3,0	2,7		2,9	2,5	
United Kingdom	1,7	1,1		1,7	1,2	
Total	15,1	10,3	68	16,0	11,8	74

TABLE 2 – OPTIMAL ENERGY CONSUMPTION FOR HEAT-CONDITIONING SOYBEANS OF 10 % MOISTURE AND 10 °C, AT TEMPERATURE OF 60 °C, 70 °C and 80 °C RESPECTIVELY

Heat conditioning temperature (°C)	Energy consumption (MJ/ton beans)	Steam consumption (kg/ton beans)
60	83	36
70	103	45
80	123	53

TABLE 3 - OPTIMAL ENERGY AND STEAM CONSUMPTION FOR DESOLVENTIZING EX-
TRACTED FLAKES, AS WELL AS THE RESULTING WATER CONTENT OF THE
DESOLVENTIZED FLAKES; OPERATING PARAMETERS:
- HEXANE CONTENT OF EXTRACTED FLAKES: 30 %; 35 %; 40 %
- TEMPERATURE OF VAPORS LEAVING DESOLVENTIZER: 70 °C, 75 °C,
80 °C and 85 °C

hexane content of extracted flakes (%)	energy consumption to evaporate hexane (MJ/ton beans)	steam consumption (101,3 kPa, 100 °C) to evaporate hexane (kg/ton beans)	water content of desolven- tized flakes (%)
temperature of vapors leaving desolventizer: 70 °C			
30	167	70	21
35	202	85	23
40	242	102	24
temperature of vapors leaving desolventizer: 75 °C			
30	178	76	22
35	214	90	23
40	255	108	25
temperature of vapors leaving desolventizer: 80 °C			
30	188	81	22
35	224	96	24
40	266	114	25
temperature of vapors leaving desolventizer: 85 °C			
30	200	86	23
35	237	102	24
40	280	121	26

TABLE 4 - AMOUNT OF HEAT AND SUPERHEATED HEXANE OF 150 °C FOR DESOLVENTIZING EXTRACTED FLAKES; OPERATION PARAMETERS ARE: - HEXANE CONTENT OF EXTRACTED FLAKES: 30 %, 35 % AND 40 % - TEMPERATURE OF VAPORS LEAVING DESOLVENTIZER: 70 °C, 75 °C, 80 °C AND 85 °C

| hexane content of extracted flakes (%) | temperature of vapors leaving desolventizer (°C): | | | | | | | |
| | 70 | | 75 | | 80 | | 85 | |
	heat MJ/t. beans	hexane vapors kg/t. beans	heat MJ/t. beans	hexane vapors kg/t. beans	heat MJ/t. beans	hexane vapors kg/t. beans	heat MJ/t. beans	hexane vapors kg/t. beans
30	167	837	178	952	188	1076	200	1233
35	202	1010	214	1139	224	1280	237	1459
40	242	1211	255	1359	266	1518	280	1722

TABLE 5 - OPTIMAL ENERGY CONSUMPTION FOR TOASTING FLAKES - CONTAINING ABOUT 22 % WATER - OF 70 °C, 75 °C, 80 °C AND 85 °C RESPECTIVELY AT 105 °C

desolventizing temperature (°C)	amount of heat for toasting flakes (MJ/t. beans)	amount of steam (101,3 kPa, 100 °C) for toasting flakes (kg/t. beans)
70	153	67
75	144	63
80	135	59
85	126	55

TABLE 6 - OPTIMAL STEAM AND AIR CONSUMPTION FOR DRYING DESOLVENTIZED TOASTED SOYBEAN MEAL OF 14-20 % MOISTURE DOWN TO 12 % MOISTURE; MEAL ENTERING DRYER AT 105 °C

moisture content of meal (%)	steam consumption kg/t. beans	air consumption kg/t. beans
14	19	95
16	39	190
18	63	295
20	86	400

TABLE 7 - AVERAGE AVAILABLE QUANTITY AS WELL AS IMPORTANT MINOR COMPONENTS OF COMBUSTION GASES FROM STEAM BOILERS, FIRED WITH NATURAL GAS, FUEL OIL AND COAL RESPECTIVELY

		emission (mg/fuel unit)					
fuel	fuel unit	carbon monoxide	sulfur oxides as SO_2	nitrogen oxides as NO_2	hydro-carbons	fly-ash	stack gases (nm^3/fuel unit)
natural gas	nm^3	30-300	15	1000-1700	10-60	10	12-13
heavy oil grade 6	kg	300	50.000	5000	300	2000-3000	15
coal	kg	500	12.000	10.000	150	15.000	16

2.1.4 Optimal energy consumption for toasting soybeans

Soybeans are toasted (cooked) to improve their nutritional value; the process is normally carried out in a steam atmosphere at about 105 °C. The temperature of the flakes leaving the desolventizing section of the desolventizer-toaster (DT) is raised to about 105 °C. The heat for denaturation the enzymes and proteins in the beans has been estimated at 90 kJ/kg.

The amount of heat for toasting flakes, depending upon the desolventizing temperature, is shown in table 5.

2.1.5 Optimal energy consumption for drying desolventized-toasted soybean meal

Depending on the hexane content of the defatted flakes and the desolventizing temperature, the water content of the desolventized flakes amounts to 21-26 % (c.f. table 3); however some drying takes place in the toasting section to 18-20 % moisture.

The assessment of the steam and air consumption for drying the desolventized-toasted soybean meal was based on the following:
- meal dryer in which the drying air is reheated inside the apparatus;
- meal entering dryer at 105 °C and 14-20 % moisture;
- meal leaving dryer at 70 °C and 12 % moisture;
- air entering dryer at 10 °C, 80 % RH, 0,0062 kg H_2O/kg dry air;
- air leaving dryer at 70 °C, 70 % RH, 0,2093 kg H_2O/kg dry air;
The results of the assessments are summarized in table 6.

2.2 Survey of the average available quantity and of the important minor components of the combustion gases from steam-boilers, fired with natural gas, fuel oil and coal respectively

The amount and properties of the exhaust gases of steam-boilers, fired with natural gas, fuel oil and coal respectively have been measured by the Heat and Refrigeration Engineering Division TNO - Apeldoorn. This division has a special coach equipped with instruments for continuous analyzing stack gases for: nitrogen oxides, carbon monoxide, soot, dust, sulfur oxides, temperature etc. The results of this investigation are summarized in table 7; they indicate that the combustion gases of natural gas are relatively clean and suitable for treating food products; however those of heavy fuel oil and coal contain considerable amounts of hydrocarbons and fly ash and are not acceptable for these purposes.

At present, the average natural gas consumption in a modern and efficiently run soybean extraction plant is 22 m^3/ton of beans, which results into 286 nm^3combustion gases of 160 °C. The available heat in these gases cooled to 60 °C is 28,6 MJ per ton of beans, equivalent with 12,4 kg of steam.

2.3 Toasting and extraction experiments

The experimental toaster is shown in figure 2. It is a double-shelled vessel; thermal oil of 120 °C is circulated between the shells.

10 kg cracked soybeans were poured into the vessel and heated to 60 °C; the vessel was closed and 2 bar steam was introduced until the beans have got the required toasting temperature. After a fixed toasting time, the steam was blown off and the beans were cooled with cold air to 70 °C, subsequently flaked and finally extracted with 6 cycles of fresh hexane at 55 °C. Some typical results of the experiments are shown in table 8.

Compared with the non-toasted flakes (no. 79) the toasted material
(no. 75) had a higher resistance to the hexane flow resulting in a higher
hexane content of the defatted flakes. The oil quality of the toasted
beans is better than that of their non-toasted counterpart.

3. CONCLUSION

According to the present state of art, the steam consumption per ton
of beans is 315 kg (heat-conditioning 45, desolventizing-toasting 140,
distillation 25, meal drying 80 and hexane recovery 25).
In the new process the sequence of operations and the steam consumption
per ton of beans will be:
toasting (110 kg), flaking, extraction, desolventizing (90), distillation
(25 kg), meal drying (25 kg), hexane recovery (25 kg); total 275 kg.
A prudent conclusion is that by applying the new process about 40 kg of
steam per ton of beans can be saved, as compared with the present state
of art, equivalent with 2,8 m^3 of natural gas.
For an extraction plant with a capacity of 1000 tons of beans per day,
the necessary investments to implement the new process are estimated at
Hfl. 800.000,-, while the payback period will be about 4 years.

TABLE 8 - TYPICAL RESULTS OF SOME TOASTING AND EXTRACTION EXPERIMENTS
WITH CRACKED SOYBEANS OF 9,0 % MOISTURE AND UREASE ACTIVITY AT
30 °C 2,5 ΔpH

Experiment no.	75	79
Toasting		
Heating time, starting at 60 °C (min.)	1	non-toasted
Steam pressure (bar)	2,1	
Toasting temperature (°C)	123	
Toasting time (min.)	1	
Urease activity (Δ pH)	0,1	2,5
Flaking		
Moisture content of flakes (%)	9,9	10,3
Average thickness of flakes (mm)	0,21	0,21
Extraction		
Percolation rate of hexane through flakes (m^3/h.m^2)	3,4	11,2
Residual oil content of flakes after 6 extraction cycles (% on moisture free base)	0,55	0,47
Hexane content of hexane-wet defatted flakes (%)	46,6	31,2
Extracted oil		
Acid value (mg KOH/g)	1,93	1,94
Peroxide value (meq/kg)	0,1	0,1
p-Anisidine value	1,7	2,3
Phosphorus content (mg/kg)		
of: crude oil	1150	850
degummed oil	15	250
Absorption of 1 % solution in a 1 cm cuvette at:		
230 nm	2,06	3,37
268 nm	0,33	0,39

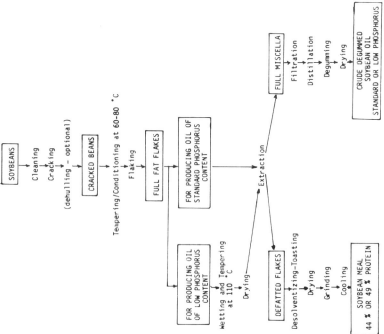

FIGURE 1 – FLOW DIAGRAM OF A SOYBEAN EXTRACTION PLANT PRODUCING SOYBEAN MEAL AND CRUDE DEGUMMED OIL OF STANDARD (200 ppm P) AND LOW (20 ppm P) PHOSPHORUS CONTENT

FIGURE 2 – EXPERIMENTAL SOYBEAN TOASTER

SOYBEANS

Cleaning

Cracking

(dehulling - optional)

CRACKED BEANS

Tempering/Conditioning at 60-80 °C

Flaking

FULL FAT FLAKES

FOR PRODUCING OIL OF STANDARD PHOSPHORUS CONTENT

FOR PRODUCING OIL OF LOW PHOSPHORUS CONTENT

Wetting and Tempering at 110 °C

Drying

Extraction

FULL MISCELLA

Filtration

Distillation

Degumming

Drying

CRUDE DEGUMMED SOYBEAN OIL STANDARD OR LOW PHOSPHORUS

DEFATTED FLAKES

Desolventizing-Toasting

Drying

Grinding

Cooling

SOYBEAN MEAL 44 % OR 49 % PROTEIN

316

ENERGY SAVING IN THE SOYBEAN EXTRACTION INDUSTRY BY REDUCING THE STEAM CONSUMPTION FOR DESOLVENTIZING – TOASTING AND DRYING EXTRACTED BEANS –

T. L. Ong

The Netherlands Central Organization for Applied Scientific
Research TNO
Institute CIVO-Technology TNO
Utrechtseweg 48, NL-3704 HE Zeist

Summary

An investigation has been made into the feasibility to save primary
energy carriers by application of a total-energy system, in the following types of edible oil processing plants: a. soybean extraction;
b. soybean oil refinery; c. margarine manufacture.
The outcome of the investigation is as follows:

Plant	Working hours/year	Payback period PBP (years)	Rate of return (%)
Soybean extraction (1000 tons per day)	6600	3,3	29
Soybean oil refinery (480 tons per day)	6000	5,5	15
Margarine manufacture (200 tons per day)	2250	11,8	6

1. INTRODUCTION

It is well known that in public electricity generation stations only
about 35 % of the total primary energy input is converted into electricity; about 65 % of this energy input is lost. A small part of the
losses is due to the transport system, such as resistance in the cables
and transformers; however, the major part is in fact waste heat discharged with the low pressure exhaust steam from the turbines.
Efforts to utilize this waste heat for town heating are not always successful, because of the high investments for transporting the hot water
over long distances.
    On the other hand edible oil processing plants – like extraction
plants, refineries etc. – utilize huge amounts of low pressure steam
(6-10 bar), beside electricity.
    In the past the application of total-energy (TE) systems was feas-
ible only in big plants, having a capacity of at least 10 MW. However recently reliable small TE-units, driven by gas or diesel engines become
available. Although the mechanical efficiency of these small units
(0,3-1,0 MW) is lower (< 30 %) than that of a big power station
(1000 MW), the application of a small unit in edible oil processing
plants could be advantageous because of the possibility to utilize the
waste heat, raising the total efficiency – based on the primary energy
input – to about 70 %, which is nearby two times that of a big power
station. Therefore substantial savings on primary energy carriers can be
achieved when an edible oil processing plant generates its own electricity and at the same time can utilize the waste heat on the spot.
However several questions have to be answered first, before the installation of a TE-system can be considered; the most important are:

a. choice of the proper type and capacity
b. the necessary investments
c. achievable savings
d. payback period
  The aim of this research is to investigate whether savings in primary energy carriers by application of a total-energy system can be im-
plemented in the following types of edible oil processing plants:
a. soybean extraction
b. refinery
c. margarine manufacture
  To achieve these goals the following data should be determined and
measured in each type of plant mentioned above:
a. the ratio of the concurrent optimal steam/power consumption
b. a breakdown of the operating times of the steam and electricity consuming units
c. based on the determinations and measurements of a. and b., the proper
   type and capacity of TE-system (steam turbines, gas or diesel engines)
   can be chosen
d. the investments for the TE-unit, building, safety and noise reducing
   measures
e. the energy and cost savings, including the payback period of the investments
f. safety and environmental, technical and non-technical barriers
  In order to obtain the necessary actual data a close co-operation
with a soybean extraction plant, a refinery and a margarine plant respectively is crucial.
In approaching several companies to co-operate in this project, a soybean
extraction plant (capacity about 1000 tons per day), a soybean oil refinery (capacity about 480 tons per day) and a margarine plant (capacity
about 200 tons per day) were found prepared to make this investigation
possible.

2. SOYBEAN EXTRACTION PLANT

2.1 Determination of the concurrent optimal heat/power consumption ratio
    in a soybean extraction plant of 1000 tons per day capacity

2.1.1 Description of the soybean extraction process
  Soybeans are normally processed to produce oil and meal by the processes shown in figure 1.
After cleaning the beans, they are adjusted to about 10 % moisture and
cracked into 4-8 pieces. For the preparation of high protein meal, the
hulls are removed by air classification. The cracked beans are softened
by tempering/conditioning with steam and subsequently rolled into flakes
having a thickness of 0.2-0.4 mm. The flakes are extracted in an extractor in counter-current with miscella of diminishing strenghts and finally
with a wash of clear hexane to reduce the residual oil content to
< 1.0 %. The defatted flakes, which contain 30-40 % hexane are desolven-
tized and subsequently toasted in a so-called desolventizer-toaster (DT).
The meal discharging out of the DT at over 100 °C and at a moisture of
18-22 % is usually dried to 12-14 % moisture. The dried meal is consecutively ground, cooled and sent to storage.
The so-called "full miscella" from the extractor, containing 20-35 % oil
in hexane is filtered; the solvent is removed in consecutively the first
and the second stage evaporators, and finally in the stripper.

2.1.2 Determination of the actual optimal heat/power consumption ratio

The extraction of soybeans is a continuous process; this means that in normal operation (except during breakdowns, shutdowns and start-ups) the steam and power demands are constant.

The plant under consideration has just finished a steam conservation programme, consisting of improving insulation, installing economizers, recovery of the heat of the air leaving the meal dryer etc. These resulted into a reduction of the natural gas consumption per ton of beans from 38 m^3 to 22 m^3. The minimum steam pressure is 6 bar.

On the average, the plant operates 275 days x 24 hours = 6600 hours a year.

As described in 2.1.1 the most important energy consuming operations are: cracking, tempering/conditioning, flaking, extraction, desolventizing/toasting, drying, grinding, distillation/evaporation and obviously pumps and conveyors for transporting beans, flakes and meal.

Besides, ventilators to keep the dust and hexane concentration in the buildings below the maximum allowable concentration (MAC value) consume a lot of electricity.

The energy consumption of the apparatuses concerned have been determined by means of standard steamflow and kWh-meters during 2 consecutive weeks at a production of 40 tons of beans per hour.

The results of the determinations of the energy consumption of the apparatuses concerned, expressed in MJ/ton of beans, are summarized in table 1.

2.2 Investments and payback period

The heat/power consumption ratio in the plant under consideration is 693/100,8 = 6,9 (cf. table 1).

Since the average hourly production is 40 tons, the TE-unit should have a capacity of at least 100,8 x 40/3,6 = 1120 kW.

There are three possible TE-systems, viz.:
a. steamturbine with high pressure boiler
b. gas-pistonmotor
c. gasturbine

A steamturbine with high pressure boiler needs rather high investments in foundation and building; besides the system needs constant supervision.

A gas-pistonmotor produces beside mechanical power – to drive the generator –, hot water of about 110 °C (from the engine cooling system) and exhaust gases of about 450 °C. Since the plant can utilize only 6 bar steam (about 160 °C), the produced hot water is useless.

A gasturbine produces beside mechanical power – to drive the generator –, only exhaust gases of about 450 °C which can be utilized to produce 6 bar steam.

The conclusion is that a gasturbine-generator is the most suitable system for the plant under consideration.

Since the gas pressure available (5 bar) is too low for feeding the turbines, a compressor of 50 kW is needed.

To keep the capital expenditures at a minimum, a TE-system running in parallel with the public power plant is chosen.

To keep the costs for stand-by power at a minimum, the system will consist of 2 gasturbine-generators of 600 kW each. In this case a stand-by of 600 kW will suffice.

```
     Other important data are:
Boiler feed water temperature                       80 °C
Natural gas price                                   0,013 ECU/kWh
Electricity price                                   0,049 ECU/kWh
     The 2 generators will produce per hour:
1200 kWh electricity and the energy balance (kWh/h) is as follows:
Natural gas                                         6250
Produced electricity                                1200
Compressor consumption                                50
Electricity available for the plant                 1150
Heat available in the exhaust gases cooled to 110 °C 3750
Total available energy                              4900
Energy loss                                         1350
```

     The efficiency of a modern boiler is 0,90. For adding 3750 kWh heat
to boiler feed water, the necessary energy will be 3750/0,90 = 4167 kWh.
The amount of natural gas necessary for generating 1150 kWh electricity
is 6250 - 4167 = 2083 kWh.
The price difference per year - 6600 working hours - is: 6600 x (1150 x
0,049 - 2083 x 0,013) = 193.189 ECU. Investment ΔI for the TE-system =
Hfl. 1.800.000,- = 642.857 ECU. Payback period PBP: 642.857/193.189 =
3,3 years.
Economic lifetime is 100 000 working hours = 15 years. Rate of return ROR
= 29 %.

3. SOYBEAN OIL REFINERY

     The purpose of refining edible oils is to remove undesirable
components out of the oils - such as gums, free fatty acids, colouring
and flavouring compounds, pesticides, oxidation products etc. - and so to
improve their quality. Today, edible oils are refined along 2 ways (see
fig. 2) viz.: a. alkali refining and b. physical refining.
     In the alkali refining process, the crude oil is consecutively
degummed (mostly with a water solution of phosphoric or citric acid), de-
acidified with a sodium hydroxide solution, bleached with activated
earth, and finally deodorized.
     In the physical refining process, the deacidification with sodium hy-
droxide is omitted; the free fatty acids are removed in the deodorization
step. The advantages of this process - compared with the first method -
are less waste water, higher yields and lower energy consumption.
     However the physical refining process is not always applicable to
highly unsatured oils, such as soybean oil, particularly when they have
incurred oxidation either in the beans or during extraction, storage and
transportation.
     The energy consumption of the 2 processes are shown in table 2.
Since soybean oil is the most important oil in The Netherlands and also
in the EEC countries, the investigation regarding a TE-system concerns an
alkali refinery, processing 20 tons/h of this oil i.e. 480 tons/d; total
working hours a year is 6000. The hourly energy consumption is 8 tons of
steam and 280 kWh electricity. In this case a 293 kW gasturbine-generator, with a stand-by power of 300 kW will suffice.
     The energy balance (kWh/h) is as follows:

```
Natural gas for the turbines                        1716
Produced electricity                                 293
Compressor consumption                                13
Electricity available for the plant                  280
```

Heat available in the exhaust gases cooled to 110 °C   922
Total available energy   1202
Energy loss   514

The efficiency of a modern boiler is 0,90. For adding 922 kWh heat to
water - for boiler and washing purposes -, the necessary energy will be
1024 kWh.
The amount of gas necessary for generating 280 kWh electricity is 1716 -
1024 = 692 kWh.
The price difference per year - 6000 working hours - is: 6000 x (280 x
0,049 - 692 x 0,013) = 28.344 ECU.
Investment ΔI for the TE-system = Hfl. 439.500,- = 156.964 ECU. Payback
period PBP: 156.964/28.344 = 5,5 years.
Economic lifetime is 100 000 working hours = 15 years. Rate of return ROR
= 15 %.

4. MARGARINE MANUFACTURE

Margarine is a solidified emulsion of a watermilk phase in a continuous fat-blend phase. A simplified flowsheet of the margarine process is
shown in figure 3.
Today margarine is manufactured by means of the so-called Votator method;
it is a continuous process in which the oil-water emulsion is turned into
margarine by churning, cooling and kneading in scraped tube coolers.
The average energy consumption per ton product of the whole process is:
45 kWh (162 MJ) electricity and 80 kg 6 bar steam (184 MJ).
The heat/power ratio is therefore 1,14, which - in fact - is far too low
for the application of a TE-system. Since the capacity of the plant under
consideration is 25 tons per hour, the hourly energy consumption is
2 tons of 6 bar steam and 1125 kWh electricity. The plant operates
5 days/week with 9 working hours/day; the average total working hours per
year is 2250.
The average boiler feed water temperature (returned condensate) is 80 °C.
Since the plant uses only a small quantity of hot water for cleaning purposes, a gasturbine rather than a gas-pistonmotor is the most appropriate
prime mover. In this particular case a 480 kW gasturbine-generator with
19,1 % electricity yield producing about 2 tons of 6 bar steam/h will
suffice.
The energy balance (kWh/h) is as follows:
Natural gas for the gasturbine   2508
Produced electricity   480
Gascompressor consumption   20
Electricity available for the plant   460
Heat available in the exhaust gases cooled to 110 °C 1368
Total available energy   1828
Energy loss   680
In a boiler having an efficiency of 0,90 the necessary energy to add
1368 kWh heat to water will be 1520 kWh.
The amount of gas necessary for generating 460 kWh electricity is 988 kWh.
The price difference per year - 2250 working hours - is: 2250 x (460 x
0,049 - 988 x 0,013) = 21.816 ECU.
Investment ΔI for the TE-system = Hfl. 720.000,- = 257.143 ECU.
Payback period PBP: 257.143/21.816 = 11,8 years.
Economic lifetime is 20 years.
Rate of return ROR = 6 %.

321

5. CONCLUSION

The payback period PBP of a TE-system for the soybean extraction
plant and soybean oil refinery is reasonably low; however the PBP of a
TE-unit for the margarine plant under consideration is considerably long,
because of the low number of operating hours per year.

TABLE 1 - BREAKDOWN OF THE ENERGY CONSUMPTION IN A 1000 TPD SOYBEAN EX-
          TRACTION PLANT - MJ/TON OF BEANS

	heat (MJ)	electricity (MJ)*
cracking		7,2
tempering/conditioning	119	3,6
flaking		36,0
extraction	40	3,6
desolventizing/toasting	297	7,2
drying	158	7,2
grinding		7,2
distillation (including usage of the heat of the vapours from the DT)	79	
pumps, conveyors etc.		14,4
ventilators		14,4
	693	100,8

* = 1 kWh = 3,6 MJ

TABLE 2 - AVERAGE ENERGY CONSUMPTION IN REFINING EDIBLE OILS ACCORDING TO
          TWO METHODS VIZ. A. WITH ALKALI AND B. PHYSICALLY

	alkali refining	physical refining
steam (kg/t crude oil)	400	300
electricity(kWh/t crude oil)	14	7

FIGURE 1 - FLOW DIAGRAM OF A SOYBEAN EXTRACTION PLANT

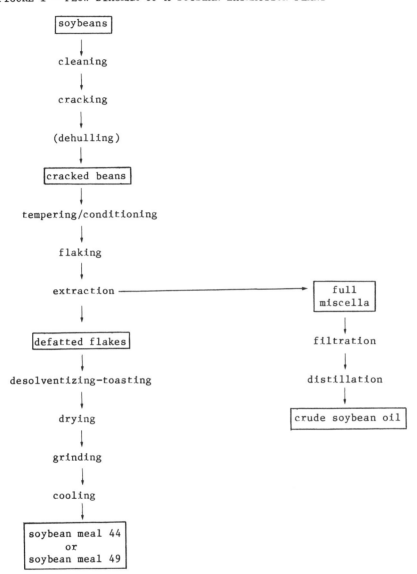

FIGURE 2 - BLOCK DIAGRAM OF TWO TYPES OF EDIBLE OIL REFINING PROCESSES

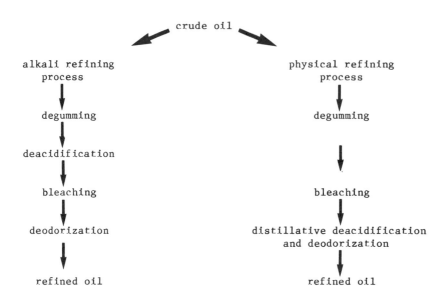

FIGURE 3 - FLOW DIAGRAM OF A MARGARINE MANUFACTURING PROCESS

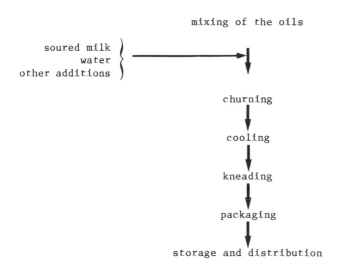

MICROWAVE APPLICATIONS

Presentation by Rapporteur
D. A. Reay, M. Sc.

International Research & Development Company Ltd
Newcastle upon Tyne, NE6 2YD, U.K.

Summary

The use of microwaves for drying and curing processes potentially
offers energy saving advantages, particularly when the material being
treated has a low thermal conductivity. Problems exist in achieving
uniform heating within structures, particular thin webs, and an
adequate knowledge of the microwave properties of materials is
necessary for successful operation of microwave ovens.
The projects supported in this sector address themselves to these
problems.

1.   INTRODUCTION

Microwave energy has been used by industry for heating and drying
processes for many years, but, unlike the use of domestic microwave ovens,
the application of microwave energy to industrial processes has, in general,
been restricted to a few specialized applications. Commercially available
microwave machines are applied to the continuous vulcanizing of extruded
(and other) rubber component, (rubber being a bad heat conductor) and the
food processing industry, particularly in the United States, uses large
microwave systems. Systems using alternative frequency ranges (eg radio
frequency (or r.f) heating) compete in some areas, and some success has been
achieved with combined fossil fuel fired and r.f. ovens. A useful description of the mechanisms involved in these processes is given in ref.(1).
One reason for the poor market penetration of microwave systems has
been high capital cost. It was recently estimated by a manufacturer of such
equipment that installed machines of 10 kW or greater power currently cost
between £1500 and £2000 per kW (2700-3600 ECU per kW). Running costs can
also be high, particularly when electricity tariffs are compared with the
low prices of natural gas which were common until comparatively recently.
A conventional microwave oven of 50 per cent efficiency overall would not
compete on an energy cost basis with a gas fired system of 25 per cent
efficiency, although of course many fossil fuel-heated systems have much
lower efficiencies. As discussed below, PVC treatment ovens may be only
5 per cent efficient.
Microwave systems have benefits in other areas. They are inherently
clean, highly controllable, and convenient. Improved product quality and/
or production rate may result from the use of microwaves. Modifications may
of course be made to the microwave system itself to improve efficiency and
reduce the cost, and the economic benefits may well be acceptable when
microwave units are used in preference to very low efficiency units operating on other fuels.
The three projects supported within the Energy R&D Programme concentrate on a number of applications where economic benefits could result.
These include the treatment of plastic (PVC) floor coverings, studied by

Eurofloor in Luxembourg, the preparation or production of construction materials, such as wood and concrete, as studied by the State University of Ghent, and the drying of thin structures such as laminated papers, also the subject of a Belgian project at the Catholic University of Leuven.

2.   CONTINUOUS PRODUCTION OF PLASTICISED PVC SHEET

Work at Eurofloor in Luxembourg was directed at building and testing a pilot microwave oven for treating PVC floor coverings. These are formed by heating a PVC paste, which then solidifies. Normally this is carried out in a thermal oven at temperatures between $175^{\circ}C$ and $210^{\circ}C$ at an efficiency of only 5 per cent. Because of the low efficiency, the process seemed to be an ideal candidate for microwaves.

The oven used has a power input of 6 kW and is designed to treat the preduct at a rate of 20-30 metres/minute. A supplementary hot air source isused to maintain the surface temperature of the sheet at a sufficiently high level.

While the curing (gelling and foaming) of the PVC can be made to take place rapidly in the oven, results to date have shown that local burning of the material can occur very rapidly due to nonuniformity of the applied energy.

Some of the raw materials used, which comprised the following by weight:

PVC	100
Plasticiser	50
Chalk	25
TiO_2	3
Blowing agent	2
ZnO	0.7

exhibited a temperature rise when exposed to microwaves, but the plasticiser did not show the same behaviour. It was concluded that the knowledge of the microwave behaviour of plastisols, in particular the loss factor - which defines the ability of the material to absorb energy - was insufficient to permit good control of the gelling process. While at low temperatures the reaction begins slowly, as the temperature rises, reaction speeds are such that charring of the plastisol can occur, (1).

Attempts were made to minimise this effect by introducing hot air as well as microwaves, but this was unsuccessful, although a speeding up of the whole process was evident. It was concluded that because of the impossibility of achieving a completely homogeneous coating of plastisol on a sheet, uneven reactions and charring were inevitable.

3.   MICROWAVE POWER APPLICATIONS AND ENERGY SAVINGS

Work at the State University of Ghent (3) has concentrated on a number of aspects of microwave systems which are each important in ensuring a successful oven. Considerable stress is given to the need for a knowledge of the microwave properties of materials, and the Ghent work has concentrated on materials of value to the building industry - concrete and wood. The microwave properties were calculated using the von Hippel method (for bulk materials) and using a slotted line method which automatically measures the permittivity of sheets.

As demonstrated on PVC, the existance of a uniform temperature gradient within the material is important. Ghent University has developed a computer simulation which enables temperature profiles to be predicted, and allows the effect of ambient temperature, forced convection across the surfaces and the power cycle to be examined. Measurement of temperatures within the

326

oven, to verify predictions and to permit accurate control, is equally important. The use of infrared detectors to monitor material surface temperatures is under investigation.

The final stage of this project has involved the development of a continuous microwave oven, which is made up using modules. It can be used for heating slabs or granular materials. Separately, a batch oven has been constructed and installed on a rubber tyre production line. Energy savings of 40% have been demonstrated, compared with the conventional steam pre-heating process, and trials have also been conducted on woods using combined hot air/microwave systems.

The contractor emphasises that if the material properties are acceptable to microwave processing, microwave heating is of interest where the product has a poor thermal conductivity and a high monetary value.

4. AN ANTENNA CONFIGURATION FOR A MORE HOMOGENEOUS POWER DISTRIBUTION TO DRY THIN STRUCTURES

The Catholic University of Leuven has been studying the use of micro-waves to dry thin structures, such as coated papers, continuously. As with PVC during, the major problem to be tackled was seen to be non-uniformity of the power distribution, leading to hot spots and thermal gradients. The work programme concentrated on a technique for overcoming this particular problem.

In previous analyses microwave ovens were idealized in the form of rectangular cavities having loss-free walls and no load. The study by this contractor takes account of the more representative situation where a load is present, and this may be simulated as a thin slab of dielectric at the base of the cavity. The cavity is assumed to be filled with air.

The calculation of the field within this new representation of the cavity is discussed fully in the paper (4), but is based on the modal expansion method, which permits calculation of the electric field at any point in a cavity as long as relevant resonant mode frequencies are known. The field distribution may then be calculated on a computer, and projected three-dimensionally.

Application of this technique has resulted in a more homogeneous power distribution.

REFERENCES

1. PERKIN, R.M. (1980). The heat and mass transfer characteristics of boiling point drying using radio frequency and microwave electromagnetic fields. Int. J. Heat and Mass Transfer, Vol.23, pp.687-695.

2. ROUSSEL, A. et al. (1984). Application of microwave heating and hot air for the continuous production of plasticised PVC sheets. (Contract EEB-2-111-L). Proc. Int. Seminar 'Energy Conservation in Industry', Dusseldorf, 13-15 Feb. 1984. VDI, Dusseldorf.

3. VAN LOOCK, W. et al. (1984). Microwave power applications and energy saving. (Contract EE-B-1-135-B). Ibid.

4. LUYPAERT, P.J. and VERDELEN, J. (1984). An antenna configuration for a more homogeneous power distribution to dry thin structures. (Contract EEB-1-137-B). Ibid.

APPLICATION OF MICROWAVE HEATING AND HOT AIR FOR THE CONTINUOUS PRODUCTION OF PLASTICIZED PVC SHEETS

A. Roussel, L. Haag and D. Marchal

Eurofloor S.A.
Rue Neuve, B. P. 10, Wiltz, Grand-Duche de Luxembourg

1.1. Summary

A microwave tunnel has been achieved for continuous gelling and foaming of plasticized PVC sheets. The reason for
this choice is the poor efficiency of the hot air pulsed
heater. The microwave tunnel is made of 6 wave guides of
1 KW each. The plasticized PVC sheet with blowing agent is
foamed very quickly, but unfortunately in a nonuniform way.
One of the reasons for this bad blowing is the nonuniform
repartition of the energy caused perhaps by the choice of
the wave guide. Another reason is the slight understanding
of all the physical, thermal and microwave properties of
the plasticized PVC. The addition of hot air during the
blowing process did not permit to find the correct foaming
of the sheet. Some formulations with different additives
(silica, aluminium hydroxide, carbon black and different
plasticizers) were also tried, but again without success.
No harmless polar additives having a good compatibility
with PVC and increasing the microwave reactivity of the
plastisol could be found up to now.

1.2. Introduction

In our work, we wanted to use the possibility of heating
PVC plastisols by microwaves for the production of floor-cove-
rings. These products are now made by successive spread-coa-
tings of plasticized PVC plastisols.

Some of the pastes may contain foaming agents which release a gas at a certain temperature, and form a PVC foam. The
ovens used for the present time are hot air ovens and they have
an efficiency of 5 percent on the primary energy. Interesting
savings could be made by microwave heating. Considering the
existing techniques, microwave heating seems to be interesting
because of the electrical characteristics of PVC. Another interesting point is the heating in the inner part of the plastisol.
This could minimize the losses of heat caused by passing calo-
ries from one medium to another (fluid - air; air - plastisol
.....), and reduce the space necessary for the volume of hot
air used for an homogeneous heating. Another important advantage of a heating in the inner part of the material is the regularity of the foaming. Because of this regularity, the mechanical characteristics of the product should be improved.

This report contains the results of a gellation and foaming of pvc plasticized sheets using a wave guide with slots.

1.3. Equipment
Preliminary tests showed that in order to have a fast gellation of PVC by microwaves (and a quick raise of temperature), the equipment has to give electrical fields of an important density for the maximum power. The equipment must also be chosen in accordance with the geometry of our products (sheets) and with the way of cure (continuous process). The choice of an applicator will depend on all those first considerations.

Orientation tests showed that the best results are made with a radiating slots guide. For our specific application, a guide with transverse slots is the best one. If we don't consider the regularity of heating, this guide allows a gellation of the PVC.

The characteristics of the product obtained in the irradiated regions of the PVC sheets are similar to the characteristics of a product gelled by a conventional process. This equipment produces a quick raise of temperature and a good gellation for short times and little power.

But the beginning of the gellation (caused by the appearance of the intensity of the electrical field) is quickly followed by a carbonization of the irradiated spot. This is caused by the little difference between gellation and carbonization temperature. Because of these results, we added a conventional pulsed hot air unit in order to control the speed of the reaction. For all these reasons, our microwave tunnel was built with the following characteristics (fig. 1)
- width of 1 meter
- 6 wave guides with 23 slots each (6 x 1 KW)
- size of the slots: 12,5 x 4o mm
- wave length: 12,2 cm (frequency: 245o MHz)
- extraction of the vapours of plasticizers
- addition of pulsed hot air between the wave guides and independant regulation of each pulsed air generator
- conveyor belt made of glass fibers covered with polytetrafluoroethylene.

The six wave guides were shifted. For this reason, the PVC sheet passing through the tunnel has the same irradiation for each point placed on a straight line accross the direction of the conveyor belt.

The regulation of the field of microwaves is possible by the use of 4 parameters:
- ceiling: difference of height between reflector and sheet
- wave guide: difference of height between guide and sheet
- breadthwise shifting of the guide
- plunger: regulation of the level of stationary waves.

1.4. Tests and results
1.4.1. Choice of the material
The phenomenon of gellation is accompanied by the transformation of a liquid phase into a solid phase. But it is

also possible to have an intermediary phase (pregellation),
and then a gellation under microwaves. In this particular case
the gellation can only be visualized by mechanical tests.

It was easier for us to do tests with foamable
plastisols, because in this case, the foaming (decomposition
of a foaming agent) is characterized by an increasing thickness of the PVC sheet. Because of these visual effects, it is
possible to locate the impacts of the waves.

For these reasons, we made a product with o,4 mm
plasticized foamable plastisol on a calandered plasticized PVC
film (o,5 mm). The foaming and gellation of such a film is
normally made at 19o° C for a period of about 2 minutes 3o
seconds (height encrease of o,5 mm).

1.4.2. Adjustment of the parameters
As we have mentioned, the technique that we used
could not produce an homogeneous electrical field. In the first
step of this study, we tried to determine the distribution of
the field in the space between the wave guide and the reflector, and then to find the best position of the sheet in this
space in order to have the best gellation.

In order to reduce in a first step the changing
parameters, we worked without a movement of the sheets in the
tunnel, and with a constant time of irradiation. For each test
the level of stationnary waves was set in order to have the
best efficiency.

Adjusting the reflector and the wave guide, we
observed an important variation of the impacts:
- the maximum of impacts (23 slots) was produced
  with a cavity of 75 to 8o mm height
- an image of the slots appeared when the sheet
  was set against the wave guide
- similar, but not identical conclusions were set
  up for each wave guide (heterogeneous impacts).

For these adjustments, and varying the exposure
time to the microwaves, we could observe that:
- the number of impacts increases with time
- the impacts are heterogeneous. (it was possible
  to have impacts at 15'', but for another sheet,
  the same impacts were not visible after 1'15'').
  These variations are certainly caused by the
  unprecise position of the sheet, or by the difference of height of the sheets.

1.4.3. Influence of hot air and of the position of the sheet.
We tried to improve the homogeneity of the electrical field at each radiating slot by the addition of hot air
and by changing the position of the sheet in the cavity.

As it was foreseen, hot air improves the sensibility of the material to microwaves. Without hot air, the
first impacts appear after 3o to 45 seconds. With hot air
(11o to 12o °C), the same impacts are seen after a 15 seconds
exposure to the microwaves.

There are more impacts at each slot, but all the

same many carbonized spots remain. For these reasons, we varied
the position of the sheet in the cavity between reflector and
wave guide in order to get a dilution of the electrical field.

Without hot air, an important part of the energy
is lost and we don't obtain many impacts. But with hot air, the
product becomes more sensitive and the impacts can be visualized. These impacts aren't any more the images of the slots,
but the result of the rebounds on the walls of the cavity and
of the interferences from one slot to another.
In this case, the homogeneity is improved, but
the result is not perfect.

1.4.4. Influence of the raw materials
It is commonly known that the power dissipated
as heat in a material under a microwave radiation is proportional to the dielectrical loss factor

$E'' = E \cdot tg\delta$ E = dielectrical constant
            δ = loss angle.

If one tries to examine the characteristics of a
PVC plastified with 35 % of dioctylphtalate (DOP), one can
find a loss factor of o,45. This factor is about ten times
higher than the average value of the other plastics (rigid
PVC included), and one thousand times higher than polytetrafluoroethylene (PTFE), but the factor of plasticized PVC
remains ten times lower than the factor of water.
A big deal of the energy must be absorbed by the
plasticizer. As we didn't know the loss factor of the plasticizers, we tried to measure the increase of temperature of the
different raw materials, when these ones were put in a multimode microwave oven for one minute, and with an electrical
power of 1 kW:
- we couldn't measure any raise of temperature
for the PVC powders, calcium carbonates, metallic oxides, or
blowing agents (azodicarbonamide)
- a raise of 5o degrees C for dioctylphtalate
and diisononylphtalate
- a raise of 55 degrees C for some stabilizers
- a raise of 75 to 8o degrees C for ethylglycol
and a mixture of diisobutylphtalate and diisooctylphtalate
(4o DIBP / 6o DIDP)
- a raise of 115 degrees C for TXIB (2, 2, 4 -
trimethyl 1,3 pentanediol diisobutyrate).
Some different formulas were tried in accordance
with the preceding results.
The following additives were put in the formulas:
- 4o phr   minex 7 (natural silicate)
- 4o phr   hydrated alumina
- 2o phr   carbon black
- 6o phr   mixture of DIBP / DIDP
- 2 phr   TXIB
The only formulation that showed an improved sensibility to microwaves (factor 2) was the formulation containing carbon black.
Unfortunately, if this material is often used in

331

the rubber industry, it can't be used for our applications, as
we must print with four colours on a white or at least clear
foamable PVC sheet.
The other additives (even TXIB) didn't show an
improved sensibility to microwaves for different times, with
and without additional hot air blowing.

1.4.5. Moving of the sheets
If one moved the PVC sheet (plus additional
blowing of hot air), we could see an expansion and gellation
of the sheet. It was however impossible to have an homogenous
reaction (the same problem couldn't be solved in the previous
static tests), and the PVC sheet was covered with carbonized
lines separated by lines of unreacted material.
Another problem is the non homogenous regulation
of the blowing of hot air (+/- 15 degrees C) that increased
the heterogeneity of the reaction.

1.5. Economical aspects
As up to this time it has not been possible to get PVC
sheet with an homogenous and continuous blowing of the foam,
no economical comparison with the classical gellation method
could be made.
If the economical aspect of microwaves is interesting for
the textile industry (drying) and for the rubber industry
(use of carbon black for the producing of tires), it is not
the same for the PVC market. This is caused by the behaviour
of the plastisols and by the impossibility of using additives
such as carbon black.
For all these reasons, no part of the work could be patented.

1.6. Conclusions
Some preliminary tests, using wet cartboards, had shown us
how to optimize our equipment. And although it is known that
a fast gellation and foaming of plasticized PVC is possible
with our equipment (radiating guides), we didn't succeed in
obtaining a regular radiation.

We think that the irregular impacts depend
- on the geometrical form of the wave guides: very little
  imperfections can produce interactions on the waves
- on the PVC plastisol itself. Indeed, the plastisol
  doesn't absorb uniformly the radiations, even with additives. We think that the loss factor suddenly increases
  with the raise of temperature. This phenomenon produces
  a better absorbtion of radiations
- on the position of the PVC sheet in the microwave tunnel, on the little variations of the thickness of plastisol and on the wavy surface.
For the moment, in order to find a solution to our problems, we try to find polar additives which could be used in
our plastisols in order to get a more regular product. We aslo
try to find a mean to have automatically the best regulation
of the stationnary waves level, and to measure the temperature

in the tunnel without perturbing the waves.

1.7. Drawings

Figure 1   tunnel oven

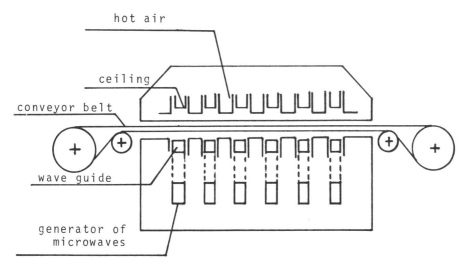

Figure 2   variable parameters

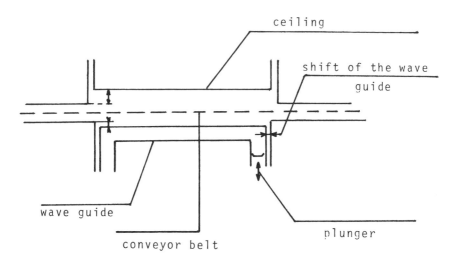

MICROWAVE POWER APPLICATIONS
AND ENERGY SAVING

W. van Loock, M. de Pourcq and C. de Wagter

Laboratory of Electromagnetism and Acoustics
State University of Ghent, Sint-Pietersnieuwstraat 41, B-9000 Ghent

SUMMARY

Two methods for determining the microwave properties of
materials are discribed. Results are given in particular for
European woods.
A computer program was developed to simulate microwave power
application. The induced power densities and the resulting
temperature rise in the material are determined.
An infrared detector was designed to control the heating
process by monitoring the surface temperature of the material.
A continuous modular microwave oven has been developed for
heating slabs or granular materials. Up to six identical
modules can be cascaded.
A batch oven was installed in a production line of rubber
tires resulting in a 40% energy saving compared with conventional process. Results on wood drying are also presented.
It is concluded that microwaves can save energy in particular
processes.

1. Introduction

Microwave power is an interesting energy technique for industrial heating and drying.
An understanding of the microwave and thermal properties of the
materials to be treated is necessary. These parameters are
needed for computer simulation and optimization of the process.
Proper applicator design and process control, including continuous temperature monitoring, assure efficient energy transfer.
Results in particular on some materials are presented.

2. Methods

2.1. Microwave properties

2.1.1. Bulk methods

The Von Hippel method is used for accurate determination of the
complex relative permittivity $\varepsilon_r^\star$ of bulk materials. A schematic
outline of the method is given in fig. 1. The TE10 mode is
excited in a short circuited waveguide. The standing wave
pattern of the empty and the sample loaded waveguide allow the
determination of $\varepsilon_r^\star$. However, a transcendental equation has to
be solved. Because the permittivity varies slowly with fre-
quency, it can be obtained for an unknown material from the
common solution at adjacent frequencies. The method has been
adapted to investigate liquids and powders. For high permittivity materials, such as liquids, up to 15 measurements per
sample are needed. Many industrial materials, e.g. rubber,
flour, textiles and wood, have been investigated with the Von
Hippel method. The method has been tested on standard lossless
materials as plexiglass and teflon. The relative error on ε_r'
is less than 5 %.

2.1.2. Slotted line systems

An automatic system to measure the dielectric properties of
sheet materials has been developed [1]. The system uses a network analyser, which is controlled by a VAX/VMS computer. A
sample of thin film or sheet material is introduced through the
0.5 mm wide slots along the axis of a rectangular waveguide.
Prior to the measurements six calibration measurements are
performed to eliminate systematic errors. The propagation constant γ_ε of the dielectric loaded section   is derived from
the S -parameters. The complex relative permittivity $\varepsilon_r^\star$ is
calculated from γ_ε using a transcendental equation, which is
solved by iteration starting with an approximate solution.
A bridge method has been used to verify the results of the
network analyser system. The results for e.g. teflon agree
within 1 %.
Broader slots (up to 5 mm) have been used to study veneers.
Centered and off-centered positions of the dielectric sheets
resulted in an error within 0.4 % for the dielectric constant
ε_r'. The S-parameters are measured with an accuracy of 0.2 dB
on the amplitude and 1° on the phase resulting in an error on
$\varepsilon_r^\star$ of about 1 %.

2.1.3. Results

Veneers of European woods as beech, ash and pine, having a moisture content ranging from 9 % to 12 %, have been investigated. Bulk measurements were carried out with the Von Hippel method. The results are summarized in table I. As the input reflection has been neglected, the error on ε_r^* increases with increasing sample thickness.

Sample	Thick-ness (mm)	Dir. of fibres against E.field	Mois-ture content (%)	Veneer (Continuous mode)		Blocks (v.Hippel)	
				ε'_r	ε''_r	ε'_r	ε''_r
Beech	0,9	⊥	9,4	1,97	0,18	2,39	0,24
	0,9	⊥	9,0	2,23	0,22	2,36	0,23
	0,9	⊥	10,0	2,09	0,24	2,43	0,26
	0,9	⊥	10,9	2,23	0,27	2,49	0,30
	0,9	⊥	10,9	2,38	0,30	2,50	0,30
Ash	0,6	//	10,0	3,00	0,51	3,18	0,68
	0,6	//	9,5	3,02	0,50	3,10	0,62
	0,6	//	9,2	2,99	0,50	3,05	0,59
	0,6	//	8,8	3,11	0,54	2,99	0,54
European pine	0,7	//	12,2	3,12	0,75	3,10	0,71
	0,7	//	11,4	3,24	0,76	2,97	0,63
	0,7	//	12,0	3,01	0,68	3,07	0,69
	0,7	//	11,3	3,22	0,74	2,95	0,62

Table I : Measurements of ε^* of some European veneers at 3 GHz.

Several rubber samples have been investigated as a function of temperature and degree of vulcanisation. The results reveal that special precautions in the microwave heating process are needed for ε_r'' increasing with temperature.

2.2. Computer simulation of microwave heating

2.2.1. Microwave power deposition calculation

In many applications of microwave heating of layered media, the electromagnetic problem can be reduced to that of the laminated slab illuminated from one or both sides at normal incidence. For the computer simulation, each layer, with constant dielectric properties, is divided into a number of sublayers. The absorbed power distribution is computed using the transmission

line equivalent of each sublayer. The resulting chain of lossy
transmission lines is described by the ABCD-matrix formalism
of network theory. The computer program allows optimization of
the distance of a metal screen, reflecting the transmitted
wave.
In case of bilateral irradiation [2], the two incident waves
of the same frequency have oppositely oriented propagation
directions. For a particular application, the absorbed power
distribution can be investigated as a function of polarization,
amplitude and phase relationship of the two waves. The analysis reveals that the absorption efficiency, being the ratio of
absorbed power to total incident power, can always be made
better than with illumination from one side.

2.2.2._ Temperature distribution_calculation

A numerical procedure has been developed to compute temperature profiles in multilayered plane media as a function of
time [3]. Starting with the absorbed power distribution, a
semi-discrete finite difference method is used to express the
temperatures of the elementary sublayers in closed form as a
function of the microwave input.
Discretizing the spatial part of the heat diffusion equation
leads to a system of ordinary differential equations in time,
which are solved analytically by making use of an eigenvector
expansion.
The computer program allows treatment of the non-linear case,
i.e. when the material permittivity is temperature dependent.
Optimization of the dielectric properties of certain layers is
possible. Temperature profiles can be evaluated for a given
sequence of incident microwave power. Fig. 2 gives an example
of a triple-layered material. The dielectric properties of the
second layer are temperature dependent and were modelled by
third order polynomials. The incident power density from the
left is 3 W/cm^2 at a frequency of 2.45 GHz. The smoothing
effect, due to diffusion of heat, in a period without power
supply, can be observed. Fig. 3 shows the computed temperature
profiles resulting from immersion of the layered structure in
hot air. Penetration into the interior of the volume is obviously poor for the duration of exposure under consideration.
Hot air heating is slow because of the poor thermal conductivi-
ties of the material.

2.3._ _ Temperature_measurements

2.3.1._ Automatic real-time temperature measurements

To measure temperature profiles in microwaves, NiCr-Ni thermocouples are placed at different positions in the material. The
thermocouples have a volume of only 0.2 mm^3, while the wires
have a diameter of 0.2 mm. They are oriented preferencially
perpendicular to the electric field, to minimize perturbation
of the microwave field and to avoid internal heating by Joule
losses. Checks for interference can be made by cycling the
microwave power on and off and observing the cooling curves.
Fast fall of temperature after switching off may indicate

interference. An automatic measuring set-up has been built
around the IEEE-488 data bus, which is controlled by the VAX-
computer. A twenty-channel scanner connects the thermocouples
sequentially with a digital voltmeter.
A temperature measurement with a resolution of 0.1°C takes
about 1 second, settling-delay of the scanner and data transfer included.

2.3.2. Contactless temperature measurements

A microwave oven load is generally rotated on a turntable or
transported on a conveyor belt. Contactless temperature measurements are sometimes preferred, although they have an important inconvenience : only the surface temperature is measured. We used an infra-red sensitive element, which produces
a signal depending on temperature variations. A mechanical
chopper generates an output signal of 10 Hz. As the device is
mounted in a microwave oven, the incident microwave power is
attenuated by means of a small circular waveguide below cut-
off.
We developed two circuits to transform the device output signal into an on-off signal suitable to switch the magnetrons.
The first one is based on the conversion of the temperature
into a pulse which duration is measured through a 8085 microprocessor circuit.
In the second circuit the temperature is measured using compa-
rators. In spite of the attenuation due to the waveguide below
cut-off, the measuring circuits are disturbed by the microwaves, so the power is switched off during the measurements.
At the moment this IR-measuring system is being improved to
allow temperature measurements in the microwave field.

2.4. Microwave applicators

A microwave batch oven and a conveyor belt system have been
developed for laboratory and industrial application. Each of
them is driven by a power source which is optimized using a
network analysis program for non-linear networks. Detection
circuits and adapted interfaces ensure reliable and efficient
magnetron operation.

2.4.1. The power source

The power source has to transform the line power into a waveform which allows the magnetron to generate the microwaves in
an efficient way. A frequently used power source is the voltage doubler of fig. 4. It has been investigated with the network analysis program NAP2 [4, 5]. This program allows the
study of any magnetron power supply, as the voltage doubler,
the single-phase full wave rectifier or any multi-phase rectifier circuit. The circuit is optimized in order to prevent
moding. The moding stability depends not only on the R.F.-
loading conditions (VSWR), but also on peak anode current, mean
anode current and current waveform.
The influence of the line voltage (V1), inductance (L) and
doubler capacity (C) on magnetron peak voltage, peak, mean and

effective current, magnetron dissipation and power supply
efficiency was investigated. Based on the calculations, a magnetron power supply was designed with L = 4.5 H, n = 8.4 and
C = 1.3 µF. The validity of the computer method was confirmed
by comparing the calculated and the measured circuit current
and output power. Good agreement was found for both quantities.
The power supply was found to have an efficiency of about 90%.
The power source has been built as a separate microwave generator and was used in combination with a batch oven in an
industrial production line 8 hours a day. It was working
satisfactory.

2.4.2. The batch oven

We have developed a microwave power system as an automatic and
programmable oven, consisting of the previously described
power source and a batch oven [6]. It has been optimized to
preheat rubber tires. The oven is fed by the microwave source
and contains also heating resistors to prevent surface cooling
of the load. To improve the power distribution in the load,
a turntable and mode stirrer are used. The oven and the power
supply are provided with detector circuits to ensure safe
operation as a min-max anode current circuit, the thermal fuse
circuit, the ventilator circuit, etc. All detector circuits
deliver a logic signal which is applied to the TTL control
register. If some defect is detected, the control register
holds the system until the defect has been eliminated. The
microwave power can be controlled using the programmable power
pack which is designed to apply intermittent power, or by
adjusting the anode voltage.
During the tests in the production line, the error detection
circuits ensured safe operation.

2.4.3. A microprocessor controlled modular conveyor belt
       microwave oven

A microprocessor controlled modular microwave oven, consisting
of 6 identical modules, for heating slabs or granular materials is under investigation. One module and the driving circuitry are constructed (fig. 5). The oven module is fed by a
meander-type resonant slot antenna. The slots are arranged to
illuminate the full width of the conveyor belt. Five tuning
elements allow the cavity matching to a wide range of loads.
To increase the efficiency, the cooling air of the magnetron
is blown into the cavity. The design is such that the dimensions of the cavity can be adjusted for other applications,
the antenna, the power supply and the conveyor belt remaining
unchanged.
Detector circuits and adapted interfaces are developed to
control the power supply and the cavity. Six interfaces for
the 6 identical oven modules are connected to the Intel 8085
microprocessor. If an error is detected, the microprocessor
switches off the 6 power supplies and the belt drive. The error
is shown on a LED display. The system can also be driven without microprocessor in the "manual" mode, the error detection
circuits remaining active. The microprocessor software performs

following functions :
- in the input mode, the microprocessor reads in the moments at which the magnetrons and the belt drive are switched on and off.
- then, in the run mode, the magnetrons and the belt drive are powered during the programmed intervals.
- if a defect in a power supply or a cavity is detected, an interrupt service routine must hold the microprocessor.

The input data and the program are stored, independent of line interruption.

The microprocessor circuitry and the oven module were tested drying wood planks provided with a LCD display showing the temperature distribution on the surface of the wood as a function of its colour. An acceptable temperature profile was obtained.

2.4.4. Narrowband Continuous Wave Microwave (CW) Generator

The majority of magnetron power supplies are LC-stabilized half-wave voltage doublers. This type of supply is normally used in multimode cavities. The bandwidth is about 50 MHz at 2.45 GHz.

Unimode cavities with high Q-factor, however, can only be matched within a very limited frequency band. To achieve a reasonable efficiency, narrowband microwave power is needed. Since the dynamic impedance of magnetrons is in general low, small variations in the applied voltage cause appreciable changes in operating current, and result in variation of power, frequency and spectrum quality. So, it is imperative to realise frequency stabilization with current regulation.

Fig. 6 shows a high voltage programmable current source for driving a commercially available 1000 W magnetron. The series control element is basically built up by a chain of commercially available voltage regulators with a minimum amount of external components. The regulator generates a fixed voltage drop across the sensing resistor combination (R1, R2). Provision is made for negligible adjustment current I1, which doesn't pass through the sensing resistor. The potentiometer R2 controls the anode current, and with it the frequency and the output power, according to the magnetron characteristics. The ripple of the anode current at the full microwave power, of 1 kW, is about 2% of the DC-value. The bandwidth is 50 kHz at 2450 MHz.

Because of the great coherence length, the narrowband power generator allows electric field measurements in the far field of a horn antenna, where the plane wave approximation is valid.

2.4.5. Energy balance for a typical microwave oven

Starting from electricity, the energy balance (fig. 7) for a typical microwave oven can be set up. The losses taken into account are the loss in the power source such as described in sect. 2.4.1, the dissipation in the magnetron (filament current, internal heating of the cavity, etc), and losses in and mismatch of the applicator. The last one can be minimized by appropriate oven design or by tuning elements.

340

As a conclusion, we may say that a typical microwave oven, such as the batch oven of sect. 2.4.2, has an overall efficiency of about 50%. In some cases the heat of the cooling air flow of the magnetron can be recovered partially by blowing it into the oven cavity.

3. Results

In the conventional process, rubber tires are preheated in a saturated steam atmosphere. They are subsequently moulded under high pressure. In the modified process, the tires are preheated with microwaves, the moulding remaining unchanged. In the calculation of the energy consumption, a conversion rate of 35% for electricity and 75% for the steam boiler is assumed.

Conventional process		Modified process	
	Energy/tire (KJ)		Energy/tire (KJ)
steam preheating	165.900	microwave preheating	11.700
steam heated mould	207.400	steam heated mould	207.400
total	373.300	total	219.100

In the modified process an energy conservation of 41% in comparison with the conventional process is realised. There was no measurable quality difference between the tires obtained from both processes. The process time is also reduced considerably. The conventional process takes about 2 hours preheating time due to the poor transfer of heat in rubber. Microwave heating takes only 45 minutes.
Oak samples of 40 x 10 x 5 cm were microwave dried in an experimental set-up. The initial moisture content was about 70%. It was found that about 2 KWh microwave energy per liter water was needed to dry until 30%-45% moisture content. More generally it can be claimed that drying of wood from water soaked condition to about 30% is performed faster and cheaper by hot air alone. Below this moisture level, a combination of hot air and microwave drying provides a fast way of water evaporation. In order to achieve a uniform moisture profile in the finished product, the final drying to about 6% should be carried out with microwave power only [7].
The drying cycle depends on the type of wood, the moisture content, the dimensions of the pieces, the orientation of the wood fibers, and many other factors.
Experiments on standard wood samples of European pine revealed that drying can be performed from 15% to 6% of moisture content with microwaves only without affecting the mechanical properties of the wood.

References

1. De Pourcq, M., De Wagter, C., Tromp, H., Van Loock, W., "Automatic measurements of the permittivity of films and sheet materials", IMPI Symposium 1980.

2. De Wagter, C., De Pourcq, M., Van Loock, W., "Microwave absorption in multilayered media due to bilateral illumination", IMPI Symposium 1983.

3. De Wagter, C., De Pourcq, M., Van Loock, W., "Microwave heating of laminated materials", IMPI Symposium 1981.

4. Rübner, T., and Petersen, "NAP2 Users Manual", Report 16/5/1973, Institute of Circuit Theory and Telecommunication, Technical University of Denmark.

5. De Pourcq, M., De Wagter, C., Van Loock, W., "Computer study of the magnetron power supply", IMPI Symposium 1981.

6. De Pourcq, M., De Wagter, C., Van Loock, W., "TTL controlled magnetron operation", IMPI Symposium 1981.

7. Resh, H., "Drying of incense cedar pencil slats by microwave power", Journal of Microwave Power, Vol. 2 (1967), n° 3, pp. 45-49.

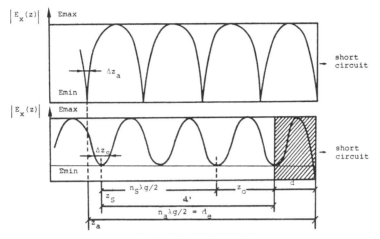

Fig.1   Von Hippel method

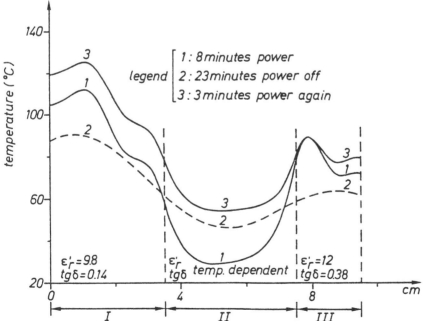

Figure 2   Computed temperature profiles in a 3-layered structure, illuminated from the left
with 3 W/cm² at 2.45 GHz. The permittivity of layer II is temperature dependent. Initial
temperature profile is uniform at 20°C. k = 0.2 W/mK, ρc = 2 10⁶ J/m³K, H = 2 W/m²K.

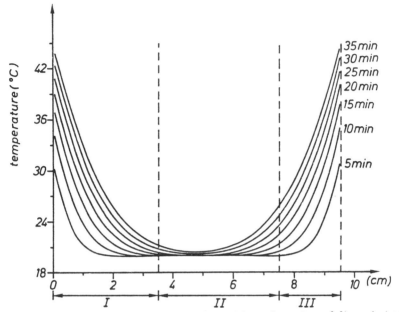

Figure 3 Computed temperature profiles for the 3-layered structure of figure 4, immersed in hot air at 100°C. Penetration of heat into the interior of the volume is poor.
$k = 0.2$ W/mK, $\rho c = 2 \cdot 10^6$ J/m³K, H = 5 W/m²K.

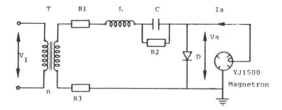

Fig. 4 Equivalent circuit of the voltage-doubler
to drive the magnetron.

T   : ideal transformer, ratio n
R_1 : loss of real transformer
L   : leakage inductance of real transformer
R_3 : resistance to monitor magnetron and diode current
C   : doubler capacity
R_2 : leakage resistor for C
V_1 : line voltage (220V, 50Hz)

344

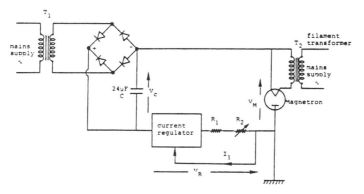

Figure 6   Basic circuit of the current regulated high voltage source.

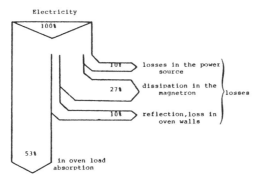

Fig. 7

AN ANTENNA CONFIGURATION
FOR A MORE HOMOGENEOUS POWER DISTRIBUTION
TO DRY THIN STRUCTURES

P. J. Luypaert and J. Verbelen

K. U. Leuven – Dept. Elektrotechniek, Microgolven Laboratorium
94 Kardinaal Mercierlaan, B-3030 Leuven

1. INTRODUCTION

For materials having high dielectric losses microwave heating is
efficient and fast.
In this work research was carried out on a special application of microwave heating : the drying of thin structures in continuous processes.
The major problem encountered in mostly all microwave applications is
the non-uniformity of the power distribution. This causes thermal
gradients and "hot spots".
Several solutions were already proposed. However the more efficient they
are the more complicated and expensive they seem to be.
In this study we try to find a simple and cheap solution based on
a special configuration of excitation sources. In that case an extensive
theoretical analysis of the field distribution inside an idealised cavity
is achieved. It is based on the Modal Expansion Method.

2. THE IDEALISED CAVITY

Fig. 1 shows a prototype of a microwave oven for drying thin
structures in a continuous process. This prototype was idealised
previously in a rectangular cavity having loss-free walls and without
any load.
In this study we take into account the influence of the load which
is idealised by a thin slab of dielectric at the bottom of the cavity
(permittivity $\varepsilon_r = \varepsilon_r' - j\,\varepsilon_r''$; lossfactor tg $\delta = \dfrac{\varepsilon_r''}{\varepsilon_r'}$).

This configuration is shown in Fig. 2.

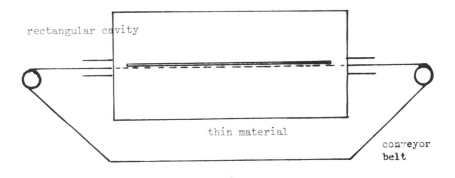

rectangular cavity

thin material

conveyor
belt

Fig. 1 : Prototype for a microwave oven for drying
thin structures in a continuous process.

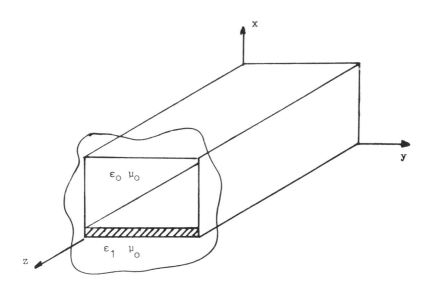

Fig. 2 : Idealised cavity with thin slab of lossy dielectric
at the bottom.

3. BASICS OF THE THEORY

3.1. Summary

The calculation of the field in the cavity is based on the modal expansion method (2). This method permits to calculate the electric field in any point of a given cavity when all possible modes are known in a certain frequency range of the excitation frequency. From the knowledge of the resonant mode frequencies and the configuration of the excitation sources the field distribution is computed by specially designed computer programmes.

3.2. Calculation of the possible modes in the cavity

In Fig. 2 we considered two different homogeneous regions. Possible modes are solutions of Maxwell equations and must satisfy the boundary conditions. A possible set of modes able to satisfy these boundary conditions are the TE_x (TE to x) and TM_x (TM to x) modes.

All TM_x modes can be found from solving a complex transcendental equation (1)

$$\frac{k_{x_1}}{\epsilon_1} \tan k_{x_1} D = \frac{-k_{x_2}}{\epsilon_2} \tan [k_{x_2} (XA - D)]$$

and $k_{x_1}^2 + (\frac{n\pi}{YA})^2 + (\frac{l\pi}{ZA})^2 = k_1^2 = \omega^2 \epsilon_1 \mu_1$ $\qquad\qquad$ (1)

$$k_{x_2}^2 + (\frac{n\pi}{YA})^2 + (\frac{l\pi}{ZA})^2 = k_2^2 = \omega^2 \epsilon_2 \mu_2$$

where :

k_{x_1} = the wavenumber for the TM_x mode inside the dielectric

k_{x_2} = wavenumber for the TM_x mode outside the dielectric

ϵ_1 = dielectric permittivity of the dielectric $\epsilon_1 = \epsilon_{r_1}' - j\epsilon_{r_1}''$

ϵ_2 = dielectric permittivity of air : ϵ_o

XA = height of the cavity

YA = width of the cavity

ZA = length of the cavity

D = dielectric slab thickness

$\mu_1 = \mu_2 = \mu_o$ = magnetic permeability of air

n and l = mode numbers.

TE_x modes can be found from similar equations (1).

We note that not all modes must be taken into account. Modes having resonant frequencies far from the centre frequency of the excitation source cause the excitation coefficients to be very small. In that case they may be neglected in the calculation of the field distribution, this saving considerably CPU time.

3.3. Calculation of the excitation coefficients

From the modal expansion theory (2) we know that the electric field in a point in the cavity can be written as :

$$E = \sum_i \frac{j\omega \, E_i}{\omega^2 - \omega_i^2} \iiint J \cdot E_i^* \, d\tau = \sum_i A_i \, E_i$$

where :

$A_i = \dfrac{j\omega}{\omega^2 - \omega_i^2} \iiint J \cdot E_i^* \, d\tau$: the excitation coefficient for mode i.

J = excitation current source

E_i^* = complex conjugate of the field in the considered point for mode i (1).

ω = centre frequency of the excitation source.

ω_i = calculated frequency of mode i.

$\iiint \ldots d\tau$ = integration should include the volumes of all excitation sources.

$\sum$ = summation includes all possible modes.

3.4. Computer programmes

Computer programmes have been developed in order to calculate the possible modes, excitation coefficients, electric field and power distribution for a given configuration of cavity with dielectric slab.
Thus far every excitation source was assumed to be a $\lambda/4$ dipole antenna. Our intention is to generalise the computer programmes for other types of excitation sources such as slots and other types of planar antennas.
Input data of the computer programme are :
 - cavity height
 - cavity width
 - cavity length
 - dielectric slab thickness
 - complex dielectric permittivity $\varepsilon_r = \varepsilon_r' - j\varepsilon_r''$
 - coordinates of $\lambda/4$ dipole antennas
 - direction of $\lambda/4$ dipole antennas
 - dimensions (height, diameter) of antennas
 - excitation frequency.
Output data :
 - Power distribution in three dimensional view at transition surface air-dielectric.

4. RESULTS

    In (1) we calculated the power distribution in a cavity having a thin water slab and excited by one λ/4 x-axis directed dipole antenna placed in the centre of the upper YZ plane. The power distribution is shown in Fig. 3.
    As we had the intention of merely drying thin structures in continuous processes this distribution is not useful due to unacceptable non-uniformity.
    In (3) we calculated the power distribution for the same cavity and water slab but with ten λ/4 y-axis oriented dipole antennas, placed in opposite side walls of the cavity. The result is shown in Fig. 4.
    As can be seen this distribution is more likely to be used for continuous drying with z-directed feed motion.

5. MEASUREMENTS

    For practical reasons former calculations were carried out for an existing cavity with dimensions 0.6 x 0.95 x 2.5 m.
    Power distribution measurements were obtained by a specially designed microprocessor controlled power distribution meter in a scaled cavity with dimensions 0.37 x 0.32 x 0.21 m and a water slab of 0.05 m thickness. Two λ/4 y-directed dipole antennas were placed in two opposite walls. This configuration is shown in Fig. 5.

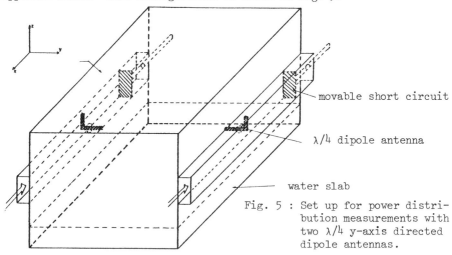

movable short circuit

λ/4 dipole antenna

water slab

Fig. 5 : Set up for power distribution measurements with
two λ/4 y-axis directed
dipole antennas.

    The measured power distribution is pictured in Fig. 6.
    From comparison of Fig. 4 and Fig. 6 we may conclude that theory and measurement agree quite well if we may assume that discontinuities in the theoretical distribution are flattened out in the measured distribution. Also differences due to scaling of cavities and mutual coupling between excitation sources should be taken into account.

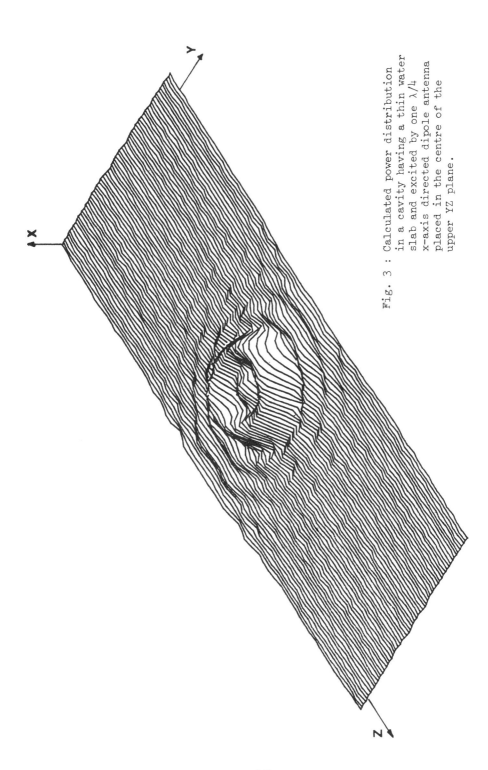

Fig. 3 : Calculated power distribution in a cavity having a thin water slab and excited by one $\lambda/4$ x-axis directed dipole antenna placed in the centre of the upper YZ plane.

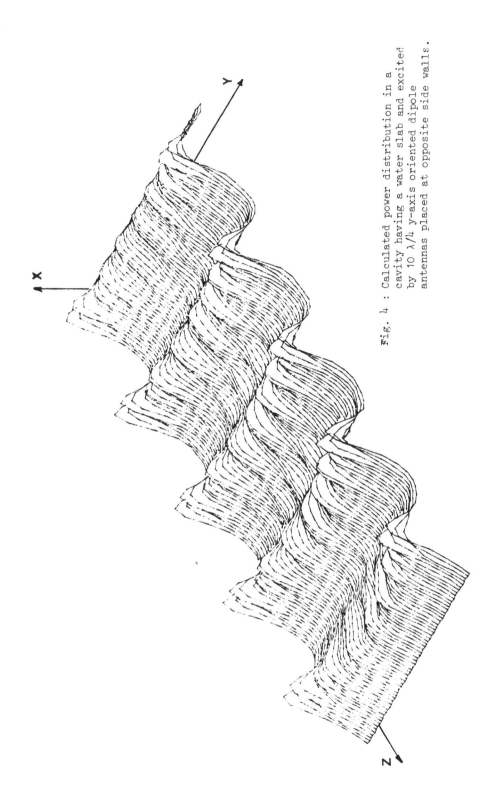

Fig. 4 : Calculated power distribution in a cavity having a water slab and excited by 10 λ/4 y-axis oriented dipole antennas placed at opposite side walls.

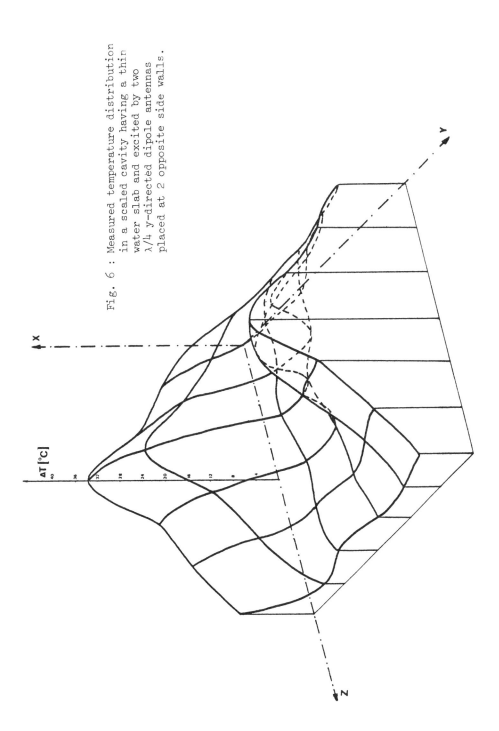

Fig. 6 : Measured temperature distribution in a scaled cavity having a thin water slab and excited by two λ/4 y-directed dipole antennas placed at 2 opposite side walls.

6. CONCLUSION AND PROJECTS

Modal expansion analysis can be used to design microwave ovens having more uniform power distributions which are of great importance in continuous drying of thin structures.

Future trends are the generalisation of the existing computer programmes for different widths of applicators and improving the efficiency and speed of the computer programmes.

REFERENCES

1. P.J.LUYPAERT, H.LEMMENS, J.VERBELEN (1982). Contract EEB-1-137-B(RS) Progress Report n° 2 (01.07.1982-31.12.1982).
2. R.F. HARRINGTON (1961). Time-harmonic electromagnetic fields. Published by McGraw Hill, New York.
3. P.J.LUYPAERT, J.VERBELEN (1983). Progress Report n° 3 (01.01.1983-31.06.1983).

CONCLUDING SESSION

Conference Chairman: Dr.-Ing. A. Strub

Concluding remarks by
Dr. -Ing. A. Strub
Prof. Dr.-Ing. R. Quack
Prof. Dr. I. E. Smith
Dr. F. Ehrhart
Prof. Dr. P. Hagenmuller
Dr. J. Limido
Dr. A. Rossi

CONCLUDING REMARKS
by the Conference Chairman
Dr.-Ing. A. S. Strub
Commission of the European Communities

To conclude the presentations and discussions we had during this conference on energy conservation in industry, I would like to start with some statistical data : 40 % of the projects presented here, dealt with the development of complete industrial installations. The others, dealt with studies, component research and applied basic research. Although a number of projects have not yet been finalised, it is my impression that most of them have achieved their objectives and that the programme as a whole has been successful.

This Seminar was attended by 400 participants coming from four Continents. The different areas dealt with will of course be discussed by the chairmen in more details, but in addition I would like to give you my personal conclusions, or better : the lessons I drew from this meeting, for our future work :

Recovery of waste heat really deserves a high priority in the Community's Energy R and D Programme. Here, a further increase of performance, prevention of fouling and development of heat exchangers for temperatures up to 1500°C will be very important topics in the future.

Heat pumps for industry currently have a marginal economic feasibility. There is hope that efficiencies will increase and that their cost will be reduced so that they become economically attractive.

Fluidized bed combustion technology has a large field of applications (e.g. with coal, gas or waste) and may contribute to use energy more rationally. From the environmental point of view this type of combustion is also very attractive, but there is much room for further improvements here. Maybe the newly developed circulating fluidized beds will achieve general economic feasibility.

There are quite a number of engines which transform waste heat, in the temperature range of 100 to 300°C, into electricity (e.g. Organic Rankine Cycles, multivane expanders, screw expanders and Peltier turbines). It would be very useful now to investigate which machine is best suitable for the different types of application (temperature range, capacity, economy). This could also be important for the further exploitation of geothermal energy.

As regards industrial processes, the variety is so large that I will not have the time to elaborate. The chairmen will no doubt enlighten us with their comments and views. I think that priority should be given in the future to the development of "new" processes, since retrofitting in existing installations implies complementary costs for installation, pipe work, etc. which reduce the economic viability of an improved system.

The transport sector is characterized by predominant use of oil products. Consequently, the development of efficient and cheap internal combustion engines remains an important task. Of course, most automobile manufacturers are working hard in this field and not everything here is suitable for Community work. Therefore quite a number of our projects dealt with long term research and new types of engine. The results of this work give me the feeling that in Europe there is still a lot of creativity.

In addition, the rational use of energy in transport requires the replacement of oil by electricity. This led us to an extensive effort in the field of electricity storage, since the main bottleneck for the promotion of electrical vehicles is their storage system. Encouraging results have been obtained in particular in the field of advanced solid state batteries.

Finally, I would like to remind that in general energy use by human beings constitutes a heavy burden to the environment. Furthermore, the resources of hydrocarbons are rapidly decreasing. Consequently, it is a predominant task of our society to intensify, on the one hand, rational use of energy and, on the other, to protect our environment. Therefore continous efforts will have to be undertaken whenever possible in order to increase the efficiency of processes, to diversify our energy resources, to make use of waste heat and to develop secondary batteries as energy storage systems.

The second EC Energy R and D Programme has reached its end. The Commission has submitted a proposal for a third programme to the Council of Ministers and its discussion is under way. Once the programme is approved, a call for proposals will be published in the Official Journal of the European Communities and we hope to see many of you back again as contractors.

Finally, before calling upon the chairmen, to deliver their concluding remarks, I would like to express my thanks to VDI for their contribution to organise this Conference in an efficient and smooth manner, to the keynote speakers for having spoken to us on their valuable experience as energy managers, to the chairmen and in particular the rapporteurs for the extensive home work they have done in compiling the results of the projects, to all those who animated the discussions with questions and comments, to the authors of the papers for presenting their work in the form of a paper and for their efforts in composing posters and exhibits, and last but not least to our interpreters, who mastered this difficult matter with elegance, notwithstanding the high speed with which some speakers tried to make an optimal use of their speaking time.

May I express the hope that the work reported at this conference will be contributing to rapid progress in the development and practical application of new technologies and processes in industry, thereby promoting rational use of energy throughout the Community.

In concluding this conference, I would like to thank all of you for coming here and I hope that you have enjoyed this stay in Düsseldorf.

CONCLUDING REMARKS
by the chairman of Session I, part A

Prof. Dr.-Ing. R. Quack

Universität Stuttgart, Germany

Of the different possible kinds of energy, the 17 papers, presented in Part A of Session I about "Energy Saving Technologies" were only dedicated to <u>heat</u>-energy. They described progress in heat transmission and in heat up-grading.

The transport of heat as latent heat has the advantage, that the heat transporting medium can accept and deliver the heat with minimal temperature loss. This advantage is most valid, if also the heat delivering medium at the beginning of the transport and the accepting medium at the end of the transport delivers resp. accepts the heat as latent heat. Under such conditions, the Two-Phase-Thermosyphons with liquid and vapour phase have found broad acceptance in industry and it depends on the actual situation, if the condensate-transport in the syphon is done by gravity or need capillary forces.

Three papers about Thermo-Syphons studies working media for temperatures above 300°C, where corrosion problems must be overcome.

Heat exchangers for very high temperatures need ceramic construction materials : two interesting recuperator designs with such materials were described, both concepted in modular structure.

Non metallic corrosion resistant materials have often a low heat conductivity. Therefore the wall thickness in recuperative heat exchangers out of such materials should be small. An example of a heat exchanger for a heat pump process was given, where the wall thickness of the polyethylene tubes was reduced to some tenth of a millimeter, because inspite of a pressure ratio of 1.4 between evaporator and condensor the absolute pressure difference over the tube wall was only 40 hPa, the evaporation taking place at 0.1 bar.

The heat transfer from a gas to a solid surface can be augmented, if the laminar gas layer on the surface is continuously disturbed by fluidized solid particles. Three papers describe special arrangements of such recuperative heat exchangers. A regenerative heat exchanger, which uses fluidized particles as heat transporting material, has the advantage of no mechanical moved construction parts, the particles being transported from the hot compartment to the cold compartment and back on a circumferential path by pneumatic forces.

Of seven heat pump papers, four describe absorption processes, demonstrating, that the absorption heat pump is especially suitable for industry. In caloric units, an absorption heat pump process can need more energy than a compressor heat pump process, but in industry waste heat is normally much cheaper than mechanical energy.

By a counterflow sorption process, the temperature level of that part of the inserted waste heat, which is upgraded, can be further raised. (To this paper the only discussion contribution, which perhaps should be introduced to the proceedings, was made, if it will be presented from Creusot-Loire in written form in right time).

Of the three papers, which describe compressor heat pumps, one describes a situation, which is almost ideal in thermodynamic sence, because both, the hot end as well as the cold end of the process can be utilised. It is an application in agriculture, where a part of the fresh earned barley is immediately dried for conservation, whereas another part of the harvest simultaniously can be chilled. The chilled barley can after intermediate storage either be used as fresh feed or seed or it can now be dried, when the peak load time in the drying section is over.

Having also visited the Poster Session in the morning and listened to the many intensive discussions at the exhibition stands, I got the impression, that the combination of such a Poster Session with a Rapporteur Session is an efficient scope for a Status Seminar. The experts, who wish to go deeper in the details, can do so in the personal direct contact with the researchers. And the others, who only will inform themselves about what is going on, get this presented by the rapporteurs in condensed form, which is more effective than a listening to an oral presentation of all papers in full extent. Therefore I congratulate the organisers of the Seminar for this scope.

CONCLUDING REMARKS
by the chairman of Session I, part B
Prof. Dr. I. E. Smith
Cranfield Institute of Technology, UK

In this session there were sixteen papers which dealt with combustion especially in fluidized beds but also with the improved control of combustion in boilers and furnaces, waste heat recovery both by direct heat transfer and through its use to generate power via Rankine type systems and one paper which surveyed the overall potential for waste heat recovery in industry.

The rapporteurs, Ir Knobbout, Mr Reay and Dr Durandet have discussed the technical aspects admirably and it is not my intention to repeat or add to their contributions.

I was very gratified to observe a high degree of quantification in most of the papers that were submitted with hard facts concerning energy and, particularly, financial savings, pay-back periods for the equipment required and so on. It is all too easy to present schemes and ideas that apparantly show a great energy saving potential but which, on further examination, fail to show themselves to be viable economically.

The fact that a large proportion of the researches carried out have been shown to be worthwhile in terms of both energy and economics must be very gratifying to the Commission, but it must not be forgotten that this also reflects the excellence of the selection of these projects which was carried out by the Commission in the first place.

Many of the projects reported on are not yet complete in the technological sense, and I believe it is important that the momentum behind these investigations is not now lost. Once a team is dispersed, or even a lone researcher deflected into another area of work, it is virtually impossible to recover the former enthusiasm and although the Commission's programme is suffering an unfortunate "pause" at present, I sincerely hope that the programme on Energy Conservation will recommence in the near future.

I have to comment on the fact that I have never before attended a conference where there has been so little discussion from the floor. This, of course, is a reflection on the excellence of the poster sessions held prior to the presentation of the papers. One of the authors of a paper in this session remarked that he had never before experienced such an exhausting yet rewarding morning, and I would like to congratulate all those who contributed towards the poster display. I believe that this pattern of meeting should be the standard for the future.

Finally I would like to record my thanks to Drs. Strub and Ehringer and their teams for organising what has been a most useful and enjoyable three days.

CONCLUDING REMARKS

by the chairman of Session II

Dr. F. Ehrhart

Pierburg GmbH & Co., Germany

The continuous efforts of the manufacturers of internal combustion engines - both for automotive and stationary applications - for improved fuel efficiency have led to remarkable results. It deserves to be mentioned, that the necessary changes did not demand that the basic concept of the engines would have to be left. We still have the piston engine, eventually combined with turbochargers, and it may be expected, that this concept will remain a workable solution for the foreseeable future. Nevertheless, as the improvement of the energy-yield of this concept will find its limitations in designs where still half of the fuel used is lost in the form of heat, parallel investigations with the target of further improvement of the fuel-efficiency at acceptable cost appear to be justified.

Besides work on the piston-engine itself optimizing the power train is also an important procedure when strifing for better fuel-economy in automotive applications.

Under consideration of the scope of the developments presented in this session the following categories may be defined :

- Improvements by development work on engine and power-train without drastic changes of design in engines and components

The developments of PORSCHE (Germany), UNIVERSITE CATHOLIQUE DE LOUVAIN (Belgium) and SOLAR 77 (Italy) fall into this category.

The results achieved by PORSCHE show that by optimizing engine and transmission fuel-economy of a Diesel-driven car can be matched with a car driven by an Otto-engine without deterioration of dynamic performance. At the same time exhaust emissions of the combination under study remained below the limits of ECE 15-04 and seem to justify expectations that the future German regulations may be met by a simple oxydizing catalytic converter and EGR-valve.

The studies conducted by SOLAR 77 SpA on the feasability of Gas-Oil/Water Emulsion Fuel for Automotive Diesel Engines have shown that by a rather simple device advantageous characteristics of engine performance can be obtained. The reliability of the device has been proven in road-tests where it was also proven, that driving characteristic remained the same when emulsion was used for fuel; although it was not possible to take reliable data on fuel consumption due to failure of instrumentation it is safe to say that exhaust emissions of unburnt fuel and nitrogen oxide decreased by amounts of between 30 % and 40 %.
In connection with the tests methodology has been developed for analysing the emulsion and its behaviour.

The matching of Internal Combusion Engines with Gas Producers as studied at the UNIVERSITE CATHOLIQUE DE LOUVAIN requires thorough knowledge of the efficiency of the energy-conversion of the gas generator, elaborate study

362

of burning properties of gases and a detailed energy conversion model of generator gas by reciprocating engines.

The developmental results show that Diesel engines with a compression ratio not exceeding 15 : 1 may easily be converted into Diesel-Gas engines without structural change. Such engines seem particularly attractive because of their versatility and low specific fuel consumption.

- Studies of improved Operating Cycles as Diesel-Rankine-Process ("Bottoming Cycle")

The developments conducted by DAIMLER-BENZ and MAN (Germany) lead to the conclusion that under the conditions of European road traffic economic feasability of the Bottoming-Cycle is not likely with the cost of fuel as it is at present. With higher cost of fuel in the future there might be a potential for economic advantage when ceramic-technology will be put to use in heat-sealed engines.

- Improving the basic knowledge required for calculation and/or prediction of phenomena in the engine and of its operating performance

The tendency of the deterioration of quality of low grade fuel as used in large diesel engines may lead to inefficient running, high maintenance cost and occasional engine failure. There is so far no satisfactory criterion for assessing residual oil quality and no guideline available to decide at which point residual fuel becomes unacceptable for large engines. Mr Dale of AERE HARWELL (U.K.) has devised an instrumented combustion chamber for conducting tests which will lead to the provision of the requested guideline.

The aim of the research task undertaken by Messrs. Benjamin, Grosman, Hutchinson and Whitelaw of BRITISH LEYLAND (U.K.) is to produce a computer program which is capable of computing unsteady 3-dimensional turbulent air-motion and heat transfer in the combustion chamber of reciprocating engines under motoring conditions. A family of geometric variations can be treated by the computer program.
Experimental data will in the next step of the study serve as means of comparison for the usability of the program.
The study presented here reports on measurements of airflow in various arrangements of valve, piston and cylinder.

- Concepts for new engines

In their experimentation of a mobile platform powered by a rectilinear engine associated with electric wheels of programmed movement, the authors, Messrs. Faul and Jarret of MOTHELEC (France), point out that the rectilinear engine seems likely to become an adequate source of current in ground vehicles in the foreseeable future and that by use of electronic control of the electric parts conversion of electric energy into mechanical energy and vice versa can be obtained with very high efficiencies. The authors expect, that for units in the range of 40 to 50 kW efficiencies can be achieved of 45 % or 50 %, the power/weight ratio should be in the area of 1 kW/kg.

In order to reduce the difficulties with seals when operating with Hydrogen and Helium under high pressure, BERTIN & CIE in their sealed Stirling engine model convert mechanical energy into electric energy within the sealed casing.
Further options of the design are dry bearings to prevent pollution of the regenerators and the use of an electric coupling instead of connecting rods. A large test programme of the whole engine has been carried out. The measured data for thermal losses proved to be well in line with the estimated value.
BERTIN will be in a position to design prototypes for defined market segments :

-   gas-burning electric generators
-   heat pumps
-   coal burning generators

The report on the two-cylinder-two-stroke internal combustion engine by Mr Hamann of FICHT (Germany) describes the experience with tests since their start in October 1982. The design was changed from air-cooled to water-cooled cylinders for reason of optimization. Efficiencies were higher than expectations. Work under progress now concentrates on the shifting of the torque-curves into a region of minimal fuel consumption.

Based on the experiences gathered with the prototype of the new rotary internal combustion engine, Messrs. Pelekis and Proussaefs of GENERAL SUPPLY (Constructions) CO. LTD (Greece) expect that the difficulties resulting from heat distortion will be eliminated with a more advanced prototype which is now under construction. The target of the development is an engine of simple design, a small number of different parts, low cost and an interesting power/weight ratio.

-   Energy storage by Flywheels

For different applications papers have been presented by NEDERLANDSE SPOORWEGEN (The Netherlands) and by KRUPP (Germany).
The projects are aimed for use in trains resp. busses where braking energy is to be stored for re-use during acceleration and for use in cranes. Both studies lead to the conclusion that technical feasability is given, however rather narrow conditions prevail for the achievement of economic success.

CONCLUDING REMARKS
by the chairman of Session III
Prof. Dr. P. Hagenmuller
Université de Bordeaux, France

ELECTRICITY STORAGE

Two ways have been followed by the E.E.C. in the scope of this research field : construction of a high mass capacity secondary battery for electrical vehicles, improving the utilization conditions of such a battery on board of a vehicle.

The aim of the programme is simultaneously to save energy used for transportation and to replace the classical gasoline vehicles by non-polluting ones.

a)   New secondary batteries

Two types of battery have been considered, according to the negative electrode : sodium and lithium (or lithium alloys particularly LiAl).

The Na/S battery using β''-alumina as electrolyte is able to yield high performances : energy densities up to 200 Wh/kg, power densities attaining 150 W/kg, constant voltage over a long period of time, utilization during several hundred charge-discharge cycles and 10 thermal cycles down to room temperature. The difficulties indeed are that the normal working temperature is around 350°C, which supposes the use of a thermally insulating container, and also severe material requirements (concerning purity for instance) (C.G.E.).

In parallel, research has been carried out on lithium secondary batteries due to theoretically higher mass capacity of the electrochemical chains using lithium.

These projects have been supported on this topic and all led to significant results :

VARTA has developed the construction of a molten lithium halide cell using LiAl/FeS electrodes. Energy densities of more than 100 Wh/kg have been realized at 450°C for a discharge current of about 30 A. The expensive and brittle BN separator has been successfully replaced by a MgO powder membrane with a large specific surface which resists such temperature.

The anglo-danish programme (U.K.A.E.A. and ODENSE UNIVERSITY are the main contractors) aims at setting up a lithium battery working at a temperature as low as possible in very stable many cycle-conditions. TiS_2 and V_6O_{13} were tested as positive electrodes, several electrolytes have been considered, a polymeric material appearing to be the most performing ($LiCF_3SO_3$ dispersed in polyethylene oxide). It seems to be suitable already at 120°C. An effective energy density of 200 Wh/kg (lithium metal anode) is expected with a cycling possibility of 200 charge-discharge cycles. An experimental battery has been built to solve the interface problems.

The purpose of the BORDEAUX UNIVERSITY project (in connection with SORAPEC) is to build a lithium battery working at room temperature to avoid using a large volume of insulating fibers in practical utilizations on board of a vehicle. The electrolyte selected is a high Li^+ conducting glass containing B_2S_3 ($\sigma > 10^{-3}\,\Omega^{-1}\,cm^{-1}$ at 25°C). The problem of the compatibility of the electrolyte with the negative Li (or LiAl) electrode has been completely solved so that any surface polarization can be ruled out. Efficient solutions have been found to largely remove the contact problems at the TiS_2 positive electrode (to make the material fully efficient). A small scale battery has been constructed with 100μ A/cm^2 current density without relaxation and was successfully tested on several cycles.

To accelerate the construction of a room temperature vehicle battery, the intention of the anglo-danish and BORDEAUX contractors is to establish systematic contacts in the future for exchanging information and "know how".

As an alternative route to the use of high performance alkaline metal secondary batteries, the E.E.C. has supported a SORAPEC project for realizing a H_2/air fuel cell. Polyamide and propylene inter-electrode matrices have been elaborated. Porous nickel foam is used as air electrode in a very efficient way, silvered active carbon reducing the polarization. Such cells have been tested for 1500 hrs at 80°C with a current density of 150 mA/cm^2.

One may emphasize that several quite different ways have been chosen in the scope of the programme to build a non polluting generator using electricity. In the present stage of evolution of this type of research this decision appears to be simultaneously a wise and prospective one. All contractors on different paths aim in any case at an industrial realization. It is too early to compare the results due to the fact that the projects are not in the same development stage as the difficulties encountered differ according to the way chosen. Strong coordination must be recommended.

b)   Improving the utilization conditions of the batteries

FIAT and ELECTRONIKCENTRALEN have developed modules for controlling battery charge, adding fluid to the battery (which in the present stage is a H_2SO_4 - Pb battery) and collecting gas. The main advantage is to reduce strongly energy waste in limiting the overcharging risks. The on board charger has a 86 % efficiency. It was tested during several months over a 2000 km distance. A high frequency 2 kW charger has also been developed (50 000 Hz), leading to a 75 % weight reduction.

In parallel, CHLORIDE LEGG LTD has developed such a high frequency "on board" charger requiring high power transistors (12 kW at 25 000 Hz). A better vehicle control is expected as far as reduced weight and size of the HF charger. The investigation is in good progress.

Advanced batteries will probably be used in a relatively near future at first for trucks and fleet cars. Mass capacity, power density, ageing problems, safety conditions still need a reasonable effort to pass beyond the Ni-Cd or Ni-Fe batteries, which are relatively expensive but have not given so far a sufficient driving range even for city vehicles. Work has also to be done for utilization with the maximum efficiency of the vehicle batteries in adapting them to real charge and traffic conditions.

CONCLUDING REMARKS
by the chairman of Session IV, part A

Dr. J. Limido

Institut Français du Pétrole, France

This session covers the three following sectors

- CHEMICAL INDUSTRY AND CATALYSIS
- COAL AND PEAT
- METALLURGY

The eight projects of the Chemical Industry and Catalysis sector can be divided into two main groups according to their main field of research :

- energy and raw material savings
- alternative energy resources (including waste products).

The Italian Company MONTEDIPE within the framework of the first group found a way of greatly improving the performance of steam-cracking units for petrochemical production by replacing the conventional monotubular coil with a new design of a split coil, and by using a new high temperature resistant alloy. The estimated saving could come close to 200 000 TOE per year on the basis of 30 % of the retrofitted EEC plants.

In a very different branch of the Chemical Industry but still in the same working group, the CITY UNIVERSITY (U.K.) project of replacing the conventional mild steel cathodes by active hydrogen catalytic cathodes in the chlor-alkali industry, aims at a 5 % reduction in electric energy consumption. The preliminary results obtained with a proprietary cathode appears to be of great interest to the chlor-alkali industry.

Six other projects focus their work on the access to new energy resources. The results obtained by SNAMPROGETTI (Italy) for the selective removal of H_2S from sour gases, opens up the availability of gaseous hydrocarbon streams whether it be from natural gas fields (sour natural gases) or from rejected refinery off gases.

An original process developed by the INSTITUT FRANCAIS DU PETROLE (France) from laboratory results obtained by the UNIVERSITE TECHNOLOGIQUE DE COMPIEGNE, showed how combustible products can be recovered by direct transformation of waste tyres. The cost/benefit ratio achieved by an industrial unit appears attractive enough to encourage the development of this process, which produces 0,52 Tons of fuel per ton of tyre feedstock.

A critical evaluation of anaerobic fermentation of waste products carried out by INTERNATIONAL RESEARCH & DEVELOPMENT CO (U.K.) emphasizes the fact that at the present stage, the main incentive for the development of such a technology, lies in obtaining solutions to the environmental problems; energy savings being a secondary matter.

In E.E.C. countries the future pattern of the hydrocarbon market leads to the increase in light and medium products at the expense of heavy residuals. Up to now, conventional conversion techniques have failed because of the unadaptability of the present day commercial catalysts and the resulting technological complexity. CERCHAR and I.F.P. (France) obtained interesting and relevant results on a pilot scale, with regard to a considerable improvement in performance and operability, by using new catalysts and original technology.

The last two projects concern the E.E.C. contribution to the longer term R & D programme of production of hydrocarbon or alcohol cuts from CO and H_2 mixtures as an alternative to natural fossil hydrocarbon resources. The work carried out by KATHOLIEKE UNIVERSITEIT LEUVEN (Belgium) in developing a new selective Fischer-Tropsch technology marks a decisive advance which is to be confirmed by on-line apparatus experimentation. In a more exploratory sense, is the attempt of the UNIVERSITE OF LIEGE (Belgium) to develop a new and cheap synthesis catalyst family in order to produce ethanol or higher alcohols. The first results show that for the time being the well known and expensive Rhodium based catalysts still remain the most efficient and selective.

Two projects share the same goal, by economically valorizing discarded fossil resources : sulphur rich coals by biological desulphurization – E.N.E.A. (Italy) and peat farming from small boglands – NATIONAL BOARD OF SCIENCE AND TECHNOLOGY (Ireland).

As opposed to the first project which is at the early stage of exploratory research, the second one has reached the commercial testing phase of the developed equipment. The additional peat resources gained by this equipment represent a potential of 3,5 M. Tons (at 25 % moisture) equivalent to 1 M. TOE.

Six projects in the metallurgy sector aim at a drastic reduction in energy consumption by the elaboration of solid products or metal parts without altering the quality of the finished product or their physical and mechanical charasteristics.

Within the sphere of liquid metal conversion into solid products, two projects strive to achieve energy savings and a reduction in surface defaults or off-cuts. The results of the research work carried out by ARMINES (France) in the continuous casting of steel, leads to a reliable model for a rational formulation of casting powder and in consequence, a better control of the lubrifying functions assured by the slag. Meanwhile the new process developed by the BRITISH ALUMINIUM COMPANY entitled "Thin Strip Casting Technique" appears to be a very advantageous alternative to the conventional "Direct Chill Casting Hot Rolling Process" since it eliminates the scalping, preheating and hot rolling stages. A variable rate of economy, depending on the type of alloy used, ranges from 28 to 38 %.

A second group of projects aims at energy conservation by reducing the number of operations necessary in the manufacture of metal parts, whether it be in forging (REGIE NATIONALE DES USINES RENAULT) or for moulding (PONT A MOUSSON/INSTITUT POLYTECHNIQUE DE LORRAINE). A reduction of up to 40 % in energy consumption is quite substantial compared to conventional cycles.

The last axe of research assembles two studies whose goal is the elaboration of parts or the assemblage of parts with defined characteristics by applying new materials in association with new methods of implementation. FIAT has made much progress in the replacing of special high allied steel with bainitic nodular iron. Positive results concerning mechanical properties and machinability have been obtained, however deformation problems have yet to be solved. AERE HARWELL (U.K.) with the help of 15 other firms is developing joining technology between composites and metals, the target of which is to reduce the weight of motor cars and trucks. The first results have yet to be completed in a project, which can be quite justified by the fact that approximately a 5 % reduction in fuel consumption can be made by reducing road vehicle weight by 10 %.

This summary shows the relevance of the research axes chosen and also the substantial results achieved. In several cases, further research is necessary and also extensive implementation of the present results.

CONCLUDING REMARKS
by the chairman of Session IV, part B
Dr. A. Rossi
Centro delle Ricerche FIAT, Italy

The session I have just chaired is the last but, I believe, not the least one in importance and in energy saving potential. The preceeding sessions involved mainly technical functions or operations. This last one involved types of industry : textile, food, cement, glass, ceramic. The activities, grouped as such, are by no means what is left over for a last cursory examination. The products now supplied by these so called "traditional" industries have provided since centuries and millennia satisfaction of basic human needs. Not only material needs such as food, clothing and shelter have been provided, but also cultural needs related to beauty, decoration, art, and even fashion.

Traditional industries have deep roots in the past at least in some specific cases. In the archeological museum of Aquileia I saw large "industrial" quantities of ceramic oil lamps, which were exported all over the world known at the time, with the factory seal printed on them. Centuries ago, a still existing now multinational company, was already making glass articles for the Kings of France and others, using not freely imported craftmanship (namely, Venetians war prisoners). The industries we are here speaking of are in general thought to be characterized by a slow pace of innovation. Automation has been probably the main recent aspect. I suspect, without having numbers in hands, that these industries are both energy intensive and extensive : in both the sense of a high energy content per unit of product and of a large quantity of product.

It appears that energy saving research in this field could bring benefits in both directions, and that bigger efforts should be devoted to a field that guarantees a multiplication effect of single improvements by the quantity produced.

The few examples given in the session seem to confirm this feeling. I will not review them again for you here as you have just heard the excellent presentations made by rapporteurs and authors.

I prefer to entertain you during these last minutes with some side considerations on the energy saving philosophy and the money saving philosophy (by energy saving I mean for brevity rational use of energy which includes savings). The two philosophies do not always run in parallel. From the macro-economic long term point of view (the nations, the Community, etc.), energy saving should be, roughly speaking, the main aim, and money saving a mean to facilitate reaching this aim.

The contrary - always roughly speaking - occurs at the micro-economic short term level (the companies, the families, the individuals) : money saving (or profit making) is mainly an aim, and energy saving the mean to reach this aim.

The connections between the two philosophies are often fluid, diverse, contradictory, conventional, and moreover they vary sometimes quickly and remarkably, with time and place. They are made up, in addition to "natural" market and economic parameters, by a whole series of artificial rules, tariffs, special regulations, fiscal measures, open or hidden helps, etc. which are valid at a certain time and in a certain location. To simplify the thinking, the research effort should lead to an objective identification of the conditions for energy saving in a given process. This task appears more technical and physical than the determination of money saving, although the above mentioned conventional rules have a certain influence on the local understanding of rational use.

During the session, we have been listening to the most varied expressions for quantifying the benefit of the research in terms of savings : savings on peak electric power, translated into Belgian Francs per month, fuel savings for mobile and stationary power plants, Gigajoule per tonne of product, Kilo French Francs per year, and finally savings of production cost per unit product. I think we should try to introduce some standardisation to make comparisons feasible and meaningful. We should try to consider energy saving systematically for a whole system, with both the positive and negative aspects for the energy accountancy : energy for operation, but also energy for the needed capital investment, the type of sources, the (thermodynamic or otherwise) quality of energy, and maybe, especially for long term operations, the "actualisation" of the energy availability and use. Energy behaves in this last respect contrary to money : the energy of tomorrow has a bigger value than the energy of today. This sometimes justifies energy storage (compared to a cash deposit at a "negative" interest rate) even with heavily unfavourable yields.

Energy "here" has more value than enegy "there". A clever Aluminium manu- facturer publicized his material as a very effective and light "energy bank" or "store", allowing to import dense packages of energy from countries which are rich in energy and mineral resources, so that local energy is saved.

Once estimated, under reasonably realistic assumptions on diffusion into the market, the prospective energy savings made by the proposed change, the problem is how to provoke this diffusion, and possibly to make it occur spontaneously.

One of the best ways to accomplish this is to transform, by a thoughtful set of rules, energy savings into money savings, appealing directly to individuals and companies.

I personally do not believe that pure uncorrected market forces could have this effect in most of the cases.

One of the possible recommendations from technical conferences like this one, to be made to competent public authorities, could in fact be the following : to promote a favourable and stable relation between energy savings and money savings, possibly harmonised in the Common Market countries. Such conditions will allow industries and other service organizations to pursue effectively and plan ahead the process of introduction of innovation into their operations, with a reasonable assurance of an acceptable return of investments in the years ahead.

LIST OF AUTHORS